Disintermediation Economics

Eva Kaili · Dimitrios Psarrakis
Editors

Disintermediation Economics

The Impact of Blockchain on Markets and Policies

Editors
Eva Kaili
European Parliament
Bruxelles, Belgium

Dimitrios Psarrakis
European Parliament
Bruxelles, Belgium

ISBN 978-3-030-65783-3   ISBN 978-3-030-65781-9 (eBook)
https://doi.org/10.1007/978-3-030-65781-9

© The Editor(s) (if applicable) and The Author(s), under exclusive license to Springer Nature Switzerland AG 2021
This work is subject to copyright. All rights are solely and exclusively licensed by the Publisher, whether the whole or part of the material is concerned, specifically the rights of translation, reprinting, reuse of illustrations, recitation, broadcasting, reproduction on microfilms or in any other physical way, and transmission or information storage and retrieval, electronic adaptation, computer software, or by similar or dissimilar methodology now known or hereafter developed.
The use of general descriptive names, registered names, trademarks, service marks, etc. in this publication does not imply, even in the absence of a specific statement, that such names are exempt from the relevant protective laws and regulations and therefore free for general use.
The publisher, the authors and the editors are safe to assume that the advice and information in this book are believed to be true and accurate at the date of publication. Neither the publisher nor the authors or the editors give a warranty, expressed or implied, with respect to the material contained herein or for any errors or omissions that may have been made. The publisher remains neutral with regard to jurisdictional claims in published maps and institutional affiliations.

Cover illustration: © dencg/shutterstock.com

This Palgrave Macmillan imprint is published by the registered company Springer Nature Switzerland AG
The registered company address is: Gewerbestrasse 11, 6330 Cham, Switzerland

Contents

1   Disintermediation Economics: An Introduction   1
Dimitrios Psarrakis

Part I   Disintermediation in Microeconomics

2   Blockchain as an Economic Optimization Problem: Value, the Firm and the Limits of Decentralization   17
Dimitrios Psarrakis

3   Economics of Smart Contracts: Efficiency and Legal Challenges   33
Guenther Dobrauz-Saldapenna and Mark A. Schrackmann

4   Corporate Strategies for Blockchain-Based Solutions   47
Hans Verheggen

5   Distributed Data Economics   69
David Shrier

Part II   Disintermediation in Macroeconomics and Finance

6   Blockchain for Growth: Applying DLTs to the UN Sustainable Development Goals   93
Jane Thomason

7	**The New Money: The Utility of Cryptocurrencies and the Need for a New Monetary Policy** *David Lee Kuo Chuen and Ernie Teo*	111
8	**Privately Issued Digital Currencies** *Dante Alighieri Disparte*	173
9	**Crypto-Assets, Distributed Ledger Technologies and Disintermediation in Finance: Overcoming Impediments to Scaling: A View from the EU** *Elisabeth Noble*	193
10	**Crypto-Assets and Disintermediation in Finance: A View from Asia** *Syren Johnstone*	215

Part III Disintermediation in Political Economy and Regulation

11	**The Political Economy of the Blockchain** *Pēteris Zilgalvis*	249
12	**Regulating Blockchain in the EU: Building a Global Competitive Advantage** *Eva Kaili*	267
13	**Advancing Digital Transformation in the Public Sector with Blockchain: A View from the European Union** *Emanuele Baldacci and Joao Rodrigues Frade*	281
14	**Disposable Identities? Why Digital Identity Matters to Blockchain Disintermediation and for Society** *Loretta Anania, Gaëlle Le Gars, and Rob van Kranenburg*	297

Conclusion	329
Index	333

Notes on Contributors

Loretta Anania works at the European Commission, DG Communication Networks Content & Technologies, Next Generation Internet unit. With a B.A. from Sussex University and a Ph.D. from MIT she worked in universities, as a journalist and a telecommunication consultant, while at the MIT Media Lab. She has published on internet policy (access pricing, broadband convergence, multimodal interfaces, social media & search computing). Twice elected *Chairman* of the Board of the International Telecommunications Society (www.its-world.org) Dr. Anania serves on the Board of QoMEX (www.qomex.org). She managed over 200 European Union R&D projects and is a panel speaker with a passion for social innovation and SDGs.

Emanuele Baldacci is the Director of Digital Services at the European Commission's Directorate-General for Informatics. From May 2015 to February 2018 he was the Director of Methodology, IT and Corporate Statistical Services at Eurostat, the statistical office of the European Union. From October 2011 to April 2015 he was the Head of the Integration, Quality and Research Department of the Italian Statistical Office. Before that, he was a deputy division chief at the International Monetary Fund, a senior economist at the World Bank and also served as chief economist at SACE, Italy's largest trade finance group. He has a Ph.D. in Demography from the Universities of Rome, Florence and Padua; he is the author of several scientific publications on fiscal sustainability, macroeconomic risk in advanced and emerging economies, population ageing and social protection and official statistics modernization.

David Lee Kuo Chuen is a Professor at the Singapore University of Social Sciences and Shanghai University of Finance and Economics. He is also an Adjunct Professor at the National University of Singapore. His other appointments are the Chairman of Global Fintech Institute, Vice President of the Economic Society of Singapore and Council Member of British Blockchain Association. As a Fulbright Scholar at Stanford University in 2015, he started researching, mentoring and investing in inclusive blockchain projects. He devotes his time to learning and sharing his knowledge on inclusive FinTech, and publish books and articles on AI, Blockchain, quantum computing and other emerging technology. He has 20 years of experience as CEOs and Independent Directors of companies involved in FinTech, Manufacturing, Fund Management and Real Estate Development. He holds editorial positions for Journal of FinTech and Journal of British Blockchain Association among others. His latest publications include The Handbook of Digital Currency, the Handbooks of Blockchain, Inclusive FinTech, AI and Quantum Computing, and Artificial Intelligence, Data and Blockchain in a Digital Economy by Elsevier and World Scientific. He is also a consultant to UNDP and ADB on blockchain, FinTech and CBDC.

Dante Alighieri Disparte Disparte is the Chief Strategy Officer and Head of Global Policy for Circle, a leading digital financial services firm building the most trusted treasury and payments infrastructure for the internet, including the fastest growing dollar digital currency, USDC. Prior to joining Circle, Dante served as a founding executive of the Diem (Libra) Association, leading public policy, communications, membership, and social impact. He has two decades of experience as an entrepreneur, business leader and global risk expert, most recently as founder and CEO of Risk Cooperative, a strategic risk advisory and insurance brokerage based in Washington, D.C. Dante also serves as an appointee on the Federal Emergency Management Agency's (FEMA) National Advisory Council, the United States' federal emergency response agency. He is also a member of the World Economic Forum's Digital Currency Governance Consortium. Dante is a frequent speaker and commentator on business and political issues shaping the world. His views on risk, economic competitiveness and security issues are regularly featured in leading media and publications, such as Harvard Business Review, BBC, Forbes, and Diplomatic Courier, where Dante serves on the editorial advisory board. Dante is a graduate of Harvard Business School and holds an MSc. in Risk Management from the NYU Stern School of Business and a

B.A. in International and Intercultural Studies from Goucher College, where he received the highest alumni recognition for public service. He is the co-author of "Global Risk Agility and Decision Making" (Macmillan, 2016) and was recognized as one of the 40 leaders under 40 by the Washington Business Journal and in the inaugural Powermeter 100 list.

Guenther Dobrauz-Saldapenna is a Partner with PwC in Zurich, Leader of PwC Legal Switzerland, a member of PwC's Global Legal Leadership Team directing the firm's global legal practice in 90+ countries and the firm's Global Financial Services Legal Leader. Guenther specializes in supporting the structuring, authorization and ongoing lifecycle management of financial intermediaries and their products. In addition he is focused on the implementation of large scale regulatory change and compliance alignment projects at Swiss and international financial institutions with particular focus on EU and Swiss regulations. Guenther is also the trusted advisor to several governments, international organisations and supervisory authorities on creating new regulatory frameworks. His passion as a practicing tech-enthusiast since 2002 is innovation linked to Exponential Technologies with a particular focus on achieving decentralization and he has also been working to promote sustainability since 2010 where he advocates a system-wide change towards a circular economy. Guenther is the author of eight books on innovation and the European, Swiss and Liechtenstein legal regulatory framework as well as of 100+ publications in international expert magazines. He received his Masters and Ph.D. degrees in law from Johannes Kepler University (Linz, Austria). Guenther also holds an M.B.A. from the University of Strathclyde Graduate School of Business (Glasgow, UK).

Joao Rodrigues Frade is a Head of Sector at the European Commission's Directorate-General for Informatics specializing in reusable solutions. Joao has extensive experience in managing complex projects including the key governance-aspects of highly distributed IT systems. In the last 18 years, Joao participated in the development, implementation, deployment and evolution of the most important large-scale distributed Trans-European Systems of the European Union. Joao holds a bachelor's degree in Economics, a master's degree in Information Systems and Technology Management and several Certifications including blockchain strategy and innovation.

Gaëlle Le Gars is a French citizen and holds a doctorate in Contemporary History from the University of Nantes specializing in International Relations & Defence. She was a Fulbright scholar at the University of Washington. She has been involved in EU digital policy for 20 years, both in and out of the European Commission, during which she worked in a range of policy areas from eGovernment to Smart and Sustainable Cities and the UN Urban Agenda. Gaëlle currently works as an independent policy analyst. Her current interests include digital identities, geocoded statistics, satellite imaging and the geopolitical implications of the ongoing push for all three.

Syren Johnstone is the Executive Director of the Master of Laws (Compliance & Regulation) Programme at the Faculty of Law, The University of Hong Kong. A member of the Securities and Futures Commission's Fintech Advisory Group (2016–2021), he has contributed thought leadership on various high-profile issues including via engagements as an expert for statutory regulatory agencies, and his work has been referenced in Hong Kong's Legislative Council and the Court of Appeal. Syren formerly practiced as a senior solicitor with Linklaters before taking up senior management roles with international investment banks. He holds two masters degrees, in neuroscience and law, from Oxford and London universities respectively. He is on the roll of solicitors in England & Wales and Hong Kong.

Eva Kaili is a Member of the European Parliament. She is the Chair of the Future of Science and Technology Panel in the European Parliament (STOA) and the Centre for Artificial Intelligence (C4AI), Member of the Committees on Industry, Research and Energy (ITRE), Economic and Monetary Affairs (ECON) and the Special Committee on Artificial Intelligence in a Digital Age (AIDA). She has been working intensively on promoting innovation as a driving force of the establishment of the European Digital Single Market. She has been the draftsperson of legislation in the fields of digital platforms, big data, fintech, AI and cybersecurity, as well as the Rapporteur of the DLT and Blockchain Resolution. She holds a degree in Architecture and Civil Engineering, and a Master's degree in European Politics.

Elisabeth Noble is a Senior Policy Expert at the European Banking Authority. She leads the EBA's work on crypto-assets, DLT and the platformisation of financial services and coordinates the European Forum for Innovation Facilitators. She represents the EBA in EU and international standard-setter policy work streams relating to FinTech, market-based finance, financial system interconnectedness, market access and the regulatory perimeter. She is contributing to the delivery of the EU Digital Finance Strategy and was a member of the European Commission's Expert Group on Regulatory Obstacles to Financial Innovation (now disbanded). Prior to joining the EBA, Elisabeth spent 7 years at HM Treasury advising primarily on the UK government's response to the financial crisis and the post-crisis domestic and EU regulatory reforms (2008–2014), including the reforms to the regulatory architecture in the EU (Banking Union). Elisabeth has also spent some time in the private sector.

Dimitrios Psarrakis is a Financial Technology and Innovation Strategy specialist of the European Parliament. He works on the design of the Digital Finance strategy of the EU and he is the draftsperson of the DLT and Blockchain Resolution of the European Parliament. He is ranked among the 100 top world influencers in the area of RegTech and Blockchain and he is a frequent speaker on topics related to FinTech, RegTech, Blockchain and Artificial Intelligence in Europe, America, and Asia. He is also the Director of the Brussels Council, an organization that promotes European high standards of governance and regulation in the digital economy and finance and links the innovation ecosystems of Europe with the rest of the world. He has a graduate degree in Finance from Harvard University.

Mark A. Schrackmann is manager on the legal, regulatory and compliance services of PWC Zurich. He specializes in Banking and Financial Market Law with a special focus on crypto and blockchain technology. He is author of numerous publications on legal and regulatory topics, and holds a Master in Law (lic. iur.) and a CAS in Financial Market Law from the University of Zurich.

David Shrier is a globally recognized authority on financial and advanced data applications, serial entrepreneur and corporate innovator, and author. He is a Professor of Practice with Imperial College London, where he leads labs on institutional digital assets and ethical applications of artificial intelligence. Previously, David created and led finTech and blockchain classes for the University of Oxford and MIT that engaged more than 15,000 innovators in over 150 countries to build the new financial ecosystem. He has published multiple books on fintech, blockchain and cybersecurity. In his private sector work, David specializes in helping established organizations to act strategically to build new revenue and new markets. He has developed more than $8.7 billion of growth opportunities with C-suite executives. He has cofounded four AI-enabled MIT spinouts. David Shrier was granted an Sc.B. from Brown University in Biology and Theatre.

Ernie Teo is a technologist, economist and game theorist with a focus on technology, fintech and blockchain. He is an Adjunct Senior Lecturer at the National University of Singapore Business School where he teaches Fintech and Blockchain. He is also Vice Chairman of Blockchain Association Singapore and Co-Founder of Dedoco, a document process solution that is built on blockchain to prevent tampering of the documents and create an audit trail for authentication and validation (signing). A pioneer of blockchain education in Singapore, he conceptualized and taught the first blockchain course as a part of a degree program at the National University of Singapore. Ernie is active in the blockchain community in Singapore, giving talks and seminars both in the industry and at universities. He also published in the area of blockchain and fintech, such as the 2018 IEEE International Conference on Cloud Engineering. He received his Ph.D. in Economics from the University of New South Wales, Australia and also held academic positions at Nanyang Technological University and Singapore Management University.

Jane Thomason is an author and thought leader in the applications of blockchain technology for social transformation. She is Co-Founder of the British Blockchain and Frontier Technology Association, Section Chief Editor, Frontiers in Blockchain, and Member of the Advisory Board of the Kerala Blockchain Academy. She is the lead author of *"Blockchain Technologies For Global Social Change"* (2019), lead author of the Chapter on *"Blockchain-Powering and Empowering the Poor in Developing Countries"* in Transforming Climate Finance and Green Investment with Blockchain (2018) Editor Alastair Marke; Lead author of the Chapter on *"Technology and healthcare opportunities in emerging markets"* with Nichola Cooper in HealthTech. Law and Regulation (2020) Editor Jelena Madir.

Rob van Kranenburg is founder of the IoT Council network (400 individual expert members). He is specialized in ecosystem management, stakeholder coordination and community engagement. He currently is a partner in the Strategy Team for Next Generation Internet, NGI FORWARD. He was co-editor of Enabling Things to Talk, Designing IoT solutions with the IoT Architectural Reference Model, Springer Open Access.

Hans Verheggen is a partner with Deloitte and focuses on emerging technology for international organizations. He has more than 15 years of business transformation experience with EU Institutions, NATO and the UN system. Currently, Hans advises the European Commission, Council and Parliament on digital strategy, cloud adoption, blockchain governance and AI use cases. Previously, Hans has worked with corporate clients in energy & resources and consumer & industrial products. Hans holds a master's degree in International Relations from the University of Antwerp and attended the Universite de Paris I Pantheon-Sorbonne and Georgetown University's School for Continuing Education.

Pēteris Zilgalvis is the Head of Unit for Digital Innovation and Blockchain in the Digital Single Market Directorate in DG CONNECT and is the Co-Chair of the European Commission FinTech Task Force. He was the Visiting EU Fellow at St. Antony's College, University of Oxford for 2013–2014, where he was an Associate of the Political Economy of Financial Markets Programme. From 1997 to 2005, he was Deputy Head of the Bioethics Department of the Council of Europe, in its Directorate General of Legal Affairs. In addition, he has held various positions in the Latvian civil service (Ministry of Foreign Affairs, Ministry of Environment). He was Senior Environmental Law Advisor to the World Bank/Russian Federation Environmental Management Project and was Regional Environmental Specialist for the Baltic Countries at the World Bank. He has been a member of the California State Bar since 1991, completed his J.D. at the University of Southern California and his B.A. in Political Science, Cum Laude at UCLA.

List of Figures

Fig. 3.1	The place of a smart contract in a transaction (*Source* The authors)	37
Fig. 5.1	The OPAL method to protect data (*Source* The author)	86
Fig. 7.1	Interbank payment landscape overview (*Source* Lai [2018])	140
Fig. 7.2	Digital tokens—Libra versus DCEP (*Source* Authors)	144
Fig. 10.1	The Determined-By-Architecture (DBA) taxonomy (*Source* Author)	235
Fig. 12.1	Lessig's four modes of regulation applied to blockchain systems (*Source* De Filippi and Wright [2018])	273
Fig. 13.1	How blockchain ledgers work (*Source* DIGIT, European Commission)	286
Fig. 14.1	The EU legislation shaping the Digital ID "governance stack" (*Source* Authors)	310
Fig. 14.2	The Europe's heterogeneous ID landscape (*Source* Asquared, 2018)	313
Fig. 14.3	Belgian user's of ITSME since 2017 (*Source* ITSME presentation, Rotterdam December 2019)	314
Fig. 14.4	Components of a Trust Framework (*Source* Makaay, E, T Smedinghoff, and D Thibeau. "OpenID Exchange: Trust Frameworks for Identity Systems," 2017)	318
Fig. 14.5	A diagram of disposable identity enabled by the Zenroom VM developed by DECODE (*Source* Authors/decode)	325
Fig. 14.6	The European Trust Framework: An alternative to the governance stack (*Source* Authors)	325
Fig. 14.7	EU citizen rights and EU sovereignty (*Source* Authors)	326

List of Tables

Table 4.1	Blockchain use-classes and their corresponding governance structures	60
Table 6.1	Blockchain for social change model	104
Table 7.1	Recent CBDC use cases by Central Banks	125
Table 7.2	Technological bottlenecks and pain points of digital money	137
Table 7.3	Attributes of various forms of money	143
Table 13.1	EBSI compared to other types of blockchain—DIGIT, European Commission	292
Table 13.2	EBSI's layered architecture	292

1

Disintermediation Economics: An Introduction

Dimitrios Psarrakis

Trust Engineered!

In the early 1990s, Francis Fukuyama published a book with the provocative title "The End of History and the Last Man". The book was based on an article published a few years earlier and the main argument was that the battle of political ideas ended with the victory of Liberal Democracy as the sole version of social arrangement after the collapse of Socialisms around the world. We remember this, now famous, book from the first part of its title, "the End of History," and we usually neglect the second part, "the Last Man," which advances an equally powerful statement: that we, people, have reached a point in our social evolution that the level of individual trust to the institutions around us cannot be improved further with more "social engineering" (Fukuyama 1992).

The idea of the "last man" is not new, though. Its origins are as old as the theoretical explorations of Hegel and Marx who worked with these research questions first and introduced systems of polity that disrupted the conservative and liberal ideas of their time. We now know that the Hegelian and Marxian assumptions of the institutional evolution of the people were

D. Psarrakis (✉)
European Parliament, Bruxelles, Belgium
e-mail: dimitrios.psarrakis@europarl.europa.eu

static and myopic because they neglected the factor of technology as accelerator of economic and social change. They replicated the ideas of Malthus who considered that change is statistically negligible, if not impossible, and saw every aspect of social interaction as a zero-sum game. Fukuyama, just like Hegel and Marx before him, was victim of the same "Malthusian fallacy". Trust can be further improved, or engineered, with the evolution of technology, or so it is the assumption of the enthusiasts of blockchain.

Blockchain, as a technological narrative, brings to Economics a very powerful promise. It claims that it can improve economic efficiency by removing the impact of information asymmetries and disincentives of collaboration. Blockchain goes in the heart of the transactions, of any kind, and promises to remove the negative effects of the inherent lack of trust between the transacting parties by *eradicating* the risk of ex post misbehaviour of those involved in an economic relationship or interaction, whenever this relationship or interaction requires a minimum level of coordination and commitment.

In one sentence, blockchain, it is said, neutralizes the negative effects of the lack of trust and enables people to act economically without the need of being confident about each other, by providing an infrastructure that guarantees the integrity of any transaction and any database in a network of ledgers. This can be accomplished without any need for a trusted third party acting as an authority to validate the transaction or the integrity of data (Swan 2015). Blockchain is claimed to be a *truth machine* (Casey and Vigna 2018) that will revolutionize our understanding of money, the markets, the governments, even our identities, and the social cooperation in general (Tapscott 2016).

This collective volume brings together economists, lawyers, market participants, and regulators from all over the world to explore what this technology can do (and cannot do) and explore its impact in the disciplines of Microeconomics, Macroeconomics, Finance, and Political Economy.

Why Disintermediation—And Not Decentralization Economics? The Problem of Dealing with Randomness

We use the term "blockchain" but it would be more accurate to speak about distributed ledger technologies (DLTs). Blockchain is one possible engineering option in a family of options, however for simplicity we call here blockchain every DLT. The very design of the blockchain, including its consensus protocol and the rules of participation and engagement, usually categorized as permissioned and permissionless blockchains, can vary. Options entail the use of distribution, encryption, immutability, tokenization, and decentralization (Furlonger and Uzerau 2019). But these are just options. The engineer selects the design that works best for her business model.

However, there is a clear-cut governance distinction we cannot ignore. A fully decentralized blockchain, decentralizes also the role of the authority who enforces the "property rights" in the ledger. A fully decentralized blockchain is a very democratic blockchain because it allocates one ballot to every node. It is obvious that hierarchical institutional systems (both in the market and the government) do not value a fully decentralized option very high. This does not prevent them though from experimenting with less strict options that enable disintermediation, or options of designing systems that reduce transaction and verification costs that accrue from the use of a trusted third party, the intermediary.

Possibly, as blockchain technology matures (or as the market matures), as well as the interaction of humans with machines or machines with machines (in an IoT dense environment) proliferates, we will move with more confidence to fully decentralized solutions. We believe though that this move towards decentralization cannot happen in a social vacuum. Social forces, at least for the time being, predispose people to feel more comfortable with disintermediation-oriented blockchain solutions.

How fast can we move from a predominantly disintermediation-oriented blockchain environment to a predominantly decentralization-oriented one? We can assume that, just like in the case of disintermediation, decentralization will follow the same track of adoption. The diffusion of innovations model is helpful for us to understand the process (Rogers 2003), but as it happens to any diffusion model in general, there is a set of behavioural requirements that we cannot ignore (Page 2018). I believe that at the core of these behavioural barriers lies the (dis-)comfort of the individuals with the notion of *randomness*. How much randomness an individual can accept in its economic interactions?

To make this point more precise let's review a truly decentralized blockchain system, the Bitcoin blockchain. What makes the Bitcoin blockchain methodologically significant is its way of removing the need to link a particular person with its signature and at the same time it allows this person to have as many signatures as it likes. In a decentralized blockchain environment, an economic agent is as good as her digital signature. De-linking the personal identity from that person's signature is counterintuitive in the economic system as we know it and it is already a significant deviation from the common practice.

What makes a person's signature so unique? It is something that brings a sense of authenticity because a signature is unforgeable and verifiable. What gives these properties to a person's signature? It is a fact that a signature is always similar but never identical. Humans generate *true randomness* in the way they write a signature that prevents replications and forgery from third parties. Our society accepts human-generated randomness as a source of authenticity, as this randomness is considered to be *true*. A decentralized blockchain system, on the other hand, generates digital signatures as a source of authenticity, but these signatures are *artificially random*. This can have significant implications.

A decentralized blockchain system, in order to be successful and reliable, must generate the properties of the physical signature, namely verifiability, and unforgeability, in a digital equivalent, the digital signature. The digital signature in the case of the Bitcoin blockchain is a 256-bits hexadecimal number generated by an algorithm, the blockchain protocol, automatically. This number is *almost* random and generated in a way that makes the reverse-engineering statistically *almost* impossible. This "almost" is what distinguishes artificial randomness from true randomness.

But the blockchain protocol goes a step further. It is designed in such a way that "honesty" is not required by the economic agents. Non-required honesty in a decentralized blockchain is another deviation from the common understanding of economic interaction that our society is hard to digest. In the case of the Bitcoin blockchain, honesty is not required because the appointment of a node in the blockchain to verify a transaction is also random. The randomness is necessary for the success of the decentralized blockchain because this prevents biases in favor of one transaction over another, prevents the prolongation of malevolent transactions that may endorse double-spending attacks, and prevents collisions that can compromise the validity of the ledgers by verifying *forking*. Randomness here is a tool strengthened by the requirement of a policy norm among the ledger participants (accept the leg of blocks that is bigger than the rest).

The first core question to ask here is: how can we trust that an algorithm, which by nature is a deterministic process, can generate randomness good enough to produce a probabilistic scenario that humans and their institutions can trust? This is a high behavioural barrier that becomes even higher when the stakes are higher and when the alternatives to this option are cost-efficient and deeply embedded in the minds and habits of legacy economic agents. The problem can become even more acute when other technologies, like a possibly very efficient hyper-performance computer, or even a quantum computer, can compromise the encryption adequacy of those random streams of numbers. Of course, there is nothing to prevent us from thinking that a quantum computer threat will be impossible to be addressed by an adequate quantum-resistant encryption mechanism, but still, this does not leave us in a better position when considering the problem of attractiveness of artificial randomness by humans and their institutions.

The second core question to ask is: how can humans blend artificial randomness with policy norms to sustain a blockchain when they know that a minority can violate these norms by creating forks? A decentralized blockchain protocol is very efficient in creating incentives for not tampering with the ledger but, effectively, blockchains are not really tamper-proof. This means that artificial randomness is a necessary requirement for sustaining the validation of decentralized blockchains but not a sufficient requirement in keeping the integrity of the architecture if a group of people wants to redefine the prevailing norms. Moreover, people are not used to solve institutional disagreements with forking.

These two problems, (1) the trustworthiness of artificial randomness and (2) the coupling of artificial randomness with the need for solid norms for sustaining the integrity of a decentralized blockchain system are both significant impediments that prevent people and institutions from accepting decentralized arrangements, especially when the stakes of failure are high and the available legacy systems are still considered as trustworthy solutions. This generates incentives for economic agents to advance disintermediation rather than decentralization-oriented blockchain solutions.

A third limitation imposed by randomness is not about the protocol itself but about the limitations of the blockchain architects to predict all the possible contingencies and emergencies in complex situations. It is impossible to foresee all the possible scenarios in advance and design ex ante an omniscient algorithm agile enough to prevent any malevolent attempt against the ledger. Humans make the code and codes usually have glitches. There is always a "smarter" or "luckier" fellow who can detect and exploit algorithmic inconsistencies. This is the case of Ethereum DAO that forced people to implement a painful forking to restore the integrity of the ledger. People are smart, but not smart enough to design algorithmic contracts that grasp every aspect of the complexity in advance. This makes decentralized constructions exposed to random events, black swans if you will, that compromise the strength of the protocol in its entirety. A decentralized blockchain is as strong as the least perspicacious smart contract design.

Decentralized blockchain solutions are already with us in numerous cases; in the case of Bitcoin, in the design (successful or not) of Decentralized Autonomous Organizations (DAOs), in significant attempts to build Decentralized Finance service providers (DeFi). Market participants and tech-savvy agents experiment with it, but DAOs and decentralized ledgers are as good as the capacity of the designers to predict what can go wrong. Bitcoin is a very illuminative case: it performs a very well-defined simple task repetitively. Contrary to the failed attempt of the Ethereum DAO a few years ago, it has limited aspirations. But even Bitcoin, the most successful case of decentralized ledger, could not escape from the limitations of its own architecture. It paid for its resilience with significant limitations to its scalability and an endless number of forks (to date 105 forks have happened to the original Bitcoin blockchain of which 74 are active projects).

Regulators and market participants cannot ignore these restrictions and feel much more comfortable to work with risks they can control and probability distributions that rely more on solid design architectures than unreliable levels of randomness. A purely decentralized blockchain, the Bitcoin, forced us early enough to think seriously about how far these innovative institutional arrangements that blockchain brings to Economics can go. This was the dawn of blockchain. When the sun raised higher in the sky, we saw that the society is not ready to allocate much of its trust to artificial randomness. It was ready, instead to experiment with more controlled solutions that advance disintermediation (the removal of the third-party verification authority from peer-to-peer transactions between interested parties).

What do we mean by *Disintermediation Economics*? We mean the impact of blockchain in Economics when economic agents (including corporations, medium and small enterprises, and the public sector) use blockchain solution architectures that advance *distribution, encryption,* and *immutability* in a wide range of cases with the purpose to remove intermediaries from the value chain with significant results in their organizational setting and their vertical or horizontal integration. We also explore how *tokenization* transforms finance and financial market structures as well as how central banks and corporations introduce *programmable money*. We explore how blockchain advances social inclusion, transforms the citizen-state relationships, and improves democracy. We explore how blockchain accelerates growth in the developing world, accelerates the efficiency of innovation ecosystems, redefines our sense of ownership and distribution of data, and forces regulators to be more open-minded and alert for significant changes in the future.

This volume reflects those market and regulatory realities. The authors of this volume do not rule out the possibility of another book, possibly with the title *Decentralization Economics*, but we are not there yet. We hope, though, to be there soon as blockchain improves rapidly along with the change in the taste and preferences of the markets.

The Structure of the Book

The book is structured in three parts. First, we explore how blockchain fits in the curriculum of Microeconomic studies. Here we place emphasis on four topics: industrial organization economics, corporate strategy, economics of smart contracts, and economics of distributed data.

Dimitris Psarrakis opens the Microeconomics part of the volume. In his chapter, he explores how blockchain changes economic organizations. Dimitris claims that the technological change that blockchain brings to the economy is not Hicks-neutral. Different choices in the architecture design of a DLT generate different organizational settings and market structures. He underlines that there is a blockchain *organizational continuum* that includes blockchain-enabled, blockchain-complete, and decentralized-complete organizational settings. How far a firm will go in this continuum is a function of transaction and coordination costs. Though he does not make any prediction on the blockchain adoption over time, he shows that any approximation to a decentralized-complete organization is constrained by four factors: first, ownership behaviour persists in blockchains, second, incomplete contracts persist in blockchains, third, blockchains cannot sustain consensus in perpetuity, and fourth, short-term behaviours in a blockchain are not necessarily aligned with long-term targets. He concludes his chapter with an exploration of techno-social factors that can affect the rapidity of adoption of blockchain in the context of variegated capitalisms.

Then **Guenther Dobrauz-Saldapenna** and **Mark Schackmann** introduce us to the topic of the economics of smart contracts. The authors support that smart contract is a significant innovation for the performance of industrial, commercial, and administrative tasks. They note that the concept of smart contracts is well developed in the field of Computer Science but its uses in the market and the legal services are not as mature yet. Smart contracts bring challenges in both economic and legal terms. Then they explain what a smart contract is and describe some possible use cases. They explore the role of smart contracts in the economic theory focusing particularly on the topics of contract completeness and dynamic contracting. Guenther and

Mark underline that functional inefficiencies and limitations in contract and algorithmic design are persistent in both the analogue and the smart contracts and prohibit contract completeness in both the versions. On the other hand, they note, the static nature of smart contracts prohibits dynamic contracting between the economic agents. This can be remedied, they claim, with deviations from purely decentralized designs with the inclusion into the smart contracts of physical intermediaries (curators) and programmable intermediaries (oracles). Finally, they explore how the property of self-executability can be improved with Ricardian contracts that can add discretion and flexibility.

Then, follows the chapter of **Hans Verheggen**. Hans links corporate strategies and blockchain solutions. He explores what blockchain means for corporates today and how they approach digital transformation leveraging blockchain concepts and technology. After a brief outlook on the blockchain market for business, he presents a picture of how enterprise blockchain and digital assets are becoming part of the corporate business model (how they create and deliver value) and the corporate operational model (how they capture their value). Next, he looks into how companies can build successful consortia, design enterprise blockchain solutions, and engage with the innovation ecosystem. Finally, he considers how corporations and markets can create business and operating models that become blockchain complete.

The first part of the volume closes with the contribution of **David Shrier** on the topic of decentralized data economics. David states that distributed ledgers offer new horizons of opportunity for the monetization of data, and new models whereby individual consumers gain more control over and benefit from their personal data, versus the predominant model of today that awards the greatest economic gains to the oligopoly platform companies. He notes that understanding distributed data economics requires reviewing the lineage of data aggregation, the characteristics of legacy data economics, the rise of a new generation of data ecologies, and finally exploration of the potential of distributed data economics in the context of technology architecture, governance, societal implications, and distributed data policy. David underscores that data ethics, and a framework for the related area of ethical artificial intelligence (and how it interacts with data) have not only moral implications, but real-world business impacts, as governments strengthen their responses to private sector activities in data monetization. Furthermore, as distributed data economies move from theory into practice, government policy interventions can smooth this transition.

Then we move on to explore Macroeconomic and Financial Implications of the blockchain innovation. Here we explore how blockchain applications and solutions can support major growth projects, including the Sustainable Development Goals of the UN. However, the impact of blockchain in monetary policy and payments infrastructures with crypto-currencies and stablecoins is a major topic to be explored. Then we turn our attention to the financial applications of blockchain, and we see how crypto-assets can improve the channeling of capital to risky projects, market structure concerns, and regulatory challenges.

Jane Thomason opens the second part of the book with her chapter on blockchain for growth. Jane claims that it is incumbent upon governments and the international community to explore how to marshal its benefits for the SDGs. Blockchain, Jane stresses, offers potential benefits for poverty, hunger, health, gender inequality, clean water, affordable clean energy, climate, and partnerships for the global commons. 2019 saw the stabilizing and maturing of the blockchain industry, becoming more about what the technology enables. She believes that 2020 will be the year that blockchain goes enterprise—research and development projects will bear results. She underscores that the areas where major blockchain progress is taking place are as diverse as the applications they are creating. The global nature of blockchain's development can help distribute opportunities for wealth creation and economic development more widely than before. It is important for governments to develop the right policies to harness the potential benefits of this technology while mitigating its risks and potential for misuse. To do so, it is essential for countries to cooperate in order to share best practices and ensure interoperability. Jane summarizes the many applications of blockchain in contributing to widespread social transformation and enabling traction against the SDGs, focusing on emerging economies. It also discusses barriers and enabling factors to achieve such a transformation.

Then we move to the opportunities and challenges that cryptocurrencies bring to the monetary policy. **David Lee** and **Enrie Teo** introduce us to the concept of the "new money". The authors stress that since their inception in 2008, cryptocurrencies are gaining adoption globally. Even though its utility may vary, the primary purpose of cryptocurrencies is to provide some form of payment (or medium of exchange) in the digital world. Lee and Teo underline that as more use cases arise from the industry, cryptocurrencies and blockchain are no longer a niche topic. Educational institutions are introducing it into their curriculum, and governments are talking about it in parliament. In particular, governments are keen to determine if the underlying technologies can form the fundamentals to issue a Central Bank issued Digital Currency (CBDC). Will these forms of currency become the "New Money"? This paper sets out to explore the utility of cryptocurrencies and

CBDC, their implications on the economy and the government's ability to use monetary policy. In their chapter, the authors examine and compare the approaches to CBDCs suggested by various governments.

Stablecoins become a major topic in the monetary policy and blockchain community after the announcement of Libra to issue its own programmable money. **Dante Disparte**, VP of Libra, shares his views about privately issued digital currencies. Dante notes that the progress and maturation of digital currencies should be welcomed by a wide range of stakeholders. Over a maiden decade, the world observed the wave of cryptocurrencies, greed-fueled or shoddy initial coin offerings (ICOs) and basic risk management failures, give way to credible opportunities to add optionality and competition in payments and banking through sound privately issued digital currencies. Dante underscores in his chapter that privately issued digital currencies or so-called stablecoins can play an important role in improving financial services. From enhancing consumer choice to spurring responsible financial services innovation and operating within the realm of regulatory and prudential oversight, rather than undermining or circumventing it, an industry is coming of age. After all, he claims, the vast amount of money in circulation in the global economy is privately issued via the two-tier banking system, credit card issuers and payment services firms, which are now turning to cryptocurrencies as a part of their own digital transformation efforts. This much holds true for the advent and likelihood of widespread public sector issuance of digital versions of fiat money in the form of central bank digital currencies (CBDCs).

Then we move into the space of crypto-asset. **Elisabeth Noble** from the European Banking Authority, gives us the view from the EU on this very critical topic, in the light of the recently introduced "Markets in Cryptoassets Regulation" and the "DLT Pilot Regime" for the crypto-asset secondary markets. Elizabeth provides some context for those regulatory proposals and reflects on some of the issues industry, regulators, and supervisors have encountered in seeking to reconcile innovative DLT applications with EU and national financial services law. Her chapter goes on to outline the key elements of the legislative proposals, which are intended to mitigate risks effectively and facilitate the scaling-up of DLT and crypto-asset applications in the EU.

Having explored the view of the EU on this topic we turn our attention to the view from Asia. **Syren Johnstone**, regulator in Hong Kong, stresses that the response in Asia to the emergence of crypto-assets has varied enormously intra-regionally. Developments in the larger capital markets have ranged from actively permissive industry-regulator partnering that has led to more granular regulation (Japan), to cautious approaches openly permitting industry development while applying existing laws where possible (Hong Kong), to banning specific activities while also promoting blockchain technology (Mainland China). After a review of the Asian narrative, he summarizes the current status of regulation in Asia. Then he addresses the hurdles to ecosystem development and questions whether regulatory incrementalism is sustainable. At the end of his chapter Synen reviews suggestions for policy development.

We conclude the Disintermediation Economics book addressing the impact of blockchain in the political economy, the regulation, the government sector, and the concept of disposable identities.

Pēteris Zilgalvis, head of the blockchain unit of the European Commission, opens the final part of the volume. Pēteris stresses that the law and political economy of decentralized digital ecosystems is the policy, economic, and legal framework surrounding the convergence of Blockchain/Distributed Ledger Technologies, the Internet of Things, decentralized Artificial Intelligence, and other emerging technologies. He claims that the key unifiers are the enablement of multilevel governance, the decentralized management of data and the distributed nature of the technologies. These new realities, Pēteris underscores, will challenge the existing more centralized economic and data management model of today's Internet and will provide self-determination to citizens in the management of their data and transactions. He believes that a major challenge for the implementation of these technologies is linked to their very essence, their decentralized nature. Much existing legislation was adopted in a time when more centralized models dominated. Finally, he analyzes the legal challenges of applying such legislation to decentralized digital technologies, and reflects on the use of regulatory sandboxes as well as novel legislation in order to enable innovation in the economy and society based on the application of these technologies.

Then, we turn to the fundamental question, how to create a global regulatory competitive advantage for the blockchain applications and solutions. **Eva Kaili**, the rapporteur of the Blockchain Resolution of the European Parliament and Chair of the Committee for the Future of Science (STOA) gives us her view on the topic. Eva stresses that the current efforts to provide institutional and legal certainty around blockchain-based innovative solutions reflect the status of the technology as it appears in the market today, which emphasizes more the "disintermediation" properties of the DLTs and less the "decentralization" properties. She believes that with the improvement of the design architectures, the algorithmic efficiency of the smart contracts, and the blending of DLTs with machine learning we can expect "decentralized autonomous organizations" to become more efficient over time and reach more strategic industries. This, she expects, will transform market structures, business and operational models and it is expected to have strong macroeconomic effects. These developments will pose significant challenges to the regulator. A principles-based approach is a sine qua non for creating a sustainable competitive advantage in order for an economy to leverage the benefits of blockchain. European Union is a pioneer regulator in the space of distributed ledgers. It adopts a technologically neutral approach. She believes that this is an appropriate approach, however technological neutrality should be coupled with business model neutrality. This is a requirement for making sure that the regulator will not be directed by short-term considerations and constraints. The European Parliament's Blockchain Resolution is a text that reflected the views of how to approach, from a regulatory point of view, a technology, which is still evolving. The Blockchain Resolution text provided the basis for the regulatory initiatives of the EU in blockchain-related topics and became the reference point for many other jurisdictions around the world.

European Union is very active in exploring cutting-edge innovative blockchain solutions to improve the functioning of the public sector. **Emanuele Baldacci** and **Joao Rodrigues Frade** from DG Digit of the European Commission work in the frontline of the digital transformation of the Public Sector. In their chapter, Emanuele and Joao discuss blockchain from a public sector perspective in Europe where interest in its adoption is accelerating. Having this goal in mind, the European Commission is currently deploying a common European Blockchain Services Infrastructure (EBSI) in close collaboration with the Member States, in addition to specific funding provided by EU Programmes. Emanuele and Joao note that despite being a recent technology, blockchain builds on classical trust enabling technologies to offer novel functionalities that open new possibilities for creating value for society. In the public sector, this happens via improved processes (internal focus) and services provided (external focus). Blockchain-based solutions, the authors believe, have the potential to increase significantly the rate of automation and modernization within the public sector in compliance with Europe's specific legal constraints, in particular when it comes to ensuring the authenticity of information in digital format.

The final chapter of this volume addresses the pioneering topic of disposable identities, accelerated by blockchain technology. **Loretta Anania, Gaëlle Le Gars**, and **Rob van Kranenburg** deal with this critical topic. The authors believe that many smart contract applications—or more precisely blockchain-based digital ledger technologies (DLTs) proliferate. And yet, without accounting for the identity dimension and the different authentication regimes, there is little chance that these technologies will gain widespread use, and their disruptive innovation potential will not be realized. A growing number of digital interactions in which we engage online require more trust and more security; choosing the right identity technologies and data policy safeguards is an important policy choice. Digital wallets are part of their proposed solution: based on disposable identities tied to events and timelines. They explain why identity technologies matter. They describe the communication network architectures and functionalities and then show how EU Treaty legislation safeguards the important elements of this identity framework. They give examples of self-sovereign identity, and other solutions adopted by the EU Member States. The authors conclude that successful deployment requires an EU legislative and regulatory framework fit for the digital society. The digital identity problem starts from the perspective of serving half a billion individual citizens, and inclusion requires public policy that strongly supports it.

Bibliography

Casey, M. and P. Vigna (2018), *The Truth Machine: The blockchain and the future of everything* (Harper Colins, London).

Fukuyama, F. (1992), *The End of History and the Last Man* (Free Press, New York).

Furlonger, D. and C. Uzereau (2019), *The Real Business of Blockchain: How leaders can create value in a new digital age* (Harvard Business Review Press, Cambridge, CA).

Page, S. (2018), *The Model Thinker: What you need to know to make data work for you* (Basic Books, New York).

Rogers, E. (2003), *The Diffusion of Innovations* (Free Press, New York).

Swan, M. (2015), *Blockchain: Blueprint for a new economy* (O'Reilly, Sebastopol, CA).

Tapscott, D. (2016), *Blockchain Revolution: How the technology is changing money, business and the world* (Random House, London).

Part I

Disintermediation in Microeconomics

2

Blockchain as an Economic Optimization Problem: Value, the Firm and the Limits of Decentralization

Dimitrios Psarrakis

Defining Blockchain Economics

Blockchain, in general terms, can be defined *as the digital technology that enables the transfer of verifiable data in a distributed network*. Taking this definition as a starting point we can define blockchain economics as *the study of how economic agents chose among different blockchain options considering efficiency alternatives associated with verification and network costs.*

What Is the Real Economic Value of Blockchain?

Answering this question is not an easy task. The perceptions about the uses and value of a technology change over time. This is a natural path for every technology as the real value a technology brings to the world reveals itself gradually through an iterative process of interaction between the technology developers, the market users and the implementing agents. Eugene Fitzgerald introduced his *iterative innovation model* to describe the dynamics of this process over time. He advises us to protect ourselves from the danger of *deterministic failure* while we experience this iterative process. Ignoring

---

D. Psarrakis (✉)
European Parliament, Bruxelles, Belgium
e-mail: dimitrios.psarrakis@europarl.europa.eu

economic or technological realities when we deal with a technological breakthrough can lead us to costly failures. Focusing solely on the technology without taking into consideration the demand and costs, or focusing solely on the economics without taking into consideration technical limits and practicalities is a common pitfall (Fidgerald et al. 2012).

From the experience of the author, in the last seven years, the prospect for a rational estimation of what blockchain can do (and cannot do) was distorted by the hype in the market and a technological enthusiasm. As it usually happens in times of irrational exuberance, neither those on the side of the blockchain enthusiasts nor those on the side of the blockchain skeptics had room to explore the sources of value of this technology. Now that the noise ceases and the information flows without distortions and aggressive narratives, it is time to explore the fundamentals.

In searching of how blockchain creates value, the first question to ask is whether DLT provides solutions to clearly defined problems or it is itself a technological option that seeks to find a problem to solve. Creating, delivering and capturing value from blockchain is indeed possible through different paths (consumption and production functions), mainly through the incremental improvement of existing products, services or processes or through the introduction of disruptive ones. In both the cases, economic efficiency is a sine qua non for the adoption of blockchain. In very general terms, blockchain, in order to be desirable for an economic agent, has to fulfill two sufficient conditions of efficiency: (a) the outcome that a blockchain solution can bring should maximize the total payoff over a set of feasible outcomes, and (b) this outcome should be strictly preferred by an economic agent to every other feasible outcome (Campbell 2018).

If we define blockchain as a general purpose technology (GPT), we can evaluate its economic value by assessing the impact of the technical improvements it brings, the innovational complementarities it creates, and the returns in scale it generates (Bresnahan and Trajtenberg 1995). However, there are important additional considerations to be taken into account. There is not just *one* blockchain. There are alternative technological architectures. Choosing among them carries significant economic consequences that generate different values in the production function.

To understand this point better, we can use the Solow model for technological change. We have the production function:

$$Q = A(t) \times f(K, L)$$

where the output Q is a function of capital K and labour L. The technological improvement A shifts the production function but does not alter the substitution rates between K and L (Solow 1957). In that sense, technological change is Hicks-neutral (Hicks 1932). However, because of the different possible architecture designs available, Hicks-neutrality is not the case for blockchain. Blockchain brings "Schumpetarian" technological change where A affects the changes of K and L disproportionally (Grossman and Helpman 1997). Different substitution rates generate different incentives for organizational design, as different types of blockchain adoption can impact both intra-organizational and inter-organizational arrangements.

Recent studies try to predict the impact of blockchain from an organizational point of view stressing the challenges it can bring to the economic institutions of capitalism. For them, blockchain is not a general purpose but rather an *institutional technology* (Davidson et al. 2016, 2018).

In this chapter, we bring together different ideas about blockchain technology stemming from an industrial organization (IO) point of view. First, we will explore the difference between blockchain-enabled, blockchain-complete and blockchain-enhanced organizations. Then, we will explore how far can we go in this continuum of organizational blockchain possibilities focusing on transaction and coordination costs. Finally, we conclude with an estimation of techno-social factors that can affect the speed and range of blockchain adoption over time in a framework of variegated capitalisms.

Any Blockchain Architecture Design Is an Economic Optimization Exercise

We defined blockchain economics as a challenge. The economic agent has to strike the balance in a trade-off between verification and network costs (Catalini and Gans 2018). This makes blockchain an economic optimization exercise that can be reduced into three major architecture questions: given the use case at hand and the value we want to create, (1) how much computational power should we allocate to every node of the network? (2) how many messages should every node exchange in order to achieve the necessary synchronization in the ledger and (3) how the network will manage the throughput of data?[1]

The use case always comes first. Before starting the design of the blockchain, economic agents need to answer a fundamental question: what problem we want to solve? This is the question that must discipline economic agents, as it is very common that technological enthusiasm and the philosophical narratives among different "tribes of blockchain disciples" prefer to

---

[1] In its simplest definition throughput can be the number of transactions per second, or TPS.

put technology, instead of the value proposition, first. Putting the problem first is what makes the Bitcoin blockchain such a powerful case. Satoshi Nakamoto had one problem in his mind: the transfer of tokens. He designed, thus, a solution that optimizes scalability based on the challenges around this problem. Concerns like smart contracts, time-stamping or interoperability with other ledgers were considered as secondary. This common-sense approach to the challenge of "how to build a useful blockchain", was lost when technology enthusiasts advanced a maximalist narrative that blockchain is the solution to everything.

Having decided what problem we have to solve to create value, the economic agent should think about two aspects, first the computational power that each node should have available to perform efficiently in the ledger. In a distributed network, this is of critical importance because, in order to have a trustworthy synchronization of data, subject to the agreed consensus mechanism, every node should be updated. Computational power is critical because, despite the efficiency of the coordination mechanism, the nodes of the network should wait for the node with the least computation power to be updated.[2]

Next to the computational power is the consensus algorithm. In the case of blockchain, the dominant role here is played by the consensus protocol that solves the problem of the "Byzantine generals" (Lamport et al. 1982). Blockchains use the Byzantine Fault Tolerant protocol (BFT) to build consensus between the nodes of the network. BFT is used by both permissioned and permissionless blockchains as the need for trust is important even in a permissioned environment (as there is no need for the participants in a permissioned blockchain to trust each other ex ante).

The BFT protocol solves, in theory, the problem of consensus in every scale but it does not solve automatically the problem of scalability of blockchains in practice. The Bitcoin blockchain, again, is a very successful case of scalability, despite that somebody cannot do a lot of things in the Bitcoin blockchain (this is often a source of critique of its scalability capacity). Thirteen years after the publication of the Bitcoin white paper (Nakamoto 2008) and despite that we have in place large-scale permissionless and permissioned blockchain projects by major technology corporations around the world, still, the case of Bitcoin blockchain provides the textbook reference point for scalability. This is true because Bitcoin was the first to address the challenge of the coordination problem between the number of nodes (today Bitcoin has around ten thousand nodes), the time you need to saturate a block and the time the

---

[2]There are different solutions to this synchronization challenge. For example Ethereum allows partial and deep synchronization so as to improve the efficiency of the ledger.

user should wait to see his transaction completed (today it takes around ten minutes to saturate a block).

The challenge that links the BFT consensus protocol with the scalability of blockchains is persistent in every architecture. How many nodes can you have onboard in your ledger? Ten? A thousand? A million? How much data do you need to use to achieve the desired synchronization between the nodes? How you optimize the throughput of data? Do you process ten thousand, hundred thousand, a million thousand transactions per second? Who sends the information that updates the ledger in a big crowd of nodes? Do you saturate the blocks with one-by-one transactions or you bundle many transactions together? How often should you update the ledger in a way that ensures the intrinsic value of the blockchain and at the same time delivers value to the user?

Academic and corporate research is focused on this type of optimization. Computer scientists and technology corporations compete on performance. They introduce solutions to improve the efficiency of the throughput of data by improving transactions per second (Gupta et al. 2019) or leveraging the properties of the protocol (Thai et al. 2019). They also compete in the value chain offering different approaches to the field of Blockchain-as-a-Service (BaaS). Some of them provide complete blockchain solutions in their own ledgers, others provide solutions building their blockchain interface in an existing ledger, and others work in the mid-ware aiming to reconcile different ledgers or couple innovative and legacy systems, neutralizing thus both the need to distinguish between permissioned and permissionless blockchains or even the need for interoperability between the ledgers.

Before moving a step forward in examining the value generation options, the main take-away is that any blockchain solution should be correctly sized so as to deliver to its value promise to the user, subject to a clearly articulated problem definition.

The Blockchain Value Generation Continuum

Having articulated the blockchain challenge as an optimization exercise, we need now to bring the economic value of blockchain closer to the economics of the firm. Models of digital transformation link the benefits of adopting digital technologies with the profitability and revenue generation efficiency of a firm as expressed by ratios like revenue per employee, fixed assets turn-over and EBIT margin. Horizontal analyses and benchmarking show that organizations with low or no adoption of digital layers in their operational and business models have -24% and -4% profitability and revenue generation efficiency, respectively, whereas digital champions (firms with high rates of digital adoption) enjoy up to 26% and 9% rates of profitability and revenue generation efficiency, respectively (Westerman et al. 2014).

We need to stress though that it is very difficult to isolate the impact of a specific technology on the profitability of a firm. Most studies speak in general about the adoption of a blend of digital technologies that may or may not include blockchain. This is also an indicator that the value of a digital technology should not be examined in isolation but in its convergence with other digital (and not) technologies. Moreover, we need to take into account that the growth of the firm is rarely the result of *mere* technological adoption. Complementarities play significant role in the growth function as digital transformation also improves the human capital of a firm as well as accelerates economies of scale (Griliches 1995).

When a firm should start considering the adoption of blockchain technology in its operational or business model? Competition generates intra-firm and industry trends over time. The gross profit margins indicate the momentum of the market. Increased competition reduces the price of sale units, reduces the volume of sales and increases the direct costs of production. A downside trend can be gradual or rapid. To reverse the trend, firms need either to reduce the total costs so as to improve the gross profit margin, or to offset the losses that occurred in the gross profit by improving the operating profit margin (by increasing the EBIT over sales ratio). A blockchain-based solution can be adopted as an improvement factor in the direct or indirect costs of production. Usually, blockchain affects the indirect costs by generating coordination and transaction efficiencies. It is important to note, though, that just like in the case of data intelligence, where firms need to assess if they really need a machine-learning capability or a simpler data analytics infrastructure, similarly, in the case of blockchain firms need to assess if they really need to be engaged in a blockchain network or if it suffice to develop a simple synchronization capability between two or more data structures.

From a strategic point of view, when the economic agent makes a blockchain decision needs to answer two questions: first, why to remove the intermediary when transacting with her peers, and second, if she enters in a network with her transacting peers, how much authority to delegate to this network? Different blockchain architectures can be engineered to accommodate different functional and governance preferences. This is another element that makes blockchain a trade-off exercise. These different strategic preferences can be satisfied by a simple architecture of distributed, immutable data structures (this is the one side of the continuum) or can be as complicated as a fully decentralized system with a network where every node can participate freely and without disclosing much information about himself (the other side of the continuum). These options span from very centralized systems of governance to very decentralized ones.

From our market observation, we see that the vast majority of organizations experiment and engage in blockchain projects close to the middle of the continuum where a combination of distribution, encryption, time-stamping and tokenization are employed in networks where the governance is strict, permissioned and controlled by protocols that allocate rights and liabilities to the nodes in a deterministic way without any reliance to *algorithmicly generated randomness.*[3]

From an Industrial Organizations point of view, the incentives system of an economic agent that compels him to choose between delegating the verification responsibility to a trusted third party or develop a peer-to-peer arrangement is related to the assessment of the costs between the two options. The centricity of the significance of "costs" in blockchain is critical. If the cost is the focal point that illustrates the incentives of the economic agents in choosing or not blockchain solutions, then the disruption that DLTs bring to the market does not seem to affect the traditional Economic Theory as the main hypotheses of Coase (1937) and Williamson (1985, 2013) remain unchallenged.

Transaction costs theory predicts that (1) the relative cost of using markets or firm's own resources, (2) the cost of drafting complex contracts across the market (Carlton and Perloff 2015) and (3) the capacity to reduce total costs in scale (Chandler 1999) determine the preference of the firm between accepting the service of an intermediary or developing a less costly network-based solution. Blockchain introduces, of course, a new cost but this cost is in aggregate less for the market participants than the cost of accepting a trusted third party as a transaction validator. In one sentence, blockchain simplifies the contractual relationships between the participants of the network, reducing the total costs of verification and generating economies of scale.

Does blockchain change the size of the firm or the size of the industrial value chain? In my view, when the discussion is about the firm, this question has not material impact in terms of performance. In theory, a firm is as big as the number of the contracts that composes it. In the case of blockchain, it is the nature of the contracts that changes (some of them are smart contracts), but this does not affect significantly the size of the firm. What is affected dramatically though, is the size of the value chain of some

---

[3]For a description of the role of randomness in decentralized blockchain environments you can review the first chapter of this volume.

industries. Blockchain disrupts the value chain and eliminates legacy factors that traditionally added value in the process, like gatekeepers, intermediaries, even regulators.

The next question to ask is: *how much of blockchain* is our society ready to accept in its value chains? As we have stressed, the majority of efforts today are concentrated around a specific blend of blockchain tools. Moving a step forward in completely decentralized operations will be determined by a set of technological and socio-political constraints.

Blockchain 4.0: Overcoming Socio-Political and Technological Constraints

In the beginning of this chapter, we stressed that blockchain is a Schumpetarian (not Hicks-neutral), institutional technology that can accelerate change in the production function and generate wider market dynamics. There is, consequently, a bridge that links the firm's transaction costs management with the overall coordination efforts of the other firms in the same industry, as well as with the overall performance of the Economy as a whole. This channel of thinking is at the core of the concept of institutional change (North 1990). Focusing entirely on transaction and coordination cost factors is necessary but not sufficient, as the decision of the firm to choose a certain position in the blockchain organizational continuum is affected by wider techno-social and institutional arrangements that the firm does not control and does not necessarily always see or grasp. The idea of change, in its nature, entails this "limited sight" element and affects how fast an organization and an economy change over time (North 2005).

Techno-social factors that affect blockchain ecosystems and ideas cannot be ignored. Blockchain is not only a technology. It is also an economic narrative, or a generator of economic narratives, itself (Shiller 2019) and as such, it reflects societal trends and mental constructs that inform economic thinking and action (Granovetter 2017). In its core, blockchain, as Hacker et al. underscore, is nested within broader political contexts and normative predispositions, ranging from private ordering, to calls to revisit fundamental concepts of money and finance, or even bring to the market of ideas visions for a new decentralized version of Capitalism. These issues cannot be easily resolved using formal economic, regulatory and legal frameworks (Hacker et al. 2019). Endorsing the view that institutional change is highly political (Haber et al. 2008), a reality that firms cannot escape, we believe that blockchain can qualify not merely as an institutional technology, but as a *political technology* as well.

We devoted the third part of this volume to the Political Economy of Blockchain and we will not repeat this conversation in this chapter. But for the needs of our analysis of how a firm architecture or a market structure can move (or resist to move), using blockchain, from one institutional setting to another, we need a framework that explains equilibrium shifts from one market variation to another. This framework is provided by the research program of the varieties of capitalism (VoC).[4]

To illustrate how Political Economy rather than Microeconomics affect the adoption of blockchain technology we can look at the case of an EU regulation. In September 2020, European Commission introduced a regulatory framework on a pilot regime for market infrastructures based on distributed ledger technology (the DTL Pilot Regime). The regulation has four objectives: (1) to bring legal certainty in the secondary markets for crypto-assets, (2) to support innovation by removing regulatory obstacles that prohibit the use of DLTs in the financial services, (3) to ensure investor protection and market integrity and (4) to ensure financial stability.[5] The editors of this volume participated in the drafting of this regulation and Elisabeth Noble describes it further in Chapter 9.

The DLT Pilot Regime is a market infrastructure regulation that aims to build an experimental design—a temporary regulatory sandbox. The intention of the Commission in introducing this text is to create space for experimentation of this new technology in a traditional (legacy) market setting that has three layers in the value chain of financial transactions of securities: the trading, the clearing and the settlement. In the EU Financial Markets regulatory framework, the trading of securities is regulated by the MIFID,[6] much about the clearing is regulated by the EMIR (especially in regard to CCPs)[7] and the settlement functions are regulated by the CSDR.[8] The fact that the securities transactions of the financial markets are separated in these three layers reflects a long tradition of unbundling the financial transactions in an attempt to ensure market integrity, to distribute liability efficiently and to promote competition. The market participants structured their role in the value chain accordingly. Multilateral Trading Facilities (MTFs), for example, have designed their operational models according to the job they need to

---

[4] For a complete account of the Varieties of Capitalism approach to political Economy see at Hall and Soskice (2013), Hancke (2009) and Macartney (2011).
[5] COM(2020) 594/3.
[6] EU Directive 2014/65.
[7] EU Regulation 2012/648.
[8] EU Regulation 2014/909.

perform whereas Central Security Depositories (CSDs) were designed accordingly to perform their job in the value chain. The DLT Pilot Regime was introduced to provide an experimental framework (an enhanced sandbox if you like) where the securities trading will be performed by "DLT MTFs" and "DLT SSS" (meaning CSDs operating a DLT securities settlement system), by temporarily removing some of the requirements of MIFID and CSDR, respectively.

Leaving aside the immediate market reactions about the narrow approach adopted (as it would be easier to include into the Pilot Regime trade facilities that are not licensed as MTFs), the major challenge comes from the fact that many of the operations carried out in the trading-clearing-settlement chain, can be consolidated in one operation using blockchain. This is a very interesting step as the MTFs suddenly can perform settlement functions without compromising transparency or increasing the verification costs, because blockchain technology allows so. How the market structure would look like then? From an institutional point of view, the performance of the settlement of securities was traditionally so centralized and so close to the governments, that it is considered as one of those "holy cows" that signify that a government is *truly* sovereign. The authority to settle a security transaction is similar to the authority of the Government to tax.

The first reflections from the market participants following the publication of the DLT Pilot Regime regulation were mixed. The Clearing Houses saw that this technology effectively leads them out of the market and they expressed their dissatisfaction to the lawmakers stressing that the separation of clearing from settlement enhances the integrity of the market. Banks and MTFs on the other hand welcomed the idea. Much of the settlement and clearing of their transactions can be now achieved in-house without the need for validation from an Authority. The moment we draft this chapter the regulation is still in the European Parliament and we expect to see the final draft in 2022, but the institutional tension that blockchain generates is apparent already indicating the socio-political constraints for a rapid adoption of decentralized blockchain solutions.

There are also technological and organizational constraints. The case of the DLT Pilot Regime gives an idea of market consolidation, but let us think by taking this example a step further. DTCC is the US post-trade financial services company that provides clearing and settlement services to financial markets. Can we blockchain the entire function of the DTCC? To build a thought experiment around this hypothetical case, following the framework of analysis we introduced in section B of this chapter, we need to answer the following fundamental questions: how much computational capacity we need to allocate to the nodes of this network of clearing and settlement? how many messages should exchange the nodes in order to achieve the necessary synchronization? who will update the blocks, how and how often? how much time will be necessary to complete the transactions and deliver value compared to the legacy system? These are the questions a blockchain architect should ask in order to design a correctly sized blockchain solution. In one sentence, what computational power and how the consensus mechanism should be organized to allow the clearing of, let's say, 100 K transactions per second (TPS) given that in the current DTCC operations, the throughput of data (the TPS) is not a problem at all?

This hypothetical scenario—the disruption of DTCC—is a case that shows the limits of decentralization because given the computational and network costs, the blockchain, as an alternative does not add much to the value chain unless the performance of the computation becomes extremely efficient (maybe with the assistance of a spectacularly more powerful hyper-performance computer). And what if we had this super-computer available? Would the market participants prefer to coordinate in a decentralized blockchain system of that scale? In the first chapter of this book, we introduced the idea of algorithmic randomness as a source of "trust generation" in decentralized blockchain systems where each node has one vote. We have also explained earlier in this chapter that the choice of having or not a trusted intermediary is related to a cost function. To complete the picture we introduce a behaviuoral layer that actually dissuade firms from engaging in decentralized-complete blockchain networks.

Richard Cyert and James March, building on Herbert Simon's idea of bounded rationality, introduced the idea of the behavioral theory of the firm (Cyert and March 1963) where the motivations for inter-organizational action and participation are constrained by bureaucratic and collectivist frictions. Economic agents optimize subject to the information available to them at a given point in time (March and Simon 1993). Williamson builds further on this view by stressing that transaction cost economics refer only to contractual safeguards, or the absence of them, and argues against the idea of complete trust (1996).

This lack of trust and the knowledge of the economic agents that they act under limited information and high uncertainty, creates deterrents that incentivizes firms to chose blockchain architectures that they own. A major finding so far is that ownership behaviour persists in blockchains (McAffee and Brynjolfsson 2017). The second finding that discourages organizations from endorsing decentralized-complete solutions is related to the incompleteness of the contracts. Going back to the example of the DTCC, the (naturally) myopic view of the financial corporations to envisage in advance the contingencies that may occur and add them in the provisions and covenants of a smart contract is a clear disincentive to participate in a decentralized network. Blockchain does not solve the problem of incomplete contracts (De Filippi and Wright 2018).

The effect of bounded rationality in organizational choices provides only one set of disincentives to join decentralized-complete blockchain systems. There are other limitations that we can explore by reviewing the limits of cooperative behaviour in game-theoretic terms. Purely decentralized blockchain systems allocate one vote to every node. This governance setting is not very attractive even in permissionless blockchains where the proof of stake plays a strong role in incentivizing the actors of the network to cooperate. In the DTCC example, not every financial firm is of the same systemic impact. As such, when we face a systemic risk, the algorithmic policy of the consensus mechanism needs to be adapted so as to incentivize more influential actors in the network to make choices that remedy the systemic problem more efficiently (Sakovics and Steiner 2012). These adaptation rules cannot be envisaged in advance, making the sustainability of consensus fragile in the long run.

The problem of sustainability of the consensus mechanisms is also associated with a fourth problem: the short-term behaviour of the economic agents in a blockchain is not necessarily aligned with their long-term goals. In a permissioned blockchain, the writer of the ledger extracts profits over her monopoly of the ledger and dynamically incentivizes honest reporting. On the other hand, in a decentralized blockchain, the writer of the ledger provides static incentives for honesty through computationally expensive proof-of-work algorithms but his rents are neutralized by the possibility of forks (Abadi and Brunnermeier 2018). The possibility of forks is a significant source of economic instability as they create to the participants of the blockchain the opportunity to play a coordination game with multiple equilibria (Biais et al. 2018). If the financial market players had the opportunity to "disrupt with blockchain" the DTCC, even in the world of perfect knowledge and endless computational power, still the insufficiency of blockchain to create a Nash equilibrium and the availability of numerous possible multiple equilibria that do not rule out the possibility of collusion when the circumstances change for some of the participants, dissuades economic agents from accepting their participation in a decentralized blockchain network.

Following this game-theoretic and behavioural reasoning we see that perfect decentralization is not necessarily the best alternative to the legacy system. Also, the idea that we can solve systemic risks with blockchain, as many enthusiasts of blockchain hold (Swan 2019), is not an easy task and further elaboration is necessary.

Conclusion

In this chapter, we defined blockchain economics and explained why any blockchain choice is by necessity an economic optimization exercise. We show what trade-offs an economic agent should take into consideration in designing a blockchain solution and the availability of blockchain options, as well as the value an organization can extract in a blockchain continuum. Finally, we explored the limits of decentralization and behavioural and strategic factors that dissuade economic agents from choosing decentralized-enhanced blockchain solutions. We suggest that four factors discourage organizations to engage in decentralized-enhanced blockchains. These factors are: the persistence of ownership behaviour in blockchains, the incompleteness of contracts, the fragility of the consensus mechanisms and the lack of alignment between short-term and long-term goals of the blockchain network participants.

Bibliography

Abadi, J. and M. Brunnermeier (2018), *Working Paper* (NBER: Cambridge, MA).
Biais, B., Bisiere, C., Bouvard, M. and C. Casamatta (2018), The Blockchain Folk Theorem, Working Papers (Toulouse School of Economics, Toulouse).
Bresnahan, T. F. and M. Trajtenberg (1995), General Purpose Technologies: 'Engines of Growth?', *Journal of Econometrics*, 65, pp 83–108.
Campbell, D. E. (2018), *Incentives: Motivation and the Economics of Information* (Cambridge University Press: Cambridge).
Carlton, D. W. and J. M. Perloff (2015), *Modern Industrial Organization* (Pearson: New York).
Catalini, C. and J. Gans (2018), Some Simple Economics of the Blockchain, Working Paper (NBER, Cambridge, MA).
Chandler, A. D. (1999), *Scale and Scope: The Dynamics of Industrial Capitalism* (Harvard University Press: Cambridge, MA).
Coase, R. H. (1937), The Nature of the Firm, *Economica*, 14, 16, pp 386–405.
COM (2020) 594/3, 2020/0267(COD): Proposal for a Regulation on a Pilot Regime for Market Infrastructures Based on Distributed Ledger Technology.
Cyert R. M. and J. G. March (1963) *A Behavioral Theory of the Firm* (Prentice Hall: Hoboken, New Jersey).

Granovetter, M. (2017), *Society and Economy: Framework and Principles* (Harvard University Press, Cambridge, MA).

Davidson, S., De Filippi, P. and J. Potts (2018), Blockchains and the Economic Institutions of Capitalism, *Journal of International Economics*, 14, 4, pp 639–58.

Davidson, S., De Filippi, P. and J. Potts (2016), Economics of Blockchain, Public Choice Conference, May 2016, Fort Lauderdale, United States.

De Filippi, P. and A. Write (2018), *Blockchain and the Law: The Rule of Code* (Harvard University Press: Cambridge, MA).

EU Directive 2014/65: Markets in Financial Instruments Directive.

EU Regulation 2012/648: European Market Infrastructure Regulation.

EU Regulation 2014/909: Central Securities Depository Regulation.

Fidgerald, E., Wankerl, A. and C. Schramm (2012), *Inside Real Innovation: How the Right Approach Can Move Ideas from R&D to Market and Get the Economy Moving* (World Scientific Publishing: Singapore).

Griliches, Z. (1995), R&D and Productivity, at Stoneman, P. (ed), *Handbook of the Economics of Innovation and Technological Change* (Blackwell: Oxford).

Grossman, G. M. and E. Helpman (1997), *Innovation and Growth in the Global Economy* (MIT Press: Cambridge, MA).

Gupta, S., Rahnama, S. and M. Sadoghi (2019), Permissioned Blockchain Through the Looking Glass: Architecture and Implementation Lessons Learned, Working Paper (Exploratory Systems Lab: University of California, Davis).

Haber, S., North, D. C. and B. Weingast (2008) *Political Institutions and Financial Development* (Stanford University Press, Stanford, CA).

Hacker, P., Lianos, I., Dimitropoulos, G. and S. Eich (2019), *Regulating Blockchain: Techno-social and Legal Challenges* (Oxford University Press, Oxford).

Hall, P. A. and D. Soscice (2013), *Varieties of Capitalism: The Institutional Foundations of Comparative Advantage* (Oxford University Press: Oxford).

Hancke, B. (2009), *Debating Varieties of Capitalism: A Reader* (Oxford University Press: Oxford).

Hicks, J. (1932), *The Theory of Wages* (St. Martins Press: London).

Lamport, L., Shostak, R. and M. Pease (1982), The Byzantine Generals Problem, *ACM Transactions on Programming Languages and Systems*, 4, 3, pp 382–401.

Macartney, H. (2011), *Variegated Neoliberalism: EU Varieties of Capitalism and International Political Economy* (Routledge: New York).

McAfee, A. and E. Brynjolfsson (2017), *Machine, Platform, Crowd: Harnessing Our Digital Future* (Norton: New York).

March, J. and H. Simon (1993), *Organizations* (Blackwell Publishers: Cambridge, MA).

Nakamoto, S. (2008), *Bitcoin: A Peer-to-Peer Electronic Cash System* (Whitepaper: www.bitcoin.org).

North, D. C. (1990), *Institutions, Institutional Change and Economics Performance* (Cambridge University Press: Cambridge).

North, D. C. (2005), *Understanding the Process of Economic Change* (Princeton University Press: Princeton, NJ).

Sakovics J. and J. Steiner (2012), Who Matters in Coordination Problems, *American Economic Review*, 102, 7, pp 3439–61.

Shiller, R. J. (2019), *Narrative Economics: How Stories Go Viral and Drive Major Economic Events* (Princeton University Press, Princeton, NJ).

Solow, R. (1957), Technical Change and the Aggregate Production Function, *Review of Economics and Statistics*, 39, 3, pp 312–20.

Swan, M. (2019), Blockchain Economic Networks: Economic Network Theory, Systemic Risk and Blockchain Technology, at Treiblmaier H. and R. Beck, *Business Transformation Through Blockchain* (Palgrave: New York).

Thai, T. Q., Yim, J. C., Yoo, T. W., Yoo, H. K., Kwak, J. Y. and S. M. Kim (2019), Hierarchical Byzantine fault-tolerance protocol for permissions blockchain systems, *Journal of Supercomputing*, 75, pp 7337–65.

Westerman, G., Bonnet, D. and A. McAffee (2014), *Leading Digital: Turning Technology into Business Transformation* (Harvard Business School Press: Cambridge, MA).

Williamson, O. E. (1985), *The Economic Institutions of Capitalism* (Free Press: New York).

Williamson, O. E. (1996), *The Mechanisms of Governance* (Oxford University Press: Oxford).

Williamson, O. E. (2013), *The Transaction Costs Economics Project: The theory and practice of the governance of contractual relations* (Edward Elgar: Northampton, MA).

3

Economics of Smart Contracts: Efficiency and Legal Challenges

Guenther Dobrauz-Saldapenna and Mark A. Schrackmann

Definition and Idea of Smart Contracts

What is a smart contract? This question came up at the latest with the ongoing blockchain hype that has been persisting for quite some time.

The principle of smart contracts was first described by American computer scientist and cryptographer Nick Szabo in the early 1990s. Szabo defined smart contracts as «*computerized transaction protocols that execute the terms of a contract*».[1] In other words, the terms of a contract are mapped directly in a code, i.e. a computer program, which then automatically executes the predefined terms as soon as the contractual conditions have been fulfilled.[2] The

---

[1] Nick Szabo, Smart Contracts, 1994, available at: https://www.fon.hum.uva.nl/rob/Courses/InformationInSpeech/CDROM/Literature/LOTwinterschool2006/szabo.best.vwh.net/smart.contracts.html.

[2] Government Office for Science, Distributed Ledger Technology, beyond blockchain, 2016, p. 22 (abrufbar available at: https://www.gov.uk/government/uploads/system/uploads/attachment_data/file/492972/gs-16-1-distributedledger-technology.pdf).

G. Dobrauz-Saldapenna (✉) · M. A. Schrackmann
PwC Zurich, Zurich, Switzerland
e-mail: guenther.dobrauz@ch.pwc.com

M. A. Schrackmann
e-mail: mark.schrackmann@pwc.ch

smart contract basically describes a technology, which allows the exchange of digitally referenced goods and services based on computable contract terms.[3]

An essential requirement for the functioning of smart contracts is that the computer program can automatically verify whether the parties have met their contractual obligations. This assumes that the respective contractual terms must be defined very clearly from the beginning; otherwise, the self-execution process generated by the program code will not be possible. As a result, there is absolutely no room for any interpretation or for discretion.[4] The program code only follows clear «if/when–then» conditions, which will then be executed automatically and completely autonomously and cannot be stopped.

From Szabo's point of view, the simplest version of a smart contract is the vending machine, which is programmed to release goods as soon as the predefined price has been paid.[5] Smart contracts follow exactly the same principle. The exchange of contractual services (e.g. exchange of goods for money) takes place automatically under precisely predefined conditions. Only the program code verifies whether the contractual conditions have been fulfilled. The contracting parties themselves have no influence on it and do not have to deal with the orderly fulfillment of the contract. This may be advantageous if the contracting parties do not know each other personally. Szabo saw the aim of smart contracts to ensure common contractual terms (such as payment terms, liens, and even enforcement), minimize both intentional and unintentional deviations, and minimize the need for external, trusted intermediaries.[6]

Although the idea and concept of smart contracts already exist for some time, there is currently no official and common definition. For that reason, the term "smart contract" needs to be defined more precisely. Contrary to what the wording of the term might suggest, it is not to be understood literally.[7] In order to understand the concept of smart contracts, it is important to know that the use of this term is misleading insofar as smart contracts are neither «smart» nor «contracts».[8] A smart contract is definitely not smart in

---

[3] Rolf H. Weber, Smart Contracts and what the Blockchain has got to do with it, in: Michele DeStefano/Guenther Dobrauz, *New Suits—Appetite for Disruption in the Legal World*, pp. 358–359.
[4] Swiss LegalTech Associations (SLTA), Regulatory Task Force Report, April 27, 2018, pp. 49–51.
[5] Nick Szabo, Formalizing and Securing Relationships on Public Networks, 1997, available at: https://archive.is/wIUOA.
[6] Szabo (fn. 1).
[7] See Reggie O'Shields, Smart Contract: Legal Agreements for the Blockchain, North Carolina Banking Institute Journal 2017, p. 177 et seq.
[8] See David Adlerstein, Are Smart Contracts Smart?, A Critical Look at Basic Blockchain Questions, Coindesk, June 26, 2017, available at: https://www.coindesk.com/when-is-a-smart-contract-actually-a-contract/.

the common sense of intelligence. It rather follows stubbornly its program code and hence executes only what the creator has programmed it for. Contracts, both in our legal and cultural understanding, are usually considered as something more than a *program* that provides temper-proofness and algorithmic executions[9]; it is a richer notion. Examined within the framework of their technological capabilities, smart contracts rather qualify as plans, not contracts.[10]

A smart contract is not a traditional contract in the sense of civil law but rather a piece of software, which can control, document and even cause a legally relevant transaction once the predefined conditions are met.[11] Smart contracts can be thus characterized by the ability to automatically execute predefined transactions without any human influence as a consequence of fulfilled conditions.[12] Taking into account all these aspects, a smart contract can be described as «*a consensual arrangement between at least two parties for an automated, independent commercial result from the satisfaction or non-satisfaction, determined objectively through code, of a specific factual condition*».[13]

Smart Contracts and Blockchain

At the time when smart contracts were first described back in the '90s of the last century, computer science was not yet advanced enough to implement Szabo's new ideas and concepts. Although the concept of smart contracts is much older than the blockchain technology,[14] smart contracts are closely linked to the booming technology as there is finally a solid and suitable technical infrastructure for their functioning. With blockchain, it is possible to

---

[9] See Cong and He, Blockchain Disruption and Smart Contracts.
[10] See Shoshana Zuboff, The Age of Surveylance Capitalism.
[11] Christoph Simmchen, Blockchain (R)Evolution, MMR 2017, p. 162.
[12] Henning Diedrich, Ethereum: Blockchains, Digital Assets, Smart Contracts, Decentralized Autonomous Organizations, London 2016, p. 167; Stephan D. Meyer/Benedikt Schuppli, «Smart Contracts» und deren Einordnung in das schweizerische Vertragsrecht, recht 2017, pp. 204–208.
[13] Adlerstein (fn. 8).
[14] The first blockchain was conceptualized by a person (or group of people) known as Satoshi Nakamoto in 2008. Blockchain can be described as a shared, distributed ledger on which transactions are digitally recorded and linked together so that they provide the entire history or provenance of an asset. Each transaction is added to the blockchain only after it has been validated using a consensus protocol, which ensures it is the only version of the truth. Every record is also encrypted to provide an extra layer of security. The records cannot be changed because all participants have access to the same version of the truth (see: What are smart contracts on blockchain?, Blockchain Pulse: IBM Blockchain Blog, July 2, 2018, available at: https://www.ibm.com/blogs/blockchain/2018/07/what-are-smart-contracts-on-blockchain/).

share data in a highly trusted way between disparate parties, without a trusted intermediary such as an entity or a person.[15]

The core function of smart contracts using blockchain as a platform[16] is to capture contractual agreements and to execute the respective transactions as soon as the predefined conditions are fulfilled.[17] The blockchain is important for the execution of smart contracts since it is a distributed ledger that is able to efficiently record transactions in a permanent way, i.e. the technology is resistant to modifications of data.[18] With the use of blockchain, the contractual fulfillment is able to take place independently and without any human intervention. The verification of the contract will be done by the blockchain for which reason the principle "Code is law"[19] applies. Only the program code decides whether the contractual conditions have been fulfilled correctly or not. At the same time, all executed transactions are permanently stored on the blockchain and cryptographically secured. These features offer contractual parties a high reliability with respect to the compliance of the contract.[20]

In summary, three main features characterize a smart contract using blockchain technology[21]:

- *Self-execution*: Once the agreed contractual conditions in the program code are fulfilled, the computer program will execute the predefined actions automatically and without any human interaction.
- *Immutability*: As transactions on the blockchain cannot be reversed, the adaption of the programmed terms of a smart contract is not possible.
- *Digital performance*: Smart contracts allow a transfer of digitally reference goods and services but not a performance in the real world.

One advantage of smart contracts is that all users of a certain blockchain network (not only the contracting parties) have the same copy of the program code, which ensures that a smart contract cannot be modified by a single

---

[15] David Fisher/Pierson Grider, The Blockchain in Action in the Legal World in: Michele DeStefano/Guenther Dobrauz, *New Suits—Appetite for Disruption in the Legal World*, p. 377.
[16] Ethereum is currently the main platform for running smart contracts. Ripple and Mastercoin offer also smart contracts based on a blockchain
[17] Karen E. C. Levy, Book-Smart, Not Street-Smart: Blockchain-Based Smart Contracts and The Social Workings of Law, Engaging Science, Technology, and Society 2017, p. 1 ff., 3.
[18] Rolf H. Weber (fn. 3), p. 357.
[19] See Lawrence Lessig, Code and Other Laws of Cyberspace, 1999, p. 3.
[20] SLTA (fn. 4), p. 36.
[21] Hans Rudolf Trüeb, Smart Contracts, in Grolimund et al. (eds.), Festschrift für Anton K. Schnyder, Zürich 2018, p. 726; SLTA (fn. 4). p. 36; Rolf H. Weber (fn. 3), p. 360.

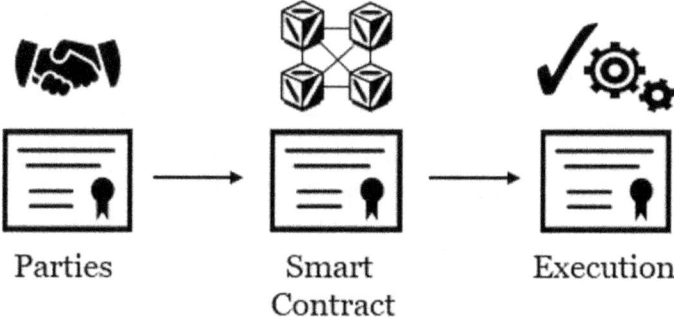

Fig. 3.1 The place of a smart contract in a transaction (*Source* The authors)

contractual party. In addition, the agreed contractual terms will be executed automatically and without any human intervention once the predefined and agreed conditions have been fulfilled. This attribute increases speed on the one hand and safety on the other, while reducing costs and operational risks. Due to the immutability and durability of the blockchain, the fulfillment of the contract can always be traced even afterwards. Another notable advantage of smart contracts consists in the fact that once the predefined conditions are met, the contractual terms cannot be refused without reason or maliciously. Thus, smart contracts also enable businesses between parties who do not trust each other. A further decisive advantage compared to a normal contractual relationship is that there is no need for an intermediary to check whether the conditions of the contract have been fulfilled. Finally, yet importantly, there are in principle no difficulties in the interpretation of contracts, as the program code automatically enforces the terms in accordance with the predefined provisions, with no room for interpretation. The legal uncertainty that may prevent the conclusion of contracts can be eliminated (Fig. 3.1).

The advantages of smart contracts using blockchain technology can be summarized as follows[22]:

- *Speed and accuracy*: Smart contracts are digital and automated. This guarantees a high degree of speed and accuracy compared to traditional systems.
- *Trust*: Smart Contracts automatically execute transactions accordingly to predefined rules. The encrypted records of these transactions are automatically shared with all participants of the blockchain. As a result, no

---

[22] See IBM (fn. 12).

contractual party has to be concerned about whether information has been altered for personal benefit.
- *Security*: Blockchain transaction records are encrypted and this makes them very vulnerable to hacking. Since each individual record is linked to previous and subsequent records on the blockchain, the entire chain would need to be altered in order to change a single record.
- *Cost savings*: From an economic point of view, smart contracts definitely entail efficiency gains by automating transaction processes and the avoidance for third parties such as lawyers, notaries and bankers, which in turn may lead to significant cost savings.

Besides the described advantages, the functioning of smart contracts nevertheless harbours certain risks, as the fundamental immutability of data, which is a core element of the blockchain, requires an error-free program code. Incorrect elements can therefore not be removed or corrected without further ado.[23] Even if there is no legally binding contract, the content of the smart contract will be executed without the possibility to adapt it (at least in theory).[24] The error-prone nature of complex smart contracts involves therefore a considerable risk potential. This is in particular the case with so-called DAOs («Decentralized Autonomous Organisations»), which are a combination of various linked and complex smart contracts.[25] One famous example which illustrates this risk is «The DAO», an investment fund operating on the basis of smart contracts, from which USD 50 million would be stolen due to such programming mistake.[26]

Possible Use Cases

When following currently discussed business ideas, there seem to be no limits to the creativity in possible application areas of blockchain-based smart contracts. Examples of use cases for smart contracts are[27]:

---

[23] Jörn Erbguth, Lösung Blockchain-basierter Konflikte, Jusletter IT, February 23, 2017; Lukas Müller/Reto Seiler, Smart Contracts aus Sicht des Vertragsrechts, Akutelle Juristische Praxis (AJP) 2019, p. 324.
[24] Gabriel Jaccard, Smart Contracts and the Role of Law, Jusletter IT, November 23, 2017, N 94. Müller/Seiler (FN 17), pp. 324–325.
[25] Melanie Swan, Blockchain: blueprint for a new economy, Peking 2015, p. 24 f.
[26] See Lee Bacon/George Bazinas, «Smart Contracts»: The Next Big Battlegroud?, Jusletter IT, May 19, 2017, N 11.
[27] SLTA (fn. 4), pp. 49–51.

- *Smart contracts for identity*: Smart contracts can let individuals own and control their digital identity with reputation, data and digital assets. This enables individuals to choose what personal information they want to disclose to their business partners, giving companies the ability to know their clients seamlessly.
- *Smart contracts for financial data recording*: Financial institutions can use smart contracts to accurately and transparently capture financial data. Smart contracts enable unified financial data across the organization, improved financial reporting as well as reduced audit and security costs.
- *Smart contracts for trade finance*: Smart contracts can facilitate rationalized international trade in goods through faster initiation of letters of credit and trade payments, while at the same time enabling greater liquidity of financial assets.
- *Smart contracts for supply chain*: Smart contracts can improve transparency at every step of the supply chain. Internet of Things (IoT)[28] devices can write to a smart contract when a product moves from the warehouse to the store shelves, providing a real-time view of a company's entire supply chain.
- *Smart contracts for securities*: Smart contracts can facilitate the automatic payment of dividends, stock splits and liability management, while reducing counterparty and operational risks.
- *Smart contracts for mortgages*: Smart Contracts can automatically connect the various parties involved in the mortgage business, enabling a smooth and less error-prone process.

Beyond the Applications: Smart Contracts and Economic Theory

Economic theory and contracts are interconnected concepts. Contract theory is a section of Microeconomics and Game Theory and deals systematically with incentives, information and economic institutions.[29] From an Industrial Organization's point of view, contracts are linked with the size of the firm. A firm is perceived as a bundle of contracts designed to improve the efficiency of the markets.[30] Here we emphasize the role of the contracts as an incentive and information mechanism. There are three fundamental topics

---

[28]The Internet of things (IoT) is the extension of Internet connectivity into physical devices and everyday objects.
[29]See Bolton and Dewatripont, Contract Theory, 2000.
[30]See Wiliamson (1985) and Coase (1988).

in the theory of contract economics: (a) static vs. dynamic contracting, (b) bilateral vs. multilateral relationships and (c) completeness vs. incompleteness of contracts.[31] We believe that the merit of evaluating smart contracts against these three axes of analysis can be an important research program with strong practical and academic impact. Here we will focus on two issues: (i) the completeness of smart contracts and (ii) the dynamics of smart contracts.

Contract Completeness and Smart Contracts

Contract (in-)completeness is the first important element we need to examine. The contract is a well-studied topic in Economics of industrial organizations. The starting point in the study of this subject is the fundamental premise that contracts are incomplete and that this incompleteness carries significant properties and material consequences in the behaviour of economic agents.[32] Are the smart contracts (more) complete? The case of Ethereum's DAO Crowdfunding project is well known. The designers of this Decentralized Autonomous Organization structured an algorithmic architecture with specific economic targets of action and activated the smart contracts to run the project. The DAO reflected an aspiration for a blockchain-complete project, or a project which entailed *all* the fundamental properties of a blockchain, namely, distribution, encryption, disintermediation, tokenization and decentralization.[33] The designers of DAO structured an architecture of code lines having in their mind a set of possible scenarios (*state-contingent*, to use the idea of Arrow and Debreu) that could occur.

However, smart contracts are as smart as the insight of their designers, just like a legal contract is as complete as the insight of the agents who draft the covenants. Even in an ideal world where all information is available, without possibility an agent to be engaged in any hidden action and secured in terms of "incentive compatibility" where everybody has strong motivations for "truth telling", it is impossible, in practice, to have available in place the resources to draft a perfect and complete contract. In a less than ideal world, like ours, the glitches in algorithmic contract structuring should be rather considered as the rule. This is what happened with DAO. Somebody spotted a glitch in the algorithm and stole a significant amount of the accounts.

There is a critical element to consider here. Drafting a smart contract requires the designer to be able to transform a human-readable language

---

[31] See Bernard Salanie, The Economics of Contracts, A primer, 2000.
[32] For an analytic account on contract incompleteness review Oliver Hart (1995).
[33] For the distinction between blockchain-inspired applications and blockchain completeness see: Furlonger and Uzureau.

into a machine-readable code. As the case of DAO eloquently tells us, the difference between legitimate transaction and theft comes down to intent, and intent is something a smart contract cannot recognize. Contracts are part of our society because they allow us to operate under uncertainty. Our legal tradition, after 4000 years of contracting, is knowledgable enough to deal with the realities of the *contractual ambiguity*. This is not the case for the smart contracts yet. Moreover, contractual ambiguity is difficult to be treated in any foreseeable digital environment no matter how advanced the smart contract's code is expected to become, or how efficient the blending of blockchain with machine learning can be.[34]

Dynamic Contracting and Smart Contracts

Smart contracts, in the current state of blockchain technology, cannot be considered as complete contracts. What is their value, then? One major property that makes smart contracts valuable is that they can regulate and enforce the covenants of the contract at the same time.[35] This introduces us to an era that Write and De Filippi call "lex cryptographia".[36] The major concern here is: what is going to happen when circumstances change or when a glitch is spotted? The DAO drama was that the designers found out promptly where the problem was and as well as the attack, but the decentralized consensus mechanism prohibited them from making a rapid change in the code to stop the attack and prevent future theft. The sole solution was to fork the Ethereum. This was a painful decision for the Ethereum ecosystem, and reminds us that we cannot ignore the fact that neither our legal tradition nor our society resolve contractual inefficiencies with forking.

Smart contracts can be easily formed between parties and the code is considered as "mutually accepted" whenever the agents reach a point of "mutual state of mind". But when conditions change, the smart contracts do not evolve, especially when they operate in a wide decentralized environment (a robust blockchain). They stay static reflecting the equilibrium when the agreement between the counterparties was reached. In an environment with pseudonymous agents, benefits can be observed in the functionality of static and rigid smart contracts. But in "more than pseudonymous" settings, this is an obvious setback that prohibits the scalability of smart contracts to a

---

[34] Kevin Werbach (2018).

[35] De Filippi and Write (2018).

[36] Lex Cryprographia: rules administered through self-executing smart contracts and decentralized autonomous organization, Write and De Filippi (2015).

wider space of industrial or administrative applications. Smart contracts need to have by design the property of "self-correction" when the principles that led to their creation are violated.

The efficient design of smart contracts will be the determinant of the rapidity of transitioning from blockchain-inspired solutions to wider blockchain-complete solutions. But, how is it possible to improve the economic efficiency of smart contracts?

Making Smart Contracts, Smarter I: Physical and Programmable Intermediation

The limits of smart contracts are evidenced. But these limits also reflect the technological limits of blockchain today to achieve decentralization in an economically efficient manner. A solution to the economic inefficiencies of decentralization can be remedied with programmable intermediation. We can identify here two possible types: curators and oracles.

Curators

One of the most recent developments in the space of crypto-assets is the emergence of Decentralized Finance organizations (DeFi). DeFis operate as quasi-decentralized autonomous organizations operating cryptoexanchages on the ledger with smart contract enabled decentralized applications (dApps). The people who build and "run" these decentralized organizations try to replicate and improve the design of DAO. However, behind the narrative of decentralization, which rather reflects an ideological interpretation of blockchain technology rather than the need to put business pragmatism first, these DeFis are rarely completely autonomous. DeFis, just like the 90% of the smart contracts we see in the market, are quasi-autonomous because they have curators to make sure that the activities of their organizations will freeze in case of an attack. The designers of Ethereum DAO have curators in place—appointed by the token-holders in a form of a "multisig" contract. The curators could be fired by the token holders in an attempt to avoid centralization.[37] The mentioning to DeFis in the context of smart contracts is that operational efficiency should be design-neutral. The facilitation of the blockchain operations by physical intermediaries is a possibility that enables

---

[37] Ioannis Lianos (2019).

the rapid experimentation with smart contracts in a wide range of applications creating institutional and legal certainty as well as a solid framework of liability that can only benefit the idea behind the smart contracts.

Oracles

The prerequisite for the autonomous execution of a smart contract is the availability of all relevant data needed to execute the terms and conditions defined in a smart contract.[38] Smart contracts can only access information that is available on the blockchain. In practice, there are many cases in which indeterminable external events or information are still required for the contract fulfillment or not available at the time the contract is concluded. In order to feed the blockchain which such external information, so-called «oracles» are used. Oracles are automated data entries or third parties, which act as an independent agent between the blockchain and real-world occurrences.

The use of oracles harbours the inherent risk that the accuracy of the provided information cannot be fully guaranteed as oracles are not part of the blockchain consensus mechanism. To ensure the correct fulfilment of a contract, an oracle must therefore have a high degree of trustworthiness in order to be capable as an independent, non-manipulable information source. Obviously, the benefit of a smart contract is greater when more information is available on the blockchain from the beginning and when someone has to rely less on external information sources.

Oracles also can serve as links with external "off-blockchain" events, in a more general form.[39] An optimal use of smart contracts and oracles can resolve the static nature and inherent rigidity of the smart contracts when conditions change or un-anticipated circumstances occur. Oracles give a genuine dynamic property to the smart contract that we do not meet in the paper-written contracts today. Contracts can be designed in such a way that will enable the adjustment of performance obligations during the term of an agreement by using this third-party source. Oracles can also perform functions of dispute resolution. This is a significant possibility especially when the smart contracting takes place between pseudonymous parties, where often the contract favours the counterpart with the greater bargaining power.[40]

---

[38] SLTA (fn. 4), p. 36.
[39] Ioannis Lianos, ibid.
[40] De Filippi and Write, Blockchain and the Law, 2018.

Making Smart Contracts, Smarter II: Ricardian Contracts

The self-execution feature of the smart contracts can be either an incentive or a deterrent in forming contractual relationships. To mitigate the risks coming from the rigid execution of the provisions articulated in a smart contract and allow further flexibility, developers explore the alternative of Ricardian contracts. The concept of Ricardian contracts was introduced by Ian Grigg in the 90s. Named after the nineteenth-century English Economist, *Ricardo* was a system for trading financial securities developed at Systems. How it works? The parties apply their cryptographic signatures on the Ricardian contract, then the contract is recorded on a blockchain (not necessarily though), and then a hash is generated automatically ensuring that the document represents the "single version of the truth".[41]

A Ricardian contract can be more desirable because, by design, the contracting parties can choose which clauses will be self-executed, possibly by using data from an oracle data feed, and will automatically perform a default action (e.g. repay a mortgage) unless overridden. Other clauses of the contract can remain open to human interpretation and action. All clauses though can be equipped with tags and metadata, making it possible for the machine to "tell" the human what these terms are and how should act about them. In one line, smart contracts blindly execute predefined instructions whereas, for Ricardians, self-executability is not a necessary feature of contract automation.[42]

Conclusion

Altogether, numerous legal questions remain open in connection with smart contracts. However, one of the major opportunities offered by smart contracts is that the contractual parties no longer have to verify compliance with the terms and conditions of a contract itself. This enables contracts to be processed quickly, efficiently and with low transaction costs without the need of any verifying intermediary. Another significant advantage is that smart contracts are considered to be very secure against fraud and counterfeiting as a result of the use of blockchain technology. Proponents of

---

[41] Clark et al. (2016).
[42] See Jurij Lampic, at www.schoenherr.eu.

Smart Contracts hope that the technology will facilitate business processes and contract processing as well as increase contract security.

There is no doubt that these advantages promise a great future for smart contracts, even though the use of smart contracts currently still harbours numerous risks. Smart contracts promise great opportunities, especially in the Fintech scene, where the focus is on digital monetary transactions against the provision of services.

Bibliography

Adlerstein, D. (2017), Are Smart Contracts Smart?, A Critical Look at Basic Blockchain Questions, Coindesk, June 26, 2017, available at: https://www.coindesk.com/when-is-a-smart-contract-actually-a-contract/.

Bacon, L. and G. Bazinas (2017), «Smart Contracts»: The Next Big Battlegroud?, Jusletter IT, May 19, 2017, N 11.

Bolton, P. and M. Dewatripont (2000), *Contract Theory* (MIT Press: Cambridge, MA).

Clark, C. D., Bakshi, V. A., and L. Braine (2016), Smart Contract Templates: Essential Requirements and Design Options. Working Paper 15 December 2016.

Coase, R. H. (1988), *The Firm, the Market and the Law* (Chicago University Press: Chicago, IL).

Cong, L. W. and Z. He (2018), Blochain Disruption and Smart Contracts, NBER Working Paper, No 24399.

Diedrich, H. (2017), Ethereum: Blockchains, Digital Assets, Smart Contracts, Decentralized Autonomous Organizations, London 2016, p. 167; Stephan D. Meyer/Benedikt Schuppli, «Smart Contracts» und deren Einordnung in das schweizerische Vertragsrecht, recht.

Erbguth, J. (2017), Lösung Blockchain-basierter Konflikte, Jusletter IT, February 23, 2017.

De Filippi, P. and A. Write (2018), *Blockchain and the Law: The Rule of Code* (Harvard University Press: Cambridge, MA).

Fisher, D. and Grider, P. (2018), The Blockchain in Action in the Legal World, in: Michele DeStefano and Guenther Dobrauz, *New Suits—Appetite for Disruption in the Legal World*.

Furlonger, D. and C. Uzureau (2019), *The Real Business of Blockchain: How Leaders Can Create Value in a New Digital Age* (Harvard Business School Press: Cambridge, MA).

Jaccard, G. (2017), Smart Contracts and the Role of Law, Jusletter IT, November 23, 2017, N 94. Müller and Seiler (FN 17).

Hart, O. (1995), *Firms, Contracts and Financial Structure* (Oxford University Press: Oxford).

Lampic Jurij (2019), Ricardian Contracts: A Smarter Way to Do Smart Contracts? Schonherr Publications, at www.schronherr.eu.

Lessig, L. (1999), Code and Other Laws of Cyberspace.

Levy, E. C. K. (2017), Book-Smart, Not Street-Smart: Blockchain-Based Smart Contracts and The Social Workings of Law, Engaging Science, Technology, and Society.

Lianos, I. (2019), Blockchain Competition: Gaining Competitive Advantage in the Digital Economy—Competition Law Implications, in: Hacker, Lianos, Dimitropoulos and Eich, *Regulating Blockchain: Techno-social and Legal Challenges* (Oxford University Press: Oxford).

Müller, L. and R. Seiler (2019), Smart Contracts aus Sicht des Vertragsrechts, Akutelle Juristische Praxis (AJP).

O'Shields, R. (2017), Smart Contract: Legal Agreements for the Blockchain, North Carolina Banking Institute Journal.

Salanie, B. (2000), *Contract Theory: A Primer* (MIT Press, Cambridge, MA).

Simmchen, C. (2017), Blockchain (R)Evolution, MMR.

Swan, M. (2015), Blockchain: Blueprint for a New Economy.

Szabo, N. (1994), Smart Contracts, available at: https://www.fon.hum.uva.nl/rob/Courses/InformationInSpeech/CDROM/Literature/LOTwinterschool2006/szabo.best.vwh.net/smart.contracts.html.

Szabo, N. (1997), Formalizing and Securing Relationships on Public Networks, available at: https://archive.is/wIUOA.

Trüeb, H. R. (2018), Smart Contracts, in: Grolimund et al. (eds.), Festschrift für Anton K. Schnyder, Zürich.

Weber, R. H. (2018), Smart Contracts and What the Blockchain Has Got to Do With it, in: Michele DeStefano and Guenther Dobrauz, *New Suits—Appetite for Disruption in the Legal World*.

Werbach, K. (2018), *The Blockchain and the New Architecture of Trust* (MIT Press: Cambridge, MA).

Williamson, O. E. (1985), *The Economic Institutions of Capitalism* (Free Press, New York).

Write, A. and P. De Filippi (2015), Decentralized Blockchain Technology and the Rise of Lex Cryptographia. Working Paper: 12 March 2015.

Zuboff, S. (2019), *The Age of Surveillance Capitalism: The Fight for a Human Future in the New Frontier of Power* (Profile Books: London).

4

Corporate Strategies for Blockchain-Based Solutions

Hans Verheggen

Although the Internet only truly came of age after 9/11 and digital transformation took a firm hold after the 2008 financial crisis, all businesses around the world have now woken up to the disruptive potential of a mix of technologies bridging the physical and digital space. Today, and especially since COVID-19, we have seen businesses with a digital layer in their business and operational model to be more efficient in absorbing the emerging dysfunctionalities of the supply chains and the intensity of protracted demand shocks, while digitally "laggard" companies suffer irreparable setbacks in their markets and finances.

Providers of cloud computing, software-as-a-service and other digital experiences and platforms have kept the NASDAQ powering ahead while companies in consumer, hospitality and leisure that are tied to physical assets are struggling to hold on to their customers as they distrust the safety of their products and services. Customers are abandoning household names in droves as they lack faith in the global supply chains and abandon brick-and-mortar stores.

The views presented in this chapter are exclusively of the author and do not represent the views of Deloitte. The author acknowledges the contribution of Koen Vingerhoets, Amy Pugh, Jamie Counihan and Antonio Senatore to this chapter.

H. Verheggen (✉)
University of Antwerp, Antwerp, Belgium
e-mail: hverheggen@deloitte.com

The first major health pandemic since the end of the First World War has forced companies to rethink how they go about their business in order to help flatten the curve and keep going concerned. There have been examples of profound difficulties for both global brands and SMEs unable to gain access to capital. With the pandemic ravaging both old and new economies, consumers are turning to the digital safety of the Internet.

This chapter explores what blockchain means for corporates today and how they approach digital transformation leveraging blockchain concepts and technology. After a brief outlook on the blockchain market for business, we present a picture of how enterprise blockchain and digital assets are becoming part of their business model (how they create and deliver value) and their operational models (how they capture their value). Next, we look into how companies can build successful consortia, design enterprise blockchain solutions and engage with the innovation ecosystem. This chapter does not look at blockchain as an alternative, digital or online method for organizing institutional or public systems. Nor does it focus on cryptocurrency.

What Blockchain Means for Businesses

Be it Bitcoin or Libra, a digital stamp, token, or twin; why would a company base its business model on the concept of disintermediation and invest in digital assets? Why would a business collaborate with its suppliers and customers, even with its competitors, to tokenize its data and assets and trust that information to a shared database for everyone in its supply chain or ecosystem?

One thing is clear by now: our global supply chains require trust. The businesses that will come out on top are those that will regain the consumers' trust first. That trust will be based on a combination of digital and physical elements. The first airline carrier that will connect with the global hospitality group and life sciences company to guarantee a safe end-to-end travel experience will lure back the high-end (business) traveler.

Little understood but crucial to regaining trust in global supply chains, are new approaches to corporate governance that rely on cryptographic and peer-to-peer communication methods such as the blockchain (Shrier 2020). Blockchain and other distributed ledger technologies (DLTs) can provide the infrastructure for enabling and scaling digital services through trust and transparency (Werbach 2018).

These extraordinary times reinforce the urgency at which businesses need to evolve to embark on the fourth industrial revolution. Just as we did not know what potential the Internet held back in the '90s, we now struggle to put disintermediation via the blockchain at the heart of the next step in digital transformation that will see us combine new telecommunications, computing and cyber technologies to revolutionize how we live, work, shop and trade (McAfee and Brynolfsson 2018).

In order to survive, many traditional businesses will need to move forward rapidly, leapfrog current digital solutions and reinvent customer experience with trust at its heart (Ross et al. 2019). Nothing prescribes that technology needs to be adopted in a certain sequence. Blockchain offers a unique "leapfrog" opportunity for lagging industry sectors that decide to put trust and transparency first.

Trust in an online world can strengthen via disintermediation. Consumers want direct insight into and control over the data they share, the assets they hold and the money they spend. So does business.

Market Outlook

Blockchain-enabled transformations are growing exponentially faster than other disruptive technologies. When we take the arithmetic mean of 10 analyst predictions, the blockchain market is expected to grow from USD 1.2 billion in 2018 to USD 23.3 billion by 2023, at an impressive compound annual growth rate (CAGR) of 80.2% during 2018–2023. The blockchain market is forecast to grow at a higher rate than artificial intelligence over a longer period. That same forecast CAGR for AI is not higher than 38%.[1]

The trade enabled by these blockchain solutions is a multiple of the market investment. According to Gartner, by 2023, blockchain will support the global movement and tracking of USD 2 trillion of goods and services annually.[2] The World Economic Forum sees similar market size growth in asset tokenization.[3]

Many companies across the globe recognize blockchain as a strategic priority for their business. The 2020 Deloitte Blockchain Survey[4] polled senior executives to understand how they see blockchain in their companies'

---

[1] Averaged data from 10 selected analysts. See bibliography for full list.
[2] https://www.gartner.com/en/newsroom/press-releases/2019-07-03-gartner-predicts-90--of-current-enterprise-blockchain.
[3] https://www.weforum.org/agenda/2019/04/data-oil-digital-world-asset-tech-giants-buy-it/.
[4] https://www2.deloitte.com/us/en/insights/topics/understanding-blockchain-potential/global-blockchain-survey.html.

digital strategy. A majority of 55% deemed it critical and positioned it in their top five strategic priorities—a sharp increase from 43% in 2018.

The vast majority of our most important clients are engaged in using blockchain to enable their digital transformation. 145 out of Deloitte's 178 largest global clients are investigating blockchain technology. Transformation solutions are being explored across all industries from launching a proof-of-concept over pilot projects to realizing the transformative opportunity that blockchain presents and using blockchain in production environments in banking, insurance, automotive, shipping, life sciences, and education, etc.

Blockchain adoption across industries is still uneven. Regulatory issues emerge as a central concern of respondents in the Deloitte survey, which may shed light on why some industries, more than other ones, have found it more difficult to identify opportunities to leverage blockchain solutions in their ecosystems.

Overall, interest remains very high with financial sector players big and small. More and more governments have joined the conversation to provide financial institutions with regulatory clarity around digital assets but also to envisage digital currencies. Supply chain remains a key use case. As blockchain enables scrutinizing and optimizing processes in a supply chain that traditionally falls outside of enterprise solutions, we anticipate that its rise could lead to an evolution of supply chain management and logistics in the not so distant future.

Why Companies Leverage Blockchain

Digital transformation remains at the heart of the corporates' strategic agenda. We may now view digital transformation as a journey towards achieving market dominance. The reality is that too many corporates have embarked upon digital transformation as a survival decision. Digital transformation is viewed widely as sine qua non to improve revenue generation efficiency (defined as revenue per employee or fixed assets turnover) and profitability (defined as EBIT margin and net profit margin) (Westerman and Bonnet 2014). Digital is happening rapidly and forcefully, whether brands are ready or not and too many leave adoption too late (Gupta 2018).

As email became the poster child for Internet connectivity, it took three development stages for Web 2.0 to disrupt most industries starting with telecommunications over advertising to consumer retail and software. Many highly regulated industries have withstood the onslaught of the Internet's free data sharing. Other ones, such as the music and media industry, have had to reinvent entire business models.

Similarly, the blockchain hype started by shaking up the financial services industry and many other more or less regulated industries that require sharing valuable or confidential data is up for grabs. As with the Internet, we have a hard time seeing the full longer-term potential of the blockchain.

The major difference with the Internet lies in the blockchain's disintermediation. Blockchain technologies (cryptography, smart contracts, peer-to-peer communications) put together allow sharing information and know-how without the need for an aggregator, verifier or broker. Contrary to digital platforms such as Uber, Airbnb and booking.com, participants in a blockchain need not another intermediary. The Internet has pushed brokers online. Blockchain pushes the broker out or at a minimum, it tracks the middlemen.

The main promise of the blockchain—for both businesses and consumers—is to cut out the middleman. Or, in economic terms, blockchain reduces transaction costs and replaces contracts by removing intermediary agency (Catalini and Gans 2019).

More than cyber security, digital contracts or due diligence, this blockchain promise is the single most important feature of any blockchain use case; it is both the least understood, and has the strongest potential for disruption in every industry. This is probably also why blockchain adoption is taking more time and more energy than an AI pilot or a robotics implementation. In order to get this right, one needs to align the full supply chain or competitive ecosystem on a future-proof blockchain-based business model against many vested interests.

In equity trading, disintermediation via the blockchain of clearing, settlement and asset servicing reduces operational costs and third-party fees. But the potential gains from eliminating economic rents and from innovating business models are unlimited.

For instance, the eTrade[5] initiative launched by the Hong Kong Monetary Authority and its 12 leading banks does not merely aim to digitize a cumbersome paper-based letter-of-credit process. The true potential is in the ingestion of much-needed liquidity from the digitized trade finance pumping idle funds back into the market, from the increased lending to SMEs supported by strong KYC checks to avoid fraud and from the demise of a monopolistic credit rating practice. Finally, companies can create new services as all credit data and contracts are shared on the blockchain.

---

[5] https://blockchain.news/news/Exclusive-Deloitte-Blockchain-Lab-on-the-3-Collaborations-with-HKMA.

Corporate Demand for Blockchain Solutions

We see three major reasons why companies seek blockchain solutions: (i) strategic competition reasons driven by the incentive to build new business models; (ii) operational model transformation reasons to deliver more efficiently with enterprise blockchain solutions; and (iii) investment management reasons in making maximal use of the blockchain's potential for digitizing assets. Below we briefly present each modus.

When Blockchain Strategy Becomes the Business Model...

In their attempt to improve their long-term strategic competitive positioning, an increasing number of firms embrace the idea of "to go far, you go together" and exchange competition for "*coopetition*" in an attempt to address shared industry problems. Solving shared problems together means solving fundamental problems with unlimited potential.

This new-age approach to problem-solving breaks the centuries-old model that would not have seen competitors collaborate. Competitors and business partners are coming together across all industries to solve shared problems by forming industry consortia and sharing blockchain platforms that enhance interoperability while preserving participants' privacy. Competitors can leverage blockchain technology to allow them to pool data, information or know-how while making sure no single competitor can control what is being shared in the pool.

The businesses that will know how to leverage such a shared ledger early on to build new businesses will stand to gain the most. Blockchain is a unique and highly functioning toolbox that, by its very nature, facilitates such disruption.

Those industry participants that will fail to see the disruption or fail to embark on the right (industry) initiative may see their market access and success greatly diminished. "For instance, an overarching working premise of the Libra concept is greater access [...], reducing barriers to entry in forming new business opportunities. Yet, reducing such barriers may change the old order and in effect 'level the playing field' of incumbents within an industry. In a Libra ecosystem context, new Fintech entrants may enter areas of activity more easily, when any such access to institutions' financial infrastructure would have required a steep investment. Consequently, new entrants may replace incumbents; yet, also, incumbent competitors may join forces in forging new, unprecedented market offerings and other cooperative initiatives".[6]

Different organizations pursue digital transformation to achieve their own strategic goals and they share common reasons to do so. Blockchain acts as an orchestrator and aligns cross-industry digital ecosystems. Major organizations transform their business models by adapting to these new ecosystems and by using the blockchain as neutral orchestrators of the value chains.

In the supply chain area, more and more ambitious projects are advancing to mature stages, including the ones led by Maersk in the shipping industry (built on Hyperledger Fabric) and Pfizer centered on the clinical supply chain (idem). Slowly but surely, corporate executives are increasingly knowledgeable about and comfortable with the technology—as we have seen in the Deloitte survey—that is being enabled increasingly by large, underlying IT platforms from major system vendors such as Oracle, salesforce and VMWare.

Overall, in the last two years, we have seen a gradual but marked shift from the numerous, early proofs-of-concept and pilot projects to multi-million dollar investments in critical industry initiatives, some of which have already gone into production. There are now a growing number of well-established well-funded blockchain consortia that are steaming ahead with the participation of both industry leaders, challengers and start-ups. These consortia will together leverage blockchain to cut costs, fight fraud and enhance compliance.

Nevertheless, collaboration models and governance based on the blockchain remain difficult to structure across all industries, be they oil & gas or pharmaceuticals, and it takes time to align competitors and collaborators on consortium agreements. In addition, the cultural resistance to change and the process redesign caused by the very disruptive nature of the shared ledger, smart contract and cryptographic concepts of the blockchain bring added complexity to the operational transformation effort. Technical challenges and risks also remain, for instance, in interoperability and security across environments for blockchain nodes, as well as in data privacy and data storage.

Or the Operating Model to Deliver Value

Bringing systems, competitors, suppliers, buyers, consumers and even regulators into a single consortium is a major intellectual and emotional challenge

---

[6]https://www2.deloitte.com/content/dam/Deloitte/us/Documents/technology/US-Libra-shaping-the-evolution-of-financial-infrastructure.pdf.

but one that blockchain's infrastructure readily supports. Interoperable with other systems, easily integrated with existing software, a mechanism for exchanging siloed data in a secure and real-time manner that increases transparency and efficiency, blockchain solutions offer an approach to digital transformation that is future-focused.

Even when a radical disruption of industry or practice is not readily on the table, blockchain solutions and platforms offer great opportunity to deliver (products and services) more effectively. From an operating model perspective, blockchain solutions allow standardizing and digitizing industry-wide data and transactions; securing transparent supply chains; preventing cross-organizational and cross-border fraud; enhancing consumer trust and providing insight into the origin and quality of products; and documenting and settling global transactions efficiently.

From an operations perspective, blockchain solutions allow making better-informed decisions to steer the business; reducing efforts to meet day-to-day reporting requirements; and managing resources efficiently and more effectively. They ensure that information is accurate, timely, and based upon a faster, less expensive and more transparent operational process.

Industry can leverage blockchain solutions to develop a single source of truth for corporate information and to produce one version of financial performance by reporting integrated, consistent source data in one shared database. Providing transparent information independent of perspective to regulators on a blockchain will inform analysts and investors in their decision-making.[7]

Today, most such information is unstructured and in various formats, including scanned or paper documents. Investors trying to analyze financial performance of (listed) companies and identifying investment opportunities turn to data vendors for aggregate and consolidated data feeds. Again, an obvious blockchain use case threatens the vested interests of incumbent industry participants, both private and public.

In this case, transparency in the financial markets is too important for efficient capital allocation and economic growth not to be disrupted by the blockchain. Rendering corporate financial reports on a blockchain will eliminate rent-seeking and spur innovation in the industry.

---

[7] https://op.europa.eu/en/publication-detail/-/publication/56fba6de-38da-11ea-ba6e-01aa75ed71a1/language-en/format-PDF/source-113099411.

Capturing Business Through Tokenization

Perhaps the greatest potential (and threat) for corporates from the blockchain lies in the opportunity to work with digital assets in the form of a blockchain token as its digital representation—a company share, a patent, a piece of real estate—that can be traded, held as collateral or used for payment.

What can we tokenize? In theory, one could tokenize (read: represent digitally, track via a digital twin and value on the blockchain) any asset, currency or commodity. The three basic types of tokens are utility, payment and security tokens:

(i) Utility tokens that provide the right to a specific product or service from the token issuer, initial coin offerings (ICOs) are common utility tokens;
(ii) Payment (or exchange) tokens represent payments for goods or services meant to function as a means of exchange, a unit of account or a store of value, e.g. cryptocurrencies created by ICOs which unlike fiat currency are not backed by a central bank; and
(iii) Security (or investment) tokens that provide to the holder, ownership of assets and entitlements to use them like dividend distribution, profit sharing and voting rights.[8]

Tokenization will change ownership rights just as much as digital changed the media and entertainment industry. The number of use cases is without limit: a rental property; shared ownership of car fleets in cities; art works and sports teams; etc.

The value of this "token economy" lies in fractioning the digital assets' ownership (where possible) and liquefying them via their trade on the secondary market. Tokenization makes an investment market more liquid for both buyers and sellers who can choose to invest in or exit from just parts of a larger asset (possibly), lowering prices and costs of ownership and making the trade quick and easy. In addition, blockchain technology can render such market trades more accessible, transparent, and efficient and cheap.[9]

Tokenization allows new business models to emerge enabled by global transactions for both traditional and underserved participants. Fractioning

---

[8] Security tokens can be classified as the digital representation of existing securities such as equities, debt instruments, funds, etc. and may qualify as transferable securities or financial instruments under the EU's Markets in Financial Instruments directive (MiFID). Some jurisdictions have outlined governance concerns on the acceptance of bearer certificates or tokens for peer-to-peer securities exchange.

[9] https://www2.deloitte.com/content/dam/Deloitte/lu/Documents/financial-services/lu-tokenization-of-assets-disrupting-financial-industry.pdf.

ownership, reducing transaction costs and taking out the middleman all serve to attract new market participants and inject liquidity into markets rife with economic rents. Every company needs to take a hard look at its business model and take into account how tokenization risks disrupting its business model.

Next to utility and security tokens, a digital currency (payment token) can make low-value transactions—so-called micropayments—feasible as cost structures are kept simple and cheap. The Libra digital asset, supported by a large number of economic participants in the Libra Network including Facebook, allows for a global integration within both existing and new digital businesses and their extensive array of products and services. Goods and services providers may spend that same payment in Libra within the same network without the use of their conventional bank accounts.

With ongoing technology investments resulting in major performance gains, e.g. Ripple handling 1,500+ transactions per second growing to hundreds of thousands vs. the original Bitcoin that handles less than 10, the prospect of a digital currency becomes very real. However, governments will need to address the regulatory uncertainty and confusion, notably on tax liability, and concerns over crypto risk as well as strengthen the governance of digital ownership.

On the one hand, we see global, large-scale, multi-player collaborations emerge, such as Facebook's Libra, with an unprecedented scale and reach of its members differentiating its unique value proposition. On the other hand, more and more sovereign states and central banks are looking actively into adopting a central bank digital currency (CBDC) as a wholesale currency next to their fiat ones. The People's Bank of China is already trialing a "digital yuan" toolkit. As a reaction, the Digital Dollar Foundation has called for a tokenized version of the US dollar, not an actual digital currency.

Businesses in Europe and the Americas need to understand that access to finance and markets will move rapidly to the digital variant. Already in China and Scandinavia, cash payments have dropped to a trickle. The stated intent by some major European regulators to block the Libra is unhelpful and will only strengthen the Chinese hand to denominate future online trade over the Internet in a digital yuan challenging the US dollar's status as the world's reserve currency and the Fed's position as lender of last resort. Unless European governments start to catch up, most future trade will be denominated in digital currencies or security tokens outside of their control.

One area at least in which Europe may occupy a leading position and that is ripe for digital securities are greenhouse gas emission rights traded in the open market. In a clearly written paper, researchers from the Frankfurt

School's Blockchain Centre[10] explain how blockchain can promote carbon resource efficiency, tracking and pricing in an automated cap-and-trade system using smart contracts and even give rise to ecological cryptocurrencies. Given the envisaged expansion of the EU's emissions trading scheme to the aviation, shipping and construction industries, now is the time to move to a blockchain-based Union registry of emission rights that embeds environmental policy in its governance and contracts.

How Companies Build Blockchain Services

We have seen why companies have been teaming up with partners in their ecosystems to build enterprise blockchain solutions across industries and value chains. We have also provided a view on how security tokens will allow the trend to digitalize investment and trade to continue unabated. How are companies responding and building blockchain-based solutions to capture the opportunities and fend off threats from the increasingly digitalized ecosystems they operate in?

For instance, the increased digitalization of patient care has pushed Pfizer to improve transparency in its ecosystem and develop a blockchain application that tracks medical products across different stages and actors in the clinical supply chain. The application also enables tracking individual products to be dispensed to patients participating in clinical trials, improving medical research inputs and patient experience. As Pfizer has embraced precision medicine in the design of new solutions, recognizing that each patient has different needs, preferences and responses to the same drug, it set a strategic goal to lead the industry in scale and value of outcome-based reimbursement.

It is in such strategic shifts that blockchain technology, in combination with digital and other assets, can bring critical success. A company needs to tackle five major hurdles to equip itself with a successful blockchain strategy and enterprise solution: (i) devise a sound blockchain strategy; (ii) build an effective consortium model; (iii) design the right future-proof platform; (iv) develop the right solution architecture; and (v) and take use cases to production. A company that executes these steps effectively will succeed in operating an efficient blockchain service and be in a position to offer its platform to its ecosystem partners.

---

[10]http://www.explore-ip.com/2018_Blockchain-and-Sustainability.pdf.

Blockchain Strategy

The chief strategy officer can work with the CEO and executive committee and map out how the organization's corporate strategy can find business value from blockchain services, often in combination with important bets in other technologies such as IoT or AI. This leads them to define "where to play and how to win" and how to drive an effective (i) ecosystem, (ii) product and (iii) delivery strategy:

(i) The ecosystem strategy focuses on the type of participants, the ownership structure, governance and commercial model;
(ii) The product strategy outlines the market(s), value proposition, core processes and target architecture.
(iii) The delivery strategy sets out the minimum viable ecosystem (MVE), the overall roadmap and milestones, and the resource plan.

In embarking on its blockchain journey, executives must carry out an enterprise risk assessment and consider global market, revenue and tax implications. Next, the company can develop strategies to pilot and implement blockchain-based solutions in an iterative and flexible approach to match the rapid changes in the ecosystem.

The Consortium Model

Probably one of the most challenging steps is to devise an effective consortium model. Consortia introduce a new way of doing business and engage in joint innovation activities, transcending the boundaries of the firm (Chesbrough 2003). A global market-leading company may choose to develop, manage or join an industry consortium, rally customers and suppliers around its use case but, very few have the clout to convince competitors to sign-up to its preferred model.

Competitors want to ensure participants and providers of blockchain services agree on both commercial and technological terms of service and acceptable use. They expect to trust blockchain service providers, partners, auditors, regulators and those involved in establishing and operating the technology surrounding the consortium's objectives.

Before a blockchain platform is developed, its owners must establish an agreement that governs the fundamental rules of the new network. The primary goal of that agreement in blockchain consortia is to enhance and underline trust. One needs to ensure to have the right controls and risk models in place to address the transformative nature of this technology. This can be a daunting process, as organizations have differing interests, policies and protocols for managing their operations. A company considering joining an existing blockchain network has to evaluate the benefits of the new arrangement against the risks of losing control over its data, processes and systems.

There are different options when it comes to selecting the operating structure of a consortium. Understanding the industry landscape, the legal and regulatory impacts and focusing on future sustainability are critical elements to making the right selection for an organization. As a consortium scales, there are a new range of considerations and decisions to be made; including jurisdiction type, regulatory landscape and economic viability. In discussions with competitors, one must be careful not to contravene anti-trust or competition laws and to protect ownership of commercial and intellectual property.

Platform Design

When choosing to integrate blockchain technology into existing or new business models, it is imperative to start simple but plan for the future to take account of the rapid evolution in the blockchain technology landscape. As more and more different blockchain solutions are put into production across many industries and expand to support more use cases, scalability and interoperability become critical success factors. In addition, companies must decide how to translate the governance model embedded in the consortium agreements into the choice of blockchain type, consensus mechanisms (and smart contracts) as well as what data to store on- and off-chain.

Over the last years, industry has categorized blockchains into public (read by anyone), private (read by a select few), permissioned (accessed by a select few) and permissionless or un-permisioned (accessed by anyone) ones. In un-permissioned ledgers, users are anonymous and there is no need to register with a central authority. Permissioned ledgers require the identity of users to be whitelisted (or blacklisted) via some form of know your customer (KYC) procedure.

These two classifications of ledgers—public vs. private and permissioned vs. permissionless—lend themselves to different use classes, each of which requires different governance structures as illustrated in the table.[11]

---

[11] https://op.europa.eu/en/publication-detail/-/publication/98da7b74-38db-11ea-ba6e-01aa75ed71a1/language-en/format-PDF/source-113099411.

Table 4.1 Blockchain use-classes and their corresponding governance structures[a]

Type of blockchain	Use classification	Governance structure
Permissionless	**Public** Reduced formal governance structure. Crypto-currencies for example	**Cooperative** Autonomous association jointly owned and "democratically" controlled (by miners)
Permissioned	**State-sponsored** Governance structures of sponsoring agencies. Land registry or identity would be typical examples	**Appointed board** Stakeholders (or the Board itself) to bring particular knowledge and skills to the team
Permissioned	**Private** Highly defined governance structure. Many platforms for business ecosystems can be listed here. HyperLedger Fabric for example	**Plutocracy or oligarchy** The individuals who make up the board are the owners or stakeholders; a form of structure in which decisions rests with a small number of people
Permissioned	**Consortium** Established by a group of organizations rather than a single entity, likely to have a more complex structure. Financial service providers e.g.	**Membership** Board members are elected to their positions with tenure for a fixed period of time
Permissioned	**State-sponsored or consortium**	**Representative** For organizations that wish to have members that are enterprises instead of individuals. Appropriate for consortium and state-sponsored blockchains

[a]Adapted from ISO TC307 SG6 Whitepaper 'Responsibility Without Power' in 'Governance for a Blockchain enabled European Electronic Access Point', https://op.europa.eu/en/publication-detail/-/publication/98da7b74-38db-11ea-ba6e-01aa75ed71a1/language-en/format-PDF/source-113099411

Corporate executives as well as system designers need to understand the limitations of these governance choices, especially as the choice for any type of blockchain is difficult to change once one has embarked on a blockchain project. Table 4.1 classifies the type, use and governance structure of alternative options.

Data storage revolves around the architectural choice of where data need to be stored: on-chain vs. off-chain. Today, a common pattern for non-cryptocurrency use cases is to store most of the data off-chain and only add e.g. a hash of a document on-chain. This allows businesses to maintain total control of their data while ensuring not to overload the chain. However, this pattern also limits the use of smart contracts, which hinders a full benefits realization of automating workflows and executing contracts, etc. Overcoming this challenge requires heavy research from both academia and practice to come up with optimization of consensus mechanisms and sharing.

The design choices of the type of blockchain and what to store on the blockchain lead to consensus mechanism choices as well. Therefore, the ultimate scalability issue lies with the consensus mechanism and which criteria it needs to fulfil, e.g. Byzantine fault tolerance vs. crash fault tolerance, its finality needed, should there be fair ordering, etc. As mentioned above, overcoming this challenge and making distributed systems as scalable as centralized systems, requires more research in consensus mechanisms.

Finally, the primary challenges for interoperability are technical. Varying consensus and hashing algorithms among the different blockchain platforms make it difficult to determine the most recent transactions as well as manage unified identities across platforms. Several POCs and hackathons have tried to solve these technical challenges, but there is still no established method working in a live production environment.

Of the many available blockchain platforms, Ethereum is arguably the most likely public one to reach a critical mass of cross-industry users. Any use case would benefit from interacting with it. Hyperledger focuses exclusively on enterprise solutions and believes that permissioned blockchains are the answer. If a company believes that permissionless blockchains have issues around privacy, scalability and interoperability that render them unsuited for global business, it may opt for R3 developed on Corda.

Using a permissioned blockchain gives solution builders a limited set of consensus mechanisms at their disposal, but on the upside, the ones that are available are Byzantine fault tolerant and can handle much larger volumes of transactions than a permissionless blockchain like bitcoin can. It is difficult to say how many transactions this type of investment would need, but one can look at already existing solutions as a proxy. TradeLens is a global supply chain platform started by IBM and Maersk built on HyperLedger Fabric which handles currently over two million shipping events per day. The network also includes a variety of different players in the value chain including authorities, shippers, ports, ocean carriers, financial services, etc. Based on this model, an investment token infrastructure could perform as well if not better as technology improves.

Solution Architecture

When a company or consortium has chosen the most appropriate governance model and blockchain architecture it will need to complement and build on these decisions to design the appropriate solution architecture that is most effective for the business. On top of the blockchain architecture, one will need to define (i) server infrastructure; (ii) back-end development for smart contracts, APIs and data integration; (iii) front-end development of user interfaces and log-ins with digital application features.

From the start, one should involve experts in cyber risk, control design, contract support, data integrity and audit readiness. Blockchain is a transformative technology that underpins new and innovative business models. By adopting strong controls and designing for scalability, one can design the right solution for successful execution.

Use Case Design

Finally, one can select the targeted use case(s), build the supporting architecture for the minimum viable ecosystem and take pilots into the market. It is advisable to start small and allow for quick wins to demonstrate the blockchain's potential and business case. As a consortium starts to operate more efficiently, it will become a market leader in the blockchain ecosystem and can provide managed blockchain services to its partners.

How to Engage with the Innovation Ecosystem

Innovation ecosystems tend to be the major factor of corporate transformation in the digital era and the modern corporation should move fast from a "eureka" approach to innovation (Birkinshaw et al. 2011), to one that leverages the know-how of a wide range of stakeholders (Murray and Budden 2017). The innovation ecosystem in the blockchain space is growing at a strong pace and experienced blockchain developers are in high demand as the technology still evolves rapidly. Companies need to invest in blockchain expertise across the business including in its commercial, logistics, financial, legal and control functions as smart contracts execute commercial agreements or logistical processes, tokenization takes off and digital assets are recorded on the balance sheet.

We see five ways in which companies can start to play in the blockchain ecosystem, build strong relationships with key partners and get prepared for future success in the blockchain space.

Lead Collaboration with Emerging Disruptors

Companies should start to incubate long-term relationships that can provide deep technical expertise leading to base use case and support rapid-scale development. Via diverse networking and rapid experimentation, chief strategy officers and investment committees can decide where to place informed bets.

Build Business Models for Mainstream Digital Assets

Companies should look at their asset portfolio and analyze how digital assets can threaten or enhance their strategic market position. To assess the impact on existing business models, they will need to invest in talent and tools to allow engaging with digital assets, designing transaction flows and consulting with regulators.

Design and Implement New Operating Models

Next, companies should create horizontal and vertical operating models, design governance models and define IP ownership that can be implemented across companies and borders. Working together with clients, suppliers and competitors companies can start to invest in high-value use cases.

Design and Implement Leading Enterprise Solutions

Once companies have figured out how to leverage blockchain, they can move from minimum viable product (MVP) to full-production, providing a full lens across the value chain and invest in high-value scalable use cases aligned with target markets. Scaling these solutions with suppliers and customers will allow transforming them into enterprise solutions for their industry.

Co-create Solutions with Alliance Partners

To sell enterprise solutions across the enterprise market place, companies can leverage their blockchain investments in building prototypes and pilot solutions with emerging vendors, large and small, incorporating intercompany payments, tax, legal and financial aspects of the supported use cases.

Blockchain and AI are two key sets of technologies that underpin the pace of change in how we do business. Digital transformation is no longer required for survival. It has become the only way to succeed. The blockchain market is set to grow much quicker than AI and the potential for disrupting business as we know it via disintermediation and digital assets is much greater. We have moved beyond the experiments and are now seeing leading companies in every industry put major blockchain-based businesses (in combination with AI and IoT) online. Blockchain networks without a coherent strategy or suitable governance are unlikely to achieve their long-term commercial goals or implementation. But shared ledgers will become fundamental to business as much as double-entry bookkeeping is today.

From Blockchain-Inspired to Blockchain-Complete

The true value of blockchain comes from its convergence with other enhancing digital technologies. The corporate leader should understand his/her needs in order to navigate and combine different technologies and find the best corporate blockchain architecture. Different blockchain architectures create different power and influence shifts that determine a framework of political and competitive calculus.

This is why corporates, and in this case public sector organizations as well, attempt currently mainly blockchain projects that rely on disintermediation rather than decentralization in their governance and market structure. The element of decentralization (along with tokenization) makes the blockchain architectures complete, whereas the element of disintermediation, along with encryption and distribution, make the design of architectures rather blockchain-inspired (Furlonger and Uzureau 2019). Marketwise, corporates seem to only depart from the blockchain-inspired architectures to start moving slowly to more decentralized architectures. Technological and cultural factors in corporations (internal) and in market structures (external) will determine the speed at which blockchain-complete architectures will see adoption.

Market structures generate more incentives for digital blockchain-complete transformations. From a technological point of view, the blending of blockchain with machine-learning and hyper-performance computing will bring us closer to the design of efficient decentralized autonomous organizations (DAOs) and more secure and trustworthy smart contracts. At the market level, the bigger the presence of human-to-machine and machine-to-machine interactions, the higher the urgency for decentralized (not just disintermediate) blockchain-complete solutions. Also, the wider the spread of the internet of things (IoT) and the more decentralized the data storage architectures (edge, fog, mist computing instead of cloud), the more precise the need for decentralization. Finally, the greater the regulatory certainty in the market, the higher the consumer trust and the better the market integration of blockchain technology (De Filippi and Write 2018).

Blockchain is not a static technology. Consequently, we need not consider corporate adoptions of blockchain solutions into business and operational models as static either. Corporations must adopt a dynamic approach and flexible response to ensure their firms' strategic agility in an "exponential" organizational setting. The agility and mentality of the exponential organization are the sole sources of competitive advantage in a digitally enhanced market.

We are only now entering the second blockchain decade. The first decade brought to market certain types of business and operational models for corporations to explore. Many more decades will follow, and new, innovative business and operational models will need inventing in order for the corporation of the future to continue creating, delivering and capturing value for its customers and shareholders.

For a corporation to be blockchain mature, it must explore its options early and spot both internal and market trends, as a digitally mature organization is more than four times more likely to develop needed digital leaders than the least digitally matured corporation (Kane et al. 2018). The success of blockchain is right there. It pushes corporate leaders to innovate on their business models altogether, not just on their products and services.

Bibliography

Birkinshaw, J., C. Bouquet, and J. L. Barsoux (2011), "The Five Myths of Innovation", MIT Sloan Management Review, at Top 10 Lessons on the new Business of Innovation: Sloan Collection, Winter 2011, pp 1–8.

Catalini, C. and Gans, J. (2019), Some Simple Economics of the Blockchain, Working Paper 22952 (NBER Working Paper Series: Cambridge, MA).

Chesbrough, H. W. (2003), "The Era of Open Innovation", MIT Sloan Management Review (Vol. 44, No. 3), pp 35–41.
De Filippi, P. and A. Write (2018), Blockchain and the Law: The Rule of Code (Harvard University Press, Cambridge, MA).
Furlonger, D. and C. Uzureau (2019), The Real Business of Blockchain: How Leaders Can Create Value in a Digital Age (Harvard Business School Press: Cambridge, MA).
Gupta, S. (2018), Driving Digital Strategy: A Guide for Imagining Your Business (Harvard Business School Press, Cambridge, MA).
https://www.weforum.org/agenda/2019/04/data-oil-digital-world-asset-tech-giants-buy-it/.
https://www.gartner.com/en/newsroom/press-releases/2019-07-03-gartner-predicts-90-of-current-enterprise-blockchain.
https://www2.deloitte.com/us/en/insights/topics/understanding-blockchain-potential/global-blockchain-survey.html.
https://blockchain.news/news/Exclusive-Deloitte-Blockchain-Lab-on-the-3-Collaborations-with-HKMA.
https://www2.deloitte.com/content/dam/Deloitte/us/Documents/technology/US-Libra-shaping-the-evolution-of-financial-infrastructure.pdf.
https://hal.archives-ouvertes.fr/hal-01382002/document.
https://op.europa.eu/en/publication-detail/-/publication/56fba6de-38da-11ea-ba6e-01aa75ed71a1/language-en/format-PDF/source-113099411.
https://op.europa.eu/en/publication-detail/-/publication/98da7b74-38db-11ea-ba6e-01aa75ed71a1/language-en/format-PDF/source-113099411.
https://www.weforum.org/agenda/2020/05/why-covid-19-makes-a-compelling-case-for-wider-integration-of-blockchain/.
https://www.gminsights.com/industry-analysis/blockchain-technology-market.
https://www.statista.com/statistics/647231/worldwide-blockchain-technology-market-size/.
https://www.deep-analysis.net/wp-content/uploads/2019/08/DA-190812-Ent-Blockchain-forecast.pdf.
https://www.idc.com/getdoc.jsp?containerId=prUS45429719.
https://www.businesswire.com/news/home/20181026005216/en/Global-Blockchain-Technology-Market-2017-2021-Advent-Artificial.
https://www.otcpm24.com/blockchain-technology-market-to-value-us-21070-2-mn-at-cagr-of-38-4-by-2025/.
https://www.netscribes.com/about-us/media/press-releases/global-blockchain-technology-market-worth-usd-13-96-billion-2022/.
https://www.newswire.com/news/blockchain-technology-market-global-forecast-to-2021.
http://www.gosreports.com/global-blockchain-technology-market-worth-5-6-billion-by-2022/.
https://www.ameriresearch.com/product/blockchain-market-size/.
https://www.ibm.com/downloads/cas/PPRR983X.

https://media.consensys.net/gartner-blockchain-will-deliver-3-1-trillion-dollars-in-value-by-2030-d32b79c4c560.

http://www.oecd.org/finance/The-Tokenisation-of-Assets-and-Potential-Implications-for-Financial-Markets.pdf.

https://www2.deloitte.com/content/dam/Deloitte/lu/Documents/financial-services/lu-tokenization-of-assets-disrupting-financial-industry.pdf.

https://www2.deloitte.com/content/dam/Deloitte/lu/Documents/technology/lu-are-token-assets-the-securities-tomorrow.pdf.

http://www.explore-ip.com/2018_Blockchain-and-Sustainability.pdf.

Kane, G. C., Palmer D., Phillip A. N. Kiron, D. and N. Buckley (2018), Research Report: Coming of Age Digitally, MIT Sloan Management Review with Deloitte Insights.

McAfee, A. and E. Brynolfsson (2018), Machine, Platform, Crowd: Harnessing Our Digital Future (Norton: New York).

Murray, F. and P. Budden (2017), Working Paper: A Systematic MIT Approach for Assessing Innovation-Driven Entrepreneurship in Ecosystems, September 2017, MIT Innovation Initiative.

Ross, W. J., Beath, C. M. and M. Mocker (2019), Designed for Digital: How to Architect Your Business for Sustained Success (MIT Press: Cambridge, MA).

Shrier, D. (2020), Basic Blockchain: What It Is and How It Will Transform the Way We Work and Live (Robison: London).

Werbach, K. (2018), The Blockchain and the New Architecture of Trust (MIT Press, Cambridge, MA).

Westerman, G., Bonnet, D. and A. McAfee (2014): Leading Digital: Turning Technology into Business Transformation (Harvard Business School Press: Cambridge, MA).

5

Distributed Data Economics

David Shrier

Part I: Foundations for Distributed Data Economics

Distributed ledgers offer new horizons of opportunity for the monetization of data, and new models whereby individual consumers gain more control over and benefit from their personal data, versus the predominant model of today that awards the greatest economic gains to the platform marketing companies such as Facebook and Google, which generally leverage the economics of data extraction. With the market cap of digitally traded tokens of distributed ledger companies exceeding US$240 billion, significant investment in the private sector is supporting the creation of the new distributed data ecology.[1]

Before we can explore distributed data economics, we need to understand where the data is derived, how it is manufactured and how it has been monetized in the past.

Blockchain systems, or distributed ledgers, are fundamentally databases. While a great deal of attention has been paid to the design, architecture,

---

[1] Coinmarketcap.com accessed March 1, 2020.

D. Shrier (✉)
Imperial College London, London, UK
e-mail: david@visionaryfuture.co

support, distribution and fundraising surrounding these databases, insufficient attention has been paid to the nature and quality of the data going into these systems, and how that data is being monetized. To paraphrase the chief innovation officer of one of the top banks in Europe, given how problematic consumer data often is in terms of its quality, we run the risk of creating immutable problems.[2]

The Potential of Distributed Data

Imagine a world where consumers dictate how their personal data is used, not a handful of corporate conglomerates. Imagine a world where there is vibrant competition, and choice among service providers, for everything from personal banking to healthcare to energy services. Imagine a world where companies pay consumers directly, instead of marketing platforms, in order to acquire their business. Imagine a world where artists get paid royalties for their work directly instead of most of the profits of small artists disappearing into the coffers of the corporations which run the recording labels and distribution systems. Imagine a world, even, where a public health crisis can be resolved through a nearly automatic collective action by a community to contain the spread of an infectious disease. Virus epidemiology information and gene sequencing could be automatically propagated through a distributed data network in seconds or minutes, instead of the current system which requires layers of human approvals and sometimes sees political intervention at the expense of public health, as with the COVID-19 coronavirus outbreak.[3]

These are all possibilities in a distributed data economy, but there are many obstacles to overcome—not the least of which the historical legacy that surrounds personal data.

The Data Aggregators

Data aggregators grew out of an opportunity to monetize the voluminous data that began to emerge out of the connected world, such as data from payments systems and telecommunications systems that offer rich sources of information about human behaviour.

---

[2] Rutter, K. Panel Discussion. February 2019. London Blockchain Foundation. London, England.
[3] Global Biodefense (2020) "Lab That First Shared Novel Coronavirus Genome Still Shut Down by Chinese Government" February 28, 2020 [online], https://globalbiodefense.com/headlines/chinese-lab-that-first-shared-novel-coronavirus-genome-shut-down/.

These data sources have been generating ever-more-greater volumes of data from billions of individuals at ever-faster rates. Consultancy IDC projects that there will be more than 44 zettabytes of data generated around the world, up from 4.4 zettabytes in 2013.[4] One zettabyte is 2 to the 70th power bytes. If this book were in printed form, and filled with a zettabyte of data, you would have 10 volumes each tall enough to reach the sun.[5]

Who are the titans of this first generation of data aggregation? Acxiom (the relevant division now owned by marketing conglomerate Interpublic Group) was the undisputed Zeus on Mount Olympus of data aggregation. Credit bureaus such as Equifax, Experian and TransUnion join them on this lofty vantage. Not unlike the Gods of Olympus, these data aggregators are extraordinarily difficult to reach, for example if you have a dispute about bad data that entered your record through fraud or identity theft. Yes, there may be a web form that you can eventually puzzle through, but oversight is weak and recourse limited. In some cases, the credit bureaus have purchased collection agencies, which enforce action based on…credit bureau data. Consumers are caught in a self-contained universe if they attempt to dispute a claim. Companies like Plaid, CreditKarma, Mint and MyLife.com now assemble and derive insights around consumer data. Dozens of vendors sell aggregated "anonymized" mobility data, information about how blocks of consumers move around a city, neighborhood or specific location.

Insight into consumers enables one to quickly pierce the anonymity of the crowd. With a few demographic dimensions (age, approximate income, city), an individual can be traced to their home address. Other, more indirect privacy penetrations are possible. For example, researchers discovered that four points of shopping data (such as date and location of purchase) could uniquely re-identify an individual out of millions of records.[6]

---

[4] Kugler L (2018) "The War Over the Value of Personal Data." *Communications of the ACM* February 2018; 61(2): 17–19, https://cacm.acm.org/magazines/2018/2/224626-the-war-over-the-value-of-personal-data/abstract.

[5] Berkan R (2012) "Big Data: A Blessing and a Curse." *SearchEngine Journal* [online], https://www.searchenginejournal.com/big-data-blessing/53528/.

[6] de Montjoye, Hidalgo, Verleysen, Blondel (2013) "Unique in the Crowd." *Nature Scientific Reports* 3: 1376 [online], https://www.nature.com/articles/srep01376.

The Emergence of Fine-Grained Human Behavioural Data

Fine-grained human behavioural insights can be extracted by understanding the digital traces, or "breadcrumbs", that people leave on ubiquitous electronic networks that pervade every aspect of modern society.[7]

The first modern payment card was issued in 1950.[8] Adoption was slow initially, but began picking up steam as data communications services improved in the 1970s and 1980s. Credit cards are expected to carry more than 850 billion purchase transactions by 2028, up from a current level of 369 billion.[9] In Europe, 2018 alone saw more than US$ 3 trillion of purchase volume.[10] With this growth in payments systems have come insights into consumer purchasing behaviours, derived from the purchasing data, that has proven highly valuable to marketers.

Mobile phones, likewise, have emerged as rich source of human factors data within the past ten to fifteen years.[11] Other data sources began emerging—for example, Catalina Marketing harvested the "scan" data from checkout registers retail stores, generating a fine-grained map of consumer shopping behaviours (albeit one that struggled with the consumer migration to e-commerce).[12] Loyalty programs (earning "points" or "miles") have further generated actionable data on consumers that merchants have used to fine tune marketing.[13]

With the World Wide Web (popularly referred to as the "internet") exploding into widespread adoption in the late 1990s and beyond, a new vehicle was created for the acquisition of personal consumer data.

---

[7] Pentland A (2013) "The Data-Driven Society." *Scientific American* October 2013; 309(4): 78–83.
[8] Steele J (2018) "The History of Credit Cards." Experian Blog March 16, 2018 [online], https://www.experian.com/blogs/ask-experian/the-history-of-credit-cards/.
[9] Nilson (2020) *The Nilson Report* January 2020: 1167 [online], https://nilsonreport.com/upload/Cover_Chart_1167.jpg.
[10] Nilson (2019) *The Nilson Report* June 2019: 1156 [online], https://nilsonreport.com/upload/Cover_Chart_1156.jpg.
[11] Kostas Konsolakis, Hermie Hermens, Claudia Villalonga, Miriam Vollenbroek-Hutten and Oresti Banos Human Behaviour Analysis through Smartphones (2018). *Proceedings* 2, 1243 [online], https://doi.org/10.3390/proceedings2191243.
[12] Springer J (2018) "How the Digital Shift Checked Catalina Into Chapter 11: The 'Big Data' Marketing Pioneer Seeks a Speedy Restructuring." Winsight Grocery Business December 17, 2018 [online], https://www.winsightgrocerybusiness.com/industry-partners/how-digital-shift-checked-catalina-chapter-11.
[13] Wise Marketer Staff (2019) "How Data Analytics Is Transforming Loyalty Rewards Programs." The Wise Marketer March 28, 2019 [online], https://www.thewisemarketer.com/infographic/how-data-analytics-is-transforming-loyalty-rewards-programs/.

This proliferation of consumer data created a virtual feast of digital information for the data aggregators to gorge themselves on. Initially, consumer brand companies such as Proctor & Gamble and Nestlé, hungry themselves for smarter and better ways to market their products, supported this nascent industry with billions in revenue. Over time, other consumer-facing sectors such as financial services and auto embraced this approach to identifying and targeting relevant audiences and individuals.

Oligopoly Platform Companies

Increasingly, oligopoly platform companies such as the BATs (Baidu, Ali Baba, Tencent) and the FANGs (Facebook, Amazon, Netflix, Google) are themselves aggregating and tying together data from disparate sources and offering marketing analytics services to their corporate customers. Continuous location streams from mobile operating systems such as Android and messing apps such as WeChat and WhatsApp enable a very fine-grained understanding of behaviour—and ability to identify not only an individual, but their preferences and even predictions on future behaviours.[14]

Part II: Legacy Data Economics

Data Depletion

A decade ago, the World Economic Forum published a white paper "Personal data: The Emergence of a New Asset Class",[15] coincident with the emergence of the expression "Data is the New Oil". Like oil and gas, data systems represent a long-term asset class with the long-cycle investment required to harvest them and maintenance investment is also required on an ongoing basis. Databases also have an analogous concept to oil and gas reserves: depletion. In the data world, this is commonly referred to as "decay" or "data decay", namely the rate at which information in a database becomes obsolete. As the world of personal data economics has become more complex and interconnected, the World Economic Forum and others are looking at new approaches for creating and apportioning value from using data in new ways.

---

[14]Bogomolov A (2018) Andrey Bogomolov "Predictive Modeling of Human Behavior: Supervised Learning from Telecom Metadata." Ph.D. Thesis, University of Trento, Italy 2018 [online], https://pdfs.semanticscholar.org/1423/704d2ca219ad657838a6086d34c1cc6030ee.pdf.
[15]World Economic Forum (2011) "Personal Data: The Emergence of a New Asset Class" [online], https://www.weforum.org/reports/personal-data-emergence-new-asset-class.

Approaches such as using federated data to uncover value in latent health information (in turn creating economic incentives to cure rare diseases, for example)[16] as we will describe later in this chapter.

For example, in parts of Europe, as many as 23% of the population has moved within the past 5 years—comparable with one of the most mobile societies, the USA, with a rate of 24%.[17] Factors ranging from employment-driven movement (e.g. Polish workers in Paris) to humanitarian crisis (e.g. Syria) have further accelerated these trends. This means that name-and-address information becomes obsolete.

This leads us to a world where consumer data sets can decay 30% per year or more. For business data in certain markets (e.g. tech job contact details in San Francisco), that decay rate can exceed 70%.[18] If you are seeking to understand society or understand customers, you therefore need to invest not in *data sets* but in *data systems*, that enable you to keep pacing with the rapidly degrading data. Data is a river, not a rock, and should be viewed as a rapidly moving resource rather than a fixed object in space and time. The systems supporting that data should incorporate a mechanism for improving *recency*.

The Value of Personal Data

Once a data system is architected, and means of acquiring and compiling information (let us say, about consumers), what is the value of that data?

Industry Valuation of Consumers

How much, fundamentally, is a person valued economically, from the perspective of data economics?

The answer is of course in the manner in which it is consumed, how it is monetized. As of this writing, an individual is worth on average, globally, $359 per year to Google but $1,793 to Amazon (in terms of revenue).[19] The

---

[16] World Economic Forum (2020) "Global Data Access for Solving Rare Disease: A Health Economics Value Framework".

[17] Chandler A (2016) "Why Do Americans Move So Much More Than Europeans? How the National Mythos and U.S. Labor Laws Influence Geographic Mobility." *The Atlantic* October 21, 2016 [online], https://www.theatlantic.com/business/archive/2016/10/us-geographic-mobility/504968/.

[18] Brence T (2016) "Customer Data Decay: Why Your Contact Data Is Rotten." Informatica Blog August 3, 2016 [online], https://blogs.informatica.com/2016/08/03/customer-data-decay-why-your-contact-data-is-rotten/#fbid=g6xcTDA0Uu4.

[19] Ngo S (2018) "Here's How Much Google and Facebook Really Think You're Worth." *Showbiz Cheatsheet* [online], https://www.cheatsheet.com/money-career/heres-much-google-facebook-really-think-youre-worth.html/.

average American Facebook user is worth about $220 per year, but EU users are worth only about ¼ as much, perhaps due to stricter advertising regulations—one would expect that it would be much closer to the US revenue, given that per capita income in EU member states like Germany and Norway are comparable to or even greater than the USA on a PPP basis.[20]

Amazon is an interesting case study. While it delivers more revenue volume through its shopping services, nearly two-thirds of its operating profit for 2019 came from Amazon Web Services (AWS), which also grew 25% faster than Amazon's core products business.[21] International business segments are still operating at a loss.[22] And AWS is very high margin revenue—23% operating margin versus 5% operating margin overall for Amazon.[23] What this means is that user data generates a large volume of low-margin revenue for Amazon, while corporate revenue tied to cloud services now comprises the majority of Amazon's profits.

Facebook, on the other hand, runs at a 34% operating margin as of 2019, even after a rise in expenses over 2018.[24] They have been able to successfully monetize user data 790+ % better than Amazon. Facebook's margins are more than double the typical media company.[25] There are some who believe they should be regulated like an oligopolistic media company and not simply a "technology provider" as they would like to be classified.[26]

Indeed, oligopoly platforms like Facebook and LinkedIn demonstrate an interesting aspect of personal data monetization—the "network effect". The more people use these platforms and the more connected they are to each other, the more valuable the platform experience is to users (making them "stickier" and spending more time interacting with the platform) and the more marketers are willing to pay to access these audiences. Two-sided

---

[20] Dazeinfo (2020) "Facebook ARPU by Region: Q2 2010–Q4 2019" updated January 31, 2020 [online], https://dazeinfo.com/2018/08/23/facebook-average-revenue-per-user-by-region-dgraph/.

[21] Condon S (2020) "AWS Brings in Nearly $10b in Sales for Amazon in Q4, Hits $40b Annual Run Rate," https://www.zdnet.com/article/aws-brings-in-nearly-10b-in-sales-for-amazon-in-q4/.

[22] Ibid.

[23] The Motley Fool Staff (2019) "How Amazon Actually Makes Money." *The Motley Fool* February 19, 2019 updated April 10, 2019 [online], https://www.fool.com/investing/2019/02/19/how-amazon-actually-makes-money.aspx.

[24] Rodriguez S (2020) "Facebook Stock Falls After Showing 51% Rise in Expenses." CNBC.com, https://www.cnbc.com/2020/01/29/facebook-fb-earnings-q4-2019.html.

[25] CSI Market "Broadcasting and Cable Profitability," accessed March 1, 2020, https://csimarket.com/Industry/industry_Profitability_Ratios.php?ind=902

[26] Bell C (2018) "Facebook: We're Not a Media Company. Also Facebook: Watch Our News Shows." Mashable.com [online], https://mashable.com/2018/06/08/facebook-media-company-news-shows/.

networks such as Airbnb or Lyft or Ola have an indirect network effect but still see this power-law value creation curve.[27]

For Facebook, at least, its consumption of user data profits may be reaching the dregs of the bottle. New data privacy laws, repeated cyberhacks, and growing awareness about the relatively weak responses Facebook has given with respect to the use of its platform to promote misinformation, are beginning to shift Facebook's interaction with regulators and policymakers, and may put pressure on its ability to monetize user data.[28] The government backlash against Facebook-sponsored Libra Project,[29] an overt attempt to acquire even more consumer data off its network (this time in the payments arena), illustrates the dangers of a data monetization policy that fails to transparently and rigorously address data ethics. Indeed, the announcement of Libra stimulated a number of governments to accelerate their Central Bank Digital Currency (CBDC) projects with the express purpose of competing with or suppressing Libra.[30] The Reserve Bank of Canada went further and said they would only launch a CBDC if Libra were successful.[31] Companies like Apple, for example, have not stimulated government response to such a degree, perhaps through more astute government affairs efforts coupled with data privacy actions perceived as beneficial to consumers.[32]

Consumer Self-Worth

The converse system is instructive to explore: how much value do consumers attribute to their various personal data elements? Someone who publishes articles on LinkedIn might not place tremendous value on their own name, since it can be found attached to the article they published. Other data elements about an individual are much more sensitive. According to research

---

[27] Flint P (2018) "70 Percent of Value in Tech Is Driven by Network Effects" [online], https://www.linkedin.com/pulse/70-percent-value-tech-driven-network-effects-pete-flint/.
[28] Guy E (2018) "Inside the Two Years That Shook Facebook—and the World." Wired.com February 12, 2018, https://www.wired.com/story/inside-facebook-mark-zuckerberg-2-years-of-hell/.
[29] Shrier D (2019) "The Future of Money Isn't Libra or Chinacoin, It's Federated" [online], https://www.linkedin.com/pulse/future-money-isnt-libra-chinacoin-its-federated-david-shrier/.
[30] Baydakova A (2020) "Central Bankers From Canada, Netherlands, Ukraine Call Blockchain Unnecessary for Digital Fiat." Coindesk.com February 24, 2020 [online], https://www.coindesk.com/central-bankers-from-canada-netherlands-ukraine-call-blockchain-unnecessary-for-digital-fiat.
[31] Baydakova A (2020) "Bank of Canada Won't Issue Its Own Crypto Unless Libra Succeeds: Deputy Governor." Coindesk.com February 25, 2020 [online], https://www.coindesk.com/bank-of-canada-wont-issue-its-own-crypto-unless-libra-succeeds-deputy-governor.
[32] O'Flaherty K (2019) "Apple Issues New Blow to Facebook and Google with This Bold Privacy Move." Forbes.com November 6, 2019 [online], https://www.forbes.com/sites/kateoflahertyuk/2019/11/06/apple-issues-new-blow-to-facebook-and-google-with-this-privacy-move/#1d9685fc481d.

conducted by the University of Trento, "where I am right now" (a user's location in time and space) is the most "valuable" personal data. Media consumption, at the other end of the spectrum (where you read news or information), is valued little or not at all, and which apps you use falls somewhere in between. This landmark "Money Walks" study also determined that people value their own data more on days, which are outliers, where unusual events or activities are occurring, versus ordinary days.[33]

Generalizations are slippery in the world of personal data values. One has only to look at the disparity among personal data protection laws in Germany, the USA, and Nigeria, to pick three countries, to see consumer sensitivities or lack thereof. With that said, consumers have generally shown a willingness to share information around activities if it will help improve their experience with a product or service. Age and gender also play into how much or little individuals value their personal data.[34] Perhaps unsurprisingly, the Millennial generation of digital natives is more prone to data sharing without remuneration.[35] Some business models have been constructed around tangible benefits for tangible personal data sharing: Waze works so well because Waze users share traffic and other road condition data with each other; Netflix's recommendation engine, a core component of its value proposition, requires that users allow for the cross-fertilization of viewing preferences ("Other viewers like you watched…")—sometimes getting the service into trouble, even when publishing "anonymized" insights into this data.[36]

---

[33] Staiano J, Oliver N, Lepri B, de Oliveira R, Caraviello M, Sebe N (2014) "Money Walks: A Human-Centric Study on the Economics of Personal Mobile Data." *UbiComp '14 Proceedings of the 2014 ACM International Joint Conference on Pervasive and Ubiquitous Computing*, 583–594. New York, NY: ACM.

[34] Liem C, Petropoulos G (2016) "The Economic Value of Personal Data for Online Platforms, Firms and Consumers." Bruegel.com blog post [online], https://bruegel.org/2016/01/the-economic-value-of-personal-data-for-online-platforms-firms-and-consumers/.

[35] Christofides E, Muise A, Desmarais S (2012) "Hey Mom, What's on Your Facebook? Comparing Facebook Disclosure and Privacy in Adolescents and Adults." *Social Psychological and Personality Science* 3(1) January 2012.

[36] Saltzman M (2018) "How to See Everything Netflix Knows About You." *USA Today* April 17, 2018 updated May 14, 2018 [online], https://www.usatoday.com/story/tech/columnist/saltzman/2018/04/17/you-can-see-what-netflix-knows-you-but-you-cant-download/510782002/.

The Societal Cost of Legacy Data Models

The Economics of Privacy

Economists have, for decades, been exploring the economic cost of privacy. Not unlike filtration systems for water, or public safety patrols by law enforcement, or security gates on buildings, data privacy has associated costs. For example, if a job applicant, for a position working at a pharmacy that dispenses prescription pharmaceuticals, conceals that he or she has been arrested for selling drugs illegally, his or her personal privacy is protected, but the business in question assumes much greater economic risk than it intended (business, regulatory, and reputational). If a private citizen is in a traffic collision, but his or her medical records are locked in a secure system that the first responders cannot access, there may be a direct and deleterious impact on health care if, for example, the individual is allergic to certain medications or has a Do Not Resuscitate (DNR) order on file. If an individual wishes to apply for a loan, certain efficiencies are introduced if a trusted third party such as a credit bureau can provide assurances to the lender (the bank, for example) that the individual has adequate creditworthiness.[37]

For each of these circumstances, there are counter-arguments that suggest an equivalent economic burden. The job seeker may have been falsely accused, and lacked the funds to adequately defend against state prosecution. The person in the traffic collision might have their medical information improperly accessed another time if it is too readily available, and suffer other harm as a result. The loan applicant might be disputing information on the credit file, but be unsuccessful in having incorrect information removed. For example, at least one of the major credit bureaus has purchased a loan collection agency where they buy debts. Even if one wishes to dispute a bureau report, the counterparty who is making false claims…is the same bureau. Or the bureau's algorithm might be discriminatory such as to disfavor the class of people to which the individual belongs.[38] Shoshanna Zuboff and others have railed against the rise of "surveillance capitalism" and the society decay

---

[37] Acquisiti A, College H (2010) "The Economics of Personal Data and the Economics of Privacy." OECD Joint WPISP-WPIE Roundtable, Background Paper [online], https://www.oecd.org/sti/ieconomy/46968784.pdf.

[38] Acquisti A, Taylor C, Wagman L (2017) "The Economics of Privacy" [online], https://www.ftc.gov/system/files/documents/public_comments/2017/10/00006-141501.pdf.

accompanied by the growth of the oligopolistic data platform companies like Facebook and Google.[39]

Generally speaking, the attitude about data privacy is weighed against public good. Someone's right to medical privacy is typically not superseded by the public's right to be aware of an infectious disease crisis; even if Patient Zero's identity is protected, the public needs to be aware that the disease is spreading from X location, so that steps may be taken to contain the infection. In some domiciles, the identities including photos of sex offenders are published; in other domiciles, this is viewed as punitive rather than rehabilitative and other measures are taken. Yet, where is the line drawn with respect to digital data? If someone threatens on a Facebook posting to blow up a school, that is certainly a safety concern; should public officials take steps around the individual, the school, or both? What if an individual simply states a preference for a political candidate who holds extremist views? In one instance, most domiciles err on the side of caution for society, in the second instance, most domiciles would protect the identity of the individual. But is a posting on a Facebook page truly private? The affirmative statement that protects classes of personal data is one that only recently has come to be codified in statute and regulation, as we will discuss later in the chapter.

Cyber (In)security

Hackers have noticed the value of personal data and have engaged in large-scale data theft over the past few years. Unfortunately, as we point out in our book *New Solutions for Cybersecurity*, these massive data stores have been inadequately secured. The Aadhaar biometric and demographic database of 1.2 billion Indians was breached with an individual record for sale for a reported Rs 500 (about €6.50).[40] Equifax saw its entire US database stolen, about 148 million Americans.[41] As more and more personal data is acquired and analyzed and stored, it creates ever-more-tempting targets for cybercriminals, both those acting purely from a profit motive as well as a growing array

---

[39] Naughton J (2019) "'The Goal Is to Automate Us': Welcome to the Age of Surveillance Capitalism." *The Guardian* January 20, 2019 [online], https://www.theguardian.com/technology/2019/jan/20/shoshana-zuboff-age-of-surveillance-capitalism-google-facebook.
[40] Tech2 News Staff (2018) "Aadhaar Security Breaches: Here Are the Major Untowards Incidents That Have Happened with Aadhaar and What Was Actually Affected." Firstpost. September 25, 2018 [online], https://www.firstpost.com/tech/news-analysis/aadhaar-security-breaches-here-are-the-major-untoward-incidents-that-have-happened-with-aadhaar-and-what-was-actually-affected-4300349.html.
[41] Electronic Privacy Information Center (2018) "Equifax Data Breach" updated February 13, 2020 [online], https://epic.org/privacy/data-breach/equifax/.

of state-sponsored data thieves. Economic analysis can reveal the trade-offs in terms of the cost of implementing better data security versus the benefits of mitigating societal, business or individual harm.[42]

Part III: New Generation Data Ecologies

We have now established the value of personal data, considered the costs of personal data privacy and impacts of poor cybersecurity, and hinted at some of the opportunity embedded in rich data streams. In this section, we are going to investigate powerful computational tools that assist with positive social change, and the necessary privacy and personal data governance regulations that accompany them—laying the foundation for the distributed data economy. Without appropriate protections, these richer data streams offer a significant challenge with respect to protecting consumers from exploitation.

Social Physics of Personal Data

More than a decade of research by Prof. Alex Pentland at the Massachusetts Institute of Technology and its collaborating institutions has derived a new computational social science of "*social physics*".[43] Placing machine-learning rigor behind Adam Smith's musings on communal good,[44] social physics has uncovered new transparency and insights into society, and has enabled interventions at scale such as mapping how vaccines could reduce the spread of malaria in sub-Saharan Africa[45] and helping a region in central Europe reduce energy usage by 17% to "go green" (enabling them to only use renewables and not rely on fossil fuels to power their homes) at a fraction of the economic cost of conventional methods.[46] These insights have been derived from analyzing anonymized, aggregated datasets consisting of the tiny digital

---

[42] Garcia ME 2013) "The Economics of Data Breach: Asymmetric Information and Policy Interventions." PhD dissertation. Ohio State University, Columbus, OH [online], https://etd.ohiolink.edu/!etd.send_file%3Faccession%3Dosu1365784884%26disposition%3Dinline.

[43] Pentland A (2015) *Social Physics: How Social Networks Can Make Us Smarter* (2nd ed.). New York: Penguin Press.

[44] Smith, A (1759) The Theory of Moral Sentiments. London: Printed for A. Millar, and A. Kincaid and J. Bell.

[45] Wesolowski A, Eagle N, Tatem A, Smith DL, Noor AM, Snow RW, Buckee CO (2012) "Quantifying the Impact of Human Mobility on Malaria." *Science* October 12, 2012; 338(6104): 267–270.

[46] Mani A, Rahwan I, Pentland A (2013) "Inducing Peer Pressure to Promote Cooperation." *Nature Scientific Reports* 3, Article number: 1735.

traces people leave throughout the day by using their credit cards and mobile phones.[47]

This naturally has lead Prof. Pentland and his collaborators to the necessary twin of social physics insights, the domain of personal data privacy. Pentland chaired the World Economic Forum privacy working group that evolved a set of principles he termed the "New Deal on Data".[48] This thinking offers direct lineage to the emergence of new privacy regulations in Europe and elsewhere.

Emergent Regulation: GDPR, PSD2, Open Banking, and the California Consumer Privacy Act

The European Union has been highly sensitive to, and progressive on, the topic of personal data and personal data monetization. Cognizant of the data privacy issues and the impacts apparent from the exploitation of consumer data by private sector interests, the EU has promulgated a body of law and regulation to change the frame.

The first major legislation, GDPR, helps establish basic rights for the individual against the corporate conglomerate, around ideas like ownership of personal data, governance (control) over personal data and "the right to be forgotten". It also introduces penalties for data breaches, a significant step towards helping consumers understand the hidden economic cost of the shadowy realm of data brokers and data aggregators. An interesting artifact of GDPR is that it is enforceable for the rights of European citizens even if they are not physically present in Europe i.e. a vacationing French family in Florida using local internet or telecom services would enjoy the same protections, in theory, as if they were in Toulouse. Lesser known is the fact that GDPR creates a de facto open banking mandate around data portability.[49] In the USA, California passed a similar regulation (the California Consumer Privacy Act).

Its sister regulation, the Second Payment Services Directive (PSD2), enables personal portability of critical data, in this case, bank data. The UK passed a very similar regulation, Open Banking. In each case, the goal is to move away from a model where an oligopoly of large corporations create

---

[47] Waldawsky-Berger I (2018) "Social Physics: Reinventing Analytics to Better Predict Human Behaviors." Wall St. Journal CIO Blog, https://blogs.wsj.com/cio/2018/09/14/social-physics-reinventing-analytics-to-better-predict-human-behaviors/.

[48] Pentland A (2009) "Reality Mining of Mobile Communications: Toward a New Deal on Data." *The Global Information Technology Report 2008–2009*, S Dutta (ed.). New York, NY: World Economic Forum.

[49] European Commission "What Are My Rights?" accessed March 1, 2020 [online], https://ec.europa.eu/info/law/law-topic/data-protection/reform/rights-citizens/my-rights/what-are-my-rights_en.

insurmountable switching costs for consumers, and towards a model where there is increased competition (accompanied by hopefully lower prices and/or better service) for consumers because their personal financial data becomes portable. An added benefit that delivers second-order economic cost improvement both for consumers and banks is better cybersecurity; API's offering a more robust cyber protocol than the previous market of "screen scrapers" that would pretend to be users and log into different banking websites to collect personal financial data on behalf of consumers. Quite harmonious in principle with GDPR, the open banking mandates that requires personal consumer financial data to become transparent and portable subject to the individual consumer's desires.[50]

In practice, compliance with these two regulations is proving to be challenging for companies.[51] New solutions that incorporate distributed ledger and artificial intelligence may enable not only compliance with GDPR and PSD2, but also enable personal monetization of distributed data for the benefit of the individual, rather than the corporate actor such as one of the FAMGAs (Facebook-Amazon-Microsoft-Google-Ali baba). We will discuss this in the section on the distributed data economy.

Part IV: The Distributed Data Economy

In this final section, we will discuss the potential and the enablers surrounding distributed data. Notice the shift in language as we progress through this chapter, from economics to ecologies to economy. We are self-consciously envisioning an evolution to a higher order of societal organization.

Laying the Groundwork for Distributed Data

We are not quite at a place in the progression of both our technologies and of our legal and business frameworks to harness the full potential of distributed data. Too, we need to improve data literacy if we hope for individuals to be able to appreciate, fully understand and take advantage of the benefits that can arise from distributed data. Before these actions can take place, we have

---

[50]Manthorpe R (2018) "What Is Open Banking and PSD2? WIRED Explains." Wired.com [online], https://www.wired.co.uk/article/open-banking-cma-psd2-explained.

[51]Mikkelsen D, Soller H, Strandell-Jansson M, Wahlers M (2019) "GDPR Compliance Since May 2018: A Continuing Challenge." CPO Magazine [online], https://www.cpomagazine.com/data-protection/gdpr-compliance-since-may-2018-a-continuing-challenge/.

core infrastructure challenges to address to create the necessary conditions for a distributed data future:

A. **First, we need to source more and better data.** Data quality remains one of the unspoken tragedies of the big data revolution. "Water, water, everywhere / Nor any drop to drink".[52] All of those zettabytes of data being produced, much of it personal data, and yet very little attention is paid to the actual quality of the information. Vicki Raeburn, who was Chief Data Quality Officer, shared that she would have to go lie down if she spent too much time considering the current quality of the "big data" that is being proudly discussed[53]… made immutable, thanks to blockchain. To bowdlerize Kirsty Rutter, former Chief Innovation Officer of Barclays UK, when she spoke on a panel about DLTs in the spring of 2019, "immutable [garbage]". Another input into the data equation is the characteristic of data transience (as stated earlier, "data is a river, not a rock"). Particularly as we start to explore social physics, we find that dynamic data flows need new management and technology processes to ensure accuracy of predictions. We need to move data systems to the point of near-real-time analysis, which perhaps can be partially enabled by systems such as OPAL that we will discuss below. Measurement and performance management of data systems has an imperative of managing and mitigating data senescence.

B. **Second, we need better analytics conducted on that data.** At this writing, we are still in the very infancy of big data analytics. Let us recall that advances such as Google-incubated TensorFlow are not even four years old.[54] Newer systems like Endor's artificial intelligence prediction engine are just barely beginning to scale.[55] Hybridized systems that combine human intuition and synthesis with machine analysis are emerging, yet need substantially more research and development before

---

[52] Coleridge ST (1798) "The Rime of the Ancient Mariner." *Lyrical Ballads, with a Few Other Poems*, 1st ed. London.
[53] In a personal conversation with the author, August 2019.
[54] Dean J (2015) "TensorFlow—Google's Latest Machine Learning System, Open Sourced for Everyone." Google AI Blog.
[55] BusinessWire (2019) "Endor Launches Predictions Protocol to Democratize Access to AI and Data Science," https://venturebeat.com/2019/04/04/endor-launches-predictions-protocol-to-democratize-access-to-ai-and-data-science/.

they become industry standard. New maths are emerging and new capabilities will arise as breakthroughs like quantum computing (today very much a laboratory technology) become commercially available.[56]

C. **Then, we can evolve into fully distributed data networks.** While DLTs are computationally expensive, this is purchased with the coin of economic benefit that can be derived from better sharing of the right information at the right time under the right controls (data governance). IPFS and other hybridized schemes that have "on chain" and "off chain" data storage enable the transparency and resiliency of a distributed ledger with the scalability of massive data sets.

Distributed Data Ethics

Increasingly attention is being paid to the ethics of big data and artificial intelligence, and the complexity of addressing these issues will only increase in a distributed data world. Research ethicists, for example, are raising questions about how conventional university approaches to protecting individuals break down in the face of big data[57]; ethicists have not yet begun to explore seriously what this means in the distributed data world.

Data systems become geometrically more useful with the application of artificial intelligence, and advanced artificial intelligence (AI) systems such as machine learning and deep learning are powered by large volumes of data. Accordingly, the data discussion and the AI discussion quickly converge. Technology scholars such as Luciano Floridi of the Oxford Internet Institute have proposed a framework approach to AI ethics, based on reviewing numerous ethical frameworks and models and converging on 5 pillars of ethical AI[58] summarized below:

(1) *Beneficence*: AI should be doing good for society.
(2) *Non-maleficence*: AI needs to go further than just doing good, it also needs to make sure that it doesn't create harm (a consumer might have a shorter commute thanks to a driving map application, but what if the

---

[56] Fan S (2019) "Quantum Computing, Now and in the (Not Too Distant) Future." *Singularity Hub* February 26, 2019 [online], https://singularityhub.com/2019/02/26/quantum-computing-now-and-in-the-not-too-distant-future/.
[57] Raymond N (2019) "Safeguards for Human Studies Can't Cope with Big Data." *Nature* 568: 277, https://www.nature.com/articles/d41586-019-01164-z.
[58] Floridi, L, Cowls, J (2019) "A Unified Framework of Five Principles for AI in Society." *Harvard Data Science Review* 1(1) [online], https://doi.org/10.1162/99608f92.8cd550d1.

data about their commute patterns is then exploited to malignant ends?). This is where issues like data privacy and data security come into play.
(3) *Autonomy*: in creating systems of autonomous machines (which become even more difficult to manage in a distributed data economy), we need to ensure that *human autonomy* isn't compromised. People still need to make decisions about things that affect them.
(4) *Justice*: the AI systems should both be fair, and promote fairness. Algorithmic discrimination by AI has been written about extensively,[59] and societal values needed to be embedded into AI-driven systems to ensure that technology aligns with law and morality.
(5) *Explicability*: the decisions made by the AI need to be understandable by humans, which helps ensure accountability for them.

A similar model might be conceived of for a distributed data economy. Indeed, as distributed systems become more widely adopted, an *ethical framework for the distributed data economy* becomes imperative, since distributed systems are intrinsically more difficult to control from a central source. How can you audit the code and activities of thousands of servers in a complex encrypted network, given the difficulties in doing so with a handful? How do you monitor the content of secure, encrypted communications streams that may be making decisions that are adverse to society?

Governance for the New Data Order

The OPAL Project (www.OpalProject.org) provides a federated approach for managing the mechanics of a highly distributed data environment that is nonetheless useful, and allows for better control of the ethical dimensions discussed in the previous section. The basic principles of OPAL focus on improving data security and data governance. They are highly congenial with a distributed data future.

The old style of handling data, which leads to a number of the data insecurity challenges seen with Equifax or Aadhaar, entails accumulating a large volume of data in a single repository, where analytics can then be conducted on it. The information theory of centralization posits that it is more efficient from a computer systems management perspective both to maintain the database and to perform analytics. Economic analysis has shown that when

---

[59] Eubanks V (2018) *Automating Inequality: How High-Tech Tools Profile, Police, and Punish the Poor* St. New York: Martin's Press.

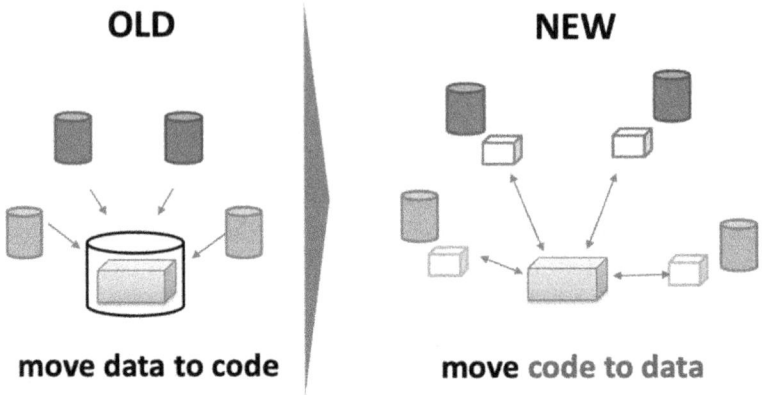

Fig. 5.1 The OPAL method to protect data (*Source* The author)

there is low uncertainty, it is more economically beneficial for a company to centralize, albeit with reduced flexibility.[60]

By bringing the code to the data, instead of the data to the code, we have an opportunity to dramatically improve information security. Contemporary information management systems, notably blockchain or current-generation distributed ledger technologies, provide for a robust code architecture to manage these more complex information flows. Next generation systems that implement near-homomorphic encryption, such as Enigma, offer the potential for exponential improvements on information security and encryption while maintaining sufficient flexibility and accessibility for the data system to be useful in a number of applications (Fig. 5.1).[61]

Distributed ledger technologies appear tailor-made for these types of distributed data systems, and standards like OPAL create a body of coherency around how algorithms and data governance are managed. Bringing these systems together pose a viable platform on which GDPR and PSD2 compliance can be maintained, while extending more control to the users and better security over the data.[62]

---

[60]Velu C, Madnick S, Van Alstyne M (2013) "Centralizing Data Management with Considerations of Uncertainty and Information-Based Flexibility." Composite Information Systems Laboratory (CISL) Working Paper, http://web.mit.edu/smadnick/www/wp/2013-02.pdf.

[61]Hardjono T, Shrier D, Pentland A, eds. (2019) *Trusted Data, Revised and Expanded Edition: A New Framework for Identity and Data Sharing*. Cambridge, MA: MIT Press.

[62]IBM Security "Blockchain and GDPR" (2018) Cambridge, MA: IBM [online]. https://www.ibm.com/downloads/cas/2EXR2XYP.

Data for the People

A distributed data economy is only possible with sufficient data literacy of consumers to understand, and take action around, the monetization (and protection) of personal data. Market demand to support data aggregators who act on behalf of consumers, a new kind of "data co-op", will only emerge at sufficient levels to support a distributed data economy if consumers attain greater levels of sophistication around how much various types of data are worth, and how those consumers can govern and manage their personal data economics.

The idea of consumer-powered personal data markets isn't new; companies like Datacoup have been trying for years to get critical mass.[63] A common expression in data-aware circles is "If you're not paying for the product – you are the product" (attributed to various individuals).[64] Too few consumers are conscious of this dynamic. The issues of consumer data illiteracy have been (1) the lack of a mandate that empowers consumers around their data (now being solved with regulations like GDPR) and (2) sophistication among users. The UN has highlighted this as a priority within its World Data Forum, with participants stating that "improving data literacy was needed".[65]

The models already exist for providing greater information literacy. Frameworks have been proposed for large-scale community engagement powered by data, posing questions about how data can be used for public good and asserting that control mechanisms built into distributed data, like OPAL, can manage the tension between personal data privacy and benefits to society.[66] Through a concerted set of actions, data literacy can be introduced to different segments of society, and create the necessary ingredients to promote the distributed data economy.

Yet data literacy by itself is insufficient. It's not only data, but *metadata* (abstractions drawn from a collection of or interpretation of data) that powers many of the artificial intelligence models today, and will even more so in the future. Informed consent by users, and therefore user data literacy, needs to

---

[63] Simonite T (2014) "Sell Your Personal Data for $8 a Month." MIT Technology Review February 12, 2014 [online]. https://www.technologyreview.com/s/524621/sell-your-personal-data-for-8-a-month/.

[64] O'Reilly T (2017) "You're Not the Customer; You're the Product." *Quote Investigator* [online], https://quoteinvestigator.com/2017/07/16/product/.

[65] United Nations (2018) "World Data Forum Wraps Up with a Declaration to Boost Financing for Data and Statistics" [online], https://www.un.org/development/desa/en/news/statistics/2018-world-data-forum-wraps-up.html.

[66] Letouze E, Oliver N (2019) "Sharing Is Caring Four Key Requirements for Sustainable Private Data Sharing and Use for Public Good" [online], http://datapopalliance.org/wp-content/uploads/2019/11/DPA_VFI-SHARING-IS-CARING.pdf.

take into account not only the specific data elements an individual might be exposed to a company (for example, the person's location to enable the use of a map application) but also the inferential insights derived from that (wealth, income, and credit score can be estimated based on pattern analysis of a collection of data points related to location[67]).

Distributed Data Policy

Policymakers globally are actively grappling with questions of how to engage with distributed data and how to regulate it, while also managing the potential for innovation and new enterprise formation it contains. Governments around the world, for example, are contemplating CBDC projects, bringing government coffers directly in line with distributed data opportunity. More than 120 national data privacy laws have been put in place,[68] risking a Tower of Babel in the absence of harmonization as data moves cross-border but is regulated locally.

Areas that the European Union, for example, could pursue with respect to data policy include:

Robust Governance. Encouragement by regulators of the private sector use of distributed ledger-based framework approaches, such as OPAL, would help to harmonize activities, streamline oversight and deliver the benefits of standards in terms of market formation and market growth. These efforts in Europe could be tied to the large-scale funding already allocated for blockchain investment.

Adaptation and Innovation Support. GDPR and PSD2 merit active review and augmentation, as would privacy and data portability regulations more broadly (particularly in light of how GDPR and PSD2 have been used as models by other jurisdictions). Now that Europe has had time to see how corporations are attempting to comply in practice, adjustments can be made to the frameworks and the interpretation guidelines. For example, an unintended consequence of GDPR has been to make it more difficult for smaller companies to comply, and introducing new costs and business and financial risks to start-up ventures, although potentially also have created areas of

---

[67] Pentland A (2019) "Building a Data-Rich Society." *Trusted Data: A New Framework for Identity and Data Sharing*, 109. Cambridge, MA: MIT Press.
[68] World Economic Forum (2020) "Shaping the Future of Technology Governance: Data Policy" [online], https://www.weforum.org/platforms/shaping-the-future-of-technology-governance-data-policy.

opportunity.[69] Steps that regulators and policymakers can take to modulate the effects of these regulations on innovation include:

(1) *Progressive regulatory models*, similar to how some jurisdictions have addressed financial services licensing (e.g. the Bank of England's e-money, "halfway" and "full" banking licenses in an effort to support challenger entry into the banking sector).
(2) More "*sandboxing*" opportunities for start-ups to engage with regulators in a contained environment, where issues can be candidly raised and addressed, and greater compliance capacity within start-ups developed. "Tech sprints" and hackathons around distributed data, data privacy, and data portability, with regulator and policymaker involvement, become another mechanism to simultaneously build government capacity around new technologies and align private sector activity with areas of opportunity.
(3) *Safe harbor exemptions* for defined activities for small and medium sized enterprises (SMEs), so that the cost of compliance does not drive them out of the market
(4) Encouragement of and potentially funding for private sector *compliance-as-a-service* providers, which could also help reduce the costs for individual SMEs while maintaining quality and rigor.

Coordination. Further coordination among the European Union, the OECD, the UN data agencies and the G20, along with other bodies such as ASEAN, African Union, OAS and Caricom, would help mitigate the risks of distributed data policy disharmonization on the one hand, and "jurisdiction shopping" by large corporate interests on the other (which run the risk of undermining data policy). The EU's Gaia-X project, on the one hand, provides some independence from the purely corporate models of virtualized data and data governance such as those offered by Amazon or Microsoft.[70] On the other hand, it's an EU-only initiative at present. Could it be offered to other nations as well? In a distributed data world, data is global, and government response needs to be global, not just regional.

By aligning these areas of Robust Governance, Adaptation and Innovation Support, and Coordination, the disruption that distributed data represents

---

[69] Martin, N., Matt, C., Niebel, C. et al. (2019) "How Data Protection Regulation Affects Startup Innovation." *Information Systems Frontiers* 21: 1307–1324. https://doi.org/10.1007/s10796-019-09974-2.

[70] Bedingfield W (2020) "Europe Has a Plan to Break Google and Amazon's Cloud Dominance." Wired UK January 27, 2020 [online], https://www.wired.co.uk/article/europe-gaia-x-cloud-amazon-google.

can be better managed, and the economic benefits realized while mitigating potential harms to society.

Acknowledgements The author wishes to thank William Hoffman of the World Economic Forum and Professor Alex Pentland of the Massachusetts Institute of Technology for their suggestions and insights that contributed to this chapter.

Part II

Disintermediation in Macroeconomics and Finance

6

Blockchain for Growth: Applying DLTs to the UN Sustainable Development Goals

Jane Thomason

Introduction

The Sustainable Development Goals (SDGs) galvanized the global community behind efforts to make the world a better place for all its people by 2030. It is an ambitious agenda, and one that will not be reached without harnessing the potential of technology. Among frontier technologies, Blockchain—deployed at scale—could accelerate SDG progress and alleviate challenges faced by the poor and marginalized.

Most people associate blockchain with the early anarchic days of Bitcoin, launched by Satoshi Nakamoto in 2007, and the heady days of Initial Coin Offerings (ICOs), where millions and billions were raised; some based on insubstantial whitepapers, which undermined blockchains' credibility as a technology capable of driving unprecedented industrial change. Bitcoin has since come far, with a market cap of over US$303.1 billion (at the time of writing) and used as a method of payment by millions of people.

Beyond cryptocurrency, there is a growing appreciation for blockchain, Bitcoins's underlying technology, for numerous use cases. Globally, 200 banks and over 40 central banks are experimenting with blockchains in financial efficiency, data management and information-sharing, for example (World Economic Forum 2019). The banks in question consider the benefits of

---

J. Thomason (✉)
Founder of Supernova Data, Industry Associate, University College London, Centre for Blockchain, London, UK

Blockchain technology to include; oversight of trades end-to-end, reduced risk of discrepancy and delayed settlement, real-time access to a shared ledger for sighting by multiple stakeholders, automation of manual processes, reduced reliance on external settlement networks, efficiency gains in capital velocity, reduced counterparty, market and credit risk (Del Rio 2019; World Economic Forum, 2019).

Digital is the future. For countries to remain competitive, it is imperative that governments look towards innovation and digital technologies to provide the basis for growth in the twenty-first century. Job creation will inevitably come from the digital economies. Blockchain enables new forms of finance to address global poverty problems. Governments and donors need to be at the forefront of understanding, preparing for, and accelerating the uptake to scale, to achieve impact.

This chapter summarizes the many applications of blockchain in contributing to widespread social transformation and enabling traction against the SDGs, focusing on emerging economies. It also discusses barriers and enabling factors to achieve such a transformation.

Blockchain and the SDGs

As the hype surrounding blockchains subsides, we can contemplate a more sober reflection of the technology and its use cases. It is becoming clear that blockchain offers the potential to build a better world; one where the poor have their identity secured on a blockchain, which they can use to access essential services or the financial system through a mobile phone and digital currencies. People living on customary land can have it titled on a blockchain and can use that title to access finance. For governments, blockchain is an opportunity to leapfrog traditional systems and achieve greater financial inclusion and transparency. For business, blockchain offers easier access to capital and significantly lower transaction costs. For donors and philanthropists, blockchain can also ensure that aid goes directly to targeted beneficiaries using a smart contract. For the ambitious, there is potential to use blockchain to create Distributed Autonomous Organisations to address global commons issues. The following section outlines some of the key use cases by SDG.

SDG 1—No Poverty

Blockchain can help leapfrog a number of challenges faced by the poor and has tremendous potential to provide scalable solutions to address issues of poverty and inequality. This includes: the potential to confer a permanent, immutable record of identity in the blockchain owned by individuals could be game-changing; using smart contracts, blockchain can be used to ensure that donor funds reach intended recipients in a transparent way without middlemen and leakage along the way. Aid delivery can be tracked with transparently recorded "way-stations" showing location in supply chain and ultimate delivery as well as financial inclusion.

Digital Identity

The World Bank (Desai et al. 2018) estimate that over one billion people globally cannot prove who they are. The window to global inclusion and economic participation is identity. The importance of trusted legal identity is recognized by the UN ID2020 agenda (www.id2020.org) to be a fundamental prerequisite for poverty reduction. Having an established identity underlies a citizen's access to a plethora of services: financial inclusion, government services, voting, employment, to name but a few. There is an opportunity to rapidly establish and scale an advanced digital identity system leveraging blockchain which will unlock many barriers faced by the poor, as well as facilitate greater economic growth through ease of transactions. The potential to confer a permanent immutable record of identity in the blockchain owned by individuals could be game-changing. Once a person has an identity, they can potentially have access to a range of services; the roll out of digital money systems could fuel rapid widespread access to financial services that was not available before. This could have a significant impact on the economic livelihoods of the large segments of rural populations that are unbanked.

There are many blockchain projects established for providing digital identity, including Bitnation, uPort, Exsulcoin, the Shyft Network and Blockstack, which can help refugees or humanitarian agencies to obtain digital ID documents and host governments can then use to verify their identity (Thomason et al. 2019).

Land and Assets Registration

Hernando de Soto, the Peruvian economist and anti-poverty campaigner, believes that the absence of formal title to property means there is $10 trillion in "dead capital" in the world economy (Casey 2016). Many people own land and assets, but due to insufficient and unverifiable records, are not able to access the value of their assets. Through digitization of assets, people would be able to borrow to improve their livelihoods and an immutable digital record (once established) means that ownership is confirmed. There are two opportunities to unlock land value. The first is to build a trusted and incorruptible system for ordinary citizens to lease their land and generate income. The second is to establish a formal registry system, tied to individual digital identities, for land to be used as collateral for citizens to borrow money and become more financially mobile. Building a formal registry scheme, based on individual digital identities, can provide the collateral necessary for larger investments and financial progression. Such capital can be used to invest in improving living standards, starting or scaling businesses, and growing the economy.

Existing technology providers actively piloting blockchain solutions for land registry schemes, include Chromaway (www.chromaway.com), a technology provider working with Sweden's land titling project (www.lantmater iet.se), and Factom (www.factom.com), a provider working on Honduras' land registry project and SESO in Nigeria (app.seso.global).

Humanitarian Settings

Mass and forced migration is a major—and growing—challenge. The UN Refugee Agency's annual Global Trends study (2018) report that 68.5 million people had been forced from their homes across the world in 2017. When refugees are forced to abandon their homes, many leave behind important documents such as birth certificates, marriage licences, passports and ID cards. These are nearly impossible to retrieve after leaving the country, assuming they have not already been destroyed (UNHCR 2018).

Blockchain has potential to help solve humanitarian problems, including identity, migration, asylum-seeking, camp management, food and remittance distribution (Ardittis 2018). Humanitarian organizations are deploying blockchain in camps to address digital identity, supply chains, cash transfers and remittances, integrity of donor funds flows, property registry, employment rights, human trafficking, education and asylum processing. This is often in conjunction with other frontier technologies such as AI, IoT, big data, drones and 3D printing.

Save The Children have been investigating a humanitarian passport (Shah 2017), the Red Cross piloted blockchain in early 2018 to test the traceability and transparency of Islamic Social Finance (The Development Circle 2018) and the World Food Programme's Building Blocks program was one of the first of its kind to facilitate cash transfers to refugees on the blockchain. To ensure these services were possible, however, fundamentals regarding satisfying identity claims were first necessary. Indeed, a task force has been established by the European Parliament to look at how blockchain technology could be used to provide digital identities to refugees (Ardittis 2018).

Financial Inclusion

There is a direct correlation between financial exclusion and poverty (World Bank 2017). An estimated two billion—or 38% of working-age adults—globally have no access to financial services delivered by regulated financial institutions, with 73% of poor people unbanked (World Bank Group 2017).

Digital currencies and mobile money systems could address this by providing widespread access to financial services, providing traceability and efficiency in disbursement which would have a tremendous impact on the economic livelihoods of the large segments of rural populations that are unbanked.

Among the financially excluded are migrant workers and their families in their home countries. In 2015, these workers sent USD500 billion home, representing a key international flow of funds. Current remittance processes are slow and expensive, penalizing the most vulnerable and impoverished groups of people. Despite technological advancement, the costs for migrants to send money across borders to their families remains extremely expensive, with fees often surpassing 5% (Cecchetti and Schoenholtz 2018) and yet remittances reduce poverty (Pekovic 2017).

Annual cross-border remittances are about $600 billion per year, three quarters of which flow to low- and middle-income countries. Yet, on average, the charge for sending $200—the benchmark used by authorities to evaluate cost—is $14. That is the result of the combination of fees (including charges from both the sender and recipient intermediaries) and the exchange rate margin, which typically comprises 7% of the amount sent (World Bank 2013). A Philippine company, Coins.ph, offers a good example of blockchain's potential. Situated in the country ranked third in the world for receiving remittances (totaling about USD$30 billion a year), Coins.ph provides Filipino users a mobile, blockchain-based platform to allow them to send money at a more affordable and faster rate. Blockchain allowed Coins.ph to build an application to facilitate fund transfers without reliance on existing bank infrastructures and to be more agile in their services at a more affordable price (Global Financing Facility 2016).

Blockchain would reduce the transaction costs for remittances, giving the unbanked access to financial systems and ensuring that funds intended for the poor actually reach them.

SDG 2—Zero Hunger: Agriculture Supply Chains

The agricultural industry ensures food security—it is a major driver of economic activity, employment, social cohesion and prosperity for many parts of rural and regional countries. Global population growth means, worldwide, demand for food is projected to rise by around 75% in the first half of this century, with three quarters of this growth in Asia (Australian Government 2014).

Key challenges across agri-supply chains are:

1. Farmers are not paid for the commodities they produce when they deliver them;
2. Buyers don't have access to flexible supply chain finance to pay farmers, as financiers lack visibility and control when financing commodities; and,
3. Consumers don't really know where their food and fibres come from restricting their ability to make informed purchasing abilities.

An efficient agriculture supply chain is especially important in low-income countries whose reliance on agriculture is 28 times greater than high-income countries (World Bank 2019). More than 60% of the world's population depends on agriculture for survival and ninety per cent of this land is found in Latin America and Sub-Saharan Africa. Half of this 90% is concentrated in: Brazil, the Democratic Republic of the Congo, Angola, Sudan, Argentina, Colombia and Bolivia.

AgriDigital (https://www.agridigital.io), for example, has used blockchain-enabled technology to create globally frictionless systems for the grains and cotton industry. Launched in March 2019, Agridigital ensures farmers continue to own their commodity right up until the moment they are paid, solving the problem of matching delivery to payment and opening up flexible financing options.

SDG 3—Good Health and Well-Being

Health Supply Chains are crucially important to ensure the authenticity and quality of life-saving medicines. Poor-quality medicines are a major public health threat, particularly in settings with a weak regulatory environment. Advances in logistic chain management leverages both digital and data analytics to not only improve the tracking and authenticity of medicines, but also ensure consistency of availability and quality. When linked to a digital identity, the digitized tracking of health supply right down to individual recipients, could be a game-changer in terms of tackling health outcomes such as maternal health and child mortality.

The blockchain brings significant operational benefits to supply chains (Provenance 2015):

- Interoperable: modular and interoperable, the blockchain can eliminate the possibility of double-spending throughout a supply chain
- Auditable: a blockchain's auditable records can be inspected and used by companies, standards organizations, regulators and customers across the supply chain
- Cost-efficient: eliminating the need for "handling companies" to be audited can drastically reduce costs across supply chains
- Real time and agile: a fast and highly accessible sign-up means quick deployment across the many participants in a supply chain
- Public: the openness of the blockchain enables innovation and bottom-up transparency in supply chains instead of burdensome top-down audits
- Guaranteed continuity: the elimination of any central operator ensures inclusiveness and longevity of supply chain management

FarmaTrust (www.farmatrust.com) offers a way to trace data about medicine moving through the supply chain on blockchain, a technology originally created for the purpose of buying and selling bitcoin without going through a server belonging to a bank or government that could be hacked (Lock 2019).

SDG 5—Gender Equality

The United Nations sees blockchain technology may dramatically improve the efficiency, transparency and accountability in international humanitarian, development or peacekeeping assistance, providing a chain of custody from generation-to-generation, woman-to-woman, each acting as a node in the transfer. Ownership registries recorded on the blockchain, will track property lineage with ownership details secured privately among the involved parties. Invisible women and children with no ID, are at risk, and fall into the hands of traffickers (sex trade, illegal human organ trade), and are missed by social programs. Commenting on the need to encourage and finance innovative approaches, Karen Ellemann, Minister for Fisheries and Equal Opportunities and Minister for Nordic Cooperation, Denmark, at a four-day event at the UN Women Headquarters in New York, said "pioneering involvement in this new territory can act as an important stamp of legitimacy enabling investment in blockchain solutions designed to help women in emergencies. For refugee women on the move, blockchain technology can help store and secure identity papers, medical records and documentation of ownership of assets" (UN Women 2018).

Slavefreetrade is a Universal Supply Chain Operating System on the blockchain. Its mission "aligns with the United Nations Sustainable Development goal 8.7 along with eradicating modern slavery by enabling and motivating business to clean slavery from their supply chains". Presently, the "distance between people in …[the supply chain ecosystem] has resulted in a lack of knowledge by consumers about who and how products are made, a lack of respect for the human rights of 45 million workers, and a lack of clear sight and responsibility to the end of every supply chain" (slavefreetrade 2020). By certifying slave-free products with a consumer-facing slavefreetrade label, those along the ecosystem will track its provenance to the origin. Using a verification framework to eradicate modern-day slavery in business supply chains, it looks at the supply chain ecosystem: world's consumers, retailers, workers, employers, businesses and suppliers, to track the provenance.

SDG 6—Clean Water

Countries spend billions of dollars to develop and implement water accounting guidelines and frameworks. By using blockchain as a foundation for water accountability and the regulation of peer-to-peer transfer of water allocations, it balances competing uses ensuring the sustainability of water for the longer term.

For example, in Australia there are multiple jurisdictions sharing responsibility for water resources management, creating a complex water market that dissuades small irrigators and an opportunity for intermediaries to enter the water market. It is a widely acknowledged goal in the Murray Darling Basin Agreement to have more individual irrigators participate more effectively in the market but there are critical barriers to participation including;

the complexity of the trading process and lack of price, volume and information transparency. The blockchain could lend transparency to the information critical to enhance market participation instilling confidence and encouraging participation by irrigators in the water market.

Civic Ledger (https://civicledger.com/) analysed how a blockchain-based platform—Water Ledger—could support an effective market for irrigators, which in economics and general equilibrium theory is defined by several conditions, collectively called perfect competition. Blockchain offers the potential for countries to manage and monitor scarce water resources.

SDG 7—Affordable and Clean Energy

The price of solar panels has dropped over 80% over the last decade—it's now cheaper to produce and buy solar energy than fossil energies (Dudley 2019). Solar panels can now be connected to the blockchain in order to enable consumers in developing countries to benefit from distributed generation. With blockchain, someone from a village can buy small solar panels and plug them to an off-grid network of cables in order to produce electricity for their local community.

Smart contracts allow individuals to buy and sell solar energy using digital tokens that can be redeemed for a local cryptocurrency. For example, the British start-up Azuri (www.azuri-group.com), produces low-cost solar panel solutions for off-grid areas in rural Africa, bringing clean energy to markets where once kerosene was the only option. Simply put, transforming the lives of off-grid rural citizens making them owners of cutting-edge technology and building a healthier safer home environment.

SDG 13—Climate Action

At the UN General Assembly in 2019, The Sustainable Digital Finance Alliance and the HSBC Center of Sustainable Finance launched "*Blockchain Gateway for Sustainability Linked Bonds: Widening access to finance block by block*". This outlines how emerging technology can enable the green bond market to scale dramatically from 2% of the current trillion-dollar bond market, unlocking capital for solutions to meet the Paris Climate Agreement. The report points to a future where the current reporting burden is alleviated to make the bond market far more efficient and accurate and lead the transformation (Fintech News 2019).

SDG 17—Partnerships for Goals: Global Commons—Technology as a Global Public Good

There are three broad types of global commons resources: common heritage domains (like the oceans, the atmosphere, Antarctica and outer space regulated by international law); resources that are under national domains but ranked as global commons issues (such as rainforests, national waters, and indigenous cultures); and shared resources that justify a common effort from the community to manage and govern (such as digital resources, the world wide web infrastructure or global financial system) (UN 2013).

Blockchain could scale local solutions to address the global commons by supporting activities to enable the sustainable management of the global commons, through systems of governance, transparent decision-making, smart contracts and decentralized mechanisms and incentives for collaboration, cooperation, consensus and trust.

A Global Commons Partnership could be enabled by blockchain and a Global Commons Trust established to fund action for Global Commons Issues and access to Global Public Goods. This could be achieved through the establishment of an International Trust to build and develop the enabling technologies for general access at minimal (or subsidized) cost—thus ensuring access to the most marginalized persons. Trustees would have a fiduciary duty to all humanity. The cost of building and maintaining the enabling technologies would be funded by financial contributions from governments and philanthropists. This remains in the "big idea" category and no one has yet created a global commons partnership, but with the current global focus on climate action, it is worthy of exploration.

The Winds of Change

Like community token economies for global commons partnerships, blockchain is a big idea that enables a reconceptualized future, where everyone can have an identity, is connected to the economy, where farmers get fair deals for their crops, and land registration is incorruptible. Where it is conceivable that everyone is educated. Blockchains may change economies and power. New self-regulating token economies will emerge that support global collaboration on global problems like climate change, diverting power from institutions to people.

While most of the development and implementation of blockchains has taken place in Western countries, arguably its greatest potential resides in emerging markets. Firstly, China and India alone together have five times the number of smartphone users than the USA (Thomason et al. 2019). Secondly, demography, the vast majority of people under 30 live in emerging and developing economies (Thomason et al. 2019). Thirdly, mobile penetration is growing rapidly and currently stands at more than two-thirds of the global population (Thomason et al. 2019). Fourthly, emerging markets simply have big problems to solve and this stimulates innovation. Finally, emerging market governments are agile and increasingly in many cases (e.g. Mauritius, Kenya, UAE, Bermuda) are driving the technology innovation agenda (Thomason et al. 2019).

The United Nations continues to take blockchains as a contributor to achieving the SDGs seriously. At the 2019 United Nations General Assembly in New York, The Women Political Leaders Global Forum, the Blockchain Charity Foundation (BCF), and the Finance Centre for South-South Cooperation, hosted *Blockchain for Social Good: Utilizing Blockchain to Aid Economic Development possibilities for blockchain to be a strong driver for inclusive growth*. Partnerships were formed, with BCF and the United Nations Development Program noting the importance of blockchain to construct a better society and partnering to support the work of blockchain for social good.

In our recently published book, *Blockchain Technologies for Global Social Change*, (Thomason et al., IGI, 2019), we make the case for blockchain as transformative for Global Social Impact, developing the *B4SC* (Blockchain for Social Change) model (seen in Table 6.1) which represents the chief social impact potential of the blockchain through three stages:

- *Cultural Influences and Drivers*; factors contributing to and/or driving the emerging environment, grouped by the following areas of influence: Technology, Governments and Communities.
- *Enabling Shifts*; factors required to transition to an environment that supports a world underscored by blockchain and a new economy. These are grouped into: Economics, Governments, Hyper Co-Collaboration, Sovereign Identity, Communities and Conversation areas of influence.
- *New World*; this presents a picture of the underlying factors of the envisioned environment after the transformational shift. These are grouped into: Empowerment, Global Economics and New Data Economy.

We propose that in order to accelerate technology adoption in satisfaction of the SDGs will require five enabling shifts (Thomason et al. 2019);

Table 6.1 Blockchain for social change model

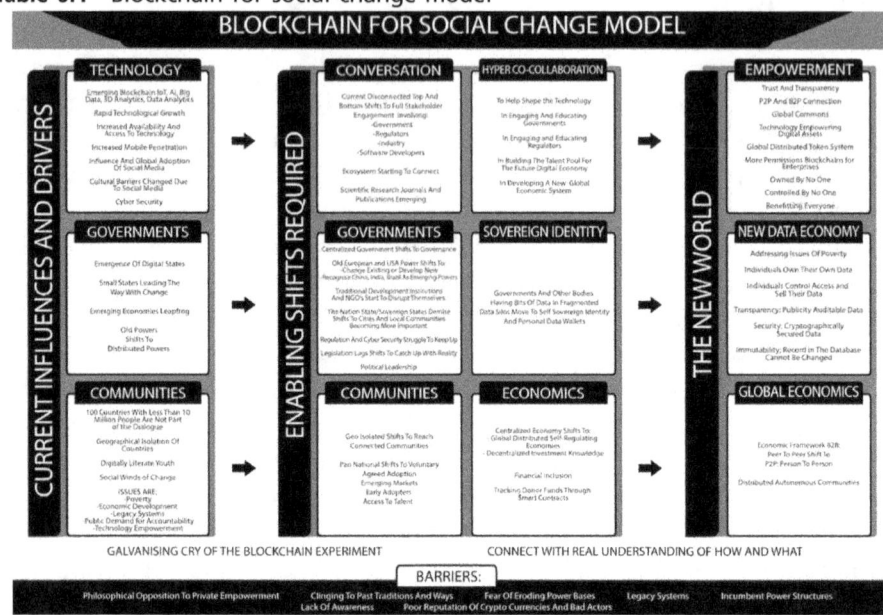

Source Thomason et al. (2019)

1. Increasing mobile and internet penetration that makes access to technology ubiquitous.
2. Perception of benefit in order to adopt the technology
3. An understanding of the move to the new data-driven economy owned and permissioned by individuals
4. A connected ecosystem with all stakeholders building hyper co-collaboration for social impact
5. International institutions support and provide models for global and national governance and enabling standards and regulations.

Global leadership for technology in general is patchy and oft ill-informed. Governments struggle to know how to approach technology, and yet the digital age is already upon them. Governments need to grapple with digital infrastructure; policy and regulation; building local ecosystems; building government capability; access to capital and reducing inequality and monitoring and benchmarks; APEC needs to look for solutions that can scale, and to unite the ecosystem which connects the blockchain systems in advanced APEC economies with those that work with the intractable problems of poverty and inequality. Yet there is a real opportunity to accelerate blockchain adoption to improve economic inclusion and citizen services and accelerate SDG progress.

Building a Digital Ecosystem

Without a digital ecosystem, the kind of SDG innovation contemplated in this chapter, will struggle to get traction. Emerging economies need to build the ecosystem that will enable the rapid acceleration of digitization. This will mean the simultaneous conjunction of the right policy and regulatory environment, incentive structures, training and skills development, funding and connections among ecosystem actors. Governments, and businesses can play a role in catalyzing the acceleration of the start-up ecosystem. The Government of Malaysia Magic Program, the Singapore Smart Nation Strategy and Code Lagos are examples of proactive leadership by the government to build digital economies.

Government

Governments have a critical role to play in getting the policy and regulatory settings in place to catalyze digital transformation. There are four key elements to a government's role: (i) political leadership; (ii) talent access; (iii) finance and (iv) infrastructure.

(i) Political leadership—There needs to be a bold political ambition to build digital transformation and the development of policies to attract talent, investors to the country and to be at the forefront of innovation. Governments need to create policy frameworks that foster, and do not hamper, digital innovation. Government interventions that can dramatically affect growth include: developing new segments via the digital economy; enhancing public and private sector competitiveness and efficiency; job creation within new segments and greater access to global job markets; attracting foreign investment as digitized economy and diversifying trade using e-commerce and online services.

Structural policies should also facilitate innovation and entrepreneurship to foster innovation and technology diffusion, ensure that competitive conditions prevail and avoid erecting barriers to cross-border digital markets.

Government can also work with donors to look at opportunities for digital solutions in aid programs. Government can promote principles and standards for digital development throughout the aid system, to ensure that more digital products and services reach, empower and improve the lives of poor people, particularly those at risk of being left behind. In relation to inclusion, governments can increase awareness, digital and entrepreneurial literacy in rural and remote areas.

(ii) Access to talent. Talent is critical. Governments need to grow the talent needed to digitize including, entrepreneurs, programmers, designers and engineers. This will only happen through proactive government policy. The example above of CodeLagos in Nigeria (www.codelagos.org) is an initiative of the Lagos State Ministry of Education aimed at educating Lagos State residents for the future of work—by teaching how to write code and creatively solve problems. Their ambitious agenda is to train 1 million coders over the next five years. Visa policy should support entrepreneurial activity to enhance labour mobility, with a skilled visa policy to attract entrepreneurs and start-ups.

(iii) Access to Finance—Governments play a key role in attracting and developing investment instruments like government-backed bonds to provide for investment in promising tech companies, and funding for start-ups and incentivizing industry to provide accelerator programs for start-ups.

(iv) Infrastructure—Connectivity is key and affordable, secure access to the internet is a fundamental priority. Also there is a need to provide physical space for start-ups and an enabling environment to allow young tech entrepreneurs to flourish and build the ecosystem will enable the digital economy to thrive.

Governments can also digitize themselves. Digital Government is a transformation of traditional "analogue government" functions towards the utilization of digital solutions for government operations, services and policies. This includes, for example, digitalization of public service systems to improve responsiveness, capability and accountability; policies and interventions to facilitate digital economic growth; and leveraging the ability of internet, email, text and social media to improve citizen participation.

Business

If the government enables the digital economy, business must drive it. It is critical for business and economic growth that digital initiatives generate and thrive. Business needs to proactively form partnerships to develop the ecosystem and provide opportunities for start-ups to incubate their ideas. Big companies are short on innovation, and the digital entrepreneurs have the ideas but no customers and no brand. Business can provide a launch pad for young entrepreneurs—by supporting co-working spaces and industry accelerator program. Business culture needs to realize that they need young entrepreneurs with ideas and energy. It can be a cultural challenge and as the young entrepreneurs and traditional executives—don't mix well, but we need to bring the cultures together to be effective!

UN and Global Community Action

Rising interconnectedness calls for international dialogue in the design of policies for the future world of work in areas such as taxation, competition, R&D incentives and standard setting. Global institutions can also play a role and continue to set targets and monitoring progress for things like: internet speed and minimum internet penetration; internet access and usage; rural inclusion and mobile network coverage. Regional collaboration is also needed to address standardization, to examine the regulatory fitness of legislation for the digital single market, and to support the sharing of best practices in areas like skills and jobs for the digital change.

A global platform of digital initiatives could play an essential role in the roll out of digitalization of emerging economies, where: experiences can be shared, collaboration and joint investments can be triggered, common approaches to regulatory problems be explored, and means for reskilling of the workforce be further exchanged. The platform could promote best practices, share information and strengthen capacity-building among countries on human resources development in the digital age in cooperation with relevant partners.

Digitization is the future for emerging economies and has the potential to close the gap. This is an area where small economies can play an active or leading role in tech innovation by being open to it and being boldly ambitious. Digitization brings unique opportunities to bypass the legacy issues that advanced economies confront, and help them "leapfrog". It is time for governments to have bold ambition and for the global community to marshall its experience and resources to support the smaller economies to harness the digital potential to close the gap.

Conclusion

The digital age is here. It is incumbent upon governments and the international community to explore how to marshall its benefits for the SDGs. There are close to five billion mobile phone subscriptions in the world, with over 85% of the world's population now covered by a commercial wireless signal. Blockchain offers potential benefits for poverty, hunger, health, gender inequality, clean water, affordable clean energy, climate and partnerships for the global commons.

Blockchain will likely be deployed in conjunction with artificial Intelligence, big data, the Internet of Things (IoT), drones, and virtual reality.

2019 saw the stabilizing and maturing of the blockchain industry, becoming more about what technology enables. 2020 will be the year that blockchain goes enterprise—research and development projects will bear results. The areas where major blockchain progress is taking place are as diverse as the applications they are creating. The global nature of blockchain's development can help distribute opportunities for wealth creation and economic development more widely than before. It is important for governments to develop the right policies to harness the potential benefits of this technology while mitigating its risks and potential for misuse. To do so, it is essential for countries to cooperate in order to share best practices and ensure interoperability.

References

Ardittis, S. (2018). *How blockchain can benefit migration programmes and migrants.* Retrieved from https://migrationdataportal.org/blog/how-blockchain-can-benefit-migration-programmes-and-migrants.

Australian Government. (2014). *Agricultural competitiveness issues paper.* Retrieved from http://agwhitepaper.agriculture.gov.au/SiteCollectionDocuments/issues_paper.pdf.

Casey, M. (2016). *Could the blockchain empower the poor and unlock global growth?* Retrieved from https://techonomy.com/2016/03/blockchain-global-growth/.

Cecchetti, S. & Schoenholtz, K. (2018). *The stubbornly high cost of remittances.* Retrieved from https://voxeu.org/taxonomy/term/8485.

Del Rio, C. (2019). *Use of distributed ledger technology by central banks; A review.* https://doi.org/10.29019/enfoqueute.v8n5.175. Retrieved from https://www.researchgate.net/publication/321883512_Use_of_distributed_ledger_technology_by_central_banks_A_review.

Desai, V., Diofasi, A. & Lu, J. (2018). *The global identification challenge; Who are the 1 billion people without identity?* Retrieved from https://blogs.worldbank.org/

voices/global-identification-challenge-who-are-1-billion-people-without-proof-identity.
Dudley, D. (2019). *Renewable energy costs take another tumble, making fossil fuels look more expensive than ever.* Retrieved from https://www.forbes.com/sites/dominicdudley/2019/05/29/renewable-energy-costs-tumble/#1874ea13e8ce.
Fintech News. (2019). *SDFA and HSBC launch pivotal report on unlocking climate financing by scaling the green bond market through emerging technology.* Retrieved from https://www.fintechnews.org/sdfa-and-hsbc-launch-pivotal-report-on-unlocking-climate-financing/.
Global Financing Facility. (2016). *GFF support for strengthening civil registration and vital statistics.* Retrieved from https://www.globalfinancingfacility.org/sites/gff_new/files/documents/GFF-IG4-10%20CRVS.pdf.
Lock, H. (2019). *Fight the fakes; how to beat the $200bn medicine counterfeiters.* Retrieved from https://www.theguardian.com/global-development/2019/jun/05/fake-medicine-makers-blockchain-artificial-intelligence.
Pekovic, P. (2017). The effects of remittances on poverty alleviation in transition countries. *Journal of International Studies, 10*(4), 37–46.
Provenance. (2015). *Blockchain; the solution for transparency in product supply chains.* Retrieved from https://www.provenance.org/whitepaper.
Shah, S. (2017). *Save the children UK CIO to pilot a 'humanitarian passport' using blockchain.* Retrieved from https://www.itpro.co.uk/strategy/28321/save-the-children-uk-cio-to-pilot-a-humanitarian-passport-using-blockchain.
Slavefree Trade. (2020). *Home.* Retrieved from https://slavefreetrade.org/.
The Development Circle. (2018). *Red Cross blockchain case study—enabling transparency of Islamic social finance.* Retrieved from https://developmentcircle.org/2018/07/05/red-cross-blockchain-case-study-enabling-transparency-of-islamic-social-financing/.
Thomason, J., Bernhardt, S., Kansara, T. & Cooper, N. (2019). Blockchain for Global Social Change. IGI Global.
UN. (2013). *Global governance and governance of the global commons in the global partnership for development beyond 2015.* Retrieved from https://www.un.org/en/development/desa/policy/untaskteam_undf/thinkpieces/24_thinkpiece_global_governance.pdf.
UN Women. (2018). *UN Women and partners to pilot blockchain technology in humanitarian action.* Retrieved from https://www.unwomen.org/en/news/stories/2018/2/news-event-blockchain-technology-and-humanitarian-action.
UNHCR. (2018). *Global trends.* Retrieved from https://www.unhcr.org/globaltrends2018/.
World Bank. (2013). *Migration and remittance flows; recent trends and outlook, 2013–2016.* Retrieved from http://pubdocs.worldbank.org/en/471191444756853938/MigrationandDevelopmentBrief21.pdf.
World Bank. (2019). *World development indicators; structure of output.* Retrieved from http://wdi.worldbank.org/table/4.2.

World Bank Group. (2017). *The global Findex database 2017; measuring financial inclusion and the fintech revolution.* Retrieved from https://globalfindex.worldbank.org/sites/globalfindex/files/2018-04/2017%20Findex%20full%20report_0.pdf.

World Economic Forum. (2019). *Central banks and distributed ledger technology; how are central banks exploring blockchain today?* Retrieved from http://www3.weforum.org/docs/WEF_Central_Bank_Activity_in_Blockchain_DLT.pdf.

7

The New Money: The Utility of Cryptocurrencies and the Need for a New Monetary Policy

David Lee Kuo Chuen and Ernie Teo

Introduction: From Digital Payments to Digital Cash

The rise of the Internet, PC, and companies like Amazon and Alibaba for the past 20 years has made e-commerce a part of everyday life. As new technologies emerge, we are entering a digital era with numerous digital footprints and digital payments, playing an increasingly important role. Traditional digital banking and payment technologies have been successful in the past, but perhaps not in the future. These electronic payment systems were dependent on bank deposits, credit cards or stored-value facilities; these payment intermediaries increased the costs and complexity of electronic payments, making it inefficient and expensive.

To support the growing e-commerce sector, make full use of the digital footprints and increase payment efficiency, truly digital cash is in high demand. Digital cash shall serve as the digital replacement of physical cash, meaning that it should fulfil criteria such as to provide a store of value, a unit of account, a medium of exchange, as well as anonymity and transferability to the users, but it is more than that—digital cash should also be able to

---

D. L. K. Chuen (✉) · E. Teo
University of Singapore, Singapore, Singapore

D. L. K. Chuen
Shanghai University, Shanghai, China

handle small transactions efficiently. On a technical level, digital cash needs to address the double-spending problem, the risk that it can be spent twice. These criteria are hard to satisfy, and the compromise usually results in high overheads, making the digital payment method inefficient and expensive. Many digital payment methods also do not meet the criteria of anonymity, and most forms of digital payments are traceable.

The invention of Bitcoin in 2008 seems to provide a potential solution, or at least a direction. It is truly peer-to-peer and offers built-in pseudo-anonymity.[1] Decentralization allows Bitcoin to remove the need to trust centralized middlemen and have no single point of failure. Incentive mechanisms were then incorporated to ensure that the interests of the participating economic agents of Bitcoin are aligned. Most importantly, ensuring transactions are correct and valid. The creation of Bitcoin also pioneered a new category termed "cryptocurrencies".

As the world gets more digital and financial institutions adopting technology to innovate on financial services, cryptocurrencies (and blockchain) are becoming mainstream and widely recognized. While searching for new and sustainable growth areas, governments have included blockchain into various national initiatives. In Kshetri and Voas (2018), the authors explain how the USA-based platform for real-estate registration, Bitland, uses a blockchain-based land registry system in Ghana, where 78 per cent of land is unregistered, and how the platform is expected to guarantee property rights and reduce corrupt practices. Geospatial applications involving blockchain can potentially unlock economic values. Similarly, in China, the use of fake export invoices to disguise cross-border capital flows has been pervasive. The government is relying on provenance, traceability, and transparency characteristics of blockchain-based systems to thwart such scandals and assist financial institutions in battles against fraud, money laundering and illegal activities. Governments (such as Kenya in Africa, China in Asia and Argentina in Latin America among many others) have also discussed issuing digital currencies of their own using blockchain technology to facilitate lower cross-border transactions, financial inclusion, reliable and provided end-to-end traceability with smart contracts (Raskin and Yermack 2018). Could cryptocurrencies or national digital currencies become the "New Money"? Will we see the end of paper money? This paper will explore this topic and discuss the implications on monetary policy and the issuance of Central Bank Digital

---

[1] Bitcoin is anonymous by design such that owners' identities are unknown to other network users unless they choose to reveal it. However, the patterns of usage or other information may reveal the identity through modern tracing using AI algorithms or via links with third parties.

Currency (CBDC). But first, we start by providing a brief introduction to cryptocurrencies and its economics.

Cryptocurrencies

What Are Cryptocurrencies?

As the name implies, cryptocurrencies are currencies based on cryptography. Most cryptocurrencies consist of a distributed network of validators where each validator holds a replicated copy of the ledger of transactions. Tokens (or currency) are minted via entries in the ledger, and this can be done with rules embedded in the code for validation (such as Bitcoin mining) or on a one-off or ad hoc basis. The ledger (or blockchain) is constructed using cryptography to make it almost impossible or very costly to change or reverse entries.

Bitcoin is the first cryptocurrency of such kind and it introduces the idea of blockchain. Features of decentralization and immutability allow it to be a form of digital cash which can be moved peer-to-peer without an intermediary and will enable it to have no central control. These features also make it different from current digital payments, and many consider it to be the chief ingredient to create the future of the digital (crypto token[2] and sharing[3]) economy.

Tokens in the Bitcoin network are represented by ledger entries, since there are no physical bitcoins. The token creation mechanism was designed to create a capped money supply (a fixed increase in its amount until the cap is reached). This mechanism is built into the code and cannot be changed without the agreement of a majority of the network. There had been various attempts to change this code and this led to hard forks (derivative currencies) as majority consensus cannot be reached (Atik and Gerro 2018). There are also instances that offline governance was heavily influenced by core developers that we saw community rolling back to an earlier version of the network voluntarily such as the 2013 Bitcoin fork from version 0.8 back to 0.7 (Narayanan 2015).

---

[2]Token Economy refers to the system of incentives based on cryptocurrencies that reinforce and build desirable behaviours the in blockchain ecosystem.

[3]An economic system in which assets or services are shared between private individuals, either free or for a fee, typically by means of the Internet.

Since the inception of Bitcoin, various forms of cryptocurrencies were introduced[4]—some have differing designs from Bitcoin such as the methods to create the money supply, and some offer alternative technologies that claim to work better. Cryptocurrencies or crypto tokens can be grouped into five general categories: (1) Transactional, (2) Utility, (3) Platform, (4) Application, (5) Asset-backed.

> **Transactional** cryptocurrencies function like Bitcoin, and their main aim is to provide a form of payment. Newer versions have enhanced privacy features and can scale better than Bitcoin. One such example is Dash[5], a cryptocurrency based on Bitcoin but with built-in privacy functions that include those providing privacy of the transactions with shielded ledgers. Its tamper-proof instant transactions, accompanied by a well-incentivized secondary peer-to-peer network, make it a stable medium of exchange (Duffield and Diaz 2018).
>
> **Utility** cryptocurrencies are tokens designed to facilitate transactions for custom blockchain networks. These can be purpose-built blockchain networks such as those for supply chain traceability or decentralized finance.
>
> **Platform** cryptocurrencies facilitate the operations of smart contract enabled blockchains. Such blockchain allows users to create smart contracts that form the basis for decentralized applications.
>
> **Application** cryptocurrencies are used for decentralized application use cases, which are built on blockchain smart contract platforms.
>
> **Asset-backed** cryptocurrencies are linked to real-world or virtual assets such as gold, fiat currency or property. These can be used to create a fractionalized investment for assets that may require a large outlay. They can also be used to provide a stable medium of exchange which can then be used for payments.

Many investors in the cryptocurrency market buy cryptocurrencies or crypto tokens not for the functions, but for speculative purposes. One of the notable earliest use cases for issuance of tokens was for fundraising. Projects (usually with a blockchain angle) would issue tokens to investors in return for funds

---

[4] As of February 2020, around 5000 of such cryptocurrencies exist.

[5] Dash is an open-source cryptocurrency forked from the Bitcoin protocol and also a decentralized autonomous organization (DAO) run by a subset of its users, which are called "masternodes". Other privacy coins are Zcash (ZEC), Zcoin (XZC), Monero (XMR), TeleCoin (TELE), Incognito (PRV) and PivX(PIVX).

(usually in the form of other cryptocurrencies). These tokens would eventually get listed on a cryptocurrency exchange. These are known as ICOs (Initial Crypto-Token Offerings). The success of such projects depends largely on its perceived value. Being speculative in nature, there were many ICO scams wherein the fundraisers had no intention of bringing the project to fruition. This prompted many governments to impose regulation or even outright banning this form of fundraising. We will discuss more about the economics, finance and challenges of cryptocurrencies in the following sections.

The Economics and Finance of Cryptocurrency: Network, Incentives and Markets

Unlike a centralized system where there is one sole authority that decides what is stored in the database, distributed networks are made up of multiple connected computers/digital devices (or nodes) working towards a common goal. In the case of cryptocurrencies such as Bitcoin, the distributed network needs to synchronize,[6] validate token transactions and record them in a replicated database. The key challenge of such a distributed network is to get the nodes to agree on the transactions that they are recording. The creators of Bitcoin designed incentives in the distributed network such that the network can achieve consensus on the validity of the cryptocurrencies transactions that are broadcasted and recorded onto the blockchain (or distributed ledger). In distributed networks, such incentive mechanisms are known as consensus protocols. The best-known example in cryptocurrencies is Proof of Work (PoW), which is also known as Bitcoin mining.

In Bitcoin mining, servers on the network commit computational resources to solve a cryptographic puzzle which is related to the set of transactions that are being verified as discussed in Nakamoto (2008). In return, the first server to find the answer to the puzzle wins a mining reward. Bitcoin mining is probabilistic in nature and the chance of winning increases with the computational power committed. Servers have an incentive to ensure that the transactions are valid if they want to keep the reward they win. This type of consensus protocol has a few problems.

First, as the network grows and becomes more competitive, it consumes large amounts of electricity making it harmful to the environment. According to Stoll et al. (2019), electricity consumption required by Bitcoin is more

---

[6]The internet is inherently asynchronous in the sense that there is no global clock and each nodes may receive messages that carries transactions' information in different sequence. This has been a major research topic in the area of distributed network involving network engineering and fault tolerance.

than the entire country of Jordan. Amassing computational power also leads to incremental chances of winning the mining reward, and this results in 65% market share being held by major mining companies such as Bitmain, Ebang and Canaan and only 8% of the market held by small scale miners. Second, since one can accumulate computation power (or machines) to gain an unfair advantage in bitcoin mining, this leads to less decentralization and ultimately results in strategic mining behaviour where miners with high computation power game the outcomes to their advantage.

The decentralized nature of cryptocurrency networks means that such consensus protocols are necessary as the servers that participate in the network are untrusted. Incentive mechanisms need to be in place such that the servers will act in the best interest of the network. Other than PoW, there is a plethora of other consensus protocols which are designed to address some of the issues with PoW. One popular alternative to PoW is Proof of Stake (PoS). PoS requires the servers to stake cryptocurrencies ("freeze" the coins in a wallet) for a chance to be selected as the verifier/miner. It trades computer resources in exchange for the time value of the cryptocurrency stake. Proof of Stake was first introduced in Peercoin, and is designed to be better in terms of energy consumption and it also better aligns the incentives between stakeholders (Ren 2014). Chepurnoy et al. (2017) discuss Twinscoin, a cryptocurrency that uses both PoW and PoS. Each time a new protocol is introduced, there will be a trade-off and another weakness, and the design thinking is to ensure that whichever consensus is used, it will provide safety[7] and liveness[8] for the distributed network.

Consensus protocols control the creation of new cryptocurrency. In Bitcoin, new coins are created on the blockchain with each new block to provide for the mining reward. Bitcoin mining rewards started with 50 bitcoins and are halved every four years. In May 2020, rewards were reduced to 6.25. This halving will continue until a cap of 21 million coins is reached, as discussed in Nakamoto (2008). This is a conscious effort by Bitcoin's creators to "hard code" the coin supply and prevent any central authority from changing it. Essentially, in most cryptocurrency networks, code controls the supply. It is difficult to change the programming, as the entire network needs to agree to upgrade code. This pre-programmed supply and cap create scarcity.

---

[7] Safety means that the consensus must never achieve agreement on a state of the ledger when nodes have not actually agreed on that given state to ensure the integrity of the ledger.
[8] Liveness means that consensus cannot stall, even in case of a tie, the consensus algorithm must always make progress

However, this is only one determinant of the market supply. Even though the creation of coins is pre-programmed, the circulation of coins is in the hands of human beings. The built-in coin creation and cap creates an expectation of future scarcity, and this causes hoarding of coins in anticipation of a higher price. This drives prices up and encourages further hoarding, making cryptocurrency mining a lucrative industry. Some coins take this further by offering "dividends" to coin holders. The choice of consensus protocol may also amplify this, for example, Proof of Stake coins organically controls supply with its staking requirements. In other cases, the creators of the cryptocurrency network pre-create or pre-mine the cryptocurrencies, essentially making them the majority owners and controllers of the coins in circulation.

One of the major challenges faced by cryptocurrencies is price volatility as current use cases are speculative in nature. Many buy and hoard cryptocurrencies in anticipation of higher future value. Athey et al. (2016) find that Bitcoin is mostly used for investing (or store of value), and its value is linked to beliefs about the future rather than exchange rates to current fundamentals. Demand for cryptocurrencies is largely speculative in nature. Sovbetov (2018) finds that (for five major cryptocurrencies) the cryptocurrency market beta, trading volume and volatility are significant both the short and long run. Liu et al. (2019) also find that cryptocurrency market size and momentum capture the cross-sectional expected cryptocurrency returns. During bull runs, the cryptocurrency market is very attractive as it is much more volatile as compared to traditional investments.

The cryptocurrency exchange industry is a fragmented one, and there are more than 250 cryptocurrency exchanges that are tracked on CoinMarketCap (a cryptocurrency tracking platform). These exchanges operate in a number of markets and offer exchanges of fiat currencies to cryptocurrencies and also among cryptocurrencies. This increases arbitrage opportunities and the speculativeness of the market. Cryptocurrencies are also commonly thought of as alternative investments, providing a hedge against the market (Lee et al. 2018). Dyhrberg (2016) suggests that cryptos and gold have similar hedging capabilities and can be used to hedge against the FTSE index. Chan et al. (2019) examine the hedging capabilities of Bitcoin, and demonstrate that while it does provide a hedge against the market, the actual amount of that hedge depends on the index and time period studied. Bouri et al. (2020) show that various cryptocurrencies respond to geopolitical risk, and during periods of heightened geopolitical uncertainty, investors can move to Bitcoin as a shelter. In regions prone to political instability and hyperinflation, cryptocurrencies are being adopted as the currency of choice for payroll and payments.

When the trust in the financial system is low, the demand for cryptocurrencies increases, leading to higher prices. In 2015, with harsh capital controls restricting the flow of bank deposits, Greeks were looking to turn physical cash into stores of value. That change in perception that fiat currency was not as reliable as previously thought, enticed a rally of 37% in bitcoin price with the thesis that bitcoin was a store of value, could be purchased with cash and had similar properties to money.

In another episode during the 2018 Venezuela hyperinflation, the volume of transactions increased with many cryptoexchanges, crypto wallet and gift cards. Aid flowed in via alternative crypto payment system. Though the actual size relative to the population of both countries are small, it still attracted the attention of international organizations in viewing underlying technology, not necessarily cryptocurrency, to be of benefits during a financial crisis caused by a loss of confidence or trust. Clearly, the collapse in the Letter of Credit services among banks during the 2008 Global Financial Crisis that led to more than 30pc drop in international trade disrupting the supply chain is still fresh in the central bankers' mind.

Another determinant of a cryptocurrency's demand is its utility. Bitcoin's main utility is for payments (and its use to pay for transaction fees), other cryptocurrencies like Ethereum are used to fuel the processing of smart contracts. Blockchain networks with well-defined use cases (such as supply chain) can provide strong utility for its cryptocurrency, forming a strong internal demand which supports the cryptocurrency price and makes it more stable. Supply-demand fundamentals such as the total number of bitcoins and the number of unique bitcoin addresses used per day have a significant impact on bitcoin price (Ciaian et al. 2016). Cryptocurrency prices could also be determined by its cost of production. As found in Hayes (2016, 2019), the marginal cost of production (mining and consumption of electric power) plays an important role in explaining bitcoin prices. The pricing model leads us to expect that during periods of excess demand (aka a price bubble), either the market price will fall and/or the mining difficulty will increase to resolve the discrepancy.

Market sentiment about the cryptocurrency and its associated blockchain networks also play a role. The trustworthiness of the cryptocurrency's blockchain and the adoption of the blockchain drive prices in the long run (using data for five major cryptocurrencies) (Bhambhwani et al. 2019). Bitcoin returns were found to be driven primarily by its popularity (Google search & number of newspaper articles), the sentiment (tone) expressed in newspaper reports on the cryptocurrency, and the total number of transactions (Polasik et al. 2015).

Incentives, social scalability,[9] consensus, utility and governance of the network have deep implications on the price of a cryptocurrency. When designing a cryptocurrency, one needs to consider the purpose of the coin and what best fits that purpose. Every choice can affect the volatility of the cryptocurrency price. One may argue that private entities (designing and creating the coin) may not have interests that are aligned to the users of the coin. Lai and Lee (2018) described the design thinking, trade-offs and implementation and adoption of a blockchain system.

For example, the issues in the Bitcoin blockchain sparkles lots of discussions. In fact, over the decade since the Satoshi paper in 2008, various schools of thought have emerged in the cryptocurrency and blockchain space. These range from the Bitcoin purists to believers of the Permissioned Enterprise Blockchain.[10] However, we also see a convergence in these schools, as experimentations with different applications reveal certain requirements. Hybrid solutions are a key emerging trend in blockchain applications where permissioned blockchain networks rely on a large public blockchain to provide data immutability and security. Many now agree that there will be multiple blockchain networks in operation and the ability to interoperate is key for a blockchain-based world. These requirements also prompted technology to evolve in an attempt to address the problems with the original Bitcoin design. The main issues with the technology revolve around scalability, interoperability and privacy. Projects such as Ethereum 2.0, EOS, Hedera Hashgraph, Zcash and Monero (just to name a few) aim to address these issues.

DeFi (or Decentralized Finance) is an emerging trend in blockchain/fintech, and the term was coined to refer to the class of tools and applications built on blockchain to facilitate a financial ecosystem. DeFi tools can come in the form of digital assets, protocols, smart contracts, and dApps (decentralized applications). Applications can be found in the area of asset tokenization, stablecoins, decentralized exchanges, alternative savings, lending and payments, and more. The aim of DeFi is to create an open financial ecosystem where one can build financial tools and services

---

[9]According to Szabo (2017), "*Social scalability is about the ways and extents to which participants can think about and respond to institutions and fellow participants as the variety and numbers of participants in those institutions or relationships grow. It's about human limitations, not about technological limitations or physical resource constraints. One way to estimate the social scalability of an institutional technology is by the number of people who can beneficially participate in the institution. Another way to estimate social scalability is by the extra benefits and harms an institution bestows or imposes on participants, before, for cognitive or behavioral reasons, the expected costs and other harms of participating in an institution grow faster than its benefits*".

[10]What sets enterprise blockchains apart from public blockchains is the permission required to participate in the network and interact with it. Unlike Open Blockchain, a node must be specifically permissioned to join the Permissioned Enterprise Blockchain.

on top of this ecosystem by combining, modifying and integrating current applications. Cryptocurrencies will facilitate the DeFi ecosystem, and this will have implications on the real-world economy as the applications grow.

However, at the current stage of maturity in the industry, real world use cases have yet to see mass adoption beyond spurts of financial speculation and fundraising activities such as token creations, Initial Token Offerings (ITO),[11] DAOs and DAICOs[12] using smart contracts. Many of these adoptions eventually led to frauds, scams and bugs that dampened the initial enthusiasm, clogging of the network, and with colossal volatility measured in fiat currency.[13]

This also makes the original intended use case of payments infeasible, and to address this a solution generally known as stablecoins has been proposed by the industry. For example, Berentsen and Schär (2019) discuss crypto-assets that are developed with the aim of minimizing price volatility by embedding a stability mechanism. In general, three methods are now used to create stablecoins: Fiat-collateralized, crypto-collateralized and non-collateralized. **Fiat-collateralized** stablecoins refer to asset-backed tokens. These assets such as fiat currency or precious metals need to be centrally held and managed by a trusted authority. Custodian costs would be incurred in this situation and there is a need for regular audits to ensure full collateralization. There are two modes of fiat-collateralization. The first is single asset-backed, this is usually in the form of currencies like the USD or gold. This means that the operational costs cannot be recovered from asset appreciation and needs to be provided through other means. The second is multi asset-backed, this is usually a basket of interest-bearing assets that are selected to cover the operational costs. These assets will need to be managed by professionals, which leads to a further increase in costs. **Crypto-collateralized** stable tokens are backed by another cryptocurrency. To handle the volatility of the cryptocurrency, usually this type of coin is over-collateralized. This requires the collateralizing cryptocurrency to maintain a certain value and also creates a large opportunity cost to the issuer. **Non-collateralized** stablecoins generally use algorithms (smart contracts) to manage the supply of the token (by issuing or destroying coins) which in turn keeps the price stable. Al-Naji et al. (2017) show how Basis, an algorithmic stablecoin, actually implements price

---

[11] Includes Initial Crypto-Token Offering (ICO), Initial Exchange Offering (IEO), Security Token Offering (STO), Initial Mining Offering (IMO).

[12] DAICO is a word association between the Decentralized Autonomous Organization (DAO) and the Initial Coin Offerings (ICO). A DAICO puts in place more stringent management rules and constraints for ICO projects to avoid certain risks for investors.

[13] In the crypto economy, volatility and stability can be measured using a benchmark based on highly traded cryptocurrencies such as bitcoin and ether, rather than fiat currencies.

stability using expansion and contraction in its three-token system. This is similar to central bank operations but decentralized. There must be perceived value and a demand-side for such methods to work.

The methods mentioned are used by private entities for the issuance of stablecoins. A derivative of Fiat is Libra Coin to be created by Facebook-led project involving 100 Libra Association members.[14] Libra has proposed to create a stablecoin backed by a basket of currencies in its initial proposal and floated the idea of single-currency-backed Libra in the revised white paper.[15] Governments have also been exploring the possibility of issuing similar digital currencies—these are also known as Central Bank Digital Currencies or CBDC.

Cryptocurrencies are usually deployed on open and public networks where anyone can join as a node on the network. These networks are also known as permissionless, as no permission is required to join. In such networks, specially designed incentive mechanisms in the form of consensus protocols such as Proof of Work are required as the network participants are not trusted (or known). Permissioned blockchain networks on the other hand are controlled, and only known parties that are given permission can join the network. Every participant in this sort of network needs to be trusted and agree on the governance of the network. This sort of network is a popular choice for CBDC. The central bank can have control over the supply and the parties that form the network. Thus, one can manage monetary and government policies using CBDCs and this will be explored next.

Monetary Policy Considerations in the Presence of Non-Sovereign Cryptocurrencies

As cryptocurrencies creep into everyday life and are used for digital payments, governments inevitably need to consider how it would affect the circulation of central bank issued money and the effectiveness of monetary policy. Money has existed in digital or electronic form for a few decades now, and those technologies have not reduced the effectiveness of monetary policy. Would cryptocurrencies be any different?

The main difference to note is that a cryptocurrency has its own price and can be used in replacement of a national currency. Oh (2018) suggests that if a new cryptocurrency becomes commonly used in a country, it can

---

[14] Libra White Paper retrieved from https://libra.org/en-US/white-paper/.

[15] A white paper in cryptocurrency is a document which includes an outline of a problem that the project is seeking to solve, the solution to that problem as well as a detailed description of their product, its architecture and its interaction with users.

cause a rise in the money supply, a fall in the interest rate and an overall rise in the exchange rate. Cryptocurrencies have demonstrated their potential for capital mobility in countries with capital restrictions, thus providing a cheap currency substitute. Relatively stable currencies such as the USD, JPY and CHF have been traditionally used as a currency substitute, and cryptocurrencies now present an alternative. Engel (2019) presents a framework for foreign exchange to examine the impact of the cryptocurrencies. In the paper, Engel suggests that the digital currency market is not a major concern for monetary policy currently as their holdings are small relative to other forms of liquid assets (in August, 2019, the market capitalization of digital currencies was approximately $260 billion, which by comparison is less than 2 per cent of US Treasury debt held by the public). He also discusses the problem of currency substitution and where consumer prices are set in the new currency, and transactions that take place using the new currency. If currency substitution occurs, inflation targeting by the central bank will lose its effectiveness.

Raskin et al. (2019) present an alternative point of view that a private digital currency may, in fact, improve welfare in a country. As mentioned in the paper: "Although private digital currencies have not replaced the dollar, their mere existence may have a counterfactual impact in that they exist as a check on both fiscal and regulatory policy". Modelling an emerging economy with a private digital currency, the authors present three key findings. First, the existence of the private digital currency imposes discipline upon monetary policy and thereby generates welfare gains for citizens. Second, a private digital currency increases local investment within an emerging market economy, as the private digital currency serves as a hedge asset. Third, citizen welfare that is increased from permitting digital currencies enables the government to raise tax rates, which in turn increases government revenue. Thus the existence of the private digital currency in an emerging economy could benefit the economy overall. The paper highlights that private digital currencies should not be analysed as a replacement for traditional money but rather as an important alternative asset.

As discussed in the previous section, non-collateralized stablecoins are being designed to mimic monetary policy. Could such coins eventually substitute the central bank? We can design such algorithms to provide a countercyclical monetary policy, however it is still a long way before it can administer policy on a discretionary basis. Thus, one middle ground that taps onto the technical advantages of cryptocurrencies, while providing central banks with the discretionary power could be CBDC.

Central Bank Digital Currencies (CBDC)

Government control of money can be traced back to ancient Egypt (more than 4000 years ago), and money innovations have never ceased throughout history. Sveriges Riksbank is the oldest central bank in the world and has been managing the monetary system of Sweden since 1668. But it was the Dutch's Wisselbank that lay the foundation for the contemporary central bank model. A critical role of central banks is to provide risk-free money and safe means of payments to the financial system. This includes retail and wholesale, or more specifically households and businesses. Despite its relatively young status of 50 years, fiat money has evolved from simple cash and banknotes to broader money that provides for bank deposits, credit cards and now electronic money. The financial institutions that provide the third-party trust and the creation of money have secured a premium for centralized trust services and the whole web of complex payment systems. However, the competing interest and complicated landscape among the different stakeholders have overshadowed the original risk-free and safety purposes.

More recently, the emergence of fintech companies with new payment methods has created opportunities to overcome these pain points, but they come with some risks. This separation between the wholesale payment system[16] and retail payment system[17] will almost surely be re-defined, and some have even suggested merging both with new players and technologies. In particular, there are new proposals from the central bankers and academics, especially in the design and structure of the Central Bank Digital Currency or CBDC using Distributed Ledger Technology (DLT) or blockchain.

It is challenging to have a precise definition but less debatable to simply define CBDC[18] as a digital form of money issued by the central bank. It has been called a digital fiat currency or digital base money to signify its similarity with fiat money. However, an expanded definition is that CBDC is a digital payment token that includes a class of digital bits and bytes which is simply treated as money by government regulation, monetary authority or legislation. The main distinction between fiat currency and digital token

---

[16]A wholesale payment system is a funds transfer system through which large-value and high-priority funds transfers are made between participants in the system for their own account or on behalf of their customers. (BIS 2003).

[17]A retail payment system is a funds transfer system which handles a large volume of payments of relatively low value in such forms as cheques, credit transfers, direct debits, ATM and EFTPOS (Electronic Funds Transfer at Point of Sale) transactions (BIS 2003).

[18]BIS (2018) defines CBDC as a new form of central bank money. That is, a central bank liability, denominated in an existing unit of account, which serves both as a medium of exchange and a store of value.

in our bank accounts is how they are issued. Commercial banks and some permitted financial institutions hold electronic fiat currency in the form of reserves that can create money. The consumers have access to money through the commercial banks, and they, in return, have to fulfil reserve requirements by the central bank. CBDC, on the other hand, allows the possibility for households and businesses to make payment to others directly and store value using an electronic form of central bank money, thereby bypassing the commercial banking system.

Many central banks are considering it, and some have started piloting CBDCs. Given the speed of innovation in central banks in devising new money, our discussions will focus on the design thinking of a few critical directions and its associated risks. Many but not all of the proposed CBDC are blockchain or DLT-based, and the debates on the benefits of using this nascent technology are still ongoing. In other words, the digital currency can be modelled either as non-cryptocurrency or as a form of crypto token.

To define CBDC in a broader sense, one should include innovations that are evolving in Asia. Some examples are China's newly proposed CBDC and Singapore's Project Ubin. China has termed its cryptography-based money as Digital Currency/Electronic Payment (DCEP) and it emphasizes the asset side of currency and its P2P payment functionalities. Singapore has different phases for Project Ubin[19] and intends to enhance the functions and capabilities of its newly proposed payment system using DLT. While the DCEP allows for the possibility of P2P payments, Singapore's model is a tokenized form of government securities that can be used for payment and as a store of value for wholesale banks. But with DLT, the possibility of P2P payments without the banks as intermediaries is real.

The Bank of Thailand (BOT) has developed a tokenized version of the Thai Baht and evaluated the impact of a tokenized Real-Time Gross Settlement (RTGS) in its first phase of Project Inthanon.[20] Project Inthanon-Lionrock is a joint DLT initiative for cross-border payments between two central banks: BOT and the Hong Kong Monetary Authority (HKMA). Cambodia, Japan, Hong Kong and Canada have all taken different approaches to design their digital currency. The Table 7.1 below is a summary

---

[19] The details of different phases are given in Appendix 2.
[20] Thailand's Project Inthanon is named after Thailand's highest mountain. The second phase involves the tokenization of bonds and the project targets coupon payments, interbank trading, bond redemption, and interbank repos (short term collateralized lending between banks). In the third phase, the Bank of Thailand explores interoperability with legal systems and other platforms, including cross-border transactions.

Table 7.1 Recent CBDC use cases by Central Banks

Target	Technology	Country(s)	Current discussions
General public or retail	CDBC without DLT	**Sweden** 1. An account-based retail CBDC is the issuance of a digital currency to the general public by directly providing an account at the central bank 2. A value-based retail CBDC is the issuance of a digital currency for which the prepaid value can be stored locally on a card or in an eWallet	1a. Will commercial banks suffer a loss in retail deposits? 1b. Should there be a lower interest rate for CBDC in account-based? 1c. Will there be a rush to safety from bank deposits during a crisis? 2. In a value-based account with partial anonymity, should a limit be placed and is that implementable?
General public or retail	CBDC with DLT	**Uruguay, Senegal, China, Tunisia, India, Israel, Lithuania, the Marshall Islands** DLT here refers to using some or all of the features of cryptocurrency. In the case of China, UTXO[21] or unspent transaction output from bitcoin transactions are used to balance the ledger. This is not popular among developed countries, according to Cœuré (2018), but it is popular in developing economies. Contrary to the assessment, this may allow the emerging economy to leapfrog as it solves many pain points for developing economies such as payment, trading and financing	1. Can developing economies enhance financial inclusion? 2. Can developing economies bypass the traditional International Payment or remittance system to lower overall cost? 3. Can household activities and illiquid be tokenized and be integrated with CBDC in the form of utility and asset tokens?

(continued)

---

[21] In cryptocurrencies, an unspent transaction output is an abstraction of electronic money with a ledger that can only append entries. Each UTXO represents a chain of ownership implemented as a chain of Digital Signatures where the owner signs a message transferring ownership of their UTXO to the receiver's Public Key. Public Key Infrastructure (PKI) is a set of requirements that allow (among other things) the creation of digital signatures. Through PKI, each digital signature transaction includes a pair of keys: a private key and a public key. Digital signature is used in Bitcoin to provide a proof that one owns the private key without having to reveal it (so proves that one is authorized to spend the associated funds).

Table 7.1 (continued)

Target	Technology	Country(s)	Current discussions
Financial institutions or wholesale	CBDC for wholesale	**Canada, Singapore, Thailand, South Africa, Eurozone, Japan** This is the most popular proposal that can integrate the traditional payment system and banking models	1. Are there benefits beyond efficiency improvement with the use of Reserve Deposits, Crypto Tokens or Assets? 2. How does the payment system integrate with other financial instruments and processes such as Delivery and Payments for securities, supply chain financing, and cross country remittances?

Source Shiral (2019), Bech and Garratt (2017) and Authors

of recent use cases by central banks, as discussed in Shiral (2019) and Bech and Garratt (2017).

Fiat is a currency issued by the government and is legal tender. Within the monetary system, money consists of the central bank and private sector money. Central bank money has two components, namely, Retail Cash and Wholesale Reserve Deposit. Traditionally, private sector money has only Retail Bank Deposit. But with CBDC, this new eMoney in the form of Crypto Tokens or eAssets will introduce several benefits and risks into the monetary system, the impact of which is still not fully known. But the benefits are clear as CBDC can manage anonymity, is easily accessible to the public, is traceable, offers online and offline peer-to-peer payments, is available 24/7, and can be designed to pay interest, among others. Neither cash nor bank deposits have all these characteristics.

What Problems Can CBDC Solve?

There is a demand for CBDC with more than 70% of governments in the world researching the topic. One primary reason is to ward off the challenge of stablecoins such as Libra which has the potential to scale globally and weaken the central banks that are not on board. Other reasons are (1) supporting competition efficiency and innovation in payments; (2) meeting future payment needs in a digital economy; (3) improving the availability and usability of central bank money; (4) addressing the consequences of a decline in cash; (5) acting as a building block for better cross-border payments; and (6) supporting a resilient payments landscape. However, it is the potential use of the CBDC that is interesting, and we summarize the specifics here:

1. To allow offline transactions of eMoney similar to physical cash.
   Near Field Communication enabled technology will lessen the reliance on the Internet/mobile network and reduce the risk of disruption of services.
2. To allow for more general value transfer via eWallet without the need of an account, or any link to financial institutions or cards for eMoney.
   At the most basic level, a simple downloading of application software replaces the complicated, inconvenient, and costly onboarding process for users. CBDC will then function similar to physical transactions using cash. It eradicates the intermediary and counterparty risk. The breakdown in trust among licensed payment institutions during crises are bottlenecks for central banks' efforts in distributing money to the ultimate beneficial

parties. CBDC may mitigate the risk of the break in the supply chain financing and trade financing during crises.
3. To ensure efficiency and security of the payment system without going through a clearinghouse or real-time gross settlement system while retaining monetary sovereignty.

   This bypassing of trusted third parties will mitigate the risk of a breakdown in any centralized system or clearinghouse system.
4. To ensure a more accurate representation of economic activities currently excluded from the calculation of national accounts statistics.

   A lot of small transactions take place without going through the banking or financial system, but they are essential economic activities. The use of CBDC for retail will capture all payments associated with primary activities currently not reflected in the national accounts.
5. To ward off the challenge of non-fiat eMoney replacing fiat money, thus weakening the fiscal policy sovereignty, which includes tax collection.

   With eMoney and e-commerce, payments using other alternative currencies may lower tax revenue as traceability may be an issue for tax authority when the goods and services traded are in digital form.
6. To reduce the cost of reliance on physical notes and coins.

   CBDC will eradicate the cost of issue, printing, storage, exchange of old notes with new ones, fraud, counterfeit, carrying, and lead to an overall improvement in hygiene.
7. To maintain privacy protection and yet have the ability to manage anonymity to prevent money laundering, terrorist financing, tax evasion and criminal activities.

   The central authority will have full information if the individual agrees to reveal that information or that transaction amount or frequency exceeds the threshold set by the body. AI and data analytics can identify patterns of money laundering and other illegal activities.

   A tier system for onboarding has several advantages. The most basic level of directly downloading an app will reduce the cost of onboarding, and thus increase social scalability beyond the country of issue. The second tier that allows for a larger amount of transactions and storage will require the opening of a bank account or linking with a credit or debit card. The third tier will require one to present physically for identification at a designated license entity. CBDC will empower the central bank in big data analysis and at the same time, lessen the control and privacy invasion at the financial institutions level.
8. To allow for digital or smart contracts to be implemented.

Digital agreements are useful when trusted parties are needed to provide trust, and when the transactions are small, decentralized digital enforcement codes (or more commonly known as smart contracts) can be executed automatically without a trusted third party. Smart contracts reduce the cost of trust. In many areas with an imperfect justice system and a weak enforcement environment for a legal agreement, smart contracts will address the pain point of non-performance of a deal and therefore may stimulate more investment. It is also possible to have a two-tier system to improve efficiency and allows the intermediary to implement decentralized apps, consistent with centralized governance and third-party trust outside the network.

9. To stimulate growth in the underserved, under-recorded, and under-represented sectors.
GDP national accounts do not capture many lowly traded, minute transactions, illiquid assets and unrecorded economic activities. Tokenization can allow tracking of household services, livestock trading, and many other unrecorded and unreported activities. By capturing the excluded economic events in the national accounts, it will lead to better policy-making for sustainable growth. In aggregation, these essential omitted statistics of primary economic activities can be substantial in agriculture and less developing economies.

The key is then to retain the desirable characteristics of cash, manage anonymity, make it easy to use, keep it secure and yet balance the need for enforcement for illegal activities. The secondary benefit of CBDC is to capture those excluded essential economic activities and devise a better sustainable growth policy. The last point is the most attractive proposition and presents the most potential to the developing economies that have yet to be entangled in a complex economy dominated by the financial sectors.

Why Do We Need CBDCs?

There are features of CBDC that are not available in traditional cash and notes. Some features are present in the DLT or blockchain-based CBDC. These features will be able to complement the existing roles performed by the monetary system. In particular, if the intention is not just to digitize money but also to have sustainable growth, well designed DLT and blockchain-based CBDC may be able to smooth the pain points and provide cost-effective solutions. CBDC can be viewed as a new form of financial design to achieve objectives such as financial inclusion, lower remittance charges, a fuller measure of GDP, and facilitating transactions with more moderate or zero cost of trust—

1. Traceability and Immutability: This will simultaneously allow for privacy protection (from intermediaries) and yet facilitate the use of big data analytics to recognize the patterns of illegal activities, while not allowing data to be easily changed by any party.
2. Smart Contract: This will allow for low-value transactions to take place where the cost of third-party trust is high. It will also allow for the non-human intervention of low-value Peer-to-Peer (P2P) as well as Machine to Machine (M2M) transactions which are too costly to track and execute at the moment. Smart contracts will bring a lot of economic activities back to the calculation of GDP. Smart Contract may also become an autonomous money-creation algorithm that allows money creation using CBDC if certain conditions are met (Rashkin & Yermack, 2018), creating a parallel to the existing fractional banking system based on bank reserves.
3. Tokenisation: This will allow the trading of goods and services and therefore release the value of illiquid assets and household services.
4. Fractionalization: This will allow for assets, livestock and durables to be divided into a smaller piece of assets. The democratization of fungible,[22] durable, livestock as an asset will lead to more liquidity and affordability.
5. Non-Fungibility: This will allow for non-fungible products and services to be tracked and assigned value for its components, weights or characteristics via a token swap or value transfer with low cost.
6. Multi-Tier Registration system (MTRS): MTRS will allow for the proportionality and materiality principles[23] to be fully applied. Depending on the activities and the amount, different tier identifications may be needed. CBDC is unlike notes and coins that have a denomination. The lower the "largest denomination" of notes, the higher the cost for laundering a large amount. However, CBDC has no "largest denomination" and carrying, storing, transferring and exchanging entails the same cost. A multi-tier registration system is an improvement as anyone trading, exchanging or transferring a significant amount will be subject to more stringent monitoring and reporting. At the same time, granting specific exemptions to those engaging in small transactions or designated activities may seem

---

[22] In economics, fungibility is the property of a good or a commodity whose individual units are essentially interchangeable, and each of its parts is indistinguishable from another part. Commodities, shares, options and dollar notes are examples of fungible goods while diamonds, land, or a cow are not fungible because each of them has unique qualities that add or subtract value.

[23] The principles seek to right-size regulations to be fit for purpose; for both traditional as well as new business models, according to the risks the activity poses.

more appropriate. Any accumulated suspicious activities will be picked up by pattern recognition and an advanced surveillance system. MTRS can combine the use of phone number identification, credit card linkages, or in-person registration. MTRS will encourage innovation and allow the regulatory system to be more flexible, allowing for less regulation for small transactions or infrequent transactions. The cost savings can be substantial for regulators, intermediaries and the end-users.

7. Data Privacy Protection: In a DLT network, the payment and settlement system may store a single copy and thus avoid the situation of a single point of failure. While secret sharing[24] or fractional filing system have not been exploited, zero-knowledge proof[25] that shields the ledger has been used in Project Ubin. Cryptography can be used to safeguard data privacy to comply with the "need to know" basis among the nodes or participating financial institutions. Other techniques such as Secure Multi-Party Computing[26] can create methods for nodes to jointly compute a function over their inputs while keeping those inputs private, thus promoting collaboration while not violating data privacy law for regulated entities.

Risks

CBDC is not without risks and warrants a careful analysis before the implementation of any new designs. Full-reserve banking requires banks to have 100 per cent cash reserve for deposits other than demand deposits to be ready for an immediate demand for withdrawals. Fractional-reserve banking, on the other hand, allows the bank to lend out the short-term deposits except for the fraction (retained as cash) that is needed to meet potential demand for withdrawal. CBDC is digitized cash and can be withdrawn instantaneously by the transfer of the private key if it resembles a cryptocurrency. If the whole

---

[24] Secret sharing is a cryptography algorithm where a ledger, in this case the secret, is copied multiple times and then each copy is divided into parts, giving each participant its own unique part of a copy. To reconstruct the original ledger, a minimum number of parts is required and so no single node can have knowledge of the whole ledger.

[25] In cryptography, a zero-knowledge proof or zero-knowledge protocol is a method by which one party (the prover) can prove to another party (the verifier) that they know the value of X in the ledger, without conveying any information apart from the fact that they know that X exist.

[26] Secure multi-party computation is also known as secure computation, multi-party computation (MPC), or privacy-preserving computation). The cryptogrphy protects participant's privacy from each other and creating methods for parties to jointly compute a function over their inputs while keeping those inputs private. Beyond the traditional cryptographic tasks of ensuring security and integrity of communication or storage and the malicious elements, this sub-field of cryptography protects participants' privacy from each other. For a need-to-know-basis interbank system, this is one vaiable solution.

amount is removed, the bank will have no deposits to lend, or in the worst case, the bank has to recall all the loans at once.

Contemporary discussions have centred on (1) whether there should be an upper bound for the conversion of deposits into CBDC; (2) whether there would be interest payment for CBDC deposit; (3) whether interest rate should be different for different tiers; (4) whether the interest rate on CBDC should be below bank deposits, and (5) whether the floor is zero or negative for CBDC; (6) whether the CBCD system is a full-reserve, fractional reserve, or a dual system. While the foundation of finance is the fractional-reserve banking system, there are arguments and proponents[27] for a full-reserve system (Mayer 2019). In 2018, the Switzerland Sovereign Money Initiative proposed a full-reserve banking as a prominent component of its proposed radical reform of the Swiss monetary system. Even though the proposal was overwhelmingly rejected (Bacchetta 2018), the idea will likely be revisited with a new interest in CBDC.

There were some discussions among the central bankers and academics[28,29] and we have summarized their findings on the significant risks of CBDC as follows[30]:

1. Facilitation of Money Laundering

There may be more money laundering with CBDC. The cost of money laundering is lower with CBDC than cash. Specific restrictions on the frequency and size of conversion of CBDC for bank deposits and a limitation in usage may be needed for prevention purposes. The saving grace is that a digital trail will be left behind, unlike that with cash. So, there may need to be a suitable set of restrictions on CBDC based on the kind of business activities separating high risk from low-risk economic activities to prevent complicated layering to avoid audit or detection.

---

[27]The chief Economist of Deutsche Bank and the former Governor of the Spanish central bank have both mentioned about the 100 per cent CBDC system and "safe money" in Mayer (2019) and Fernández Ordóñez (2018).

[28]Long (2019) discussed about risk prevention in the practice of central bank legal digital currency (in Chinese) especially in reference to DCEP. Barrdear and Kumhof (2016) discussed in detailed about the macroeconomics of Central Bank issued digital currencies.

[29]Klein et al. (2020) discussed about the digital Euro and the role of DLT for CBDC.

[30]The material in this section is entirely drawn from Long (2019) with the authors' inputs.

2. Risk of a Bank Run on Banks with Low Credit Rating

The possibility of a run on the bank as an event may trigger a preference for lower risk CBDC over bank deposits. CDBC has lower risk than bank deposits, and during a credit crisis, it may be the root cause of a bank run as more people convert their bank deposits to CBDC. CBDC is classified as M0 and it is a liability of the central bank. Bank deposits are classified as M1/M2, which is a liability of commercial banks. Holding CBDC subject one to sovereign risk whereas holding bank deposits has an additional risk of a bank default. Therefore, there is a strong incentive to convert deposits to CBDC during a period when a bank is known to have a credit crisis. The central bank may impose limited conversion from bank deposits to CBDC. But any such measures will defeat the purpose of having CBDC, which is to have a lower risk while having more convenience.

3. Systematic Risk of the Banking System

A unique event at one bank may trigger a run on the whole banking system. A bank run can be instantaneous, given that it is in electronic form. The race to CBDC can spread within a short period from a single bank to the entire banking system. The order and magnitude of the run on the banking system may be much larger than a single bank run and can happen instantaneously.

4. Risk of Deleveraging of Banks Without a Diversified Portfolio

A bank without a diversified liquid asset portfolio can become illiquid in a very short period. According to regulatory requirements, all deposit liabilities of banks need to be supported by corresponding assets, and the asset requirements corresponding to different currency types of deposits are different. Cash reserve does not generate interest and is a form least preferred but kept simply to meet the needs of users. Unlike the 100% requirement of cash reserve, general deposits only require a partial reserve. Assuming that the deposit reserve rate is 10%, one unit of a commercial bank's reserve in the central bank can create a ten-fold deposit currency. When the reserves of commercial banks in the central bank are insufficient, commercial banks can borrow reserves from the central bank by collateralizing their liquid assets to the central bank. The size of a commercial bank's liquid assets constrains its ability to create a deposit currency.

Commercial banks create deposit currency through loans, however, the scale of commercial banks' liquid assets limits the size of credit creation.

Similar to cash reserves, CBDC requires a 100% reserve. Therefore, the switch from retail bank deposits to CBDC forces banks to transfer deposits of equal size from partial reserves to 100% reserves, which will quickly consume liquid assets held by commercial banks. The tighter liquidity will seriously shrink the amount and increase the pricing of credit, especially for banks without a large portfolio of diversified assets. The money multiplier will decrease. When the bank runs out of liquid assets, it cannot support the conversion of the user's deposit to CBDC, and the bank is forced to recover the loan assets at a discount. Banks may quickly become insolvent.

5. Risk of a Bank Run Caused by Interbank Payments

Interbank payment of CBDC may cause a bank run when conversion depletes reserves. When there is a deleveraging happening by banks depositing CBDC as reserves and when there is a transfer of CBDC to another bank, the payee bank has to use 100% backing to settle through RTGS. That in itself is a deleveraging process as the payee bank needs to recall loans to reduce lending to 100% reserve. This may create a deposit run because the bank reserves may have to be converted to CBDC reserve that requires 100% backing. Previously, there is a limited supply of cash and therefore there is a limit of how much cash can be deposited. However, CBDC is a circular flow and if there is no physical or strict limit of the conversion of CBDC into deposits, the circular flow ends in a rapid deleveraging of the monetary system. Assuming that the entire non-banking sector needs more CBDC, and that the entire banking sector has run out of reserves to exchange for CBDC, it still cannot meet the demand. Banks need to sell/mortgage eligible assets to the central bank to obtain reserves to exchange for CBDC. Given the scale of interbank payment, the banking sector may quickly deplete its qualified assets.

The central bank may have to expand the list of qualified collateral or even completely remove the collateral requirement for large-scale unsecured loans. Therefore, the credibility of this guarantee depends on the central bank's commitment as the lender of last resort. Given the potential scale of liquidity requirements, it may bring unprecedented risks to the central bank's balance sheet. There is a strong case to "set appropriate mechanisms to restrict" the conversion of bank deposits to CBDC.

Not only do we need to restrict the exchange of bank deposits to CBDC, but we also need to prohibit the free conversion of reserves to CBDC. Under the current currency issuance system, commercial banks can borrow reserves from the central bank's mortgaged national debt. The Bank of England study also recommended that commercial banks use qualified collateral to exchange CBDC with the central bank. A two-tier reserves system separating into one with CBDC that pays lower or no interest, and the other as the existing fractional bank reserves may be a solution.

6. The Risk of Inconsistency

Under the premise that neither reserves nor bank deposits can be freely exchanged with CBDC, it will bring challenges in maintaining the consistency of CBDC and their face value. The central bank needs additional mechanisms to achieve this goal. The Bank of England's 2018 research report recommended the setting up of the CBDC exchange, which sold/purchased treasury bonds to the central bank in exchange for CBDC, and exchanged bank deposits with the household and corporate sectors for CBDC. As long as the central bank promises to pay 1 unit of CBDC for bonds worth 1 unit of "deposit currency", there is an arbitrage mechanism in the market that drives the difference between the face value of CBDC and deposits to zero.

This will call for a limit or cap on wholesale CBDC accounts to limit the volume both in terms of size and the number of small transactions. Central bank scholars Gürtler et al. (2017) point out in their paper that the setting of the cap of the CBDC account is an art rather than a science. If the cap is set high enough, it cannot effectively limit the wholesale payment function and may cause bank deposits to run to CBDC. If the cap is set too high, it will damage the effectiveness of CBDC as a payment tool and may cause parity risk.

7. The Issue of Competition

The advantage of CBDC is convenience. It has the additional benefits of lower risk, offline payment and partial anonymity. As a result, the interest rate of bank deposits can be viewed as a risk premium. Those who hang on to CBDC view convenience premium higher than the risk premium and vice versa. If the interest rate is near zero, the risk premium will not be enough to cover the inconvenience, and therefore there will be a tendency to hold CBDC. In the event of economic downturn or market panic, holders will be more concerned about asset security than financial income, and more bank deposits will be switched to CBDC. At this time, the interest rate instrument will become more ineffective. This will then have a counter effect of expansionary monetary policy.

8. The Risk of Ineffective Monetary Policy

If the CBDC supply exceeds the demand for various reasons, the central bank will not be able to recover CBDC liquidity at zero interest rates. Traditional physical cash has similar problems but has no real impact, because (1) physical cash accounts for only 5% of the M2 supply, and (2) physical cash flow efficiency is much lower than bank deposit (the reasonable assumption is one-tenth of the deposit). Therefore, physical cash contributes less than 1% to the overall social liquidity, and the central bank only needs to control the liquidity supply of bank deposits.

But CBDC will be very different because (1) CBDC is not only a substitute for physical cash, but also a substitute for bank deposits and it is reasonable to assume that CBDC will account for 20% of the M2 supply; (2) The circulation efficiency of CBDC is higher than bank deposits. In 2016, the Bank of England's research by Barrdear and Kumhof (2016) showed that CBDC's turnover efficiency is twice that of bank deposits. Therefore, CBDC contributes nearly one-third to overall social mobility.

In the case where CBDC's impact on social liquidity is comparable to bank deposits, if the supply of social liquidity is excessive, the central bank will lack effective monetary policy tools to recover the CBDC liquidity. The central bank traditionally used interest rates and open market operations tools to regulate liquidity, but now nearly one-third of liquidity is not affected by interest rate instruments, which in turn will significantly weaken the effectiveness of existing interest rate instruments. The direct consequence of excess liquidity is inflation.

Challenges of Digital Money

It is essential to return to the basics to understand the concerns of central banks. The four primary functions of money or eMoney are that it is a medium of exchange, a store of value, a unit of account and a means of deferred payments. Other vital attributes that enhance the function of money include Portability, Durability, Divisibility, Verifiability, Fungibility and Limitations in Supply. The Table 7.2 below outlines the disadvantages of fiat and the technological bottlenecks and pain points of digital money in terms of its functions and attributes.

Much of the literature focuses on the extension of fiat money and its mechanism, partly because they fear that innovative money instruments may not fit in with century-old regulation, legacy systems and existing stable systems. The discussion tends to be centred on the approach of comparing physical

Table 7.2 Technological bottlenecks and pain points of digital money

eMoney functions	Explanation	Central Bank digital currency non-DLT based	Non-Central Bank digital currency DLT based
Medium of exchange	eMoney functions as a reference value to facilitate trade.	Digitizing coins and notes to have minimal impact on the fractional-reserve system	Limited Supply, low acceptance, low circulation, low transaction per second, high energy consumption for PoW, congestion, high storage cost, high transaction fees, no finality, governance issues
Store of value	eMoney is an asset that can be saved, retrieved and exchanged at a later time, and be predictably useful when retrieved, and it also maintains value without depreciating	No different from the existing system	Illiquidity, universally recognizable, readily exchangeable for other assets, fluctuates in value
Unit of account	eMoney allows different things to be compared to each other	May be able to digitize other goods and services not traded frequently	Not a standard measure for trade in goods and services, Not a benchmark to measure the value
Standard of deferred payments	eMoney is a widely accepted way to value debt, thereby allowing goods and services to be acquired now and paid for in the future	New products on digitized goods and services	Inflation and deflation, no recourse in case of counterfeit, instability and loss of purchasing power

(continued)

Table 7.2 (continued)

eMoney functions	Explanation	Central Bank digital currency non-DLT based	Non-Central Bank digital currency DLT based
Attributes	*Requirements*	*Advantages*	*Disadvantages*
Portability	Money is mobile and can be exchanged with ease with other currencies	More portable than cash and notes with possible 24/7 exchange	In reference to fiat currencies, there needs to be a regulated exchange
Durability	Money is immutable and can withstand continuous use by a large number	Forgery is more complicated and there is no wear and tear	May lose its value if there is a loss of trust with attacks or bugs
Divisibility	Money has small increments for the exchange of things of varying value	eMoney can have more than two decimals	Divisible up to 10^{-8}
Verifiability	Money is impossible to forge and easily identifiable as legitimate	eMoney is comparatively more traceable, authenticated and verified	Double spend and subject to malicious attack if there are fault or bugs
Fungibility	Money is interchangeable that two equal units have to be equivalent and indistinguishable	Fractional eMoney can have many digits and is an advantage of its fungibility	It is possible to trace the transaction history and the individuals who use them
Limits in supply	Money can retain its value	If backed and conditional on fiat, it is relatively stable	Can be created with no limits

Source Authors

and electronic form, as well as comparing peer-to-peer and trusted third party. The creation of the asset and the smooth functioning of the exchange mechanism is the foundations of the monetary system. Naturally, the concerns are the response of the current system to the innovation, and whether there exists a systematic risk. From our discussions above, the general form of CBDC does have significant systematic risks beyond single bank risks, among other concerns such as the diminished role of the traditional banking business models.

Interbank Payment Network

Let us have an overview of the interbank payment landscape in relation to M0 and M1. Figure 7.1 below maps out the interbank payment landscape.

Lai (2018) discusses in detail the Interbank Payment Network (IPN). A payment system consists of a set of instruments, banking procedures and, typically, interbank funds transfer systems that ensure the circulation of money (BIS 2003). In any country, either a wholesale payment system or a retail payment system is used as the IPN.

Wholesale Payment

A country's central bank usually operates a wholesale payment system (also known as large-value payment systems) for the transfer of systemically important, low volume, and high-value funds among banks and large corporations. There are generally two types of wholesale payment systems:

1. A **Real-Time Gross Settlement (RTGS):** This system is used for settling funds between accounts on a per transaction basis in real time.
2. A **Deferred Net Settlement (DNS):** This system is used for the settlement of funds between accounts at designated times of the day on a net basis, usually done by consolidating a batch of transactions between accounts. Instead of settling them individually, only the net positions are settled after offsetting the batches.

However, most wholesale systems are hybrid and employ special techniques to minimize liquidity risks and credit risks. Given that these are centralized system, there are scopes for central banks to use DLT to achieve better efficiency as discussed in the Monetary Authority of Singapore's Project Ubin. The stages of references are given in Appendix 2.

Retail Payment

The **retail payment system**[31] (also known as **low-value payment systems**) is used for processing non-urgent, low-value and high-volume transactions

---

[31] A retail payment system is a funds transfer system which handles a large volume of payments of relatively low value in such forms as cheques, credit transfers, direct debits, ATM and EFTPOS (Electronic Funds Transfer at Point of Sale) transactions BIS (2003).

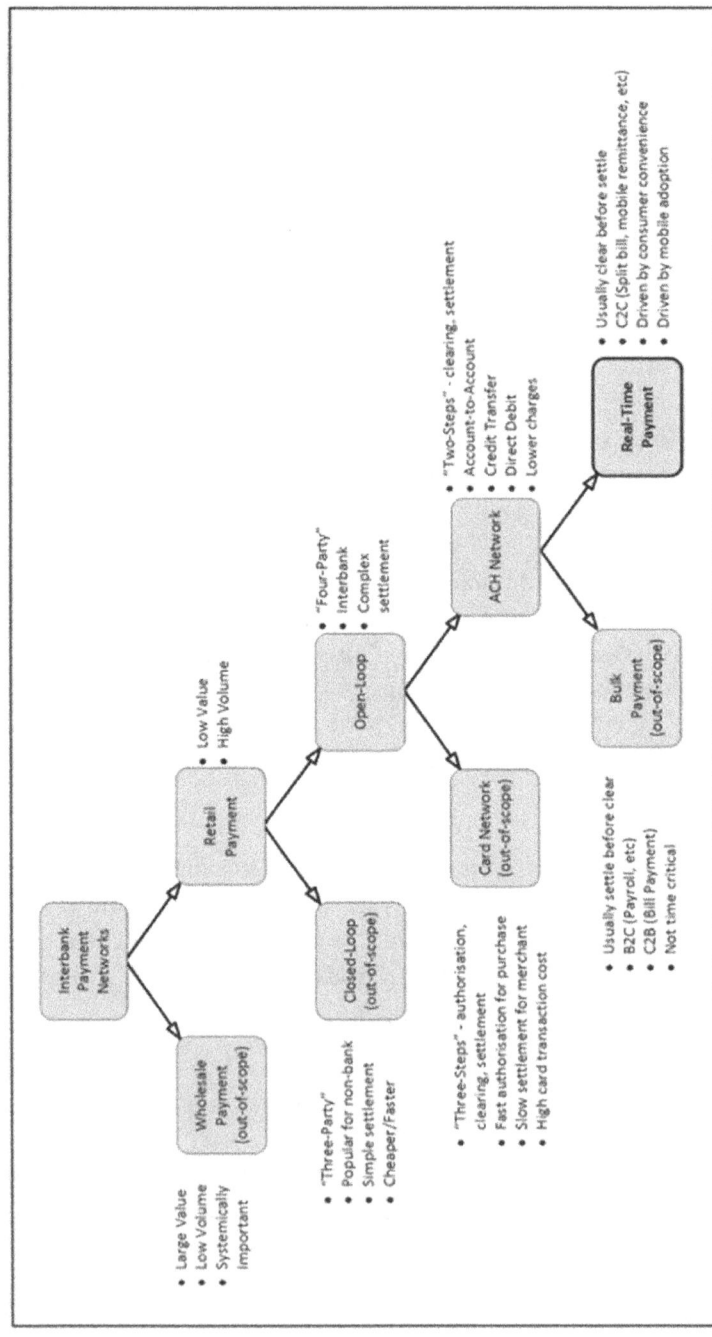

Fig. 7.1 Interbank payment landscape overview (*Source* Lai [2018])

such as consumer payments. Retail payment systems can exist in two forms: closed-loop and open-loop.

Closed-loop

A **closed-loop system**, also known as the "three-party" payment system, requires both payer and payee to be on the same platform. It is usually adopted by non-bank entities for end-to-end, simpler, cheaper and faster transactions. Settlement can be achieved in one step via internal book transfer as the transactions are managed by one entity.

Open-loop

An **open-loop system**, also known as a "four-party" payment system, is used to facilitate the transfer of funds between a payer and payee belonging to different banks. Since it involved a network of banks, settlements are more complex. Therefore, the banks have to appoint a licensed and trusted centralized third party to process and coordinate the transactions. There are two types of open-loop networks: Card Payment (CP) and Automatic Clearing House (ACH).

a. Card Payment (CP) Network

A **Card Payment** network is an open-loop electronic fund transfer point of sale system (**EFTPOS**) for international payments between a payer and payee belonging to different banks. Notable examples are Visa and Master Cards. Here, the merchant holds an account with its bank to receive payments. The entire payment process involves authorization, clearing and settlement. The network usually has high transaction cost, slow settlement for the merchant and fast transaction for the purchase.

b. Automatic Clearing House (ACH) Network

An **Automatic Clearing House** network is another open-loop retail payment system that facilitates domestic fund transfer directly between banks (also known as **Account-to-Account** or **A2A** transfer). The original purpose of an automatic clearing house was to provide clearing and settlement services for paper checks between banks. The ACH is account-to-account credit transfer or direct debit with lower charges.

i. Bulk Payment

ACH batch payment systems operate only during normal working days. A specific clearing window of the day known as the outward clearing window is open for banks to submit payment instructions from their account holders to the ACH for validation and processing.

ii. Real-Time Payment

One of the most commonly publicized examples of RTPS is the United Kingdom's Faster Payment System (FPS) that was implemented in 2008. It has most of the characteristics of what most countries will expect out of having an RTPS. In 2014, FPS handled more than 1 billion transactions worth over $1 billion.

Naturally, with such complex and critical systems in place, it is natural to proceed with great care. Table 7.3 looks at how the existing system can accommodate the innovation of CBDC. In particular, in row 6, the Non-DLT Electronic Substitutes that focus on centralized ledgers may be more comfortable for adoption. The payment system infrastructure is an extension of the existing system with an emphasis on (1) Centralized Interbank Payments, (2) Bi-lateral Payments and (3) Peer-to-Peer exchanges with third-party trust. DLT Electronic Substitutes (in row 7) may be a form too innovative for the existing regulation and system to digest and accommodate.

We defined four types of new infrastructure settings for the systems described in the table:

1. Centralized Interbank Crypto and Fiat Payments;
2. Bi-lateral Payments;
3. Peer-to-peer exchanges with third-party trust;
4. Peer-to-peer decentralized exchanges.

All these new infrastructures will have implications for the existing system. Given the complexity of legacy issues, the inertial cost of the central bank to transform is higher for matured financial centres than merging markets or agriculture-based economies with lower linkages with international payments. It will be interesting to see if countries with similar characteristics such as Cambodia or Marshall Island will have a first-mover advantage and leapfrog their economies through digitalization. The inertia cost associated with the possibility of instability in the banking system and the inefficacy of monetary

Table 7.3 Attributes of various forms of money

1. Private Physical Substitutes	Tokens and notes	Non-legal tender	Private money physically held	1. Peer-to-Peer, B2C or via Peer-to-peer Exchanges 2. No infrastructure needed
2. Physical Fiat	Cash and notes	Legal tender	From Central Bank and can be physically held, in Central or Commercial Banks	1. Through Central Banks, B2C or Peer-to-Peer 2. No infrastructure needed
3. Electronic Fiat	Bank deposits	Legal Tender eMoney	In Central Bank	1. Centralized Interbank Payments 2. Bi-lateral Payments
4. Electronic Fiat	Deposits	Legal Tender eMoney	In Commercial Banks	1. Centralized Interbank Payments 2. Bi-lateral Payments
5. Electronic eMoney	eMoney in other forms including Credit and Debit Cards	Legal Tender eMoney	In Commercial Banks	1. Centralized Interbank Payments 2. Bi-lateral Payments 3. Peer-to-peer exchanges with third-party trust
6. Non-DLT Electronic Substitutes	New Form of Central Bank eMoney	Digital currencies	Centrally Issued and in Centralized Ledgers	1. Centralized Interbank Payments 2. Bi-lateral Payments 3. Peer-to-peer exchanges with third-party trust

(continued)

Table 7.3 (continued)

7. DLT Electronic Substitutes	eMoney	Crypto-currencies	By algorithm or decentralized organizations and on the DLT	1. Centralized Interbank Crypto and Fiat Payments 2. Bi-lateral Payments 3. Peer-to-peer exchanges with third-party trust 4. Peer-to-peer decentralized exchanges

Sources BIS and Authors

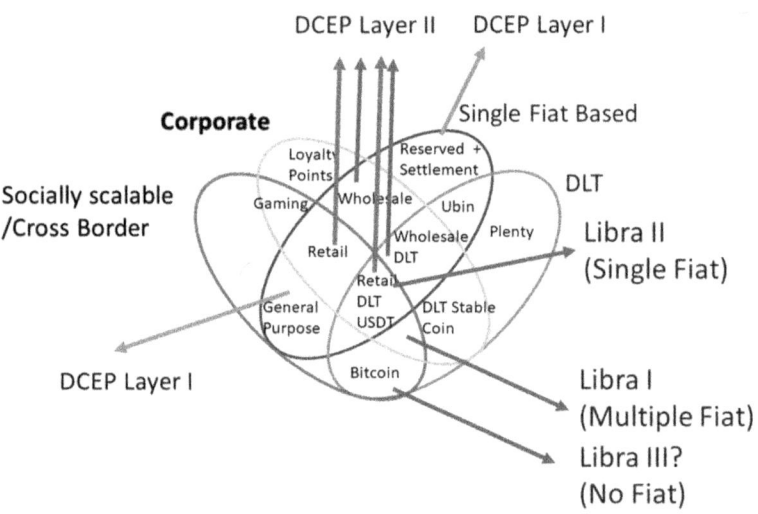

Fig. 7.2 Digital tokens—Libra versus DCEP (*Source* Authors)

policy may slow down the transformation process. The more advanced and more internationalized the financial sector is, the higher the inertia cost.

Figure 7.2 below presents the diagrammatic classification of currencies and looking at the possible paths of Libra coin and Chinese's DCEP within the payment and settlement system. The possible configuration of Libra in the future (Libra III) and the second layer of the DCEP are purely speculative and a natural extension of the current design.

But the cryptoexchanges are now trading with 5,500 cryptocurrencies with a trading volume of USD102 billion with the domination by Bitcoin of 66%. Tether (USDT) is usually the most heavily traded cryptocurrency with digital tokens designed to replicate the value of the US Dollar. As of 23 May 2020, Tether (USDT) which claimed to be backed by the US dollar, has a market cap of $8.92B and a 24-hour USDT volume of $36.93B. It has a market cap ranked 3 behind Bitcoin and Ether with a circulating supply of 8,913,502,390. Tether is traded on 125 exchanges. Tether had an all-time high of $1.1059 over two years ago. Over the last day, Tether has had 5% transparent volume and has been trading on 8,188 active markets. By markets, it means the number of fiat or crypto token markets using USDT to trade.

While there are close to 200 centralized exchanges, there are also decentralized exchanges (DEX) that operated without a central authority that allows P2P trading of cryptocurrencies. DEX does no rely on third-party services to hold customer's funds. Despite the small trading volume as compared to USD daily volume of USD5.1 trillion, the distributed nature of the payments and settlement network is interesting. The decentralized exchange network will change the way metals and other commodities are traded and funded, just as how they will stimulate M2M trading and settlement. While they are far from making an impact, the potential of decentralized exchanges will facilitate barter and minute trades when goods and services are tokenized and fractionalized. This innovation has future implications on the demand for fiat currencies and the CBDC.

The Europe and Asia Perspective

The Europe Perspective

Given the risk that we mentioned above about a general class of CBDC, it is not surprising that the focus of the developed economy is more towards maintaining stability and the effectiveness of its monetary policy. For example, the decrease in cash usage has led to the push for e-payments in Europe. Still, the existing regulations, the system of fiat money, and channels dictate the innovation of digital currency and payment systems. Some interesting discussions are in Mersch (2017), Bank of England (2020); Ward and Rochemont (2019), and BIS (2015, 2018, 2020a, b).

The adoption of above-mentioned infrastructure requires a considerable leap in mindset and a revamp of the entire payment system. Instead of worrying about the transition that can disrupt critical services, Switzerland's financial regulator Finma was the first to issue two Crypto Bank Licences to Sygnum[32] and SEBA[33] with guidelines on payment on blockchain and rigorous approach to combating money laundering on the blockchain.[34] These entities can perform the functions of both traditional banking services as well as crypto token related services, which mainly is a form of private key custody and involves a whole new set of crypto compliance. As computation law and crypto governance evolve, we will see more decentralized exchanges while such "banks" will be providing the infrastructure for open APIs and dApps. While trust cannot be distributed, there are new centralized entities to take on the role of private keys custodian of tokenized goods and services, while disrupting the traditional commercial bank model that thrives on bank deposits.

FINMA recognizes the innovative potential of the "shift in trust" and applies the relevant provisions of financial market law in a technology-neutral way. It does not allow crypto banks to circumvent the existing regulatory framework, especially the rules for combating money laundering and terrorist financing, where the inherent anonymity of DLT and blockchain technology present increased risks. Financial Action Task Force (FATF) guidance on financial services in the context of blockchain technology must be closely followed. Institutions supervised by FINMA are only permitted to send cryptocurrencies or other tokens to external wallets belonging to their own customers whose identity has already been verified and they are only allowed to receive cryptocurrencies or tokens from such customers. SEBA Crypto AG registered in Zug and Sygnum AG registered in Zurich will offer services for institutional and professional customers only. While restrictive, it is considered a giant leap in Europe. However, in Asia, the regulations, innovation and experiments are moving at an even faster speed that has surprised many observers.

The Asia Perspective

The People's Bank of China (PBOC) was the first central bank to initiate a research group on cryptocurrency on the prospects for the introduction of a CBDC in 2014. We have summarized notable announcements by various agencies and associated news in Appendix 1.

---

[32] https://www.sygnum.com/.
[33] https://www.seba.swiss/.
[34] https://www.finma.ch/en/news/2019/08/20190826-mm-kryptogwg/.

However, Singapore was one of the first to launch the open-source code for a tokenized digital currency under the Project Ubin proposal which involved several international banks such as Bank of America Merrill Lynch, Credit Suisse, Hong Kong and Shanghai Banking Corporation (HSBC) Limited, JP Morgan, Mitsubishi Financial Group, two local Singapore banks and several other blockchain companies (R3) in 2016. The associated timeline of Project Ubin and Acts are summarized in Appendix 2.

In 2017, Japan recognized Bitcoin and other digital currencies as legal property under the Payment Services Act.[35] Japan's Financial Services Agency confirmed bitcoin and several cryptocurrencies as legally accepted means of payment in the country.

Subsequently, in the same year, the Bank of England initiated a global discussion on the prospect of the introduction of a CBDC. In 2018, the International Monetary Fund began examining the potential innovative nature of digital coins (crypto-assets) and supported CBDC proposals publicly. Finally, in 2019, the tokenized debt was issued by the World Bank. Other initiatives by International Agencies and the USA are summarized in Appendix 3.

The three fundamental aspects of digital currency design are the asset, the payment and the utility. Most of the discussion focuses mainly on the first two aspects except PBOC that has mentioned the use of DCEP for tokenization of currently untraded services and goods.

Even though CBDC and DCEP can generally be classified by most as fiat money, there is a distinct difference. The Chinese have so far refrained from calling the DCEP as digital fiat yuan but only refer to it as digital money. One purpose of DCEP is to stimulate the trading of services and goods, China has given the DCEP enough flexibility to facilitate the selling of products and services that are currently not actively traded in the market. Some of these critical components of economic activities are excluded from the calculation of the actual GDP statistics but may constitute a large part of economic activities. Examples are time-based services or a stable asset token with underlying value. The timeline of the development of the Chinese DCEP can be found in Appendix 1.

While the earlier discussions of CBDC were centred around the payment functions, recent talks have switched to fiat currency in the form of digital tokens and assets. From the simple idea of money for transaction, speculative and precautionary motives, the studies have extended towards tokens as a form of money that serves as a unit of account, a store of value, a

---

[35] http://www.japaneselawtranslation.go.jp/law/detail/?id=3078&vm=02&re=02.

medium of exchange, and a standard of deferred payments. Money must be durable, portable, divisible, and difficult to counterfeit. PBOC has extended the discussion to tokenizing services and illiquid goods.

The potential innovations associated with digital currency designs refer to both the tokenization of the asset and services, as well as the P2P payment aspect. Any asset and services can be tokenized as an asset-bearing token, and whose liability is backed by the physical asset, legal entity, an object or just an everyday service. The digital currency or token can be designed to be automatically created as an asset and yet not a liability of any party. The P2P payment allows for transfers between parties without the involvement of trusted third parties. Still, some other designs aim to create a network that works in isolation from (or with only a marginal connection to) existing payment systems. The model can cater to value-based applications that directly open accounts in a distributed ledger with payments of such tokens native to the network.

The only connection with the existing payment system would be the exchanges and trading platforms, where the digital tokens would be exchanged for sovereign currency, and where transaction fees are charged and the exchange rates determined by demand and supply. The earlier discussions were focused on efficiency improvement for existing regulated entities such as the banks in setting up a decentralized payment mechanism between payment service providers to improve back-office clearing and settlement processes. From end-users being unaware of digital currencies and distributed ledgers to a whole new mechanism that changes the way assets are stored, and payments are executed. These will change the way the society views currency and existing activities not captured in GDP calculations to be explicit prices and trade. These latest discussions are certainly deviating from the earlier norm that distributed ledgers could be re-engineered and adopted to existing payment systems without involving the issuance of digital currency. This is a much broader mindset than the distributed ledgers which are simply used with a sovereign currency. PBOC has deliberately left the layer II architecture, beyond the level I creation of DECP, to the private sector, awaiting them to innovate and work hand in hand with the central bank. While this is true, not all central banks think like the PBOC research team.

A General Framework

There are two-tier considerations for CBDC. The first is the approach to the currency issue, i.e. how the digital currency will be issued. The second is the payment method among wholesale banking and retail. The central bank can centralize the decision for the approaches, or they can relax the control on the payments once the digital currency is in circulation.

The major pain point for cash or M0 is the high costs associated with the issuance, print, withdrawal and storage of physical money in the form of notes and coins. Physical cash lacks portability, traceability and anonymity. It is vulnerable to counterfeit, money laundering, terrorism, and unknown criminal use. Meanwhile, existing non-cash payment tools such as credit and debit cards, Internet and app payment cannot replace M0 as they are dependent on trusted third-party payment services. Furthermore, these other payments are dependent on institutions accounts that fail to support offline and anonymous payment services.

The main advantage of using the bitcoin UTXO (Unspent Transaction Output) is the possibility of offline payment, managed nonymity, and P2P payment without a centralized ledger. The design can be viewed as M0.5 as it retains the P2P offline Anonymity characteristics of M0, and yet traceability is similar as in M1. Unlike cards and institutional dependent payments, M0.5 can replace M0 with the added advantage of managed anonymity. However, this M0.5 concept is lacking in most central banks' design except China.

M0.5 combines the best features of a distributed system such as blockchain with the central bank's central management. As in Lee (2017), there is no conflict between decentralized ledger technology with central bank's centralized management. Although the technical characteristics of blockchain are not dependent on centralized institutions, they do not necessarily run contrary to the purpose of effectively integrating distributed operations with centralized governance and control. If appropriately designed, blockchain and DLT can effectively integrate distributed operations and better achieve centralized control of CBDC. There is no inevitable conflict between the two. For example, China utilized a three-layer general framework to understand and design their CBDC.

Layer 1 decision: The issuance of CBDC
Layer 2 decision: The Core-Satellite payment system that links the user
Layer 3 decision: The authentication, registration and query functions.

In the first layer, the decision regarding the digitisation has to be made of how CBDC is issued. There is a choice between a centralized or distributed technology to sign and issue the encrypted digital string of money guaranteed by the central bank. Only the central bank is allowed to issue and burn the digital money or tokens created. However, these coins can be created and burned on a single or multimode blockchain or DLT where the central bank controls this core node.

Layer 2 refers to the underlying payment system. The core node of the system can be controlled by the central bank and other nodes can be either directly managed by the retail or there can be delegated nodes of commercial or wholesale banks. One design is to have central bank core deposits the CBDC on the core that can be a dedicated node on the private cloud or independent core node, which can be viewed basically as the central bank's cash operation management system. The satellite nodes or the user nodes can have their payments on the core node or have their own CBDC's dedicated cloud node. There seem to be no reasons why there cannot be two tranches, those that are designed as 100pc reserves account needs to designate 100pc CBDC holding and the fractional CBDC can create new credit.

The third layer consists of three clients: tokenization, registration and analytics. Tokenization or certification is to ensure that supply is limited and whether the underlying is an asset or just created as a balance sheet item.

To entice usage of CBDC, eMoney must be more convenient and less risky than the current payment system. Here are the critical designs behind a new breed of CBDC:

1. CBDC is guaranteed by the Government and retains its fiat currency legal tender status. Not all digitized fiats are legal tender and CBDC has to be directly backed by the Government to ensure universal usability.
2. The usage and deposit of CBDC do not take on corporate and credit risks of licensed entities or financial institutions. Not all digitized fiat are of the same risk, and therefore there are issues of bank runs and freedom of usage across different platforms.
3. Public–Private sector collaboration is essential in designing a new CBDC. There are a lot of considerations and no one party can claim to have the solution for scalability, both technical and social. So for cross-border remittances and exchange, it becomes important to leave room for innovation amidst the tight regulatory environment.

The Board of the Bank for International Settlements (BIS) has established BIS Innovation Hub with central banks in Switzerland, Hong Kong SAR and Singapore to foster international collaboration on innovative financial technology within the central banking community and the following[36]:

---

[36] BIS to set up Innovation Hub for central banks.

1. identify and develop in-depth insights into critical trends in technology affecting central banking;
2. develop public goods in the technology space geared towards improving the functioning of the global financial system; and
3. serve as a focal point for a network of central bank experts on innovation.

Central banks are sharing their findings and open source of their pilot programs to ascertain what would be the acceptable designs for a decentralized system for banks. As a new wave of private payment solutions arrive, the urgency is felt as these innovations may potentially leave incumbent financial institutions obsolete. Both China and Singapore are involving more private sector participation.

It is interesting to note that the structure and restrictions of CBDC, the payment system, and how complex the monetary system, will all affect the speed of adoption and experimentation. China is in a unique position because it is the second-largest economy in the world, and yet it is very isolated from complex financial instruments. Its fairly close system without exposure to international instruments trading, as well as more trading that will be done in RMB gives an added advantage and added urgency for it to adopt CBDC, since less complexity and lower risks mean fewer outcome uncertainties, unlike many central banks. Another important fact is that since China internationalized its currency, it needs to exert certain control over the direction of the RMB and hence its reserves. Matured financial centres and many central banks do not have the luxury or appetite for testing the resilience of using a CBDC as the cost of disruption is much too high for international standing.

At the end of the day, it is about a balance between legality and convenience, innovation and a one-size-fits-all regulation, substance and cosmetics, and cost and security. There is an opportunity to improve international payment systems with CBDC and banking regulation would have to keep pace with the use of DLT and blockchain. There is not much time left before many central banks are left behind with ineffective payment and monetary systems.

The concerns of central banks are about private sector issuers taking advantage of their unique positions to possibly increase fees and lending rates, and privacy invasion if the public relies entirely on private money. The purpose of a central bank is to provide a fair, safe, liquid payment system equally to both the retail and wholesale sector. COVID-19 may trigger further financial crises and bankruptcies, and the public will suffer losses as well as interruptions in payments and settlements as seen in the global financial crisis. The collapse in the letter of the credit system that caused three months of severe shrinkages in trade and disruption in the supply chain was an important lesson for international payment and related financing activities.

Comparing Different Central Bank Approaches to Issuing Digital Currency

Banque or bank Gold or Banco was conceptualized in the early 1940s by John Maynard Keynes and E.F. Schumacher (1943). The value of any currency is inherently related to the demand and supply based and that in turn is based on the demand for international trade. Similar to the 1940s, the interest rate may not have enough policy potency to solve unemployment in the coming years. A unit of trade account may eventually be back in fashion, and this time, it is a unit of e-account to track the international flows of assets and liabilities. These may not be necessarily be tracked by an International Clearing Union, but instead through DLT of blockchain technology. While Keynes's idea was replaced by establishing the US dollar as a reserve currency convertible to gold at a fixed price on demand by other governments previously, Libra and China may revive the idea. Libra Association, if successful, may resemble the Banco proposal with coins backed by the volume of trades. China, on the other hand, may execute the idea.

Keynes's Banco proposal has been revived several times since the GFC by Zhou Xiaochuan, the former governor of the People's Bank of China. He proposed the adoption of the International Monetary Fund (IMF) special drawing rights (SDRs) as a global reserve currency. His view was echoed by the United Nations and the International Monetary Fund during the same period. To simultaneously meet the demand for reserve currency and the twin goal of domestic monetary policy goals, there were calls for the reform of the existing system. Zhou Xiaochuan subsequently set up the Digital Currency Research Institute in Beijing with the view that digital payment systems and CBDC can compete with each other, and innovation can take place in private sector's infrastructure under the guidance and supervision of the government. We may just see a new DCEP system evolving together with BRI[37] modelled after the Banco, starting with a few fiat currencies.

Coincidentally, International Swaps and Derivatives Association (ISDA) has devised many standards for smart contract exploring issues of legal and regulatory uncertainty as market participants seek to apply new technologies, such as smart contracts and DLT, to derivatives trading. Legal guidelines

---

[37] Zhou Xiaochuan's (2009) speech on 23 March 2009.

for Smart Derivative Contracts from Master agreement, collateral, Equities, to Interest Rate Derivatives have been presented in a series of whitepapers and contracts since 2019.[38] Such ideas and established standards can be extended to tokenizing commodities and services by China. DCEP is in the process of internally tested in four large cities—Shenzhen, Suzhou, Chengdu and Beijing satellite city Xiong'an. Blockchain Service Network (BSN), ChinaChain, has now launched globally. ChinaChain, architected in part by Red Date Technology, launched an internet of interoperable blockchains that includes Ethereum, Hyperledger and EOS. ChinaChain or Blockchain Service Network (BSN) will connect 128 cities in China to seven countries. McDonald, Starbucks and Subway have been named together with 16 other retail firms & restaurants to experiment and transact in DCEP.[39]

Meantime in the United Kingdom after Brexit, the two purposes of liberalizing the pounds by the Bank of England originally are made known publicly, especially the second one. First, the BoE is to regain its regulatory power that seems to have been given to the third-party payment units. Second is to revive the sterling as a universal currency so as to challenge the dollar hegemony. The second reason was voiced by the former Bank of England governor in the USA on 23 August 2019. These two reasons are perhaps expressed and pursued by many other central bankers. European nations have exported medical supplies to Iran as part of a mechanism set up to circumvent US sanctions on Tehran, ending their struggle over the past year to establish the INSTEX[40] barter system.[41] The creation of the INSTEX mechanism has enabled the export of medical devices from Europe during the COVID-19 Pandemic, and the arrangement would allow many other transactions to proceed. The USD dominant position is not automatically guaranteed.

Furthermore, CBDC resembles the controversial 1920's "100 per cent reserve" idea of English Nobel prize-winning chemist Frederick Soddy and later presented to US President Franklin Roosevelt by the Chicago School's Frank Knight and Henry Simons at the end of the Great Depression. The idea of "100% Money" was popularized by Fisher's book published in 1935 on the same title after receiving a summarized letter from Henry Simon that sparked his interest (William 1993). The essential effect is to separate the money lending function from the money-creation function, thus allowing

---

[38] https://www.isda.org/2019/10/16/isda-smart-contracts/.
[39] https://medium.com/coinmonks/chinas-chinachain-launched-globally-starbucks-mcdonald-s-subway-to-test-china-s-dcep-12742832d778.
[40] The Instrument in Support of Trade Exchanges (INSTEX) is a European special-purpose vehicle (SPV) established in January 2019.
[41] https://www.dw.com/en/europe-and-iran-complete-first-instex-deal-dodging-us-sanctions/a-52966842.

control of the size of the money stock being solely a government function. CBDC is undoubtedly a revival of the original ideas linked to Sovereign Money System, Full-reserve banking, Plain Money, and 100 per cent money. None of these ideas has taken root before. With technology, coupled with social and political pressure from inequality, governments may eventually be incentivized to adopt and accelerate these "unconventional" proposals. With a full-reserve system, the idea of tontines and mutual aid on a blockchain can potentially be revived as a new approach to banking and to reach the financially excluded.

The BoE has commented that DLT is not necessary for CBDC, as they may have been focusing solely on the importance of transaction purposes and regulating. They may have missed the empowerment by the distinct features of blockchain and associated cryptography techniques such as fractionalization of ownership, data privacy, programmable currency and multi-party sharing and computing. The convergence of blockchain technology with the Internet will be the future that no central bank should ignore. The idea of having an Internet of many blockchains[42] aided by other technologies such as IoT with external data verification with oracles is perhaps the ultimate infrastructure of the central bank in transforming the economy.

Most of the discussions outside China seem to have shied away from discussing the function of programmable money, smart contracts, oracles, Internet of Blockchain and Convergence of Technology. CBDC can perform a more prominent role and solve the pain points of the currency economies, which presently rely on QE Infinity to prevent the economy from sliding. The long-term solution can only be available if central banks are willing to broaden the discussion beyond transactionality and supervision objectives. Open comprehensive design for CBDC based on blockchain may be an exciting opening to a journey with a steep learning curve for all stakeholders. With Sovereign Wealth Fund such as Temasek Holdings[43] becoming a member of Libra Association and China venture into DCEP with many stakeholders, no governments can afford to be complacent, and rigidity is no more in the vocabulary.

---

[42] Polkadot and Cosmos are predicated on the thesis that the future will have multiple blockchains that need to interoperate with each other rather than individual blockchains existing in isolation. https://polkadot.network/ and https://cosmos.network/.

[43] https://www.reuters.com/article/facebook-cryptocurrency-temasek/singapore-state-investor-temasek-joins-facebooks-libra-project-idUSL8N2CX07V.

Conclusion: What Would Likely Happen in the Future?

The suspension of the gold window in 1971 saw the end of the conversion of the metal to USD at a fixed exchange rate of $35 per ounce. That led to the Bretton Woods system being replaced by the current freely floating fiat currencies since 1973. Since then, the monetary system has been driven by the fractional-reserve system with USD acting as a global reserve currency. Besides, USD also serves as the default trading currency for commodities trading and in particular crude oil. Since 2008, the USA field production of crude oil has increased from 5 million barrels a day to a record of more than 12 million in 2020.[44] Demand for the USD has been growing over time. Continuous quantitative easing (QE) and the asset allocation strategy of Risk-Parity fuelled further demand for the USD and US debts. It is not coincidental that Satoshi Nakamoto launched the Bitcoin Network in 2009 immediately after the global financial crisis.

The value of gold-backed currencies was rooted in the trust in gold. Free-floating fiat shifted the trust to the issuing Government in providing stability for the exchange system. Bitcoin, however, is viewed as a hedge against the collapse in the trust of the monetary system. Its value has a negative coherence with stability and trust in the fiat system. During a crisis of confidence, the trust in a Government may shift to the use of bitcoin as a medium of exchange, a store of value, and a unit of account, which is essentially the trust in the Community or Cryptography. While the loss in trust in the global system is unlikely, the loss in trust in a country monetary system happens frequently. However, the launch of bitcoin is a direct challenge to the notion of USD being the reserve currency of the world and therefore a replacement candidate for the entire fiat system. It is unlikely that it will happen but cryptocurrencies, like many other alternative forms of currencies during unstable times, are likely to be in existence for a long time, given that several countries have declared some of these cryptocurrencies as legal tender or part of the legal payment system.

Even as China begins regulation on cryptography and software, potentially making codes legal entities, there are still a lot of challenges for international law and governments to define cryptography, computational networks and code. Thus, it is difficult to have an international agreement on how to regulate cryptocurrencies. With cryptocurrencies making up a small composition

---

[44] https://www.eia.gov/dnav/pet/hist/LeafHandler.ashx?n=pet&s=mcrfpus2&f=a.

of the monetary system, it is unlikely to destabilize the fiat system in the near term.

A more direct challenge to the fiat currency system and in particular the USD reserve system will be the non-fiat stablecoin. Stablecoins issued by non-government entities such as technology giants may stand a good chance of destabilizing the USD-based monetary system if regulation fails to keep up with technology development. On top of this, countries with limited resources may turn to the technology provided by these private entities (such as the Libra project) to create digital versions of their currency. With wide adoption, a country or a group of countries with massive trade and capital accounts collectively may exert pressure on the USD reserved based system in a very short period. That is a very likely scenario that we may see soon.

The fiat-backed corporate-issued stablecoin may be less of a threat as these coins are likely to be heavily regulated even though they have a vast user base. However, as the use cases of these technology corporations grow, this may change. As mega apps emerge from tech giants with their own social platforms, telecom network, online broadcast, mobility, proptech, telemedicine and e-commerce with a large volume of trades, corporate-based stablecoins may play a much more significant role than we can imagine at this moment. With its reputation and financial muscle, a fiat-baked corporate stablecoin can transform into a coin based solely on the trust of the corporation. A cross-border community-based monetary and payment system may evolve and may pose a threat to the blockchain or DLT payment system initiated initially by governments.

Acknowledgements We thank our SUSS research fellow Cheryl Wang Yu and research assistant Pranav Pandya for the invaluable background research that went into this paper.

Appendix 1: The Timeline of Chinese Study of the CBDC

Date	Content	Source
Central Policy Statement 中央政策声明		

(continued)

(continued)

Date	Content	Source
2014	央行就成立了发行法定数字货币的专门研究小组,论证央行发行法定数字货币的可行性 The central bank set up a specialized research group to issue and demonstrate the feasibility of the central bank digital currency	中国人民银行 People's Bank of China
October 2016	《中国区块链技术和应用发展白皮书(2016)》 China Blockchain Technology and Application Development White Paper (2016)	中国工信部 China Ministry of Industry and Information Technology
December 2016	国务院印发《"十三五"国家信息化规划》,首次将区块链技术列入国家级信息化规划内容 The State Council issued the "13th Five-Year Plan" National Information Action Plan, and for the first time included blockchain technology in the national informatization plan	中国国务院 State Council of China
January 2017	中国人民银行正式成立数字货币研究所 The People's Bank of China officially established the Digital Currency Research Institute	中国人民银行 People's Bank of China
June 2017	中国人民银行引发了《中国金融业信息技术'十三五'发展规划》:积极推进区块链、人工智能等新技术应用研究 The People's Bank of China has initiated the "13th Five-Year Plan" for the development of information technology in China's financial industry: actively promoting the application of new technologies such as blockchain and artificial intelligence	中国人民银行 People's Bank of China

(continued)

(continued)

Date	Content	Source
September 2017	国内数字货币交易所被勒令关停,对加密货币持禁止态度;监管当局决定关闭中国境内虚拟货币交易所 Domestic digital currency exchanges ordered to shut down and cryptocurrencies banned; Regulators then decided to close virtual currency exchanges in China	中国人民银行、中央网信办、工业和信息化部、工商总局、银监会、证监会、保监会 People's Bank of China, Central Cyberspace Office, Ministry of Industry and Information Technology, General Administration of Industry and Commerce, China Banking Regulatory Commission, Securities Regulatory Commission, Insurance Regulatory Commission
August 2018	官方出台《关于防范以"虚拟货币""区块链"名义进行非法集资的风险提示》 The official released of the "Reminder on Preventing Risks of Illegal Fundraising in the Name of 'Virtual Currency' and 'Blockchain'"	银保监会、中央网信办、公安部、人民银行、市场监管总局 Banking and Insurance Regulatory Commission, Central Cyberspace Office, Ministry of Public Security, People's Bank of China, General Administration of Market Supervision
January 2019	官方出台《区块链信息服务管理规定》以明确责任、规避安全风险,2019年2月15日实施 Officially issued "Regulations on the Management of Blockchain Information Services" to clarify responsibilities and avoid security risks, which would be implemented on 15 February 2019	国家互联网信息办公室 Cyberspace Administration of China
March 2019	《关于发布第一批境内区块链信息服务备案编号的公告》 First batch of licensed blockchain service providers was released (197 licences)	国家互联网信息办公室 Cyberspace Administration of China

(continued)

(continued)

Date	Content	Source
August 2019	央行将推进中国法定数字货币研发归入2019年下半年八项重点工作之一；央行有关负责人在公开场合表示正在进行数字货币系统开发，"数字人民币时代"即将到来；央行出台《金融科技(FinTech)发展规划(2019–2021年)》 The central bank decided to promote the development of China's legal digital currency as one of the eight key tasks in the second half of 2019; relevant officials of the central bank stated in public that the digital currency system development was underway, and the "digital yuan era" was to be launched—FinTech Development Plan (2019–2021)	中国人民银行 People's Bank of China
September 2019	中国人民银行行长易纲表示数字货币研究目前取得了积极进展,但数字货币推出目前没有时间表 People's Bank of China Governor Yi Gang said that digital currency research had made positive progress, but there was no timetable for the launch of digital currency	中国人民银行 People's Bank of China
October 2019	《关于发布第二批境内区块链信息服务备案编号的公告》 Second batch of licensed blockchain service providers was released (309 licences)	国家互联网信息办公室 Cyberspace Administration of China
October 2019	中共中央政治局就区块链技术发展现状和趋势进行第十八次集体学习,习近平强调区块链技术的作用 The Political Bureau of the Central Committee of the Communist Party of China conducted the 18th group-study lesson on the current status and trends of blockchain technology. President Xi Jinping emphasized the role of blockchain technology	中共中央政治局、中共中央总书记 Political Bureau of the CPC Central Committee, General Secretary of the CPC Central Committee
October 2019	第十三届全国人民代表大会常务委员会通过了《中华人民共和国密码法》 The Standing Committee of the 13th National People's Congress passed the "Cryptography Law of the People's Republic of China"	中央委员会 Central Committee

(continued)

(continued)

Date	Content	Source
November 2019	《中国产业结构调整指南目录》拟稿中加入的加密货币挖矿(包括比特币挖矿)已移除,从2020年起将其从要禁止的行业清单中删除 Cryptocurrency mining (including bitcoin mining) added to the draft "Guide to the Catalog of China's Industrial Structure Adjustment" and will be removed from the list of industries to be banned from 2020	中国国家发展和改革委员会(发改委) National Development and Reform Commission (NDRC) of China
December 2019	深交所发布深证区块链50指数 Shenzhen Stock Exchange released the Shenzhen Stock Exchange 50 Index	深圳证券交易所、深圳证券信息有限公司 Shenzhen Stock Exchange, Shenzhen Securities Information Co., Ltd.
January 2020	央行、国务院等多个部门机构公布了11则促进区块链与各领域结合的政策信息 The central bank, the State Council and other departments announced information on 11 policies to promote the integration of blockchain and various fields	中国人民银行、国务院、银保监会、交通运输部、国家外汇管理局、广电总局、司法部等 People's Bank of China, State Council, Banking Insurance Regulatory Commission, Ministry of Transport, State Administration of Foreign Exchange, State Administration of Radio, Film and Television, Ministry of Justice, etc.

(continued)

(continued)

Date	Content	Source
February 2020	央行发布、多家机构参与的《金融分布式账本技术安全规范》 "Technical Security Specifications for Financial Distributed Ledgers" issued by the central bank and involving multiple institutions	中国人民银行;由中国人民银行数字货币研究所负责起草,由中国人民银行科技司、中国工商银行、中国农业银行、中国银行、中国建设银行和国家开发银行等20余家机构参与 Drafted by the People's Bank of China Digital Currency Research Institute, with the participation of more than 20 institutions including the Science and Technology Department of the People's Bank of China, Industrial and Commercial Bank of China, Agricultural Bank of China, Bank of China, China Construction Bank and China Development Bank
April 2020	《关于发布第三批境内区块链信息服务备案编号的公告》 Third batch of licenced blockchain service providers was released (224 licences)	国家互联网信息办公室 Cyberspace Administration of China
Important Reports on Central Bank Digital Currency		
2016	《中国金融》专题:央行数字货币研究与探讨 "China Finance" Special Topic: Research and Discussion on Digital Currency of Central Bank	《中国金融》、巴比特网站 China Finance, 8BTC Website
2019	中国研发央行数字货币这五年 Five years of China's central bank digital currency R&D	《环球》 Global Times
2020	央行数字货币已开始内测;法定数字货币专利助力我国数字金融发展 The start of China's DC/EP piloting; Patents related to CBDC would aid the development of digital finance in China	新华社 Xinhua News
Local Government		

(continued)

(continued)

Date	Content	Source
February 2020	全国已有22个省(自治区、直辖市)将区块链写入2020年政府工作报告;更多地方政府有关区块链政策信息 22 provinces (autonomous regions, municipalities) included blockchain in the 2020 government progress report; more local government information on blockchain policy.	Various
April 2020	北京已开始使用区块链技术进行行政审批 Beijing's administrative approval process driven by blockchain technology	国家互联网信息办公室 Cyberspace Administration of China
Corporate Development		
February 2020	互联网巨头和传统金融机构均开始涉足金融科技 Internet giants and traditional financial institutions are both getting involved in fintech	Various

Appendix 2: MAS Timeline of Project Ubin, Digital Bank Licenses and Payment Services Act

Date	Phase	Source and content
Initiated: 16 November 2016 Concluded: 9 March 2017	Phase 1: Tokenized SGD	https://www.mas.gov.sg/schemes-and-initiatives/Project-Ubin https://www.mas.gov.sg/-/media/MAS/ProjectUbin/Project-Ubin–SGD-on-Distributed-Ledger.pdf MAS announced on 16 November 2016 that it would partner with R3 and a consortium of financial institutions on a proof-of-concept project to experiment with interbank payments using Blockchain technology
Initiated: 5 October 2017 Concluded: 11 November 2017	Phase 2: Re-imaging RTGS	https://www.mas.gov.sg/-/media/MAS/ProjectUbin/Project-Ubin-Phase-2-Reimagining-RTGS.pdf?la=en&hash=02722F923D88DE83C35AF4D1346FDC2D42298AE0 MAS and The Association of Banks in Singapore (ABS) successfully developed a software prototype of three different models for decentralized interbank payment and settlements with liquidity savings mechanisms

(continued)

(continued)

Date	Phase	Source and content
Initiated: 24 August 2018	Phase 3: Delivery versus Payment (DvP)	https://www.mas.gov.sg/-/media/MAS/ProjectUbin/Project-Ubin-DvP-on-Distributed-Ledger-Technologies.pdf?la=en&hash=2ADD9093B64A819FCC78D94E68FA008A6CD724FF MAS and Singapore Exchange (SGX) announced on 24 August 2018 that it was collaborating to develop Delivery versus Payment (DvP) capabilities for settlement of tokenized assets across different blockchain platforms This would allow financial institutions and corporate investors to carry out simultaneous exchange and final settlement of tokenized digital currencies and securities assets, improving operational efficiency and reducing settlement risks. Three companies, Anquan, Deloitte and Nasdaq were appointed as technology partners for this project. They would leverage the open-source software developed and made publicly available in Project Ubin Phase 2 The successful conclusion of the DvP project was announced on 11 November 2018. The project demonstrated that DvP settlement finality, interledger interoperability and investor protection could be achieved through specific solutions designed and built on blockchain technology

(continued)

(continued)

Date	Phase	Source and content
	Phase 4: Cross-border Payment versus Payment (PvP)	https://www.mas.gov.sg/-/media/MAS/ProjectUbin/Cross-Border-Interbank-Payments-and-Settlements.pdf?la=en&hash=5472F1876CFA9439591F06CE3C7E522F01F47EB6 https://www.mas.gov.sg/-/media/MAS/ProjectUbin/Jasper-Ubin-Design-Paper.pdf?la=en&hash=437222C94FD39314FB4C685EA31FC3AAA5CA5DA1 The Bank of Canada (BoC), Bank of England (BoE) and the Monetary Authority of Singapore (MAS) jointly published a report on 15 November 2018 which assessed alternative models that could enhance cross-border payments and settlements. The report examined existing challenges and considered alternative models that could in time result in improvements in speed, cost and transparency for users The report, cross-border interbank payments and settlements: Emerging opportunities for digital transformation, provided an initial framework for the global financial community to assess cross-border payments and settlements in greater depth. Specifically, it discussed how a variety of payment models could be implemented, from both a technical and non-technical perspective. MAS and BoC subsequently linked up their respective experimental domestic payment networks, namely Project Jasper and Project Ubin, and announced on 2 May 2019 a successful experiment on cross-border and cross-currency payments using central bank digital currencies. MAS and BoC jointly published a report, Jasper-Ubin Design Paper: Enabling Cross-Border High-Value Transfer using DLT, which proposed different design options for cross-border settlement systems

(continued)

(continued)

Date	Phase	Source and content
	Phase 5: Enabling Board Ecosystem Collaboration	MAS announced on 11 November 2019 the successful development of a blockchain-based prototype that enabled payments to be carried out in different currencies on the same network
		The prototype network, developed by MAS in collaboration with J.P. Morgan and Temasek, had the potential to improve cost efficiencies for businesses. The payments network would provide interfaces for other blockchain networks to connect and integrate seamlessly, and would also offer additional features to support use cases such as Delivery versus Payment (DvP) settlement with private exchanges, conditional payments and escrow for trade, as well as payment commitments for trade finance
		The network was currently undergoing industry testing to determine its ability to integrate with commercial blockchain applications. Beyond technical experimentation, this phase of Project Ubin sought to determine the commercial viability and value of the blockchain-based payments network
		The project report would be published in early 2020. The report would describe the blockchain use cases that would benefit from a blockchain-based payments network, and set out additional features that the network could provide. In addition, the technical specifications for the connectivity interfaces that were developed will also be released for public access under Apache License Version 2.0

(continued)

(continued)

Date	Phase	Source and content
7 January 2020	Digital Bank Licences	https://www.mas.gov.sg/news/media-releases/2020/mas-receives-21-applications-for-digital-bank-licences https://www.mas.gov.sg/regulation/Banking/digital-bank-licence https://www.mas.gov.sg/regulation/payments/application-for-a-payment-service-provider-licence MAS announced on 7 Jan 2020 that it received 21 applications for digital bank licences as at the close of application on 31 December 2019. This comprised seven applications for the digital full bank (DFB) licences, and 14 applications for the digital wholesale bank (DWB) licences. Applicants included e-commerce firms, technology and telecommunications companies, FinTechs (such as crowdfunding platforms and payment services providers) and financial institutions. The majority of applicants were consortiums, with entities seeking to combine their individual strengths to enhance the digital bank's value proposition This was in response to its announcement on 28 June 2019 that it would issue up to two digital full bank (DFB) licences and three digital wholesale bank (DWB) licences. These new digital banks were in addition to any digital banks that Singapore banking groups may already establish under MAS' existing internet banking framework The digital bank licences would allow entities, including non-bank players, to conduct digital banking businesses in Singapore. These new digital bank licences marked the new chapter in Singapore's banking liberalization journey, and ensured that Singapore's banking sector continues to be resilient, competitive and vibrant. A DFB would be allowed to take deposits from and provide banking services to retail and non-retail customer segments. A DWB would be allowed to take deposits from and provide banking services to SMEs and other non-retail customer segments.

(continued)

(continued)

Date	Phase	Source and content
28 January 2020	Payment Services Act	https://www.mas.gov.sg/news/media-releases/2020/payment-services-act-comes-into-force https://www.mas.gov.sg/regulation/acts/payment-services-act On 28 Jan 2020, MAS announced the commencement of the Payment Services Act (PS Act). The new PS Act would enhance the regulatory framework for payment services in Singapore, strengthen consumer protection and promote confidence in the use of e-payments. It was a forward-looking and flexible framework for the regulation of payment systems and payment service providers in Singapore. It was to provide regulatory certainty and consumer safeguards while encouraging innovation and growth of payment services and FinTech

Appendix 3: Other Notable International Initiatives, Research and Recommendations

European Central Bank	Digital Base Money: an assessment from the ECB's perspective	https://www.ecb.europa.eu/press/key/date/2017/html/sp170116.en.html Digital Base Money: an assessment from the ECB's perspective Speech by Yves Mersch, Member of the Executive Board of ECB, at the Farewell ceremony for Pentti Hakkarainen, Deputy Governor of Suomen Pankki—Finlands Bank, Helsinki, 16 January 2017
ADBI	Money and Central Bank Digital Currency	https://www.adb.org/sites/default/files/publication/485856/adbi-wp922.pdf This paper gave an overview of the concepts and features of central bank money and private sector money and focused on the actual performance of these types of money in selected advanced and emerging economies. In addition, digital coins (crypto-assets), such as bitcoin, were newly emerged private sector money. Much attention was given to digital coins because the underlying distributed ledger technology (DLT) could enable a decentralized verification process while maintaining features similar to cash

(continued)

(continued)

IMF	Designing Central Bank Digital Currencies	https://www.imf.org/en/Publications/WP/Issues/2019/11/18/Designing-Central-Bank-Digital-Currencies-48739 This was a technical paper on the optimal design of a central bank digital currency (CBDC) where CBDC could be designed with attributes similar to cash or deposits, and can be interest-bearing. It argued that the optimal CBDC design would trade-off bank intermediation against the social value of maintaining diverse payment instruments. When network effects mattered, an interest-bearing CBDC would alleviate the central bank's trade-off
IMF	Central Bank Digital Currencies: 4 Questions and Answers	https://blogs.imf.org/2019/12/12/central-bank-digital-currencies-4-questions-and-answers/ This blog discussed the role of the IMF and addressed the issues of financial stability, legal foundation and regulation
Financial Stability Board	Addressing the regulatory, supervisory and oversight challenges raised by "global stablecoin" arrangements: Consultative Document	https://www.fsb.org/2020/04/addressing-the-regulatory-supervisory-and-oversight-challenges-raised-by-global-stablecoin-arrangements-consultative-document/ This consultation set out 10 high-level recommendations to address the regulatory, supervisory and oversight challenges raised by "global stablecoin" arrangements
Federal Reserve System	Update on Digital Currencies, Stablecoins and the Challenges Ahead	https://www.federalreserve.gov/newsevents/speech/brainard20191218a.htm Governor Lael Brainard speech on the Monetary Policy, Technology, and Globalization Panel at "Monetary Policy: The Challenges Ahead", an ECB Colloquium Held in Honour of Benoît Coeuré, Frankfurt, Germany 18 December 2019
Federal Reserve System	The Digitalization of Payments and Currency: Some Issues for Consideration	https://www.federalreserve.gov/newsevents/speech/brainard20200205a.htm Governor Lael Brainard At the Symposium on the Future of Payments, Stanford, California 5 February 2020

(continued)

(continued)

US Congress	The draft legislation "Keep Big Tech Out Of Finance Act"	https://www.consumerfinancemonitor.com/wp-content/uploads/sites/14/2019/07/Facebook-crypto-bill-HFSC.pdf	A proposed bill to prohibit large platform utilities from being a financial institution or being affiliated with a person that is a financial institution, and for other purposes. It was proposed on 15 July 2019 by the Democratic majority of the House Financial Services Committee targeting Libra
US Congress	A draft bill titled "Stablecoins Are Securities Act".	https://financialservices.house.gov/uploadedfiles/bills-116pih-ssa.pdf	To establish the treatment of managed stablecoins under the securities laws, and for other purposes. It was proposed on 18 Oct. 2019. This legislation was meant to regulate stablecoins, a cryptocurrency that would work as a non-volatile, stable source of value, under the familiar Securities Act of 1933

References

Al-Naji, N., Chen, J., & Diao, L. (2017). *Basis: A Price-Stable Cryptocurrency with an Algorithmic Central Bank.* Formerly Known as: Basecoin Version 0.99. 7.

Athey, S., Parashkevov, I., Sarukkai, V., & Xia, J. (2016). *Bitcoin Pricing, Adoption, and Usage: Theory and Evidence.* Stanford Institute for Economic Policy Research, Working Paper No. 17-033.

Atik, J., & Gerro, G. (2018). *Hard forks on the Bitcoin Blockchain: Reversible Exit, Continuing Voice.* Stan. J. Blockchain L. & Pol'y, 1, 24.

Bacchetta, P. (2018). *The Sovereign Money Initiative in Switzerland: An Economic Assessment.* Swiss Journal of Economics and Statistics. 154:3.

Bank of England (2020). *Central Bank Digital Currency: Opportunities, Challenges and Design.* Retrieved from https://www.bankofengland.co.uk/paper/2020/central-bank-digital-currency-opportunities-challenges-and-design-discussion-paper.

Barrdear, J. & Kumhof, M. (2016). *The Macroeconomics of Central Bank Issued Digital Currencies.* Bank of England Staff Working Paper No. 605. Retrieved from https://www.bankofengland.co.uk/working-paper/2016/the-macroeconomics-of-central-bank-issued-digital-currencies.

Bech, M. L., & Garratt, R. (2017). *Central Bank Cryptocurrencies.* BIS Quarterly Review September. Retrieved from https://www.bis.org/publ/qtrpdf/r_qt1709f.htm.

Berentsen, A., & Schär, F. (2019). *Stablecoins: The Quest for a Low-Volatility Cryptocurrency.* In The Economics of Fintech and Digital Currencies. CEPR Press.

Bhambhwani, S., Delikouras, S., & Korniotis, G. M. (2019). *Do Fundamental Drive Cryptocurrency Prices?*. Available at SSRN 3342842.

BIS (2003). *A Glossary of Terms Used in Payments and Settlement Systems.* Retrieved from https://www.bis.org/cpmi/glossary_030301.pdf.

BIS (2015). *Digital Currencies, Committee on Payments and Market Infrastructures.* Retrieved from https://www.bis.org/cpmi/publ/d137.pdf.

BIS (2018). *Central Bank Digital Currencies, Committee on Payments and Market Infrastructures.* Retrieved from https://www.bis.org/cpmi/publ/d174.htm.

BIS (2020a). *Impending Arrival—A Sequel to the Survey on Central Bank Digital Currency*, by Codruta, Henry Holder and Wadsworth, Monetary and Economic Department, BIS Papers No 107. Retrieved from https://www.bis.org/publ/bppdf/bispap107.pdf.

BIS (2020b). *The Technology of Retail Central Bank Digital Currency.* Rachel Auer and Ranier Bohme, BIS Quarterly Review. Retrieved from https://www.bis.org/publ/qtrpdf/r_qt2003j.htm.

Bouri, E., Gupta, R., & Vo, X. (2020). *Jumps in Geopolitical Risk and the Cryptocurrency Market: The Singularity of Bitcoin* (No. 202015). University of Pretoria Department of Economics Working Paper Series. Working Paper No. 2020-15.

Chan, W. H., Le, M., & Wu, Y. W. (2019). *Holding Bitcoin Longer: The Dynamic Hedging Abilities of Bitcoin.* The Quarterly Review of Economics and Finance. 71.

Chepurnoy, A., Duong, T., Fan, L., & Zhou, H. S. (2017). *TwinsCoin: A Cryptocurrency Via Proof-of-Work and Proof-of-Stake.* IACR Cryptology ePrint Archive, 232.

Ciaian, P., Rajcaniova, M., & Kancs, D. A. (2016). *The Economics of BitCoin Price Formation.* Applied Economics, 48(19).

Cœuré, B. (2018). *The Future of Central Bank Money. Speech by a Member of the Executive Board of the ECB at the International Center for Monetary and Banking Studies.* Geneva. Retrieved from https://www.ecb.europa.eu/press/key/date/2018/html/ecb.sp180514_4.en.html.

Duffield, E., & Diaz, D. (2018). *Dash: A Payments-Focused Cryptocurrency.* Whitepaper.

Dyhrberg, A. H. (2016). *Hedging Capabilities of Bitcoin. Is it the Virtual Gold?.* Finance Research Letters, 16.

Engel, C. (2019). *Lessons for Cryptocurrencies from Foreign Exchange Markets.* Retrieved from https://www.ssc.wisc.edu/~cengel/WorkingPapers/MASCryptoPaper.pdf.

Fernández Ordóñez, M. (2018). *The Future of Banking: Secure Money and Deregulation of the Financial System.* Retrieved from http://sgfm.elcorteingles.es/SGFM/FRA/recursos/doc/AGORA/220802394_542018121416.pdf.

Gürtler, K., Nielsen, S. T., Rasmussen, K., & Spange, M. (2017). *Central Bank Digital Currency in Denmark?* Retrieved from https://www.nationalbanken.dk/en/publications/Pages/2017/12/Central-bank-digital-currency-in-Denmark.aspx.

Hayes, A. (2016). *Decentralised banking: Monetary technocracy in the digital age.* In Banking Beyond Banks and Money (pp. 121–131). Springer, Cham.

Hayes, A. S. (2019). *Bitcoin price and its marginal cost of production: support for a fundamental value.* Applied Economics Letters, 26(7).

Klein, M., Gross, J., & Sandner, P. (2020). *The Digital Euro and the Role of DLT for Central Bank Digital Currencies.* FSBC Working Paper, Frankfurt School Blockchain Centre.

Kshetri, N. & Voas, J. (2018), *Blockchain in Developing Countries.* Vol. 20. IEEE IT Professional.

Lai, R. & Lee, D. K. C. (2018). *Blockchain—From public to private.* Handbook of Blockchain, Digital Finance, and Inclusion, Volume 2. By Lee. DKC & Deng. R. Elsevier.

Lee, D. K. C. (2017). *Decentralization and Distributed Innovation: Catch-up and Leapfrog.* Preprint. SSRN. https://papers.ssrn.com/sol3/papers.cfm?abstract_id=3476510.

Lee, D. K. C., Guo, L. & Wang, Y. (2018). *Cryptocurrency: A New Investment Opportunity?* Journal of Alternative Investments, 20 (3).

Long, B. (2019). *Risk prevention in the practice of central bank legal digital currency* (in Chinese). 龙白滔. (2019). 央行法定数字货币实践中的风险防范. Retrieved from https://news.caijingmobile.com/article/detail/402236.

Liu, Y., Tsyvinski, A., & Wu, X. (2019). *Common risk factors in cryptocurrency* (No. w25882). National Bureau of Economic Research.

Mayer, T. (2019). *To Save the Euro, Turn it Into a Digital Stablecoin. Financial Times Online.* November 18th 2019. Retrieved from https://www.ft.com/content/476d85f8-07cf-11ea-a958-5e9b7282cbd1.

Mersch, Y. (2017). *Digital Base Money: an assessment from the ECB's perspective, Speech by Yves Mersch, Member of the Executive Board of the ECB, at the Farewell ceremony for Pentti Hakkarainen, Deputy Governor of Suomen Pankki* – Finlands Bank, Helsinki, 16 January 2017.

Nakamoto, S. (2008). *Bitcoin: A peer-to-peer electronic cash system.* Retrieved from https://bitcoin.org/bitcoin.pdf.

Narayanan, A. (2015). *Analyzing the 2013 Bitcoin fork: centralized decision-making saved the day.* Center for Information Technology Policy. Princeton.

Oh, J. H. (2018). *The Foreign Exchange Market With the Cryptocurrency and "Kimchi Premium".* Retrieved from https://www.econstor.eu/bitstream/10419/190386/1/E1_1_Oh.pdf.

Polasik, M., Piotrowska, A. I., Wisniewski, T. P., Kotkowski, R., & Lightfoot, G. (2015). *Price fluctuations and the use of Bitcoin: An empirical inquiry.* International Journal of Electronic Commerce, 20(1).

Raskin, M., & Yermack, D. (2018). *Digital Currencies, Decentralized Ledgers, and the Future of Central Banking.* Edward Elgar Publishing.

Raskin, M., Saleh, F., & Yermack, D. (2019). *How Do Private Digital Currencies Affect Government Policy?* (No. w26219). National Bureau of Economic Research.

Ren, L. (2014). *Proof of stake velocity: Building the social currency of the digital age.* Self-published white paper.

Schumacher, E. F. (1943). *Multilateral Clearing*. Economica. 10 (38).

Shiral, S. (2019). *Central Bank Digital Currency: Concepts and Trends*, VOX CEPR Policy Portal. Retrieved from https://voxeu.org/article/central-bank-digital-currency-concepts-and-trends.

Sovbetov, Y. (2018). *Factors influencing cryptocurrency prices: Evidence from bitcoin, ethereum, dash, litecoin, and monero.* Journal of Economics and Financial Analysis, 2(2).

Stoll, C., Klaaßen, L., & Gallersdörfer, U. (2019). *The carbon footprint of bitcoin.* Joule, 3(7).

Szabo, N. (2017). *Money, blockchains, and social scalability.* Retrieved from http://unenumerated.blogspot.com/2017/02/money-blockchains-and-social-scalability.html.

Ward, O. & Rochemont. S. (2019). *Understanding Central Bank Digital Currency (CBDC).* Institute and Faculty of Actuaries. Retrieved from https://www.actuaries.org.uk/system/files/field/document/Understanding%20CBDCs%20Final%20-%20disc.pdf.

William, R. A. (1993). *Irving Fisher and the 100 Percent Reserve Proposal.* Journal of Law and Economics, 36 (2). Retrieved from https://www.fullreservebanking.com/Irving%20Fisher%20and%20the%20100%20Percent%20Reserve%20Proposal.pdf.

Zhou Xiaochuan (2009). *Reform the International Monetary System.* BIS Review. Bank of International Settlements. Retrieved from https://www.bis.org/review/r090402c.pdf.

8

Privately Issued Digital Currencies

Dante Alighieri Disparte

Introduction

The Rise of Cryptocurrencies

There is a unique feature in humanity and our societies. As the historian Yuval Noah Harari notes, our ability and propensity to ascribe collective beliefs into systems, institutions or concepts not only animates them, it gives them power.[1] The same holds true in how we accept the wonderment of money and the edifice of value, whether it is ascribed in physical form or digitally native. From the earliest prototypes of standardized units of exchange, stores of value and units of measure, whether they were used to track and barter by our ancestors or to hold up the post-war financial system, how people and the economy writ large interacts with money is as enduring a societal construct as ever.

Arguably, the rise of cryptocurrencies (most of which have been used for speculative gain as the market searched for a proverbial winner in truly decentralized digital assets erring on the side of bitcoin as a form of digital gold),

---

[1] Harari, Yuval, Noah, *Sapiens: A Brief History of Humankind,* Harper, February 10, 2015.

D. A. Disparte (✉)
Chief Strategy Officer at Circle, Washington, DC, USA
e-mail: ddisparte@riskcooperative.com

© The Author(s), under exclusive license to Springer Nature
Switzerland AG 2021
E. Kaili and D. Psarrakis (eds.), *Disintermediation Economics,*
https://doi.org/10.1007/978-3-030-65781-9_8

is a continuation of a process of collective belief systems, rather than something radically new. Afterall, it would stand to reason that a generation of people born into the Internet age with a smartphone in hand and accustomed to instant gratification (or settlement to import the concept into the world of payments and value transfer), would find analog, slow, expensive and opaque financial systems abhorrent. The 2008 financial crisis, which forestalled many a retirement and college savings aspiration, also demonstrated the fundamental imbalance of too-big-to-fail economic backstops, that socialized losses and privatized gains as countries threw trillions of dollars to prop up a faltering financial system.

The somewhat varnished origin story of cryptocurrencies holds a number of first principles that are as enduring in their ideals. This is especially true as blockchain records are designed to be permanent in their storage, creating opportunities for scarcity and uniqueness to exist in digital form. These ideals include concepts of self-sovereignty, ownership, control and rights-access empowering the end-user in a system rather than the intermediary or rent seeker. The darker version of this story has animated many regulatory and financial compliance concerns with cryptocurrencies. Namely that their opaque, anonymous, or pseudonymous nature gives the dark web a criminal thrift which has spurred a wave of online illicit activity, as insidious as election interference and as ubiquitous as ransomware or botnet and phishing attacks.

The truth and certainly the current state of play in the market is somewhat more nuanced and optimistic, given the number of well-regulated firms that are seeking permission rather than forgiveness in their plans for privately issued digital currencies or support of the asset class more generally. Moreover, as people conflate the rise of cryptocurrency with the rise in cybercrime, it is well-advised to remember that correlation does not equal causality and cyber-attacks often say more about the poor state of cyber hygiene and vulnerability, than the methods used to extract value.[2] Along these lines, by today's stringent regulatory and financial crime compliance standards, if an innovation called "cash" was proposed for regulatory approval it would likely be denied. This denial would cite the opacity and risk-prone nature of cash, along its ability to be a vector for spreading diseases in the context of the COVID-19 pandemic. Indeed, some countries resorted to physically laundering their cash to avoid the spread of disease. Others still, like the USA at the height of the pandemic had to exhort the public and banks to put coinage back into circulation due to scarcity. This, together with the growing

---

[2]Disparte, Dante, *WannaCry on Cyber Monday,* International Policy Digest, May 14, 2017.

trend among merchants and vendors to not accept cash due to its impracticalities and potential risks, calls for more payment optionality not less. Privately issued digital currencies are filling this global void for trusted, internet-native thrift, while the debate about CBDCs remains abstract.

Circulation in Code

The words *In God We Trust* are emblazoned on physical versions of US currency. To a new generation of users, the words *in code we trust* could mark the seal of value in digital currencies, assets and fundamental trust in technology. This, notwithstanding persistent global breaches and erosions or outright distortions of that trust. The rise of bitcoin and its stabilization as a permanent fixture in global financial markets has driven improvements in the virtual asset domain. Despite bitcoin's inherent price volatility, competitive dynamics and market demands for consumer protection and common operating standards have created a cottage industry of intermediation in a field that was supposed to shift autonomy to end-users and disintermediate traditional financial services.

In this vein, just like the earliest days of the formal banking system where gold and other precious cargo was ferried around the world on risky galleons and stagecoaches, the perennial threat of risk, caused the industry to harden into the structures we know (and often take for granted) today. If value can be stored in banks, on plastic cards, enshrined in metal or paper, among countless other forms, then why not in intangible, ethereal, internet-ready form? This question underpins the internet of value and the digitization of everything, including with the advent of privately issued stablecoins, the digitization of fiat currency itself. The growing boom of non-fungible tokens or NFTs, has created an entirely new asset class or a digital Veblen good exploiting the ability for blockchain to create digital scarcity.

Compressing Innovation

There is a maturation in the digital asset space that betrays its comparative infancy as the wave of fintech innovation takes hold of the world and shapes regulatory and public policy conversations. Companies and projects that have barely crossed a decade in age, are on the cusp of being more valuable than banks that have had a centuries' long head start, as well as all the protections and comforts afforded to too-big-to-fail industries, whether in the form of regulatory clarity, public backstops and capital buffers, or increasingly limited competition over time. This market compression cycle where upstart fintech's are challenging the entire financial services value chain, is now starting to see large, dominant global players emerge, who have amassed great wealth and a vast user base at the nexus of e-commerce, mobile money and, increasingly, the mass adoption of crypto.

Companies like PayPal in the USA, for example, have entered the digital currency market by announcing plans to support digital assets across their platforms. This will introduce on-ramps to digital currencies and assets to PayPal's more than 346 million users.[3] A proverbial blockchain-based applications layer in financial services now includes well-run and well-regulated firms, from the coterie of wallet providers (or virtual asset service providers (VASPs) in the parlance of international compliance bodies), to exchanges and market makers, among many others. While the industry is a little over ten years old, the last five years courtesy in no small measure to increasing regulatory clarity (and some glaring cases of basic risk management failures, like Canada's QuadrigaCX), has started to see world-class operators emerge.[4] The stratospheric initial public offering (IPO) of the crypto-native company, Coinbase, which paid homage to crypto's first principles of democratization and decentralization, opted for a direct listing and had no headquarters address in its filing. Coinbase's stock market debut at $85 billion in valuation, made the nine-year-old firm the most valuable exchange in the USA, despite other exchanges being around for hundreds of years.[5] Banking and high finance it would seem are coming off their bank holiday and entering the era of the always on, 24/7/365 internet of value.

Digital Numismatics

Stablecoins, as they are known courtesy of attempts to provide underlying asset backing, are designed to inherit the underlying price or value stability of the assets they reference. Like most waves of creative destructive innovation in a market, the early days of so-called stablecoins were anything but stable.[6] Courtesy of the ICO mania that was a frenzied, greed-filled bubble inflated

---

[3] Irrera, Anna, *PayPal to Allow Cryptocurrency Buying, Selling and Shopping on its Network*, Reuters, October 21, 2020.
[4] Disparte, Dante, *QuadrigaCX: How to Lose $140 Million in an Instant*, Forbes, February 5, 2019.
[5] Barry, Emily, *Coinbase Is Most Valuable U.S. Exchange after First Day of Trading*, Market Watch, April 14, 2021.
[6] Disparte, Dante, *Culling Unstable Coins: Crypto Correction or Market Crash?* Forbes, December 14, 2018.

by the issuance of all manners of "internet funny money" with a few credible solutions in the mix, produced a market correction in 2018 reminiscent of the dot com bubble of the late 90s. This market correction, which was given the moniker "cryptowinter" took a number of these utility tokens, stablecoins and other digitally minted instruments out of circulation and gave rise to a more exacting model (if punitive) for all the digital numismatists who saw the opportunity in auguring an era of programmable money—the veritable ultima Thule of the crypto-purists, who see the value in democratizing control in how people, send, spend, save and secure their money.

The difference between physical money and money in digital form is simply programmability and efficiency in conveying over long distances and in near real time. You cannot code a physical coin or bill to be "auto-executable", and never miss a payment for example. You cannot code physical species to liquidate an insurance claim parametrically in the event of a large-scale disaster where the physical banking system might fail.[7] And, lastly, you cannot execute low-cost micropayments, let alone convey value over long distances with the instantaneity, assurance and user control afforded by the internet to all forms of information and communication, but for the transfer of value.

Fintech entrepreneurs aim to exploit the value of digital transformation, which presupposes that the next instance of a solution or service is comparatively free compared to the first. Thus, the creation of infinitely new growth possibilities and lifting the constraints of traditional business models that are often confined by brick-and-mortar, fixed-lines or the limitations of tangible assets can be unlocked. The technologists that understood these dynamics did not only capture lasting first-mover advantages, they created entirely new categories of business and self-perpetuating ecosystems. It would stand to reason that their sights would eventually turn to the future of money and the movement of value.

Programmable Money

While the opportunity for programmable money remains of great interest to the public and private innovators and proponents of digital currencies, the practical reality is that the only way to unblock this value is through public–private collaboration. In some countries, this is being spurred through open banking requirements, in which basic access to the financial system

---

[7] Disparte, Dante, *Insurance: A Great Form of Protection, A Terrible Form of Liquidity*, Forbes, April 29, 2018.

is designed to be portable for the end-users in the system. In others, the approach is to lay down proverbial digital commons and fast payment networks designed for instant and often free settlement layers between banks and payment system operators. In others, particularly those countries that recognize the direction of travel around the world is increasingly cashless, the very two-tier banking system that is widely in use today must evolve. This evolution can support a safe and secure digital twin in the form of CBDCs, hybrid approaches or the coexistence of privately issued digital currencies, which after all is the dominant model for how most value-added money is circulated in the economy already.

The decline of physical cash in circulation is a sign of the increasing dependence on e-commerce and other forms of payment settlement, from ubiquitous card networks to the encroachment and merger of technology partnerships (such as Apple and Goldman Sachs powering the Apple Card), which have enabled vast (and growing) networks of contactless payments. With the backdrop of a global public health emergency buoyed by the COVID-19 pandemic, the deceleration of the use of physical money is underway. As obvious limitations of traditional money were exposed, including potential perils in spreading communicable diseases, new meaning was given to "money laundering" in which some countries resorted to physically washing bills.[8] In other cases, the use of cash was discouraged at the point of sale or because of scarcity of coinage or bills adding short supply to fears of infection.[9]

The challenges and limitations of physical money and how value is conveyed in a digital age were exasperated by the pandemic. Like many countries, including fortress nations like the USA, contemplated how to effectively deploy government-to-citizen payments to help stabilize the economy and shore up vulnerable households, the reality and vulnerability of a largely analog value transfer system was laid bare. Those inside the perimeter of payments could benefit from comparatively faster government support in the form of electronic funds transfers (EFT), while others waited for the proverbial "check in the mail" to arrive. This resulted in multi-billion dollars of loss, erroneous payments, and unclaimed checks.[10] An additional challenge in deploying this direct stimulus, was the lack of a universally accessible, open payment standard.

---

[8]Purdy, Chase, *China Is Literally Cleaning its Money to Stop the Spread of Coronavirus*, QZ, February 15, 2020.

[9]Heflin, Jay, *Mnuchin Asks Public to Spend Coins to East Shortage*, Washington Examiner, August 11, 2020.

[10]Crutsinger, Martin, *The US Sent $1.6 Billion in Stimulus Checks to Dead People – And About $500 Million Never Came Back*, Chicago Tribune, September 1, 2020.

The next generation of digital currencies built on public blockchain is filling this void and they should be embraced by public authorities not as a fringe innovation by crypto nativists, but as the core infrastructure for broadly raising prosperity. Such a system would have helped governments deploy a more focused, needs-based approach in disbursing money to the people who would need it the most. Instead, the USA opted to send $1,200 to the entire tax-paying population, irrespective of need.[11]

In the era of high-assurance technologies that can settle these types of population-scale payments at speed and without sacrificing auditability, it was unsurprising that calls for the launch of a digital dollar and the corresponding digital wallets grew louder in the USA (notwithstanding the fact that dollar digital currencies and open wallets were already widely accessible at the time as free-market innovations). So much so, that the initial draft language of the CARES Act, which triggered the $2.2 trillion first wave of economic intervention to stave off economic paralysis or ruin, called for the creation and issuance of a digital dollar.[12] How this is done and what type of public-private infrastructure needs to be laid down may be unclear depending on the country, but the need and case for change in digital numismatics is now a mainstay in the fintech, regtech and traditional banking sectors. The voices calling for prudent deployment of new approaches for the movement of money and digital issuance of currency are increasingly prominent and arguably inside the system, rather than from crypto-utopians or anarchists.[13]

Fintechnocrats

The promise of fintech, a coined term denoting the marriage of finance and technology, will bring with it a reduction of complexity, friction and costs, without sacrificing quality or compliance—or so its proponents would argue. Yet, like all waves of rapid innovation with start-ups and innovators tinkering on the edges of mature, heavily regulated industries, there are bound to be risks and teachable moments. Just because you can do something with code that otherwise takes thousands of people to execute, does not always mean you should. By the same token, mature industries and

---

[11] 116th U.S. Congress, *CARES Act*, Introduced on January 24, 2019.
[12] Brett, Jason, *Congress to Hold Hearing on 'Digital Dollar' Options for Possible Future Stimulus Payments*, Forbes, June 8, 2020.
[13] Various Authors, *The Digital Dollar Project: Exploring a US CBDC*, Digital Dollar Project (https://www.digitaldollarproject.org/exploring-a-us-cbdc), May 2020.

public services, simply cannot extend their perimeter of coverage and inclusion, without embracing digital transformation. In order to balance the risks and opportunities promised by the fintech revolution, which is linked to the regtech, insurtech, medtech (and so many other "techs"), will be the emergence fintechnocrats to help pave the way for a balanced approach.

On balance, a fintech effort must strive to achieve regulatory approval, basic risk management, which can be especially perilous with novel technologies, customer adoption and protection, among other standards. When it comes to projects involving so-called exponential technologies like blockchain, cryptocurrencies and high-frequency trading, as examples, there are many lessons that have chastened early movers. This demonstrates the need for bridge builders between the largely "analog" worlds of financial services, regulation and financial stability, and the often utopian worlds of entirely self-sovereign control of financial services with no guard rails. These need not be treated as opposing forces, interests or objectives, but rather areas warranting equal treatment if the opportunities of fintech are to be managed along with the potential perils.

The unfortunate case of QuadrigaCX in Canada is a teachable moment. While the ultimate outcome of this case had less to do with the underlying technology or virtual assets, the comparative risk management immaturity, due diligence and outright fraud caused more than 115,000 investors on the cryptocurrency platform to lose more than $190 million.[14] In a case like this one, what recourse should customers have? How do you hold parties accountable in such an amorphous service model? How do appropriate, risk-adjusted regulations emerge that do not trade-off innovation for consumer protection? Insidiously these protective instincts may lead to the maintenance of consumer protection rules that "protect" consumers so much, they are left on the margins of the financial system altogether or starved of choice.

Fintechnocrats (and forensic accountants) are often left picking up the detritus of these types of market and management failures are the ones trying to strike the right balance between risk and reward. There is a fine line between the needed innovations to make financial services more accessible, affordable and fit for purpose in the twenty-first century and regulatory overreach that favours incumbents. The job of ensuring regulatory regimes are not only up to par, but that they are harmonized around the world in order to avoid a race to the bottom arbitrage that has made aspects of traditional financial services a porous, shadowy market where bad actors can thrive, rests

---

[14] Deschamps, Tara, *Crypto Exchange Quadriga was a Fraud and Founder and Founder was Running a Ponzi Scheme, OSC Report Finds*, CBC, June 11, 2020.

on the work, minds and outputs of the fintechnocrats and responsible fintech players working in free markets.

Looking further back in time, the case of Knight Capital, a high-frequency trading firm that was once thought to be best-of-breed, was brought to its knees by a "rogue" trading algorithm that bought positions the company could not afford.[15] In this case, in a matter of minutes, Knight Capital had to cease its operations and was sold for salvage value in part because of the excess need for speed and the deployment of unchecked technology. Here too, there are teachable lessons about the boundaries of financial technology and appropriate regulations, as well as checks and balances in a marketplace. The ever-present spectre of flash crashes or other technological risks emerging in the world's trading platforms is a reminder that complex systems tend to fail in complex ways.[16] Here too, the necessary human interventions at both the managerial levels and the market oversight and regulatory levels are key to ensuring innovation can continue apace, while allowing standards and duties of care to catch up. The cadre of fintechnocrats standing watch, meticulously documenting the evolution of financial services and how compliance and regulation should evolve to make important contributions in market outcomes is essential—even if this work is perceived to be onerous and slow by impatient fintech entrepreneurs.

A fintechnocrat, a coined term marrying financial technology with a technocrat, is not meant to be a pejorative term, but rather a *nom de guerre* for an emerging class of professionals conversant in code, conduct and in the application of emerging technologies in mature financial services. If the promise of digital currencies, as one example, is ever to be fully achieved, it will be owed in no small measure to this group of global professionals who are diligently pouring over every white paper, consultation document and business plan detailing how the application of technology can fulfill many unmet promises and needs in financial services. In order to prove that financial innovation, inclusion and compliance are not competing objectives, fintechnocrats will need to continue following a trust but verify approach. They must also take heed, however, that the consequences of being a fintech laggard has potentially dire national security and economic competitiveness implications as the future of money is not an abstraction in many regions in the world and the threat of being left behind is very real.[17]

---

[15] Popper, Nathaniel, *Knight Capital says Trading Glitch Cost it $440 Million*, The New York Times, August 2, 2012.

[16] Disparte, Dante, and Franzetti, Andres, *Replacing a Broken Model*, Risk Management, vol. 60 no. 7, September 2013.

[17] Matthews, Barbara, C., and Tran, Huang, *Advanced Economies Under Pressure in the Central Bank Digital Currency Race*, Atlantic Council, New Atlanticist, August 25, 2020.

Lest the world of fintech innovation moves upmarket favouring large firms or projects, fintechnocrats have a unique obligation to develop and adhere to technology neutrality and a risk-weighted, activity-based approach to regulation. For example, many in the banking sector have long advocated for a "same risk, same rules" model as a first principle for allowing fintech competition onto the banking playing field. For their part, fintech developers must seek permission rather than forgiveness, especially when they are compelled to "tinker" with heavily personal, delicate and regulated matters like people's money. The fintechnocrats, for their part, must also ensure that activity-based, technologically neutral regulations do not cluster all digital assets, cryptocurrencies or stablecoins into the same category. Rather they must contemplate the economic behaviour, security and intent of digital assets in formulating new rules that enable innovation and compliance to coexist.

In short, no one gains by running unchecked science projects with an economy, which is why one of the favoured models of fintechnocrats is to put innovative start-up projects into sandboxes or observatories for regulators to formulate appropriate rules. This model is used in more than 25 countries around the world but may not be fit for purpose for all projects and could potentially imperil intellectual capital or tie up launch timelines in otherwise hyper-competitive markets—starving ideas of oxygen and entrepreneurs of capital, their lifeblood. For this latter category, the adoption of consensus-based multi-stakeholder pre-licensing reviews or regulatory and supervisory colleges are a favoured model, but this too can quickly devolve into regulatory theatre and yield no real market outcomes begging the question: if novel approaches to money and payments are risky, what about the risks of status quo? A world with more than three billion people on the margins of the banking system is a great source of global risk, as is the single point of failure financial infrastructure, emblematic in the Equifax breach, that imperils the privacy of entire populations.[18]

A Thousand Flowers Blooming

If the wave of technology innovation has created tech titans, and the era of bitcoin and virtual assets has created blockchain billionaires, appropriately drawing the line of public and regulatory interest is in the hands of the fintechnocrats. This group of professionals are also the custodians of work

---

[18]Disparte, Dante, *The Equifax Breach and a Lifetime of Vulnerability*, Huffington Post, September 9, 2017.

underway at more than 90% of the world's central banks, which are evaluating the promise and perils of circulating a digital twin of their national currencies.[19] For some countries, this is no longer theory or a monetary abstraction, as they move into the production or circulation phase of their digital currency projects. The most ambitious among these in terms of scope and likelihood to reach hundreds of millions if not billions of people as an export capability are the efforts underway by the People's Bank of China (PBOC), via the Digital Currency Electronic Payment or DCEP initiative.[20]

Most of the geoeconomics and geopolitical debates on the future of CBDCs are heralding the end of the US dollar and dollar dominance as a global reserve currency. The most oft cited reason is that China's ambitions are to extend its technological and digital currency influence via the Belt and Road Initiative (BRI) making the Renminbi or Yuan and export product. While this may be the case, the arguments negate the fact that US dollar is already enshrined in billions (and growing) of dollar digital currencies in circulation built on open blockchain infrastructure and across blockchain platforms. Collectively these dollar digital currencies have safely and compliantly transacted trillions in payments over the open internet, while broadly preserving global macroprudential and compliance standards. This is a breakthrough in the future of money and payments and one of the most important innovations, which is calling the US home. These platforms enjoy budding partnerships with global merchant services firms, credit card companies and the banking system itself, ostensibly reaching global scale. That a free market is building digitally native financial services firms, who are bringing the banking system along for the ride to the future.

The world has clearly entered a thousand flowers blooming phase of digital currency innovation, evidenced by the non-stop annual cadence of conferences and Zoom events either glamorizing or fearing the future of money. Merely digitizing the existing perimeter of payments would not yield globally desired social outcomes on financial inclusion. If basic access to banking and payments is a human right, there is much work to be done in order to reach the more the three billion people who are on the margins and lower the cost of basic financial access. Many analyse the risks of breakthrough fintech innovations, blockchain and digital currencies, but not nearly enough is said about the risks of doing nothing for financial inclusion. While part of this

---

[19] Boar, Codruta, et al., *Impending Arrival: A Sequel on Central Bank Digital Currency*, BIS Papers no. 107, Bank for International Settlements, Monetary and Economics Department, January 2020.
[20] Hoffman, Samantha, et al., *The Flipside of China's Central Bank Digital Currency*, Australian Strategic Policy Institute, International Cyber Policy Centre, October 14, 2020.

financial inclusion challenge is explained by the lack of evolution and acceptance of new forms of identification and verification in financial services (e.g. digital identities and electronic know your customer or step ladder e-KYC standards), there are also gaps in how so-called de-risking is carried out in global financial services levying a heavy penalty on the poor.[21]

Double-Blind Digital Currencies

Privacy, compliance and financial innovation should not be at odds with each other. This includes commitments to enshrining human rights and values into the code, conduct and governance of new forms of money, whether publicly or privately issued along with the rails on which they will move. Critically, these rails should not be proprietary or closed-loop systems, which risk devolving internet-level money into the financial equivalent of airline loyalty miles masquerading as digital currencies. This is an area of opportunity to hardwire certain standards and value systems into new innovations and the ongoing work among global bodies, such as the Financial Stability Board (FSB), the Financial Action Task Force (FATF), which has stood up a virtual asset contact group in order to bridge a conversation between private and public interests for financial integrity and compliance, are key to achieving a harmonized regulatory standard.[22]

As the prospect of digital currencies coexisting from both private and public issuance gradually becomes a reality, the competitive differentiation of stablecoins, CBDCs and other hybrid iterations may begin to narrow. Today, digital currencies aim to differentiate themselves on the stability of their underlying assets, from which they counter the deleterious effects of other forms of hyper-volatile cryptocurrencies. As more and more central banks weigh the merits of digitizing their fiat currencies, the question of how to navigate monetary digital transformation in some respect hinges less on economic safety and soundness, and more on consumer choice, digital wallet optionality and privacy. This last area may be the next frontier for digital currency proponents to fully describe. The temperament among central bankers to not jump into the perilous and privacy eroding "all-seeing" state of government-led CBDC efforts is laudable. This is especially true as a new era of responsible free-market actors are scaling trusted, compliant and

---

[21] Disparte, Dante, *Could Digital Currencies Make Being Poor Less Costly*, Harvard Business Review, August 4, 2020.

[22] Various Authors, *Regulation, Supervision and Oversight of "Global Stablecoin" Arrangements*, Financial Stability Board, Final Report and High Level Recommendations, October 13, 2020.

secure asset-referenced digital currencies on transparent public blockchains that preserve monetary policy and result in no new money creation or fractionalization. Critically, as regulatory harmonization and clarity improve, these operators are also well within the orbit of central banks and other regulators.

On the one hand, fully entering the retail layer of digital currency issuance and management may be a line too far for many of the world's central banks of which a preponderance are contemplating some degree of technological experimentation with their national thrift. For others, the pathway to launch a CBDC is clearly paved through making wholesale applications more efficient. The real breakthrough, at least in order to unlock the true potential of open, low-friction digital money and all the cost savings, empowerment and other advantages it may present, is to figure out how to embed the openness, privacy and trust that traditional fiat currencies issued by trusted, independent central banks enjoy—all of this, but in digital form. This is a difficult proposition for the public sector to countenance, especially since one of the most powerful attributes of physical species is that it is the ultimate privacy-preserving payment instrument (one of the reasons it is the favoured tender for illicit actors). Can privacy at scale coexist with publicly issued digital currencies?

The best approach is to err on the side of public–private collaboration with digital currencies to not only unlock an open and competitive space where private sector operators, digital wallets, banks and other providers can differentiate their offerings. In this structure the public sector preserves the two-tiered banking system, monetary policy and guaranteeing the full faith and credit of all tender, public, private and digital in use in an economy. With an often checkered citizen experience when it comes to abusive states, the next hurdle to overcome is how to ensure that digital currencies are not misused to pry into people's lawful transactions, their identity or location and other areas that should be protected as first principles. To the right of lawful, the use of money in free societies should not be encumbered by a "terms of use agreement" or other forms of censorship.

The way to achieve this standard where privacy is enjoyed in a digital currency as a design principle is to have a "double-blind" digital currency issued by a central bank or under its purview, which a growing number of digital currencies are already achieving. This would not be for the direct use of consumers and businesses, but rather this digital mint would flow through an open and competitive wallet environment. Beyond requisite know your customer screening, which in a domestic setting is the first line of defense and entry of the banking system, users will be able to have liberal access to an open, user-directed payment environment that should not only be privacy-preserving, it should offer a level of technological encryption and pseudonymity akin to cash. Risk-based payment thresholds established on a stepladder basis depending on the financial magnitude of a transaction might trigger further checks and validation, not dissimilar to the current banking system.

A major improvement offered by blockchain-based payment systems, however, compared to traditional transactions, is that it would be materially easier to identify suspicious patterns or activities in the aggregate. This would increase the cost (and transparency) for illicit actors to leverage this type of public–private digital currency infrastructure, while not penalizing the most legitimate actors in an economy. A lower cost, open digital currency infrastructure of this nature would lower the barriers of user participation, improving financial inclusion. Thus, increasing the costs and likelihood bad actors would get caught, opening entirely new business models and forms of economic participation. The advent of digital currencies is not about cash, credit or other forms of displacement and competition in an economy. Rather, these forms of monetary innovation have more to do with optionality as complements to existing forms of money and payment, rather than as their competitors.

To add an extra dimension of privacy preservation, these "double-blind" digital currency projects should also enjoy statutory forms of protection and other public guarantees, eventually attaining the status of digital legal tender. The risk management and compliance burden, much like existing banks and payment system operators, should exist at the private sector layer and not encumber public sector monetary policy nor move central banks into an area of operation beyond their core competency. Simply put, blockchain and cryptocurrencies are not nearly as disruptive to the two-tiered banking system, from whence monetary policy is conveyed, as the advent of CBDCs. If central banks want to disrupt their banking, payments and financial systems, the launch of a centrally managed, privacy eroding CBDC is the best way to do it.

Digital Currencies in Circulation

There are more than 4,800 digital currencies, assets, or tokens in circulation today with a combined market cap of over $2 trillion for the top 200 coins in circulation (with bitcoin representing the lion's sharing of value).[23] Of these, a small fraction can be classified as stablecoins or high-standard, high-assurance virtual assets where the insidious issue of buyer or receiver's remorse would not be present due to value fluctuation or the risk of "vaporware". Now that regulators, including central banks and enforcement agencies are making their low levels of tolerance for fraud, circumvention of rules and expectations of basic consumer protections known, it is likely that the "culling of unstable coins" will continue to gravitate towards few trusted assets. The closer proximity these assets get to "zero-risk" central bank custody, either through stabilization, reserve management and liquidity mechanisms, or through direct custody or interface inside the regulated two-tier banking system, the better in terms protecting public interest and sovereignty over monetary policy, while letting the internet of value thrive.

The advent of privately issued digital currencies, which follow the sheer volume and operating standards of how money is moved and issued today, will likely enhance the two-tier banking system helping to complete it, rather than compete with it. An environment such as the one espoused by Sweden's central bank the Sveriges Riksbank, in which an eKrona can be issued under the oversight of public authorities while promoting a widely interoperable and vigorously competitive "app layer" or digital wallet and banking services environment offers compelling insights into how even in a cashless society, well-harnessed technology does not erode the public interest, but rather enhances it. Indeed, as the COVID-19 pandemic has shown, the lack of payment optionality and ubiquitous internet-ready rails for how value is transferred (whether across the public–private lines or in the form of peer-to-peer user-directed payments), is clearly an area of domestic and international financial vulnerability.

Competition or Completion?

While much has been said about the potential risks of digital currencies and the distortion or circumvention they may pose to the rules-based financial system. Not nearly enough has been said about the challenges posed by the status quo, in which fundamental building blocks of fast, secure, democratized access to banking and internet-ready payment services leave a lot to be expected. This is true in a domestic setting in many countries or regions around the world, including those that boast competitive economies and

---

[23] CoinMarketCap website: https://coinmarketcap.com/2/ (accessed, April 24, 2020).

banking sectors. This challenge, however, is much more pronounced when it comes to emerging and developing countries and the cross-border use cases for digital currencies or fintech innovations that purport to offer greater speed, access and lower costs, thus helping drive a wedge on pernicious rates of financial exclusion.

Through this lens, digital currencies do not pose competition to the financial system, but rather may represent a way of completing unfinished work. This unfinished work has excluded billions of people and exacted the highest cost from those who can least afford it for even basic financial access or services. This work cannot be meaningfully completed if the premise of being fully banked presupposes the existence and ubiquity of brick-and-mortar infrastructure. As is shown by the early days of mobile money networks such as M-Pesa in Kenya, among others, even in environments with scant banking access the marriage of technology, finance and regulatory oversight can drive step-change improvements in rates of financial access.[24] This much holds true in the rise of China's fintech and e-commerce behemoths, Ant Financial, Alibaba and WeChat Pay, among others, that are working to fill a void of traditional banking, lending and payment services, among other areas in the financial value chain.[25]

Scaling the Walled Gardens

With the prospect of central banks entering the digital transformation tide, the case for completing a system will be made clear. The most likely outcome will be public sector oversight of monetary policy and digital currencies in circulation and private-sector competition for the use and movement of money, irrespective of its physical or ephemeral for—a veritable convergence of physical and digital legal tender. The most meaningful pursuit should be breaking down the walled gardens of even highly efficient and large-scale payment systems that not only operate on proprietary technologies and protocols, they often do so at the expense of small businesses, merchants, banks and, ultimately, end-users in these systems. Insidiously, the too-big-too-fail nature of some of these platforms and companies, privatizes gains and socializes losses, while reaching nothing close to population-scale or public utility-like access, notwithstanding taxpayer underwriting. This general lack

---

[24] Reuters Staff, *M-Pesa Helps Drive up Kenyans' Access to Financial Services – Study*, Reuters, April 3, 2019.
[25] Unknown, *What Ant Group's IPO Says About the Future of Finance*, The Economist, October 10, 2020.

of interoperability and the cost for the "convenience" of executing an out of network or off banking hours transaction introduces a "death by 1,000 cuts" model, often takes days or weeks to settle and subjects both ends of a payment or transaction to friction, fees and, in many cases, risk.

While policy and regulatory directives such as those espoused by open banking, free basic banking rules or instant settlement networks, can address sources of friction in how value is transferred, the reality is the technology stack used by the most of the world's largest payment networks has not had a protocol-level upgrade in decades. The advent of blockchain technology and the implied trust, record keeping and traceability of digital currencies offer the suspension of long-held norms that the only safe payment in a financial system requires often costly and potentially perilous forms of intermediation, especially when considering the scorecard on illicit activity that flows through cash-based or many bank-based transactions. The opacity, competitive nature and multi-jurisdictional approach to combating illicit finance in traditional networks would also benefit from an update at the core protocol level for how value is transferred in a safe, secure and compliant manner in the internet age.

Removing the penalty on the poor from de-risking activities, which are an important set of requirements for anti-money laundering and countering the financing of terrorist activities, among others, can at once lower the cost of services, without lowering standards of security. This is one of the most powerful attributes of open blockchain-based networks, which even in cases where there is a perfectly decentralized network, such as the bitcoin blockchain, the ability to carry out real-time transaction monitoring is a game changer for financial integrity efforts. The recent Twitter hack, which compromised high-profile accounts and sought ransom payments in bitcoin and the 2015 WannaCry ransomware dragnet, which hit more than 150 countries over three days, are but two examples of how the value of a transparent transaction ledger enabled law enforcement to verifiably "follow the money"[26].

While many of the use cases that are heralded by the era of programmable money describe what can be done with the digital asset itself. High-assurance and novel approaches to financial intelligence, integrity and privacy preservation (prerequisites for mass adoption of virtual assets), over time will be heralded as the true breakthroughs. Marrying this with interoperability and breaking the chains of end-user financial lock-in effects courtesy of proprietary financial technologies with high barriers to exit, will be seen as the

---

[26] Post, Kollen, *Twitter Hack Shows That Crypto Is Easier to Investigate Than Fiat, Say Industry Law Experts,* Cointelegraph, August 4, 2020.

other lasting difference from the era of blockchain experimentation with the movement of value.

Geoeconomics and Geopolitics

How or by whom digital currencies are issued, provided of course they meet basic standards of solidity, liquidity and security, will matter much less than the underlying rails that securely transfer value. The countries, companies and coalitions that develop trust in this infrastructure, irrespective of the technology stack or standards, will be the lasting contributors to the future of money. It is critically important that the right level of regulatory compliance, alignment, public license and value systems are built into the designs of these new systems, lest their rise to prominence in the global financial landscape will pose new sources of risk, distortion or circumvention.

The fact remains, blockchain-based financial systems ought to give ne'er-do-wells no place to hide and ought to benefit from the collective cybersecurity and operating defenses implied by distributed or entirely decentralized infrastructure. Indeed, when compared to much of the infrastructure employed in the traditional financial services sector, which tends to funnel into a single source of failure systems or databases, distributed ledger technologies offer transformational gains in cybersecurity, consumer privacy, redundancy and operating continuity. This robustness alone argues for the deployment of blockchains across a range of essential services, from identity and authentication, to land titling, insurance and, in the broadest sense, financial services, which continue to labour under insidious rates of mistrust, opacity and some fundamental system vulnerabilities. Large-scale data breaches such as in the credit reporting arena, have reached population scale. Groups the size of the US labour force are caught up by these breaches, amplified the twin vulnerabilities of alphanumeric personal identifiers such as the US social security number (often granted to people at birth), and vast and vulnerable honeypot databases that hold personally identifiable information and are the gateways to accessing the financial system and credit, which makes people and their personal data the product.[27]

While the spectre of risk borne by those so fortunate to have won the birth country or postcode lottery to have access to financial services as a birthright differs from the risks faced by the world's 1.7 billion unbanked people, the reality is that the world has an imperative to improve digital

---

[27]Disparte, Dante, *The Equifax Breach and the Case for Digital Identity,* Forbes, October 2, 2017.

financial commons. If access to financial services is a human right, then the first principles spurring the wave of fintech innovation (especially those espoused by crypto-purists who argue for the democratization of value and self-sovereignty) are powerful ideals that should set the standard for future innovations and projects in the digital currency arena. Striking the right balance between innovation, compliance and inclusion will have to reframe these three objectives not as trade-offs or sources of friction, but rather as co-equal priorities.

When it comes to money, banking, and financial services as basic as payments, the veritable bottom rung of the ladder of economic mobility, the direction of travel is digital. This is especially true because the rest of the world's traditional financial infrastructure has reached a point of diminishing returns. There are hundreds of billions in investor capital and trillions in economic activity waiting patiently for the regulatory certainty to unlock a wave of responsible fintech innovation around the world. As more and more regulators, public authorities and politicians begin to balance the promise and perils augured by the advent of digital currencies, the prospects of regulatory harmonization is also within reach. It would seem digital currencies have not only come of age, but they are also here to stay. What remains is to ensure appropriate balancing between the unique upside these innovations represent, especially when it comes to enhancing user control in what can be characterized as the 4S' of payments, namely how we spend, send, save and secure our money, with the potential downsides.

Risk always follows breakthrough innovations. When it comes to risk, the last decade of digital asset innovation has had its fair share of losses, near misses, fraud and epic 101-level risk management and compliance failures. From the ICO bubble bursting, to the many lapses of digital fiduciary obligations, to the constant reminders that the long-arm of the law will exert control over ignorance of rules and basic consumer protections, digital currency proponents can now see a path where technology-neutral, same risk, same rules regulations are no longer anathema to lowering friction and increasing user control in financial services. We should all be optimistic of what the future of money can bring and realistic that the future of money is now.

9

Crypto-Assets, Distributed Ledger Technologies and Disintermediation in Finance: Overcoming Impediments to Scaling: A View from the EU

Elisabeth Noble

Introduction

Over the last decade, applications of distributed ledger technologies (DLT) and crypto-assets have been increasingly observed in the European Union (EU).[1] However, regulatory fragmentation and legal uncertainty have dampened levels of investment and limited scaling cross-border. This chapter reflects on the key challenges and goes on to consider initiatives intended to facilitate the scaling-up of DLT and crypto-asset applications in the EU while mitigating effectively the risks.

---

[1] For an overview of DLT and crypto-asset developments see, for example, the publications of the Cambridge Centre for Alternative Finance, including the annual global benchmarking studies on crypto-assets: https://www.jbs.cam.ac.uk/faculty-research/centres/alternative-finance/publications/.

The views expressed in this paper those of the author and should not be taken to represent those of the European Banking Authority (EBA) or to state EBA policy. Neither the EBA nor any person acting on its behalf may be held responsible for the use to which information contained in this paper may be put or for any errors which, despite careful preparation and checking, may appear.

E. Noble (✉)
European Banking Authority, Paris, France
e-mail: Elisabeth.Noble@eba.europa.eu

Part I: In Search of Clarity and Consistency: One Application, One Set of Rules?

From a technological perspective, successful experimentation and pilot projects have demonstrated the reliability and potential utility of DLT in multiple financial sector use cases, such as the issuance and settlement of bonds and other securities, the creation and management of crypto-assets, derivatives transactions, cross-border payments and trade finance.[2] However, technological success is not by itself sufficient to guarantee technological transformation. Instead, compliance and legal teams must respond satisfactorily to questions such as *"what are the legal risks?"*, *"how will this be viewed by the supervisor?"*, *"do we need another licence?"* and *"can we do this cross-border?"* in order to secure a green light for investment. For firms seeking to roll out DLT and crypto-asset applications in EU Member States these questions will not have been easy to answer in recent years due to challenges in reconciling emerging technologies with existing EU and national regulatory and supervisory approaches. Variations from one jurisdiction to another will have also posed further complications for those firms seeking to scale up their applications cross-border.

The reconciliation of emerging technology use cases with existing regulatory and supervisory approaches has also posed challenges for EU financial regulators and supervisors. In general, financial regulation and supervision should not prefer or prevent the adoption of a specific technology but where activities present similar risks, regardless of the technology used, they should be subject to similar regulation and supervision (technological neutrality and the "same risk, same rule" principle).[3] However, increased market experimentation with DLT and crypto-asset applications has exposed inconsistencies

---

[2] The EU Blockchain Observatory & Forum issues regular publications highlighting market developments, including use cases in the EU financial services sector: https://www.eublockchainforum.eu/. Industry associations such as the Association for Financial Markets in Europe (AFME) and European Banking Federation (EBF) also issue regular publications summarising market developments.

[3] For an overview of the challenges in achieving technological neutrality in practice, see the March 2020 speech of José Manuel Campa (the Chairperson of the European Banking Authority) at the fourth annual conference on 'FinTech and Digital Innovation: Delivering for the Future': https://eba.europa.eu/calendar/jos%C3%A9-manuel-campa-delivers-keynote-speech-4th-annual-conference-%E2%80%98fintech-and-digital. The principle of technological neutrality is explored in the December 2019 report of the European Commission's Expert Group on Regulatory Obstacles to Financial Innovation: https://ec.europa.eu/info/publications/191113-report-expert-group-regulatory-obstacles-financial-innovation_en.

in the application and interpretation of EU and national law and demonstrated a need for clarifications of, and in some cases changes to, regulatory and supervisory approaches.[4]

In this part we outline five key challenges with which firms, regulators and supervisors have had to grapple and which have informed initiatives intended to mitigate risk and facilitate responsible experimentation with, and the cross-border scaling of, DLT and crypto-asset applications in the EU (see Part 2—a Digital Finance Strategy for Europe).

Challenge 1: Establishing a Dialogue—Building a Culture of Openness to Experimentation

Following the emergence of so-called cryptocurrencies in 2008, regulators and supervisors in the EU initially focussed their efforts on mitigating money laundering risks and consumer detriment, notably with the European Supervisory Authorities (ESAs)[5] issuing warnings to EU consumers and financial institutions about the risks posed by virtual currencies and advising on actions to strengthen the EU framework for anti-money laundering (AML) and counter-financing of terrorism (CFT).[6]

Against this background, firms seeking to pilot DLT and crypto-asset applications within the EU financial sector reported that they initially encountered varying levels of openness towards experimentation and challenges in obtaining early steers about possible supervisory acceptance and compliance expectations.[7] As DLT and crypto-asset applications began to

---

[4]For examples, see the January 2019 reports of the European Banking Authority (EBA) and European Securities and Markets Authority (ESMA) on, respectively, crypto-assets https://eba.europa.eu/sites/default/documents/files/documents/10180/2545547/67493daa-85a8-4429-aa91-e9a5ed880684/EBA%20Report%20on%20crypto%20assets.pdf?retry=1 and initial coin offerings and crypto-assets: https://www.esma.europa.eu/sites/default/files/library/esma50-157-1391_crypto_advice.pdf.

[5]The ESAs were established following the (2008) global financial crisis with a view to strengthening supervision of the EU financial sector. The ESAs comprise the European Banking Authority (EBA), the European Insurance and Occupational Pensions Authority (EIOPA) and the European Securities and Markets Authority (ESMA). For further background on the establishment of the ESAs see: https://www.europarl.europa.eu/factsheets/en/sheet/84/europaisches-system-der-finanzaufsicht-esfs-.

[6]For information about the actions taken by the ESAs, see section 1.1 of the European Banking Authority's January 2019 report on crypto-assets: https://eba.europa.eu/sites/default/documents/files/documents/10180/2545547/67493daa-85a8-4429-aa91-e9a5ed880684/EBA%20Report%20on%20crypto%20assets.pdf?retry=1.

[7]For an overview of some of the challenges faced by firms in seeking to experiment with and launch DLT applications see this session summary from the April 2019 EUROFI in Bucharest: https://www.eurofi.net/wp-content/uploads/2019/11/dlt-and-digital-tokens_opportunities-and-challenges_bucharest_april2019.pdf.

gain traction in a wider set of use cases and started to demonstrate real potential for efficiency gains (e.g. in the context of trade finance, cross-border payments and the trade and post-trade settings), regulators and supervisors started to augment their approach.

Notably, and against a wider background of accelerating technological innovation in the EU financial sector, many supervisors established innovation facilitators (typically in the form of regulatory sandboxes[8] and innovation hubs[9]) to provide greater proximity with the industry to enable a more open and real-time dialogue about the opportunities and risks presented by novel technological applications in the financial sector.

These opportunities for closer dialogue via innovation facilitators are much welcomed by industry, but challenges remain. First, when engaging with supervisors via innovation facilitators communications tend to be bilateral, reflecting traditional approaches to the design of access points for innovation facilitators (typically, telephone lines, online portals and application processes operated by supervisory authorities). Second, of course supervisors express views as regards the application and interpretation of the regulatory perimeter and supervisory measures applicable in the Member State concerned. This means that a firm seeking to roll out a DLT solution cross-border may need to engage separately with supervisory authorities via their respective innovation facilitators, potentially receiving from each authority rather different steers as to acceptability of the application and supervisory expectations (see further Challenge 3).[10]

To help address these challenges, measures are now in place in the EU to help facilitate greater cross-border cooperation and coordination between

---

[8]'Regulatory sandboxes' are schemes that enable firms to test, pursuant to a specific testing plan agreed and monitored by a dedicated function of the competent authority, innovative financial products, financial services or business models. For further information about regulatory sandboxes in the EU, see the January 2019 joint ESA report: https://eba.europa.eu/esas-publish-joint-report-on-regulatory-sandboxes-and-innovation-hubs. For a list of regulatory sandboxes currently operational in the EU, see the webpages of the European Forum for Innovation Facilitators (EFIF): https://esas-joint-committee.europa.eu/efif/innovation-facilitators-in-the-eu.

[9]'Innovation hubs' provide a dedicated point of contact for firms to raise enquiries with competent authorities on FinTech-related issues and to seek non-binding guidance on regulatory and supervisory expectations, including licensing requirements. For further information, see the links available in the previous endnote.

[10]For a further discussion of this issue, see section 3 of the January 2019 joint-ESA report: https://eba.europa.eu/esas-publish-joint-report-on-regulatory-sandboxes-and-innovation-hubs. See too the Terms of Reference of the European Forum for Innovation Facilitators (EFIF): https://esas-joint-committee.europa.eu/efif/efif-homepage.

innovation facilitators via the establishment of the European Forum for Innovation Facilitators (EFIF).[11] The EFIF provides a platform for supervisors to meet regularly to share experiences from engagement with firms through innovation facilitators, to share technological expertise and to reach common views on the regulatory treatment of innovative products, services and business models, thereby promoting multilateral discussion and consistency in supervisory approach towards applications of innovative technologies in the EU financial sector.

However, a common framework for cross-border experimentation monitoring is not yet in place and firms continue to have to engage with supervisors on a largely bilateral basis, potentially slowing down experimentation and roll-out of applications cross-border. Second, and crucially, although supervisors can exercise existing levers for proportionality in the context of the operation of regulatory sandboxes, they cannot use their powers to disapply regulatory requirements mandated under EU law.[12] This may mean that some potential technological applications cannot be tested, even under tightly controlled sandbox conditions, because of technical breaches of EU law; yet without the opportunity to test the case for regulatory change may not be borne out (a so-called "chicken and egg" situation). Finally, prior to the coming into force of an EU-wide approach (see further Part 2), challenges continue to arise from variations in the approach to regulating and supervising DLT and crypto-asset applications as explored below.

Challenge 2: Squaring the Circle: Traditional Intermediary and Process Requirements and Potential New Alternatives

The body of EU financial services law evolves continuously, tracking and in some cases even facilitating, the disintermediation of financial services from a relatively limited to a much broader range of market participants, and new business models and delivery mechanisms for financial services. For example, changes to the regulatory framework have enabled a disintermediation of some types of financial service, notably payment services,[13] and

---

[11] The EFIF was established further to the January 2019 joint ESA report: https://eba.europa.eu/esas-publish-joint-report-on-regulatory-sandboxes-and-innovation-hubs. The webpage of the EFIF is accessible here: https://esas-joint-committee.europa.eu/efif/efif-homepage.
[12] For further information, see section 2 of the January 2019 joint ESA report: https://eba.europa.eu/esas-publish-joint-report-on-regulatory-sandboxes-and-innovation-hubs.
[13] See Directive 2007/64/EC (the first Payment Services Directive) and Directive (EU) 2015/2366 (PSD2). Other notable measures include the Electronic Money Directive (Directive 2009/110/EC).

market forces have prompted a rise in activity by "other financial intermediaries", including those carrying out lending activity pursuant to schemes of national regulation.[14]

Taking account of the different consistent parts of the EU financial services sector, EU financial services law assumes, or in some cases even requires, the use of specific intermediaries (e.g. a central securities depository) or procedures (e.g. book entry) for risk management. However, applications of DLT may offer alternative processes for effective risk management. In this context, firms, regulators and supervisors face the challenge of determining whether these processes are capable of being reconciled with requirements under existing EU (and in some cases national) law, or whether clarifications or legislative changes are needed in order to achieve a fully technological neutral and harmonized approach in light of these technological advancements.

This challenge can be illustrated by a simple example drawn from the securities and markets context. Let's assume a bond (a "transferable security" within the meaning of EU securities and markets law[15]) is to be issued and traded on a regulated trading venue using DLT. In accordance with Article 3(2) of the Central Securities Depositories Regulation (Regulation (EU) 909/2014) (CSDR),[16] where a transaction in transferable securities takes place on a trading venue, the issuer must arrange for the securities to be represented in book-entry form with an authorized central securities depository as defined under Article 2(1) CSDR. EU legislation does not prescribe any particular method for initial book-entry form recording (so, potentially DLT could be used) but national rules may make specific provision which have the effect of precluding, for example, DLT-based records.[17] In this case, although the EU legislation is "technology neutral" in the sense of not prescribing a specific mode for record keeping, the *absence* of specific provision leaves room for national discretion that may mean, depending on where a firm is established, DLT may or may not be used for this purpose,

---

[14] For information about non-bank financial intermediation in the EU, see the European Systemic Risk Board's monitoring work: https://www.esrb.europa.eu/pub/reports/nbfi_monitor/html/index.en.html, which complements global monitoring carried out by the Financial Stability Board: https://www.fsb.org/work-of-the-fsb/policy-development/enhancing-resilience-of-non-bank-financial-intermediation/.

[15] See in particular the Directive on Markets in Financial Instruments (Directive 2014/65/EU) (MiFID): https://eur-lex.europa.eu/legal-content/en/TXT/?uri=CELEX:32014L0065.

[16] The CSDR is available here: https://eur-lex.europa.eu/legal-content/EN/TXT/?uri=CELEX%3A32014R0909.

[17] For a further discussion, see ESMA's January 2019 report on initial coin offerings and crypto-assets: https://www.esma.europa.eu/sites/default/files/library/esma50-157-1391_crypto_advice.pdf and February 2017 report on distributed ledger technology applied to securities markets: https://www.esma.europa.eu/sites/default/files/library/dlt_report_-_esma50-1121423017-285.pdf.

highlighting a challenge firms, regulators and supervisors are facing in reconciling DLT with existing regulation and navigating different approaches at the national level.[18]

Challenge 3: Identifying the Applicable Regulatory Requirements Where Activities Involve Crypto-Assets

Continuing the theme of challenge 2 (fragmentation), industry and regulatory and supervisory communities have had to grapple increasingly with the question of whether and how EU financial services regulation applies to applications of DLT entailing crypto-assets.

In the EU there is not yet an established "taxonomy" of crypto-assets.[19] Instead, a case-by-case assessment must be carried out to determine whether: (a) a crypto-asset falls within the scope of EU financial services law, in which case specified activities involving such assets must be carried out in accordance with EU regulation, and (b) a crypto-asset falls within the scope of any Member State bespoke national law.[20]

In terms of applicable EU financial services law, it is relevant to consider whether a crypto-asset qualifies as:

- "electronic money" pursuant to the second Electronic Money Directive (Directive 2009/110/EC), or
- a "financial instrument" under the Markets in Financial Instruments Directive (Directive 2014/65/EU).[21]

If a crypto-asset falls within either of these categories then a person carrying out specified activities involving such assets is required to be authorized or registered pursuant to EU law and to conform to a wide range of regulatory

---

[18] For further examples, see the ESMA reports cited in the previous endnote and the EBA's January 2019 report on crypto-assets: https://eba.europa.eu/sites/default/documents/files/documents/10180/2545547/67493daa-85a8-4429-aa91-e9a5ed880684/EBA%20Report%20on%20crypto%20assets.pdf?retry=1.

[19] For further analysis, see the EBA's January 2019 report on crypto-assets https://eba.europa.eu/sites/default/documents/files/documents/10180/2545547/67493daa-85a8-4429-aa91-e9a5ed880684/EBA%20Report%20on%20crypto%20assets.pdf?retry=1.

[20] Ibid.

[21] The Electronic Money Directive is available here: https://eur-lex.europa.eu/legal-content/EN/ALL/?uri=CELEX%3A32009L0110 and the Markets in Financial Instruments Directive is available here: https://eur-lex.europa.eu/legal-content/en/TXT/?uri=CELEX:32014L0065.

requirements.[22] Additionally, "passporting" arrangements apply such that services can be extended across the EU enabling the firm to carry out services beyond its home Member State without the need for separate authorization or registration. However, analysis by the European Banking Authority (EBA) and the European Securities and Markets Authority (ESMA)[23] has exposed that the majority of crypto-asset activities currently in circulation fall outside the scope of this EU law, resulting in uncovered risks (e.g. to consumers and investors) and, in the absence of common EU measures, fragmentation as to the acceptability and regulation of activities within the Member States noting, in particular, that some Member States, such as France and Malta have adopted bespoke national regimes[24] as interim measures in the absence of an EU-wide scheme.

Overall, this means that firms face considerable challenges in navigating regulatory requirements, face considerable uncertainties about supervisory acceptance and expectations regarding crypto-asset applications, and sometimes incur significant additional compliance costs as firms seek to conform to different local prudential or conduct of business requirements in the Member States in which they wish to operate.

For supervisors, this divergent approach poses problems for the cross-sector monitoring of risks, oversight of crypto-assets ecosystems (for example, involving issuers, wallets and exchanges) and coordination of supervisory actions. Different levels of regulation also leave scope for forum shopping, regulatory arbitrage and vulnerabilities to financial crime across the Single Market. Finally, consumers face challenges in understanding the regulatory status of crypto-assets and in navigating differential standards of protection depending on where they engage crypto-asset services, often being left confused by a lack of clarity and consistency concerning their rights (e.g., in the event of a complaint or the need for redress) impeding demand.[25]

---

[22] For further analysis, see the EBA's January 2019 report on crypto-assets https://eba.europa.eu/sites/default/documents/files/documents/10180/2545547/67493daa-85a8-4429-aa91-e9a5ed880684/EBA%20Report%20on%20crypto%20assets.pdf?retry=1.

[23] For a further discussion, see the January 2019 reports of EBA and ESMA: https://eba.europa.eu/sites/default/documents/files/documents/10180/2545547/67493daa-85a8-4429-aa91-e9a5ed880684/EBA%20Report%20on%20crypto%20assets.pdf?retry=1 and https://www.esma.europa.eu/sites/default/files/library/esma50-157-1391_crypto_advice.pdf.

[24] For a comparison of the French and Maltese approaches see Buttigieg C. and Cuyle S. 'A Comparative Analysis of EU Homegrown Crypto-asset Regulatory Frameworks', European Law Review, Issue 5 2020.

[25] For further discussion see Haben P. and Noble E. 'Crypto-assets: A Test Case for Technological Neutrality', International Banker, September 2020.

Challenge 4: Reconciling the Operation of DLT with EU Data Protection Law

Another of the challenges that has received extensive attention is the reconciliation of DLT use with the EU's flagship data protection rules established by the General Data Protection Regulation (Regulation (EU) 2016/679) (GDPR) and applied since May 2018.[26]

The GDPR regulates the processing[27] (including by automated means) of personal data[28] with the objective of facilitating the free movement of personal data between Member States[29] while protecting the fundamental rights and freedoms of natural persons, in particular, the right to the protection of personal data as enshrined in Article 8 of the Charter of Fundamental Rights.[30] This is achieved through the imposition of obligations on data controllers[31] and specific rights for individuals, for instance, to obtain access to personal data[32] and to request that personal data be erased when it is no longer needed or where processing has been found to have taken place unlawfully.[33]

Early DLT experimentation involving the processing of personal data (e.g. in the context of payment transactions and identity verification) has exposed challenges in reconciling the operation of DLT with data protection authorities' interpretation of the requirements of the GDPR,[34] highlighting the

---

[26] The GDPR is available here: https://eur-lex.europa.eu/eli/reg/2016/679/oj.

[27] 'Processing' is defined in point (2) of Article 4 GDPR as 'any operation or set of operations which is performed on personal data or on sets of personal data, whether or not by automated means, such as collection, recording, organisation, structuring, storage, adaptation or alteration, retrieval, consultation, use, disclosure by transmission, dissemination or otherwise making available, alignment or combination, restriction, erasure or destruction'.

[28] 'Personal data' is defined in point (1) of Article 4 GDPR as 'any information relating to an identified or identifiable natural person ('data subject'); an identifiable natural person is one who can be identified, directly or indirectly, in particular by reference to an identifier such as a name, an identification number, location data, an online identifier or to one or more factors specific to the physical, physiological, genetic, mental, economic, cultural or social identity of that natural person'.

[29] For material and territorial scope, see Articles 2 and 3 GDPR.

[30] The Charter is available here: https://ec.europa.eu/info/aid-development-cooperation-fundamental-rights/your-rights-eu/eu-charter-fundamental-rights_en.

[31] 'Controller' is defined in point (7) of Article 4 GDPR as 'the natural or legal person, public authority, agency or other body which, alone or jointly with others, determines the purposes and means of the processing of personal data; where the purposes and means of such processing are determined by Union or Member State law, the controller or the specific criteria for its nomination may be provided for by Union or Member State law'.

[32] Article 15 GDPR.

[33] Article 17 GDPR.

[34] For a detailed discussion see the 2019 report of the European Parliament Research Service 'Blockchain and the General Data Protection Regulation' https://www.europarl.europa.eu/RegData/etudes/STUD/2019/634445/EPRS_STU(2019)634445_EN.pdf.

need, on the one hand, for developers to have an early cognizance of GDPR obligations to implement compliance by design[35] and, on the other, the need for public authorities to provide guidance on the acceptability of different technological solutions for GDPR compliance.

By way of example, the GDPR is based on the assumption that data can be modified or erased where necessary (e.g. at the request of the data subject or in accordance with the purpose limitations specified in the GDPR). However, by its nature, DLT is intended to provide an immutable ledger to ensure data integrity and to increase trust in the network. Therefore, how can compliance with the GDPR be secured? For instance, are encryption methods sufficient if they have the effect of limiting the "public" visibility of the personal data? As observed by the European Data Protection Supervisor (EDPS), national data protection authorities have been cautious about expressing opinions,[36] leaving firms again exposed to the challenge of grappling with potentially divergent approaches at national level.

Challenge 5: Determining Governing Law

Finally, one critical legal issue has contributed to the limited cross-border scaling of DLT to date: the challenge of identifying governing law. Of course if DLT exists in a vacuum this question is irrelevant—it is just a technology. But in the financial sector, the creation, transfer and store of information using DLT has a function, indeed value. Financial counterparts need ex-ante certainty regarding their position for the scenario where things go wrong, in particular in cases of default, insolvency, error, or theft, including in the context of legal opinions for the purposes of establishing accounting and prudential treatment.[37]

In this context, the virtue of DLT as a borderless technology enabling multiple parties in multiple jurisdictions to effect transactions can also be a vice: in the event of dispute, enforcement or insolvency proceedings counterparts may seek to assert different governing law—the conflict of law

---

[35] In the use cases observed to-date in the EU financial sector, permissioned systems have been preferred at least enabling the controller(s) and processor(s) to be identified. In permissionless systems this may not be possible (ibid.).

[36] See the EDPS' Annual Report 2019: https://edps.europa.eu/sites/edp/files/publication/2020-03-17_annual_report_2020_en_0.pdf. The EDPS is the EU's independent data protection authority. The mission, tasks and powers of the EDPS are established in Regulation (EU) 2018/1725: https://eur-lex.europa.eu/legal-content/EN/TXT/?uri=CELEX%3A32018R1725. For further information, see the website of the EDPS: https://edps.europa.eu/.

[37] For a detailed analysis see Paech P. 'The Governance of Blockchain Financial Networks' https://papers.ssrn.com/sol3/papers.cfm?abstract_id=2875487.

issue—and yet another challenge for firms seeking to roll-out the technology for use cross-border. This means that a financial institution in a dispute about, for example, who has rights over a token issued using DLT may first have to go through expensive and lengthy proceedings in order to establish which State's law will be applied, before even getting to the determination of the dispute in accordance with the identified applicable law.

A full and proper explanation of why the conflict of law issue may arise justifies a book of its own. But, by way of illustration, let's use the following simple example: A DLT system has been created to enable the issuance of securities-like tokens to investors. An issuer, located in State X, creates 5000 tokens using the DLT. A financial institution in State Y agrees to purchase 4000 tokens from the issuer. Transfer of the private keys for the agreed 4000 tokens to the purchaser's "wallet" is expected to take place automatically on receipt of funds. However, the private keys for only 3500 tokens are received. The financial institution intends to take action to enforce its rights for the remaining 500 tokens. But which governing law applies: X, Y or another? Albeit impossible to answer in the abstract, the example highlights the problem of identifying the "hook" connecting the issue to a specific State's legal system. Courts in different jurisdictions will go about the analysis in different ways but may find it relevant to consider matters such as:

- the white paper or documents (if any) regarding the issuance of the tokens in case a governing law is indicated;
- the place of incorporation of the issuer (*lex societatis*) (as, in this example, there is an identifiable issuer whereas for some "native" tokens there may be no identifiable issuer, just code (Bitcoin is a good example of such a token));
- the place of incorporation of the financial institution albeit in this scenario the private keys for tokens are held on DLT and are not physically in a vault or in a traditional custody account which would be the "normal" way of determining the location of securities (*lex rei sitae*);
- any other potentially relevant documentation such as the DLT Protocol in case it should indicate a governing law.

In the absence of well-established norms and practices for specifying or otherwise determining governing law for DLT and crypto-asset applications, legal outcomes are by no means predictable and stable thereby undermining confidence in DLT-based financial transactions.

In recognition of the conflict of law issue, some states have started to introduce domestic law to provide greater certainty for counterparts using DLT in specified circumstances. For example, under French law, issuers of initial coin offerings towards French investors are obliged to publish information documents indicating the law applicable to the tokens and the competent court.[38] For comparative purposes, under Liechtenstein law, local laws are applicable if (a) tokens are issued by an entity based in Lichtenstein (place of issuer) or (b) the parties agree that Liechtenstein law applies (choice of law).[39] However, these unilateral attempts to clarify the question of the governing law are of limited effect and firms continue to face challenges in identifying governing law.

Part II: A Digital Finance Strategy for Europe

Taking account of the stated priorities of the European Commission's digital agenda,[40] the advice of the ESAs (including reflections on the challenges outlined above),[41] the outcome of various public consultations[42] and other important inputs,[43] on 24 September 2020 the European Commission published its Digital Finance Strategy accompanied by legislative proposals for a regulation on a pilot regime for market infrastructures based on distributed ledger technology (the Pilot Regime), a regulation on markets

---

[38] For information about the Loi PACTE (loi no. 2019-486 of 22 May 2019) see the website of the Autorité des Marchés Financiers (AMF): https://www.amf-france.org/en/node/59937.

[39] For information about the Liechtenstein Law on Tokens and Trusted Technology Service Providers (referred to as the Blockchain Act) see https://digital-assets-custody.com/liechtenstein-blockchain-act-in-force-since-1-january-2020/.

[40] See in particular the September 2019 mission letter of (the then) European Commission President-elect Von der Leyen to Vice-President Dombrovskis: https://ec.europa.eu/commission/sites/beta-political/files/mission-letter-valdis-dombrovskis-2019_en.pdf.

[41] In particular, the January 2019 reports of EBA and ESMA: https://eba.europa.eu/sites/default/documents/files/documents/10180/2545547/67493daa-85a8-4429-aa91-e9a5ed880684/EBA%20Report%20on%20crypto%20assets.pdf?retry=1 and https://www.esma.europa.eu/sites/default/files/library/esma50-157-1391_crypto_advice.pdf.

[42] In particular, the December 2019 European Commission consultation on an EU framework for markets in crypto-assets: https://ec.europa.eu/info/law/better-regulation/have-your-say/initiatives/12089-Directive-regulation-establishing-a-European-framework-for-markets-in-crypto-assets/public-consultation.

[43] For example, the December 2019 report of the European Commission's Expert Group on Regulatory Obstacles to Financial Innovation https://ec.europa.eu/info/publications/191113-report-expert-group-regulatory-obstacles-financial-innovation_en and the April 2020 study requested by the ECON Committee of the European Parliament on crypto-assets, key developments, regulatory concerns and responses: https://www.europarl.europa.eu/RegData/etudes/STUD/2020/648779/IPOL_STU(2020)648779_EN.pdf.

in crypto-assets (MiCA) and a directive and regulation on digital operational resilience (DORA).[44]

The main objectives of the Digital Finance Strategy are to:

- tackle fragmentation in the Digital Single Market for financial services, thereby enabling European consumers to access cross-border services and help European financial firms scale up their technology-enabled business;
- ensure that the EU regulatory framework facilitates digital innovation in the interest of consumers and market efficiency;
- create a European financial data space to promote data-driven innovation, building on the European data strategy, including enhanced access to data and data sharing within the financial sector;
- address new challenges and risks associated with the digital transformation, in particular, to ensure conformity with the "same risk, same rule" principle.[45]

The legislative proposals for the Pilot Regime and MiCA represent the first concrete actions within the Strategy's identified priority of ensuring that the EU financial services regulatory framework is (a) innovation-friendly and does not pose obstacles to the application of innovative technologies that have the potential to benefit EU consumers, firms and the overall functioning of the EU financial system and (b) mitigates effectively risks posed by innovative technologies. In particular, the proposals are intended to secure appropriate levels of consumer and investor protection, legal certainty and, ultimately, ensure financial stability.[46]

At the time of writing, the legislative proposals are subject to the co-legislative procedure (in the European Parliament and Council)[47] and the content may change as a result of this procedure and therefore the overview of the proposals that follows should be checked against the final texts when adopted.

---

[44]The full Digital Finance package, including the legislative proposals, is available on the European Commission's website here: https://ec.europa.eu/info/publications/200924-digital-finance-proposals_en.

[45]See further the European Commission's Digital Finance Strategy: https://eur-lex.europa.eu/legal-content/EN/TXT/?uri=CELEX:52020DC0591.

[46]See the explanatory memoranda for the legislative proposals on the Pilot Regime and MiCA: https://eur-lex.europa.eu/legal-content/EN/TXT/?uri=CELEX:52020PC0594 and https://eur-lex.europa.eu/legal-content/EN/TXT/?uri=CELEX:52020PC0593.

[47]For information about the procedure see: https://www.europarl.europa.eu/olp/en/ordinary-legislative-procedure/overview.

The Pilot Regime

The legislative proposal for the Pilot Regime[48] has four general and related objectives which reflect four of the five challenges identified in Part 1 of this chapter. Firstly, the Pilot Regime is intended to facilitate DLT experimentation in the EU securities and markets sector by providing a common framework that enables, where appropriate and necessary, the *disapplication* of EU law that could otherwise impede experimentation. By so-doing this will facilitate the identification by regulators and supervisors of any areas of EU securities and markets law that pose potential obstacles to DLT and crypto-asset application and, as appropriate, determine the steps necessary to address these issues. In turn this:

- provides confidence and certainty in the capacity to experiment and, in turn, exposes and presents the evidence base for potential areas of the EU regulatory framework that may not be fit-for-purpose and warrant clarification or change;
- promotes the uptake of technology and responsible innovation by providing a designated and EU-wide regime for experimentation;
- secures consumer and investor protection and market integrity by specifying appropriate parameters to frame experimentation and mitigate risks (e.g. by limiting the types of financial instruments that can be traded);
- mitigates consistently any risk to consumers, investors and to financial stability by limiting the requirements under EU law that can be disapplied under the regime.[49]

In summary, the Pilot Regime provides a time-limited framework,[50] that enables market participants who wish to operate (on a purely voluntary basis) a "DLT market infrastructure" (defined as a "DLT multilateral trading facility"[51] or a "DLT securities settlement system"[52]) for DLT transferable securities (i.e. crypto-assets that qualify as "transferable securities" within the

---

[48] https://eur-lex.europa.eu/legal-content/EN/TXT/?uri=CELEX:52020PC0594.

[49] See further the explanatory memorandum for the legislative proposal on the Pilot Regime: https://eur-lex.europa.eu/legal-content/EN/TXT/?uri=CELEX:52020PC0594.

[50] The Pilot Regime has been conceived as a temporary measure, albeit the European Commission may proposal an extension or permanence of the regime if experience acquired with the operation of the regime implies such a need (Article 10(2) of the legislative proposal).

[51] Article 2(3) of the legislative proposal.

[52] Article 2(4) of the legislative proposal.

scope of MiFID[53]) to experiment with the DLT and crypto-assets for these purposes.

DLT market infrastructures must be operated in accordance with the conditions specified in the regulation intended to mitigate operational risks and risks to consumers and investors,[54] but benefit from two key privileges. First, operators may seek from their supervisory authorities temporary and duly limited exemptions from specific requirements under EU financial services legislation that could otherwise prevent the development of solutions for the trading and settlement of transactions in crypto-assets that qualify as financial instruments.[55] Second, operators of DLT market infrastructures can provide their services across the EU without needing to acquire a licence or registration beyond that required in their home Member State.

As a central element of the Pilot Regime, operators of DLT market infrastructures, supervisors and ESMA must cooperate closely in order that all parties can benefit from experience acquired with the operation of DLT market infrastructures, exemptions requested, granted or refused.[56] In particular, operators must report every six months to the relevant supervisor and ESMA on specified matters,[57] and ESMA is mandated to fulfil a coordination role between the supervisors with a view to building a common understanding of DLT and DLT market infrastructures as well as to help build a common supervisory culture and convergent supervisory approaches and outcomes.[58]

Within five years following the entry into application of the regulation, ESMA is required to present a report to the European Commission on a wide range of matters relating to the application of the Pilot Regime, including the functioning of DLT market infrastructures, the exemptions requested and granted, benefits, risks and interoperability issues.[59] Based on this report, the European Commission must present a report to the European Parliament and Council on whether the regime for DLT market infrastructures should be extended, amended, made permanent or terminated, and may set out any proposed modifications to the EU framework on financial services legislation

---

[53] The Markets in Financial Instruments Directive is available here: https://eur-lex.europa.eu/legal-content/en/TXT/?uri=CELEX:32014L0065.
[54] See further the explanatory memorandum for the legislative proposal on the Pilot Regime: https://eur-lex.europa.eu/legal-content/EN/TXT/?uri=CELEX:52020PC0594 and the recitals of the proposal.
[55] Articles 4 and 5 of the legislative proposal.
[56] Article 9 of the legislative proposal.
[57] Article 9(4) of the legislative proposal.
[58] Article 9(5) of the legislative proposal.
[59] Article 10(1) of the legislative proposal.

or proposed harmonization of national laws to facilitate the use of DLT in the financial services sector.[60]

In its presentation of the legislative proposal for the Pilot Regime the European Commission acknowledges plainly that EU financial services legislation was not designed with DLT and crypto-assets in mind and that there are provisions of existing EU law that may preclude or limit the use of DLT in the issuance, trading and settlement of crypto-assets that qualify as MiFID financial instruments and that regulatory gaps may also exist resulting in uncovered risks.[61] Through the creation of a framework that facilitates responsible experimentation, firms, regulators and supervisors will have the opportunity to learn together about the opportunities and risks posed by the application of the technologies in securities markets contexts thereby accelerating the identification of potential issues and potential legislative or non-legislative solutions thereby overcoming many of the challenges identified in Part 1.

Markets in Cryptoassets (MiCA)

The legislative proposal for MiCA[62] is intended to bring in the scope of EU law activities that are not currently within scope and to address gaps in the framework for the regulation of crypto-assets in the form of "electronic money".[63] Importantly, it does not extend to crypto-assets that qualify as "financial instruments" within the scope of MiFID (in view of the Pilot Regime).[64] Some other exclusions and exemptions are also proposed.[65]

In presenting the legislative proposal, the European Commission emphasized the acceleration in crypto-asset experimentation and application in the EU financial sector and the need both to leverage the opportunities presented by DLT and crypto-asset technologies and address the risks identified in the

---

[60] Article 10(2) of the legislative proposal.

[61] See further the explanatory memorandum for the legislative proposal on the Pilot Regime: https://eur-lex.europa.eu/legal-content/EN/TXT/?uri=CELEX:52020PC0594 and the recitals of the proposal.

[62] https://eur-lex.europa.eu/legal-content/EN/TXT/?uri=CELEX:52020PC0593.

[63] 'Electronic money' is defined in Directive 2009/110/EU (the Electronic Money Directive; https://eur-lex.europa.eu/legal-content/EN/ALL/?uri=CELEX%3A32009L0110) as 'electronically, including magnetically, stored monetary value as represented by a claim on the issuer which is issued on receipt of funds for the purpose of making payment transactions as defined in point 5 of Article 4 of Directive 2007/64/EC, and which is accepted by a natural or legal person other than the electronic money issuer'. The Directive was not conceived with crypto-assets in mind and therefore does not address all risks in relation to the issuance of electronic money in this form.

[64] Article 2(2) of the legislative proposal.

[65] Article 2 and Articles 4(2), 15(3) and (4) and 43(2) of the legislative proposal.

advice the EBA and ESMA.[66] In particular, the European Commission highlighted that the majority of crypto-assets currently fall outside the scope of EU financial services law and that even where they do fall in scope effective application of the law is not always straightforward.[67] In light of these issues, and acknowledging the potential opportunities that some crypto-assets may offer and recent developments in relation to so-called stablecoins,[68] the European Commission identified the following as objectives for the proposal:

- to provide legal certainty by creating a sound legal framework that clearly defines the regulatory treatment of crypto-assets that do not currently fall within the scope of EU financial services law;
- to support innovation by establishing a consistent, safe and proportionate framework that enables services to be provided cross-border in accordance with common rules (MiCA will replace any bespoke frameworks under national law that extend to crypto-assets within the scope of MiCA[69]);
- to instil appropriate levels of consumer and investor protection and market integrity, thereby enhancing confidence to engage crypto-asset products and services where appropriate; and
- to ensure financial stability by addressing risks in a consistent manner across the EU, including in relation to so-called stablecoins.

MiCA defines a "crypto-asset" as a digital representation of value or rights which may be transferred and stored electronically using DLT or similar technologies and establishes regulatory regimes for specified activities involving different sub-categories of crypto-asset:

- "asset-referenced token": a type of crypto-asset that purports to maintain a stable value by referring to the value of several fiat currencies that are

---

[66] In particular, the January 2019 reports of EBA and ESMA: https://eba.europa.eu/sites/default/documents/files/documents/10180/2545547/67493daa-85a8-4429-aa91-e9a5ed880684/EBA%20Report%20on%20crypto%20assets.pdf?retry=1 and https://www.esma.europa.eu/sites/default/files/library/esma50-157-1391_crypto_advice.pdf.

[67] See the explanatory memorandum for the legislative proposal on MiCA: https://eur-lex.europa.eu/legal-content/EN/TXT/?uri=CELEX:52020PC0593.

[68] Including political statements regarding proposals for global stablecoins, for example the December 2019 joint Council and European Commission statement on stablecoins: https://www.consilium.europa.eu/en/press/press-releases/2019/12/05/joint-statement-by-the-council-and-the-commission-on-stablecoins/.

[69] See the explanatory memorandum for the legislative proposal on MiCA: https://eur-lex.europa.eu/legal-content/EN/TXT/?uri=CELEX:52020PC0593 and the recitals of the proposal.

legal tender, one or several commodities or one or several crypto-assets, or a combination of such assets[70];
- "electronic money token" or "e-money token": a type of crypto-asset the main purpose of which is to be used as a means of exchange and that purports to maintain a stable value by referring to the value of a fiat currency that is legal tender[71];
- "utility token" a type of crypto-asset which is intended to provide digital access to a good or service, available on DLT, and is only accepted by the issuer of that token[72];
- other: crypto-assets which are not asset-referenced, e-money or utility tokens and not otherwise excluded from the scope of the regulation.[73]

The term "stablecoin" is not used in the proposal, but depending on the features of the coin in question, the coin may fall within the definition of "asset-reference token", "e-money token" or as other.

MiCA establishes regulatory regimes for:

- the issuance of crypto-assets in the form of *asset-referenced tokens* and *e-money tokens* (respectively, Titles III and IV);
- crypto-asset services,[74] including custody and administration of crypto-assets and the operation of crypto-asset trading platforms and exchanges (to fiat or to other crypto-assets) (Title V).

Firms will be required to obtain (national) authorization as "crypto-asset service providers" and to conform with a wide range of regulatory requirements (including governance, operational resilience, and consumer protection requirements) in order to carry out in the EU crypto-asset services such as exchange or wallet provision.[75] Firms will also be required to obtain authorization and conform to a more extensive set of regulatory requirements[76] in order to issue asset-referenced tokens and, in the case of e-money tokens,

---

[70] Point (3), Article 3(1) of the legislative proposal.
[71] Point (4), Article 3(1) of the legislative proposal.
[72] Point (5), Article 3(1) of the legislative proposal.
[73] For example, Title II (crypto-assets, other than asset-referenced tokens or e-money tokens) applies in relation to such tokens, as do the provisions of Title V in relation to crypto-asset services (defined in point (9) of Article 3(1) of the legislative proposal)).
[74] Point (9), Article 3(1) of the legislative proposal.
[75] See further Title V of the legislative proposal.
[76] For example, requirements to issue a white paper in conformity with the requirements under MiCA, governance and operational requirements, requirements regarding communications and marketing, complaints handling procedures, own funds, and requirements to maintain a reserve of assets (see further Title III).

must be authorized either as an electronic money institution or as a credit institution.[77] Authorization is not required to offer other types of crypto-asset (e.g. utility tokens) to the public or seek to admit them for trading on a crypto-asset trading platform, however, some limited regulatory requirements are foreseen, including the requirement to have prepared and published a white paper in conformity with the regulation (Title II).

Firms benefitting from authorization from their home authority as crypto-asset service providers and issuers of asset-referenced and e-money tokens will be able to offer their services across the EU without the need for additional authorization or a registration in the host states in which they wish to operate.

Typically supervision will be carried out at the national level. However, it is proposed that supervision will be elevated to the EU level and be carried out by the EBA for issuers of "*significant asset-referenced tokens*"[78] and issuers of "*significant e-money tokens*"[79] (but only in relation to compliance with provisions of MiCA),[80] or where the issuer wishes to voluntarily submit to EU-level supervision,[81] with significance determined on the basis of criteria established in the regulation (supplemented as appropriate by a delegated act of the European Commission), including:

- the size of the customer base of the promoters and shareholders or other relevant third parties;
- the value of the tokens or, where applicable, their market capitalization;
- the number and value of transactions;
- the significance of cross-border activities;
- interconnectedness with the financial system.[82]

In relation to issuers of significant asset-referenced or e-money tokens, the EBA is required to establish supervisory colleges to facilitate coordinated

---

[77] Article 43(1) of the legislative proposal.
[78] Article 39 of the legislative proposal.
[79] Article 50 of the legislative proposal.
[80] Article 98(4) of the legislative proposal. This reflects the fact that to issue e-money tokens an entity must be authorised already as a credit institution or as an electronic money institution and therefore is subject already to an extensive set of regulatory requirements under, respectively the Capital Requirements Directive and Regulation (amended most recently by Directive (EU) 2019/878 (CRDV) and Regulation (EU) 2019/876 (CRR2)) and the Electronic Money Directive (Directive 2009/110/EU). The additional requirements under Title IV of the legislative proposal are intended to cover additional and specific risks relating to the issuance of e-money tokens. As such Title IV does not specify all of the requirements that appear in Title III (for issuers of asset-referenced tokens) as this would otherwise be duplicative and potentially contradictory with other requirements applicable to credit institutions and electronic money institutions.
[81] Articles 40 and 51 of the legislative proposal.
[82] Articles 39 and 50 of the legislative proposal.

oversight of the wider ecosystem for the issuance, store and exchange of the crypto-assets, bringing together supervisors of the most relevant crypto-asset service providers, ESMA, the ECB and relevant third country and other authorities as appropriate.[83] The supervisory colleges are intended to support the early identification of issues, and coordination of any necessary remedial actions, that could otherwise undermine the operational resilience of the ecosystem, consumer protection, market integrity and financial stability.

Finally, it is worth highlighting the regulatory requirements applicable to issuers of asset-referenced tokens which include obligations to prepare and publish a white paper,[84] to provide clear, fair and transparent marketing and other communications to holders/prospective holders of tokens,[85] to have in place complaints handling procedures, sound governance and organizational arrangements,[86] to hold own funds in accordance with the requirements of the regulation (higher in the case of issuers of significant asset-referenced tokens),[87] and to maintain a reserve of assets in conformity with the requirements of the regulation to which holders of tokens may have rights as specified in clear and detailed policies and procedures[88]; additional obligations apply in the case of issuers of significant asset-referenced tokens.[89] In the case of e-money tokens, as issuers are required to be authorized as credit institutions or as electronic money institutions, they are subject to already extensive obligations under existing EU law (e.g. regarding governance, own funds and conduct of business requirements). Additional requirements are proposed to apply under MiCA, which are intended to address specific risks relating to the issuance of crypto-assets, including the obligation to issue a whitepaper and in relation to marketing and communications. [90]

Overall MiCA represents a bold and important step in creating a harmonized, proportionate and robust framework for the regulation of crypto-asset activities in the EU (thereby addressing the majority of the challenges set out in Part 1) and is expected to promote confidence on both the supply and demand side for crypto-asset products and services by instilling high levels of confidence in the governance, prudential and operational resilience, and conduct of business of crypto-asset issuers and service providers.

---

[83] Articles 99 and 101 of the legislative proposal.
[84] Article 17 of the legislative proposal.
[85] For example, Article 24 to 26 of the legislative proposal.
[86] Articles 27 and 30 of the legislative proposal.
[87] Articles 31 and 41 of the legislative proposal.
[88] Articles 32 to 25 of the legislative proposal.
[89] Article 41 of the legislative proposal.
[90] See endnote lxxx.

Importantly, the legislative proposals for the Pilot Regime and MiCA demonstrate that the European Commission will not hesitate to act, on the one hand, to remove obstacles to financial innovations where they are shown to have real potential benefits for consumers, businesses or for the functioning of the EU financial system and, on the other, to address inconsistently covered or uncovered risks. These initiatives also signal the European Commission's priority to make Europe fit for the digital age and ambition to leverage the full potential of innovative technologies and are part of a long-term strategy to embrace and lead the digital revolution.[91]

Other Actions Underway

Pending the outcome of the legislative process, the ESAs are continuing to monitor DLT and crypto-asset developments in the EU and, in the context of the EFIF, promote cross-sectoral knowledge-sharing, coordination and consistency of approaches to the acceptance and supervision of DLT and crypto-asset applications in the EU.[92] The EBA and ESMA are also continuing to monitor emerging crypto-assets with a view to supporting the European Commission in the preparation of interpretative guidance on the application of existing EU rules to crypto-assets.[93] The ESAs are also continuing to contribute to international work underway on DLT, crypto-assets and so-called stablecoins, including that of the Financial Stability Board (FSB), the Basel Committee on Banking Supervision (BCBS), the Financial Action Task Force (FATF) and Committee on Payments and Market Infrastructures and the International Organisation of Securities Commissions (CPMI-IOSCO). Additionally, following industry calls for clarity about DLT and the GDPR, the European Data Protection Board (EDPB)[94] indicated in its 2019/20 work program possible work on blockchain[95] which could result

---

[91] See further the political guidelines referred to in endnote xl.
[92] For further information on monitoring work of the EFIF see the Terms of Reference and event minutes available from the EFIF webpage: https://esas-joint-committee.europa.eu/Pages/Activities/EFIF/European-Forum-for-Innovation-Facilitators.aspx.
[93] See further the actions under section 4.2 of the Digital Finance Strategy: https://eur-lex.europa.eu/legal-content/EN/TXT/?uri=CELEX:52020DC0591.
[94] The EDPB was established by the GDPR (Article 68) and can, among other tasks (Article 70), issue guidelines, recommendations, and best practices on procedures for erasing links, copies or replications of personal data from publicly available communication services as referred to in Article 17(2), and examine, on its own initiative, on request of one of its members or on request of the European Commission, any question covering the application of the GDPR and issue guidelines, recommendations and best practices in order to encourage consistent application of the GDPR. For further information see the website of the EDPB: https://edpb.europa.eu/edpb_en.
[95] https://edpb.europa.eu/our-work-tools/our-documents/work-program/edpb-work-program-201920 20_en, building on its 2019 Annual Report in which the EDPB indicated it would intensify its

in guidelines, best practices or the issuance of recommendations to the European Commission for legislative clarification. The EDPB and EDPS are also continuing to monitor innovative technologies,[96] including the evolution of blockchain, noting compliance challenges in areas such as storage limitation, controllership and the rights of individuals. It is also relevant to note that the European Commission is working with the ESAs to strengthen the EFIF, in particular, to offer by mid-2021 a procedural framework for launching cross-border testing and other mechanisms to facilitate firms' interactions with supervisors from different Member States.[97] The European Commission and ESAs are also continuing to monitor and support the exploratory work of central banks, including the European Central Bank (ECB),[98] on the feasibility of retail central bank digital currencies (CBDC).[99] Finally, in the course of 2021, the European Commission is likely to publish its legislative proposal to strengthen the framework for mitigating money laundering and terrorist financing risk and, in the context of that proposal, is likely to extend AML/CFT obligations to the categories of new regulated firm established by MiCA.

---

work in the context of advanced technologies, including blockchain: https://edpb.europa.eu/about-edpb/board/annual-reports_en.

[96] For information about the EDPS' work on innovative technologies, see: https://edps.europa.eu/data-protection/our-work/technology-monitoring_en.

[97] See the actions under section 4.1. of the Digital Finance Strategy: https://eur-lex.europa.eu/legal-content/EN/TXT/PDF/?uri=CELEX:52020DC0591&from=EN.

[98] See, for example, the ECB's October 2020 report on a digital euro: https://www.ecb.europa.eu/pub/pdf/other/Report_on_a_digital_euro~4d7268b458.en.pdf.

[99] See further the actions under section 4.2 of the Digital Finance Strategy: https://eur-lex.europa.eu/legal-content/EN/TXT/?uri=CELEX:52020DC0591.

10

Crypto-Assets and Disintermediation in Finance: A View from Asia

Syren Johnstone

The Crypto Narrative

The legal jurisdictions that comprise Far East Asia ("Asia") vary dramatically across a number of key factors relevant to crypto-assets[1] and crypto-finance. This includes cultural values, political ideologies, economic and social development, maturation of financial systems, and the comprehensiveness of the laws, practices and enforcement mechanisms that regulate commercial and financial activity. The legal systems of the larger financial centres derive either from the English common law model (Hong Kong[2] and Singapore) or a civil law model heavily influenced by a mix of either continental law and US law (Japan) or continental law and Japanese law (Mainland China[3]).

---

[1] In view of the variants of terminology, typically based on explicit or implicit embedded meanings and assumptions, this Chapter generally adopts "crypto-assets" as a more neutral term that covers all types of digitally written instances cum tokens based on cryptographic consensus technologies that are capable of being owned. This is comparable, though not identical, to the definition of crypto-asset provided in the European Union consultation document "On an EU framework for markets in crypto-assets", p. 7 (undated, 2019).
[2] I.e. Hong Kong Special Administrative Region of the Peoples Republic of China.
[3] Mainland China refers to the Peoples Republic of China excluding Hong Kong and Macau, which operate under different legal systems.

S. Johnstone (✉)
Faculty of Law, The University of Hong Kong, Hong Kong, Hong Kong
e-mail: syrenj@hku.hk

All major jurisdictions in Asia have recognized the importance of financial technologies ("Fintech") to the development of its financial markets and have responded with facilitative regulations.[4] However, the same cannot be said of the challenges and opportunities presented by crypto-assets and crypto-finance. Responses have generally revolved around concern about the integrity of the primary and secondary markets that have developed around crypto-assets. The differences cited above are significant in this regard and underpin widely varying approaches to crypto-assets. As such, there is no one "regional response"; heterogeneity is the rule. This Chapter will focus on the largest capital markets that are most active in the crypto-assets and crypto-finance space—Japan, Hong Kong and Mainland China—and touch on other jurisdictions where relevant.

The development of crypto-assets and crypto-finance in Asia, and the evolution of regulatory responses to it, roughly falls into four phases: emergence, counteraction, traction, point of no return.

Emergence

The collapse of the Tokyo-based Mt Gox Bitcoin exchange in February 2014[5] crystallized concerns about the prospects for unregulated, decentralized cryptocurrencies. On the other hand, it triggered a wave of Chinese investment.[6] At this time there was effectively no regulatory oversight of Bitcoin trading in Asia. Crowdfunding, which had started to get a fledgling foothold in Asia despite struggling with problematic securities cum investment laws and negative incidents,[7] was quickly overtaken and largely replaced by initial coin offerings ("ICOs"), which offered a faster route to capital and appeared to bypass legal constraints.

By the time of the Mt Gox hack, Mainland China[8] had already made it clear that cryptocurrencies such as Bitcoin were not legal currency, thus formally removing virtual currencies from the traditional banking system. A primary concern was capital flight and this led to the People's Bank of China ("PBOC") establishing, in March 2016, the National Internet Finance

---

[4]Specific laws and regulations related to e-money payment systems and financial services have been actively developed in essentially all major jurisdictions in Asia.
[5]As a result of an alleged hack causing the loss of around US$473 million in Bitcoins.
[6]More than 30,000 Bitcoins changed hands in China compared to just 300 in the United States (Lee 2014).
[7]For example, the Ezubao P2P Ponzi scheme in Mainland China involving around 50 billion yuan from over 900,000 investors (circa 2015–2016).
[8]People's Bank of China et al. (2013).

Association, a self-regulatory organization ("SRO"). However, the SRO was essentially comprised of institutions from traditional financial markets whose interests may not be aligned with the growth in crypto-assets via ICOs or crypto-financing.[9] In Hong Kong, the view was taken that virtual commodities such as Bitcoin do not qualify as a means of payment or electronic money, and accordingly are not regulated by the Hong Kong Monetary Authority ("HKMA"), nor was it necessary to either legislate for or prohibit participation in crypto-assets.[10]

ICOs had made their way onto the radar screen of regulatory agencies in Japan, Hong Kong, Mainland China and Singapore by the end of 2016. The common concern was the high risk of mis-disclosure and fraud as a consequence of no regulatory oversight, and that the activity could be connected to actors barred from utilizing the public capital market.[11] Several regulators in Asia had by this time already established expertise in Fintech.[12] However, it was oriented towards technology as an evolution within an existing model of the financial services industry, not a fundamental disruption of it. Regulators typically possessed extremely limited or no understanding of the newly available cryptographic consensus technology ("CCTech"), such as blockchain and distributed ledger technology, which forms the basis of crypto-assets and crypto-finance.[13]

During this phase the other possibilities offered by CCTech started to be recognized, such as tokenization of assets more generally. So too were the problems in the development of a new system of digital commerce, ranging from the need for an enabling digital ecosystem, to unresolved problems in the technology itself.[14] Regulatory agencies, with little expectation as to whether or how this market might grow, and reluctant to inhibit evolution of a technology that could have potential, generally took a cautious wait-and-see approach. They increasingly pursued a path of information gathering, typically at a distance from the industry. The exceptions were Japan and Hong Kong. The Financial Services Agency of Japan ("JFSA") maintained close contact with cryptoexchanges in what is best described as a voluntary

---

[9]The SRO was comprised of more than 400 institutions from the traditional finance segment – banks, securities companies, funds etc. See https://www.nifa.org.cn/nifaen/.
[10]Financial Services and Treasury Bureau (2015). Hong Kong Monetary Authority (2015).
[11]I.e. connected to money laundering or funding terrorist activities.
[12]In particular, the banking and securities regulators in Hong Kong, Mainland China, Japan and Singapore.
[13]Blockchain and distributed ledger technology are examples of iterations of CCTech.
[14]For example, The DAO incident in June 2016, which created many issues in relation to the concept of immutability. For a review see Johnstone (2018b), Section 4.2.

industry-regulator partnership as the JFSA's ambit of authority was unclear. In Hong Kong, in February 2016 the Securities and Futures Commission ("SFC") established the Fintech Contact Point[15] to enhance communication with businesses involved in the development and application of Fintech, and formed the Fintech Advisory Group[16] to assist identify the opportunities, risks and regulatory perimeter implications of Fintech and to broaden the understanding of Fintech as an evolution of the financial services industry.

Counteraction

2017 saw a rapid growth in money being raised via ICOs. In Mainland China, the first seven months of 2017 witnessed 65 ICOs raising around US$398 million[17] despite heightened concerns being expressed about the operations of cryptoexchanges in January 2017.[18] On 4 September 2017 seven central government regulatory agencies announced a complete ban on ICOs.[19] The ban, which is at intervals reemphasized,[20] led to the closure of more than a hundred crypto-asset trading platforms within a year.[21] South Korea, which had its first ICO in May 2017,[22] experienced frenzied interest in ICOs until the Financial Services Commission indicated, in September 2017, that it would apply securities laws to ICOs and proposed an outright ban be effected via legislative amendment. However, in both jurisdictions many consumers had already acquired crypto-assets, with a particularly deep penetration rate in South Korea,[23] meaning that simply shutting down cryptoexchanges presented issues that shifted regulatory efforts to control trading and implement reporting and disclosure requirements. Counteraction in Mainland China also prohibited banks and payment institutions from

---

[15] https://www.sfc.hk/web/EN/sfc-fintech-contact-point/.
[16] https://www.sfc.hk/web/EN/sfc-fintech-contact-point/fintech-advisory-committee/. By way of disclosure, the author has been member of the Fintech Advisory Group since its establishment.
[17] Per the National Internet Finance Association, a body established by the PBOC in 2016.
[18] Statement by PBOC Shanghai Headquarters, https://shanghai.pbc.gov.cn/fzhshanghai/113571/3230012/index.html; Statement by PBOC operations Office, https://beijing.pbc.gov.cn/beijing/132005/3245162/index.html.
[19] Persons who had completed ICO financing at the time of the Announcement were required to terminate the investment contracts and return the funds raised or otherwise "dispose of risks in an appropriate manner". See People's Bank of China et al. (2017a, b).
[20] https://shanghai.pbc.gov.cn/fzhshanghai/113571/3926566/index.html.
[21] https://www.xinhuanet.com/fortune/2018-07/06/c_1123089788.htm.
[22] The ICO of South Korean fintech company Blockchain OS, through a Swiss-based foundation, finished in nine minutes in exchange for 6900 Bitcoins.
[23] A survey dated December 2017 reported that one-third of salaried workers in South Korea have investments in crypto-assets (Jo 2017).

dealing in virtual currencies or providing related services including opening bank accounts and insurance services.[24] Although fiat money could not be exchanged for virtual currencies, the September 2017 announcement did not explicitly forbid transactions among virtual currencies, most likely because that would not affect the government's capital control policies.[25]

Where ICOs had not been banned, actions taken by regulators in the USA were influential. In July 2017 the Securities and Exchange Commission ("SEC") issued the "21(a) DAO Report", which concluded that an ICO token known as "Slock.it" was a security.[26] Two years earlier, the Commodity Futures Trading Commission had taken the view that cryptocurrencies were commodities under the Commodity Exchange Act of 1936,[27] a view subsequently confirmed by the court.[28] This galvanized regulatory attitudes as to how crypto-assets might be positioned into existing regulatory silos. Regulatory agencies in Asia started to publish advisories to the industry that crypto-assets may be securities or futures products subject to existing laws, and risk warnings to investors. Both Hong Kong and Singapore took this approach, only regulating ICOs where they fell within existing securities legislation, the Securities and Futures Ordinance ("SFO") in Hong Kong, and the Securities and Futures Act ("SFA") in Singapore. Positioning tokens under these laws brought focus to the activities of cryptoexchanges in Asia, which were by now handling significant daily turnovers, and increasing amounts of fiat currency raising systemic and money laundering concerns. However, appreciating the various and often conflicting roles cryptoexchanges undertook was not as yet fully grasped. Japan, culturally receptive to cryptocurrencies and cryptoexchanges, was a notable exception to this—large scale hacks[29] caused the JFSA to stay close to the operational activities of cryptoexchanges despite acknowledged vagueness as to what law might apply[30] and uncertainty as how best to identify and manage risk.

---

[24] People's Bank of China et al. (2017b).
[25] Xie, R. (2019).
[26] A later report of the SEC was also significant for regulators in Asia. See United States Securities and Exchange Commission (2017).
[27] In the Matter of Coinflip, Inc., d/b/a Derivabit, and Francisco Riordan, CFTC Docket No. 15–29. 17 September 2015.
[28] *CFTC v. McDonnell*, et al., Case 1:18-cv-00361-JBW-RLM Document 29 Filed 03/06/18.
[29] Such as Mt Gox, vide supra.
[30] Payment Services Act and/or the Financial Instruments and Exchange Act, discussed below.

Traction

In the jurisdictions where ICOs had not been banned, regulatory agencies began to more clearly adopt conservative, risk-based approaches to digital financing activities that tap the public capital market. Japan continued to be the most receptive country in Asia, embracing ICOs including secondary market trading on cryptoexchanges. Regulatory oversight had become a matter of necessity as a consequence of the growth of Japan's secondary market—by the end of 2017 Japan's Bitcoin market accounted for almost two-thirds of the global trading volume.[31] A basic regulatory framework was introduced via legislative changes, in April 2017, to the Payment Services Act ("PSA") and the Act on Prevention of Transfer of Profits from Criminal Activities. The changes recognized virtual currencies as having value and constituting a legal payment method—although that did not go so far as to treat them as a legal currency. Importantly, the amendment of the PSA enabled the JFSA to license and regulate cryptoexchanges. This was initially directed at oversight by way of information gathering, as opposed to standard setting[32]—a shortcoming that was laid bare by the Coincheck hack in January 2018.[33] In April 2018 a group of 16 cryptoexchanges established the Japan Virtual Currency Exchange Association ("JVCEA") as an industry body that promoted standards that must be complied with by its members.[34] In October 2018 the JFSA authorized the JVCEA as a self-regulatory organization ("SRO"). In December 2019 it had 19 exchange members with an in-kind trading volume of over 250 billion yen and margin trading in excess of over 3.8 trillion yen.[35]

Open support in Japan and more tentative support in Hong Kong and Singapore led, in view of similar moves internationally, particularly the USA, to the industry in Asia making a shift in 2018 from ICOs to securities token offerings ("STOs"). STOs held out the expectation that a capital raising exercise could be undertaken in full compliance with securities laws—normally via private placement or similar exemptions—thus enabling investors to

---

[31] Japan Times (2017).
[32] Standard setting had initially taken the form of de facto applying adapted versions of their existing exchange and securities industry practices.
[33] US$532 million in funds were lost.
[34] Covering, for example, insider trading, margin limits, the management of online wallets and speculative trading.
[35] Source: website of JVCEA.

obtain legal opinions on the offering[36] and regulatory agencies to exercise their powers to investigate and enforce, typically by curtailment of the offering rather than by any stronger sanction such as fines.[37] While this greatly clarified the position in Hong Kong, the situation in Japan suffered from a continuing lack of clarity as to which law applied—the PSA or the Financial Instruments and Exchange Act ("FIEA"), Japan's securities and exchange law. In October 2017 the JFSA indicated that ICOs characterized as investments or securities will be subject to the FIEA and that ICOs issuing coins which are a virtual currency would be regulated under the PSA. However, uncertainty remained as the investment use of virtual currencies could nevertheless cause the JFSA to regard tokens in an ICO as "deemed securities" subject to the FIEA. This led to the drying up of both ICOs and STOs in Japan.

In parallel with these developments, which had to some extent assuaged regulatory concerns about the abuse of the primary capital market (other than the money laundering and terrorist financing concerns), greater attention began to be placed on secondary market activities.[38] Hong Kong had become an important regional alternative to Japan for cryptoexchanges to operate from,[39] partly because of its status as an international financial centre and because the regulatory framework was more receptive than other leading international financial centres. This included over-the-counter brokerages such as Octagon Strategy Limited. While the ban on ICOs in Mainland China led to some large cryptoexchanges shifting their legal status and some operations elsewhere,[40] it remained active in blockchain development[41] and mining operations. However, that is subject to significant headwinds. The Leading Group of Internet Financial Risks Remediation, established in 2016, remained active in closing down domestic websites related to trading crypto-assets and ICOs and banning payment services from accepting crypto-assets such as Bitcoin. In August 2018 local authorities took steps to ban

---

[36] Prior to this time it had become common for ICO issuers to seek "non-security" legal opinions. However, it had by this time become increasingly difficult to give such an opinion and many law firms adopted a policy approach that they will not provide such opinions.

[37] For example, in Hong Kong see Securities and Futures Commission of Hong Kong (2018a, b, c).

[38] For a review, see Johnstone (2020a).

[39] Globally significant platforms include OKEx, BitMEX, OKCoin and ANX. According to the Securities and Futures Commission of Hong Kong (2019b), dozens of cryptoexchanges were operating in Hong Kong at the time.

[40] Including Binance, often regarded as the largest cryptoexchange globally (now headquartered in Malta), and Huobi (now incorporated in the BVI and listed in Hong Kong, stock code: 1611).

[41] The Office of the Central Cyberspace Affairs Commission has indicated over 500 projects are in progress encompassing trade finance, asset management, cross-border payments, and supply chain financing. See Cyberspace Administration of China (2019).

hotels, office buildings and shopping malls in Beijing from hosting events promoting cryptocurrencies[42] and it was reported that the websites of over 120 foreign cryptoexchanges would be blocked.[43] Mining activities have been the subject of discouragement and repeated speculation that they may be simply shut down.[44] Other jurisdictions in Asia had also attracted large numbers of cryptoexchanges. Malaysia, for example, was the home to around 40 cryptoexchanges by the end of 2018.[45]

Point of No Return

As will be apparent from the foregoing phases, the general approach has been to assess crypto-assets against silos established by existing regulatory frameworks—really the only option for regulatory agencies whose powers are prescribed by statutes conceived in a pre-CCTech era intended to cover the core triarchy of money, securities and commodities/futures, and the activities related to them. In the current phase, most regulatory agencies in Asia outside of Mainland China have in effect acquiesced in the inevitability of crypto-assets, a development influenced in significant ways by common underlying concerns that have been crystallized in FinCEN's and FATF's 2019 position on crypto-assets.[46] Learning and experiences over the past 5 or so years have resulted in clearer directions about where crypto-assets fit within legal systems, and this is discussed next.

The Current Status Quo

There is at present significant regional variation in the treatment of crypto-assets. The three largest financial markets in Asia—Japan, Hong Kong, and Mainland China—continue in divergent directions. Japan has continued to introduce legislative changes, Hong Kong has introduced adapted non-statutory regulatory responses without any change in the law, and Mainland China has maintained its ban.

---

[42] Huang (2018b).
[43] Huang (2018b).
[44] For example, see Huang (2018a, b).
[45] Source: Fintech News Malaysia.
[46] Financial Crimes Enforcement Network (2019). Financial Action Task Force (2019). FATF formally adopted amendments on June 21, 2019 that detailed an interpretative note to Recommendation 15 which sets out standards and expectations applying to virtual assets and virtual asset service providers.

Status and Treatment of Crypto-Assets

Possibly the only Region-wide common ground, as with the international approach generally, is to treat cryptocurrencies as not being legal tender. In this regard there has been some confusion in relation to Japan, which has made legislative amendments that provide for crypto-assets as having proprietary value. While this means crypto-assets can be used for the purposes of making good payment through a payment services channel, it does not render them legal tender.[47]

The status of crypto-assets as property remains unclear in Asia. In Japan, the Tokyo District Court ruled in 2015 that the definition of property in the Civil Code does not support Bitcoin as a possible object of ownership, which appears in part based on the provision that only tangible things can be owned and the Court's (somewhat surprising) finding that a Bitcoin is not the subject of exclusive control.[48] While not addressing the issue directly, amendments to the PSA assist in relation to claims in insolvency situations, as discussed below. On the other hand, in 2019 the Singapore International Commercial Court accepted that virtual currencies do possess the characteristics of property, although the point was not argued in Court, leaving the issue potentially moot.[49]

While several jurisdictions in Asia position crypto-assets according to pre-existing regulatory silos established by statutory law the treatment is not always consistent. Hong Kong applies existing securities laws on a case-by-case basis to determine the status of a crypto-asset[50] as does South Korea; Malaysia has generally prescribed all crypto-assets as securities[51]; Indonesia regards crypto-assets as trading commodities which can only be traded on futures exchanges[52] and are banned as payment instruments or currency[53]; and Thailand distinguishes between virtual currencies that are

---

[47] "Legal tender" essentially means that if a person offers to settle a payment obligation in legal tender that is refused to be accepted then they can't be sued for non-payment. Most countries typically have laws that provide for their fiat currency to be legal tender.

[48] An unofficial translation of the judgment can be found at https://www.law.ox.ac.uk/sites/files/oxlaw/mtgox_judgment_final.pdf. See also Gullifer et al. (2019).

[49] *B2C2 Ltd v Quoine Pte Ltd* [2019] SGHC(I) 03 at 142. The focus of the case was on the application of contract law, in particular the doctrine of mistake involving algorithmic trading.

[50] In practice, the functional definition of security provided by the SFO's "collective investment scheme" reflects the *Howey* test.

[51] Capital Markets and Services (Prescription of Securities) (Digital Currency and Digital Token) Order 2019 and Capital Markets and Services Act 2007.

[52] Ministerial Regulation No. 5/2019.

[53] Bank Indonesia Regulations 18/40/PBI/2016 and 20/6/PBI/2018.

used as a medium of exchange and digital tokens that are used to determine rights.⁵⁴ In contrast, Japan and Singapore have made bespoke legislative changes that take a broadly similar approach. Both work to position crypto-assets under either securities/financial instruments laws or under payment services laws, depending on the characteristics of the crypto-asset. However, as discussed below, important distinctions in these two jurisdictions may create inconsistencies.

Japan

In keeping with its overall approach, Japan has continued to evolve its regulatory framework in relation to the secondary market. The JFSA has taken a firm direction change from monitoring and information gathering towards standards and practices via amendments in 2019 to the PSA and FIEA that have recently come into effect (May 2020). The approach has been to more clearly distinguish the treatment of crypto-assets under the PSA and the FIEA, to specifically provide for "virtual assets" as having proprietary value and as a payment mechanism cum means of settlement, and expanding the definitions of securities and financial instruments and attendant obligations and rights to encompass virtual assets, including in relation to insolvency situations. The change has led to the recognition by the JFSA of a second SRO, the Japan Security Token Offering Association.

The amended PSA has established the basis for more granular requirements specific to the digital environment. Cryptoexchanges, now defined under the PSA as "crypto-asset exchange service provider" ("CAESP") will become subject to tightened regulations including obligations related to disclosure, margin transactions and, importantly, the handling of client money and the segregation of customers' crypto-assets from their own and other's assets. Because the PSA frames "crypto-assets"⁵⁵ as part of a means of settlement, CAESPs will need to be a member of the Certified Association for Payment Service Providers,⁵⁶ and speculative trading has been criminalized.⁵⁷ The

---

⁵⁴Emergency Decree on the Digital Asset Businesses B.E. 2561 (C.E. 2018). To be used in a token offering, a virtual currency must be approved by the Office of the Securities and Exchange Commission - Bitcoin, Bitcoin Cash, Ethereum, Ethereum Classic, Litecoin, Ripple, and Stellar have been approved for this purpose.

⁵⁵The term "virtual currency" has been replaced in the PSA with "crypto asset" (*ango shisan*) in order to avoid the implication that a legal currency is involved.

⁵⁶Else establish that it has equivalent internal regulations and compliance systems. Article 63–5, Item 6 of the revised PSA.

⁵⁷The PSA makes it a criminal offence to induce sales or purchases of a crypto-asset (whether for money or another crypto-asset) for purposes other than a means of payment, such as for the exclusive purpose of promoting the interests in a particular crypto-asset.

amended law clearly contemplates the use of crypto-asset custody services, however, such services are currently treated as a CAESP even if their activities do not include dealing or similar brokerage services.[58] In the event of the insolvency of a CAESP, subject to limited exceptions, the PSA gives priority over general creditors to users who have delegated the management of their crypto assets to the CAESP.[59] These legislative changes in principle introduce important consumer safeguards. However, regulatory effectiveness will depend on how the changes are implemented in practice via more granular regulations, such as the method of achieving asset segregation, details of which are yet to be released. In the interim, the JFSA has issued explanatory material that covers the use of hot and cold wallets.[60]

The amended FIEA has introduced the concept of electronically recorded transferable rights ("ERTRs")[61] to more clearly delineate crypto-assets (as defined in the PSA) from the kind of rights typically associated with tokens issued in ICOs and STOs. ERTRs are rights represented by proprietary value that will include "collective investment scheme interests", a concept involving a broadly similar analysis as the *Howey* test. Crypto-assets have also been included in the definition of financial instruments in order to capture derivatives transactions in which the underlying is a crypto-asset. These amendments bring a raft of the usual requirements into play, ranging from registration statements/prospectuses, reporting and intermediary licensing to market abuse and unfair practices provisions.

However, the exact boundary lines of ERTRs and crypto-assets are yet to be defined pending implementing regulations. For example, utility tokens nevertheless could be treated as crypto-assets (*qua* a means of payment) rather than as ERTRs. Clarity is essential in order to provide commercial certainty in view of the very different obligations that arise depending on whether a token falls under the PSA or FIEA.

Hong Kong

ICOs are generally permitted but if a token issued in an ICO possesses characteristics normally associated with securities it will be regulated by the SFO[62] and possibly by Hong Kong's prospectus law.[63] Acts taken in relation

---

[58] Article 2, Paragraph 7, Item 4 of the revised PSA.
[59] Article 63-19-2, Paragraph 1 of the revised PSA.
[60] https://www.JFSA.go.jp/common/diet/198/02/setsumei.pdf.
[61] *denshi kiroku iten kenri*.
[62] Securities and Futures Commission of Hong Kong (2017).
[63] Companies (Winding-up and Miscellaneous Provisions) Ordinance (Cap. 32).

to a crypto-asset may invoke licensing requirements under the SFO arising out of: dealing in, advising on or managing virtual assets, or establishing platforms for alternative trading services[64] where the crypto-asset is a security, or in relation to futures contracts traded on recognized markets where the underlying is a crypto-asset.[65] To date there has been one enforcement action taken by the SFC, in March 2018, in relation to the ICO of Black Cell Technology Limited.[66] While the SFC regarded the Black Cell ICO as possibly constituting an unauthorized collective investment scheme being offered to the public, the basis of its assessment was brief and provided little or no further guidance to the market.[67] In practice, the absence of case law or regulatory guidance in Hong Kong means that the best assessment of whether an ICO will be treated as a security under Hong Kong law is to consider the SFO's functional definition of collective investment scheme in light of the *Howey* test, and the more detailed 2017 reports of the US SEC's 21(a) Report and report on the Munchee ICO.[68] Where a crypto-asset falls outside of the scope of the SFO it is essentially unregulated.

In November 2018 the SFC announced two important initiatives. First, it established a licensing sandbox for cryptoexchanges, referred to as "virtual asset trading platforms" ("VASP").[69] The sandbox is premised on a cryptoexchange trading at least one crypto-asset classified as a security, since otherwise the SFC would have no statutory authority to issue a licence. An applicant for a licence would need to accept conditions on its licence that would apply not only to its securities-related activities but also to its operations more generally, including all crypto-assets traded on the cryptoexchange irrespective of whether they are securities. In November 2019 the SFC released regulatory standards applicable to VASPs. These seek to address concerns related to, inter alia, safe custody of assets, requirements pertaining to KYC and AML/CTF, market manipulation, risk management and conflicts of interest. As at the date of writing no cryptoexchange has been granted a VASP licence though it is widely understood that some cryptoexchanges are in discussions with the SFC. To date only one company has announced its application for a licence—OSL Digital Securities Limited, a subsidiary of the HKEX listed

---

[64] Called automated trading systems in Hong Kong under the SFO.

[65] For example, this would include exchanges authorized in the United Kingdom by the FCA (such as Crypto Facilities) and in the United States by the CFTC (such as CME, TD Ameritrade, TeraExchange, LedgerX, NADEX, etc.).

[66] Securities and Futures Commission of Hong Kong (2018a, b, c).

[67] Ibid.

[68] For a review, see Johnstone (2018b).

[69] Securities and Futures Commission of Hong Kong (2018b) & (2019b).

BC Technology Group Limited.[70] While the SFC's proposal is highly laudable in an admittedly difficult legal environment, and will undoubtedly bring a higher level of consumer protection via regulatory oversight, there are a number of difficult issues that remain outstanding for its approach to be regarded as sustainable.[71]

Second, the SFC announced regulatory standards for firms managing crypto-asset portfolios or distributing crypto-asset funds, and this is discussed below.

Mainland China

In October 2019 President Xi Jinping stated that China must seize the opportunities presented by blockchain technology to innovate and transform industries.[72] The focus in Mainland China is on public purpose as opposed to public use. Thus, while cryptographic technologies continue to be actively developed in connection with the traditional financial marketplace, such as by banks looking for efficiency gains, Mainland China's position established in 2017 remains essentially unchanged. Considerable sensitivity in the crypto space remains. Binance's Weibo[73] account has been closed, WeChat has prohibited crypto trading,[74] cryptoexchanges have been subject to a renewed crackdown (39 based in Shenzhen alone),[75] and mining activities have been added to a list of industries that are to be discouraged or eliminated.[76] Other than previously expressed concerns about the retail public, etc., a significant driver of the approach in China is its push on two fronts. First, the DC/EP (Digital Currency Electronic Payment),[77] a central bank digital currency which in April 2020 entered a pilot testing phase in four cities, operates on a two-tiered issuance structure, is distributed by commercial banks and tech firms (not the central bank directly), and initially targets retail users.[78] Second, its Blockchain Service Network ("BSN") which launched in

---

[70]Announcement dated 7 November 2019. https://www1.hkexnews.hk/listedco/listconews/sehk/2019/1107/2019110700800.pdf.
[71]Johnstone (2020a).
[72]Remarks made at the 18th collective study of the Political Bureau of the Central Committee. Foxley (2019).
[73]China's messaging service, broadly similar to Twitter.
[74]Lielacher (2019).
[75]Suberg (2019).
[76]By the National Development and Reform Commission. See Li (2019).
[77]https://www.nbd.com.cn/articles/2020-04-16/1425918.html.
[78]The DC/EP is issued to a regulated intermediary which then distributes to the public - the Agricultural Bank of China and payment service providers AliPay and WeChat Pay (respectively

April 2020 and aims to make available to the public a low-cost blockchain development infrastructure.[79]

In January 2020 a new law came into effect regulating cryptographic works and established the State Cryptographic Administration to create guidelines and policies.[80] This has been described as implicit cryptocurrency regulation that will negatively impact on blockchain development as a result of concerns it makes networks transparent to the government.[81] While the law does require commercial entities to be subject to audits on standards it does not require commercial cryptographers to hand over source code that is not subject to the state secrets law. However, the latter is notoriously vague and the impact of the new law is likely to require time to assess.

Other Jurisdictions

ICOs are now generally permitted in Singapore, Malaysia, Thailand and Indonesia, albeit on different grounds.

In Singapore, the conditions for an ICO now depend on the application of the SFA and the revised Payment Services Act ("SPSA") that became effective in January 2020. The SFA will apply where the ICO structure and characteristics, including rights attached to tokens, is regarded as a "capital markets product", i.e. a security.[82] On the other hand, the SPSA provides for the concept of a "digital payment token",[83] being a digital representation of value distinct from e-money[84] and from securities covered by the SFA. Importantly, the SPSA brings digital payment tokens within a regulatory framework covering dealing and cryptocurrency exchange services. While guidance has been provided by the MAS that provides useful case studies,[85] it remains open to question whether the approach taken is sufficient to address the legal risks involved in ICOs.[86]

Malaysia, which had originally taken a negative stance towards ICOs, in January 2019 took the approach of defining all crypto-assets as securities to

---

owned by Alibaba and Tencent) are involved in the pilot. The four cities are Shenzhen, Xiong'an, Chengdu and Suzhou.

[79] See https://www.bsnbase.com/ (Chinese) and https://global.bsnbase.com/ (English).
[80] Xinhua (2020).
[81] For example, see Zmudzinski (2019).
[82] Securities and Futures Act (Cap. 289), specifically section 2(1) thereof.
[83] Section 2(1) SFA.
[84] Monetary Authority of Singapore (2019), Section 3.
[85] Monetary Authority of Singapore (2018).
[86] Basak et al. (2019).

bring them under regulatory oversight.[87] This allows ICOs subject to registration requirements,[88] and requires cryptoexchanges to be licensed—as at the end of the grace period in March 2019, of the 42 cryptoexchanges that had been operating only 22 had applied for a licence, the rest being required to cease operations and return client assets.[89] In Thailand, ICOs are permitted as a result of the Emergency Decree on the Digital Asset Businesses B.E. 2561 (C.E. 2018), and they are permitted in Indonesia because no specific laws apply or have been introduced.

South Korea has changed its stance following the policy report by the Fourth Industrial Revolution Commission under the Presidential Office, which contemplates licensing cryptoexchanges, providing for crypto-custodians, OTC and derivatives trading, and integrating crypto-assets into the financial system.[90] In March 2020 a bill was passed that will legalize crypto-assets and cryptoexchanges as from March 2021, subject to meeting compliance requirements.[91]

Developments in Other Financial Products Related to Crypto-Assets

The creation of funds with a focus on crypto-assets led to Hong Kong adapting its existing regulatory framework. As part of its crypto-assets related initiatives in 2018 and 2019, the SFC introduced a new framework covering fund managers of investment portfolios where either the investment objective of the portfolio is to invest in virtual assets or the manager intends to invest 10% or more of the gross asset value of the portfolio in virtual assets. Such "virtual asset fund managers" will be subject to additional terms and conditions on their licence, the proforma of which were released in October 2019,[92] with the first such amended licence being created in April 2020.[93] The terms and conditions for licensing such funds will be relevant for crypto hedge funds to consider.

---

[87] Per the Capital Markets and Services (Prescription of Securities) (Digital Currency and Digital Token) Order 2019, dated 14 January 2019. See also Securities Commission Malaysia (2019a).
[88] Securities Commission Malaysia (2019b). See also the Act on the Regulation of Conducting Fundraising Business without Permission 2010.
[89] Fong (2019).
[90] Yoon (2020); Palmer (2020).
[91] Amending the Act on Reporting and Use of Specific Financial Information.
   https://likms.assembly.go.kr/bill/billDetail.do?billId=PRC_S1W9V1R1K2Y5J1A5K3V1Z0L4X1H3W9
[92] Securities and Futures Commission of Hong Kong (2019a, b).
[93] Venture Smart Asia.

The potential for blockchain to enable fractional ownership of tangible and intangible assets, i.e. tokenization via tradable crypto-asset-backed securities ("DABS"), has been discussed in Asia since around 2016. The later development of STOs had in theory fostered the issuance of DABS in receptive jurisdictions but until quite recently found little traction in Asia, which lags behind developments in the USA. In August and September 2019 FinFabrik[94] successfully launched two DABS on its CrossPool platform: a private credit instrument for a Hong Kong construction machinery rental and trading company, and a private equity participation in rights for a film.[95] In Japan, the traditional retail interest in securitized real estate provides a likely avenue for DABS.[96] The roughly 6x growth of Asian private equity over the past decade, now representing 26% of the global private equity market,[97] also provides clear opportunities for DABS to generate access to high net worth investors, though no successful private equity DABS have been launched to date.

Issues for Ecosystem Development

The development of a digital ecosystem, capable of operating on a cross-border basis, is essential if society is to benefit from the potential of CCTech. However, it is far from clear that the approaches taken in Asia have supported this objective. An ecosystem can be defined as a complex system composed of all the units found in a particular environment, interacting with it and with each other. The different units may to a significant extent be interdependent.

Units in a CCTech ecosystem, such as a particular blockchain implementation, face survival challenges in an environment determined by the prevailing political, economic and legal infrastructure. Supporting legal conditions and an efficient economic organization are factors that have correctly been put forward as precursors to the growth in western capitalist societies[98] and are no less essential for the development of a digital ecosystem. Such factors shape the course of human events and facilitate economic and social change, including the restructuring of relationships of control.[99] The latter is of

---

[94] https://www.finfabrik.com/. The DABS are described in the Lightpaper https://www.crosspool.io/
[95] Frater (2019).
[96] For example, see https://www.securitize.io/press/new-research-suggests-digital-securitization-facilitates-greater-real-estate-investment.
[97] Yang, K. et al. (2019).
[98] North and Thomas (1973).
[99] Bowman (1996), p. 35.

particular concern as the possibility for fundamentally different commercial relationships, including disintermediated economics, rests at the heart of CCTech.[100] However, regulatory responses to date have not adequately addressed this element, which has slowed the development of the ecosystem. A short-list of concerns in this regard, which have been expanded upon elsewhere,[101] are as follows.

The Problem of Diversity

When looked at on a regional basis, the diversity of approaches in Asia gives rise to fundamentally different commercial conditions for activity in each jurisdiction. Engaging in an act in relation to a particular crypto-asset may in different jurisdictions be treated as falling under domestic securities or commodities laws, under payment services laws, under bespoke crypto laws or outside any regulatory oversight. This creates uncertainties around enterprise development and sustainability issues. The lack of consistency and regional coordination is amply demonstrated in the case of Japan and Singapore—while both have recently made legislative amendments to bring a similar type of crypto-asset under their respective payment services laws, the two jurisdictions provide for definitions that are different in material ways, thus opening up a distinct possibility of the same crypto-asset being treated very differently.[102]

The Problem of Patchy Integration

Applying financial regulation has had patchy success. While it has to an extent de-risked markets subject to oversight, it has been less successful in de-risking the regional cum global market in crypto-assets. A not insignificant volume of trading has moved to cryptoexchanges that operate in jurisdictions that provide little or no regulatory protection to investors, which merely pushes the problem to be someone else's problem. There remains a residual risk that local investors remain exposed to those venues. In this environment, regulatory efficiency fares poorly.[103] Where the opportunities for crypto-assets to be transacted in

---

[100] See for example May (1988) and Dai (1998).
[101] Johnstone (2020b).
[102] Compare Article 2(5) of the JPSA and section 2(1) of the SPSA.
[103] There are a number of technical definitions of regulatory efficiency that do not affect the key argument being made out here. For example, regulatory efficiency could be defined as the efficacy

regulated jurisdictions are diminished, liquidity may be pushed to unregulated environments, increasing the risk of abusive practices that have been problematic in well-regulated markets. While an investor can choose to participate only in a regulated market, crypto-asset prices are not solely determined by transactions in regulated marketplaces. Concerns such as these have given rise to the argument that regulatory agencies and lawmakers must respond to the development of CCTech by adopting "attraction regulation".[104]

In jurisdictions that may treat crypto-assets as securities, insufficient attention has been given to the role of intermediaries from the traditional marketplace of stocks and bonds, yet these are the intermediaries accustomed to the policy objectives of regulatory oversight. It remains a problem that labelling a crypto-asset as a security does not mean that granular securities regulations are capable of being applied in any meaningful way. For example, securities dealers from the traditional markets have been unable to comply with rules relating to accounts, audits and asset segregation. This leaves the crypto-asset as a special class of "security" that would appear to necessitate bespoke regulatory solutions. In practice, securities dealers in Asia have been unable to participate in this "securities" market.

… and Patchy Support

The need to develop a legal environment more attuned to the characteristics of CCTech remains to be squarely addressed. Courts have struggled with what laws apply to crypto-assets, a problem in no way resolved by a restrictive categorization as a security. There is in general an absence of policy direction that will facilitate laws and regulations having a positive impact on ecosystem development. This ranges from governance (the governance of crypto-assets is not subject to any constraints whatsoever meaning they can be created poorly, gamed, abused or simply provide inadequate means of resolving issues moving forward), to code standards or benchmarks that promote interoperability (in the absence of any guidelines for crypto-asset development a rapid population of crypto-assets is emerging that are creating barriers for interaction), to clarity over the relationship between a token holder and the network on which the token resides. Developments that promote the licensing of cryptoexchanges may in principle seek to address market abuse, but there

---

of regulatory rules in achieving stated policy objectives, or the maximisation of the general welfare through the adoption of optimal rules designed to correct market failures. *See generally* Winston (2006).

[104] *See generally* Johnstone (2018b), Section 5.3.

are no clear supporting laws that address market manipulation and insider dealing in crypto-assets that do not fall under securities laws.[105] In short, policymaking and regulatory development has suffered from shortcomings in applying financial regulations, and it has not sufficiently addressed the ground conditions for positioning CCTech as a tool capable of serving wider social purposes. However, there are nascent steps being taken in these regards, such as the newly formed "Blockchain Governance Initiative Network" ("BGIN") launched on 10 March 2020, which is supported by the JFSA.[106]

Taxonomies and Technology Neutrality

The resolution of policy problems is often influenced by tacit and explicit knowledge about the nature of the problem,[107] and there is a tendency to look for solutions from within the extant regulatory framework in priority to possibly more innovative and effective solutions.[108] To date, policymakers have sought to fit crypto-assets into a taxonomy typically based around payment, investment or utility functions. Such a fit-to-existing-regulations taxonomy ("FER taxonomy") engages familiar tools and concepts, implicitly assumes existing regulation as an enduring metric of relevance to policy objectives, and is oriented to risk reduction based around existing models of risk and opportunity.

Taxonomies are systems that identify, describe and classify based around a priori constructs (i.e. ideas or theories) or purposes. Questions that must be asked of a taxonomy include: what purpose is it intended to serve; does it provide information germane to that purpose; does the a priori construct it is based on presuppose outcomes; and is it likely to be sustainable as "new species" emerge.

FER taxonomies achieve very little and are essentially recursive, appearing to "solve" the question of what laws should apply, or should be developed to apply, to crypto-assets.[109] They perform poorly in relation to the key characteristics of crypto-assets, which may be capable of simultaneously falling into more than one category according to how they are used, or might be regarded as morphing from one category to another over time[110] in accordance with

---

[105] Johnstone (2020a), Secion. 6.3.
[106] Financial Services Agency Japan (2020).
[107] Nonaka (1994).
[108] Winn (forthcoming).
[109] Johnstone (2019).
[110] Hinman (2018).

the semantics of the regulation that is applied to it (not the technology).[111] By its nature, an FER taxonomy is incapable of responding meaningfully to changed underlying assumptions—see "Considerations for a Setting New Bearing" section below.

FER taxonomies also make achieving technology neutrality more difficult because the objectives of incumbent agencies have been significantly influenced by their own origins. This often presupposes a model of activity—how commercial relationships, institutional arrangements and interactions are formed—that is at odds with different possibilities presented by CCTech. For example: cryptoexchange regulation remains largely premised on centralized structures despite the availability of decentralized models undertaking exchange functions[112]; more generally, CCTech has the potential to bring institutional innovation to economic coordination and governance.[113]

The regulatory enforcement of an FER taxonomy therefore tends to cause digital ecosystem development to cycle back to the extant ways of doing things—which results in the possibilities offered by CCTech being constrained, pre-empted, or bypassed altogether. The idea that policymakers following a principle of "same business, same risks, same rules" will be sufficient to promote technology neutrality in relation to crypto-assets is misguided.[114]

An Alternative—DBA Taxonomy

In response to these concerns, a Determined-By-Architecture ("DBA")[115] approach to taxonomy has been proposed as an alternative lens to bring to bear on some current issues.[116] The focus of a DBA taxonomy is on the genesis and nature of (and subsequent operation of) the connection (i.e. relationship) being established between two or more persons. The key "genetic" components of CCTech primarily comprise three elements: (i) cryptographically secure technology (ii) able to implement a consensus mechanism (iii) across a decentralized network—hence CCTech. Similar to the GATC bases

---

[111] Ether is a prime example of this taxonomic failure as it can be used as means of payment, as an investment, or as providing a utility. In contrast, a security such as a share is unable to perform a variety of such other functions and unsurprisingly presents no difficult issues for an FER taxonomy.
[112] Johnstone (2020a), Section 5.
[113] Davidson et al. (2016). See Section 3.
[114] Although this quote may be apt in relation to traditional banking (see the Statement by Sabine Lautenschläger "Digital na(t)ive? Fintechs and the future of banking" 27 March 2017), see the response to the EU Consultation provided by the World Federation of Exchanges (undated).
[115] The similarity to "DNA" is intentional.
[116] Johnstone (2020b).

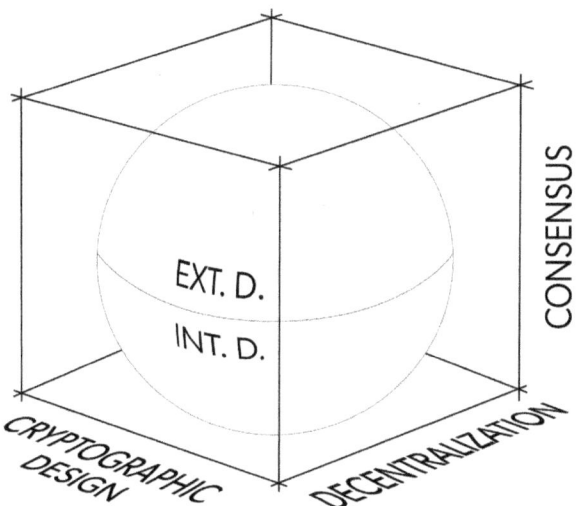

Fig. 10.1 The Determined-By-Architecture (DBA) taxonomy (*Source* Author)

comprising DNA, these elements can be implemented in innumerable ways. As such, a DBA taxonomy would be concerned with the fundamental operation of CCTech, and less so with labelling the things exchanged (such as capital, services, rights, permissions, etc.). This introduces bottom-up considerations to regulating the technology.

A DBA taxonomy may also be more sensitive to different levels of code behaviour. The internal dimensions of the code (the engineering of the stack) pose issues distinct from the external dimensions of the code (the social elements of the code, its functions and operations).[117] Figure 10.1 shows the internal and external dimensions of a CCTech iteration against the three axes of a DBA taxonomy. A DBA taxonomy therefore permits a regulatory approach that may be more responsive to the unique operations and issues presented by CCTech. Topics such as governance and interoperability may be understood and addressed at a more granular level of the technology's operation. For example, there has been little exploration of how the ability to write self-executing regulatory mechanisms into the underlying code might be relevant to regulatory clarity and/or objectives. Because the DBA approach does not depend on existing commercial structures, it may also promote technology neutrality—technology neutrality does not equate to technology agnosia. Moreover, a sustainable ecosystem is likely to create

---

[117] Johnstone (2020b).

new types of problems that will demand a taxonomy well attuned to the enduring characteristics of CCTech.

Considerations for a Setting New Bearing

Subject to intra-regional variations in their detail the direction in Asia is to fit crypto-assets into one of two main silos—as a payment mechanism or as a security (derivatives can be built on either of these)—failing which there will be no regulatory oversight, thus leaving the status of the crypto-asset in a lacuna. While there has been some meaningful progress in pursuing regulatory objectives, significant difficulties in providing appropriate and more comprehensive responses to CCTech remain. The benefits of such progress to the industry and the consumer have been mixed. Whether the much sought-after goal of ecosystem development has been hampered rather than facilitated by existing approaches likely turns on the singular question of whether de-risking has prevented irreparable damage to a burgeoning industry by successfully excluding bad actors, while at the same time allowing good actors the opportunity for advancement.

Regulatory Incrementalism

Many of the foregoing issues can be traced back to a starting point that presumes financial regulation and the related regulatory agencies are best placed to regulate crypto-assets because of the intersection with the capital market. This has fundamentally shaped regulatory thinking around CCTech in what can be characterized as regulatory incrementalism. To date it has served the purpose of providing various stopgap solutions that seek to address risk. De-risking is not the sole measure; prospects for innovation and growth also must be considered. Concerns have been expressed that the "lack of a workable regulatory framework has hindered innovation and growth… [and] offer[s] no clear path for a functioning token network to emerge".[118] The European Commission's 2019 consultation "On an EU framework for markets in crypto-assets" also acknowledges the applicability and suitability of financial regulation to digital assets is problematic and could limit the use of CCTech, yet continues to tie digital assets more narrowly to finance.[119]

---

[118] Pierce (2019).
[119] See pages 4 and 3 respectively of the consultation document.

Regulatory incrementalism is not, per se, a bad thing. For existing regulated markets it provides a gradual evolution of standards that permit responses to be developed in lockstep with the relevant changes. As such, it minimizes disruption and facilitates acceptance and adoption. However, as Charles Lindblom amply demonstrated, incrementalism has its limits.[120] In the present context of complex problems, incrementalism suffers from a variety of problems including limited policy alternatives being adopted; a greater preoccupation with risk reduction than with facilitation of goals; danger in the misapplication of legal/regulatory requirements to an inappropriate factual matrix; and the analysis preceding incremental change exploring some not all of the possible consequences.[121] Incrementalism has supported FER taxonomies that are insensitive to the underlying characteristics of CCTech. It is less than clear that incrementalism around a financial regulation model will provide optimal solutions that meet overarching social objectives. For example, if one imagined that personal data was an unregulated, packageable commodity that could be sold into the public capital market, financial regulation could be applied and could sensibly operate within the parameters of its own objectives—though it would not achieve the overarching social objectives of safeguarding the use of personal data. Despite these problems, whether existing laws remain fit for purpose has been subject to only very limited questioning.[122]

It is arguable, if not self-evident, that the underlying assumptions on which extant laws are built have changed in material ways. Changed fact patterns raise doubts about the sustainability of continuing to apply existing regulations. For example[123]: that one can identify and geo-locate an actor; that all actors subject to oversight mechanisms are by nature centralized and able to be held accountable for a network/ecosystem; that trust at scale can only be provided by a trusted third party; that a public market must occur on a centralized platform that acts as a trading gateway; that voting mechanisms by which decisions are made cannot be unwound; that decision-making is essentially centralized and hierarchical[124]; that a token generation is comparable

---

[120]Lindblom (1959) & (1979). Since Lindblom, there has been increased emphasis on the role of the status quo in incrementalist processes that suggest the quality of policy development is frequently negatively impacted by economic, political or institutionally sourced influences that bring about marginal, if any, adjustments to the status quo.

[121]Lindblom (1979), p. 522.

[122]The application of existing silos, fostered by regulators possessed of specialized toolkits, has been well supported by a variety of industry professionals looking to redirect their experience in the traditional markets to new business opportunities and by the institutional providers of financial capital looking for familiar investment contexts under STO structures.

[123]See further Johnstone (2020b).

[124]As compared to dynamic, distributed management structures, e.g. holacracy.

to a security being issued by an issuer with centralized accountability; that once a crypto-asset has been classified as a security (or as a payment device), the laws and regulations that apply to it are fit for purpose; that a completed transaction in a security or other asset (or payment device) is inviolable except under operation of law. Conversely, in the instances where securities laws are appropriate to apply, it does not follow that they should be applied more broadly across the panorama of the crypto-asset landscape.

If the choice to apply securities laws is underdetermined[125] by new fact patterns, the policy choice between different regulatory approaches comes down to the opportunity cost of choosing one approach over the other, which may change over time.

Positioning the CCTech discussion around financial regulation has already had evolutionary consequences. Commercial decisions taken by developers, and hence ecosystem development, have been redirected by the need to comply with securities laws. For example, enthusiasm around the ICO model did not "wane" because other forms of virtual asset fundraising such as STOs have attracted interest[126]—the possible commercial relationships offered by ICOs were essentially evicted from contributing to ecosystem development by being positioned under a legal infrastructure that reinforced the traditional relationship, and barrier, between capital users and capital providers. This has not helped and may instead have inadvertently bolstered an existing speculative interest in crypto-assets that has come to overshadow the concept of CCTech providing new avenues for commercial activity. The result is an inverted development situation—the business proposition of disintermediated commerce undertaken digitally that might be settled in a digital currency medium now competes with a cryptocurrency market that continues to be volatile, subject to abusive practices, and generally subject to limited pockets of effective oversight.[127] This is consistent with the narrative of technological revolution suggesting that the irruption of a new technology such as CCTech will be initially dominated by "financial capital", which serves to push the revolution forward, and subsequently by the involvement of "production capital", which serves to grow the technology and propagate the paradigm across the economy.[128] While this is not to ignore the de-risking achieved as regards dishonest or dubious ICO schemes, equally one

---

[125] In the sense of the underdetermination thesis. *See generally* Quine (1951).
[126] Securities and Futures Commission of Hong Kong (2019b), para 14.
[127] Underwood (2018).
[128] Perez (2002). Perez uses "financial capital" to refer to actors using wealth in the form of money to create more wealth and "production capital" to refer to the motives and behaviours of actors who generate new wealth via the production of goods or provision of services; pp. 71–72.

cannot ignore the considerable telescoping of concepts underlying ICOs and DAOs—or concepts that might further evolve from them—that has caused CCTech in various ways to become pinioned by securities laws. If the irruption of CCTech remains yoked to financial capital there is a danger that today's risk-averse financial regulation could stifle innovation and stall entry into a production capital phase, leaving CCTech delivering little more than a technical reinvention of existing financial products and economic relationships.

A Paradigm

The emergence of CCTech as a new technology can be seen as challenging the extant regulatory paradigm—in the sense meant by Thomas Kuhn[129]—and has resulted in lawmakers and technologists inhabiting different realities.[130] This is the result of the application of incompatible frameworks to organize their respective diagnostic and prescriptive enquiries—in each case, the elements contained in the framework generate the type of question that needs to be addressed.[131] However, paradigms constitute powerful forces and it is of interest if not troubling to observe that the comments cited above to the effect that regulation has hindered innovation and growth were made by a regulator whose mindset remains that securities law nevertheless prevails as the appropriate approach.[132]

The new possibilities offered by CCTech have not been matched by a shift in how to think about CCTech in regulatory terms. The appropriateness and sustainability of the incrementalist approach taken to date deserves far more attention than it has received. This would require a more fundamental discussion and assessment of whether it provides a basis or an obstacle for CCTech to be developed in ways beneficial to society. It would explore how to evolve legal constructs that better align with the particular characteristics of CCTech. It would also necessitate questioning the appropriateness of industry regulation falling under the financial regulatory umbrella, and what kind of regulatory oversight body with what overarching priorities might be better suited to the task. While a wholesale disposal of incrementalism is

---

[129] Kuhn (1970).
[130] Johnstone (2020b).
[131] Ostrom (2005), pp. 28–29.
[132] Pierce (2019), suggesting a safe harbor.

unwarranted it does require, as Lindblom put it, supplementation "by broad-ranging, often highly speculative, and sometimes utopian thinking about directions and possible features, near and far in time".[133]

Suggestions for Policy Development

How might we begin to think about regulatory progress? The present author has made five proposals for policy development.[134]

First proposal: Develop policies based around a DBA taxonomy addressing the key "genetic" components of CCTech. As different iterations of CCTech build on each other, evolve or begin to be interoperable, regulation based around these elements are more likely to remain sustainable.

Second proposal: Regulatory development should distinguish between the internal and external dimensions of the code and determine what the regulatory objectives and possibilities are in relation to each before proceeding to more granular regulation.

Third proposal: High-level principles need to be developed around several cornerstones: technology and business model neutrality; attraction regulation; restated regulatory objectives based on broader social objectives; and review processes.

Fourth proposal: Policymakers should consider using regulation to set boundary conditions via permissive regulations that stimulate the discovery of private market solutions which align with public policy concerns. Such boundaries would need to provide adequate regulatory certainty around the characterization of the activity.

Fifth proposal: It will be necessary to explore, having regard to the first four proposals above, what type of agency will need to be created to foster industry and ecosystem development. The new agency would need to have powers sufficient to ascertain and limit the boundary lines of where financial regulation might apply. This must be wrapped into an international approach.

Asia Tomorrow

At the time of writing, at least in Asia, there is a notable lack of cross-jurisdictional coordination to achieve any of this, despite the obvious issues

---

[133] Lindblom (1979), p. 522.
[134] Johnstone (2020b).

created for a borderless technology. As jurisdictions introduce policies to de-risk or to attract development capital to get a slice of the economic activity, further regulatory reversals, stopgap solutions and other regulatory tinkering should be expected. This, together with differing political views on the technology and its potential uses, may result in trial-and-error approaches that achieve limited success in promoting genuine innovation and development on a regional basis. For the time being, incrementalism seems well entrenched.

Initiatives in various jurisdictions are nevertheless of interest. Mainland China's BSN assists the developer community, although is likely to embody elements of control that restrain more open-ended possibilities and may remain specific to the Chinese context. Developments in Hong Kong based around licensing conditions provide meaningful opportunities for the discovery of private market solutions, albeit remaining captured within a financial regulatory framework. The JFSA's BGIN may provide some helpful directions for policy thinking, although it remains a new initiative yet to prove itself.

If one believes in the new prospects offered by CCTech, it seems highly probably that an international approach will be needed. Broadly speaking, Asia has in relation to CCTech leaned in the direction of the USA, primarily due to capital market considerations. Change of the more fundamental sort discussed above likely requires the emergence of initiatives driven by social opportunity cost considerations, more likely from the EU than the USA, or a G20 initiative much like those necessary to get countries working together on a coordinated approach to over-the-counter derivatives and credit rating agencies.

Bibliography

Basak, S., Kho, J.H., and Tay, V. (2019). Initial coin offerings and capital market regulation: Singapore's perspective. *International Company and Commercial Law Review*, 30(1), 533–549.

Bowman, S.R. (1996). *The modern corporation and American political thought*. The Pennsylvania State University Press.

Cyberspace Administration of China (2019). *Announcement of the National Internet Information Office on the release of the second batch of domestic blockchain information service record numbers*. 18 October 2019. www.cac.gov.cn.

Dai, W. (1998). *b-money*. https://www.weidai.com/bmoney.txt.

Davidson, S., De Filippi, P., and Potts, J. (2016). *Disrupting Governance: The New Institutional Economics of Distributed Ledger Technology.* 19 July 2016. https://ssrn.com/abstract=2811995.

Financial Action Task Force (2019). *Public Statement-Mitigating Risks from Virtual Assets.* 22 February 2019. www.fatf-gafi.org.

Financial Crimes Enforcement Network (2019). *Application of FinCEN's Regulations to Certain Business Models Involving Convertible Virtual Currencies.* 9 May 2019. www.fincen.gov.

Financial Services Agency Japan (2020). *Launch of a new global network for blockchain "Blockchain Governance Initiative Network"* [BGIN]. 10 March 2020. www.fsa.go.jp.

Financial Services and Treasury Bureau (2015). *LCQ4: Regulation of trading activities of bitcoins.* Press Release 25 March 2015. www.fstb.gov.hk.

Fong, V. (2019). *22 Crypto Exchanges Now Seeking Approval from Securities Commission Malaysia.* 6 March 2019. www.fintechnews.my.

Foxley, W. (2019). China Should 'Seize Opportunity' to Adopt Blockchain. *Coindesk.* 25 October 2019. www.coindesk.com.

Frater, P. (2019). Cannes' 'Papicha' Receives Tokenized Investment from Hong Kong Financiers. *Variety.* 9 September 2019. www.Variety.com.

Gullifer, L., Hara, M., and Mooney, C.W. (2019). *English translation of the Mt Gox judgment on the legal status of bitcoin prepared by the Digital Assets Project.* 11 February 2019. www.law.ox.ac.uk/business-law-blog/blog/2019.

Hinman, W. (2018). *Digital Asset Transactions: When Howey Met Gary (Plastic).* 14 June 2018. https://www.sec.gov/news/speech/speech-hinman-061418.

Hong Kong Monetary Authority (2015). Press Release. *The HKMA reminds the public to be aware of risks associated with Bitcoin.* www.hkma.gov.hk.

Huang, Z. (2018a). China wants an "orderly exit" from bitcoin mining. *Quartz.* 8 January 2018. www.qz.com.

Huang, Z. (2018b). China to block more than 120 offshore cryptocurrency exchanges as crackdown escalates. 23 August 2018. *South China Morning Post.* www.scmp.com.

Japan Times (2017). *Cryptocurrency's worrying boom. Japan Times.* 26 December 2017. www.japantimes.co.jp/opinion/2017.

Jo, H. (2017). In a country known for its "bitcoin zombies," one-third of workers are crypto investors. *Quartz.* 8 December 2017. www.qz.com.

Johnstone, S. (2018a). ICO utility tokens and the relevance of securities law. *Hong Kong Lawyer*, March, pp. 30–33. https://www.hk-lawyer.org/content/ico-utility-tokens-and-relevance-securities-law.

Johnstone, S. (2018b). *Regulating Cryptographic Consensus Technology: Oxymoron or Necessity?* 8 October 2018. https://ssrn.com/abstract=3264556.

Johnstone, S. (2019). Taxonomies of digital assets: recursive or progressive? *Stanford Journal of Blockchain Law and Policy*, Vol. 2 No. 1, January. https://stanford-jblp.pubpub.org/pub/taxonomies-digital-assets.

Johnstone, S. (2020a). Secondary markets in digital assets: rethinking regulatory policy in centralized and decentralized environments. *Stanford Journal of Blockchain Law and Policy*, Vol. 3 No. 2, June.

Johnstone, S. (2020b) *Inhabiting different realities: incrementalism, paradigms and the New Prospect.* The working paper is https://ssrn.com/abstract=3605107.

Kuhn, T.S. (1970). *The structure of scientific revolutions.* Second Edition, enlarged. The University of Chicago Press, London.

Lee, D. (2014). *Mt Gox exchange shutdown sparks Chinese bitcoin gold rush.* 26 February 2014. www.scmp.com.

Li, C. (2019). China, a Major Bitcoin Source, Considers Moving Against It. *The New York Times.* 9 April 2019. www.nytimes.com.

Lielacher, A. (2019). China's bitcoin ban intensifies as WeChat prohibits crypto trading. *Brave New Coin.* 15 May 2019. https://bravenewcoin.com/insights/.

Lindblom, C.E. (1959). The Science of 'Muddling Through'. *Public Administration Review*, Vol. 19, No. 2 (Spring), pp. 79–88.

Lindblom, C.E. (1979). Still Muddling, Not Yet Through. *Public Administration Review*, Vol. 39, No. 6 (Nov.–Dec.), pp. 517–526.

May, T.C. (1988). *The crypto anarchist manifesto.* https://activism.net/cypherpunk/crypto-anarchy.html.

Monetary Authority of Singapore (2018). *A Guide To Digital Token Offerings.* 30 November 2018. www.mas.gov.sg.

Monetary Authority of Singapore (2019). *Consultation on the Payment Services Act 2019: scope of e-money and digital payment tokens.* 23 December 2019. www.mas.gov.sg.

Nonaka, I. (1994). A Dynamic Theory of Organizational Knowledge Creation. *Organization Science*, Vol 5, No. 1 (Feb) 14–37.

North, D.C., and Thomas, R.P. (1973). *The Rise of the Western World.* Cambridge University Press.

Ostrom, E. (2005). *Understanding Institutional Diversity.* Princeton: Princeton University Press.

Palmer, D. (2020). South Korean presidential committee wants to bring crypto into mainstream finance. *Coindesk.* 6 January 2020. www.coindesk.com.

People's Bank of China, Ministry of Industry and Information Technology, China's Banking Regulatory Commission, China's Securities Regulatory Commission, & China's Insurance Regulatory Commission (2013). *Announcement of Preventing Risks of Bitcoin by People's Bank of China, Ministry of Industry and Information Technology, China's Banking Regulatory Comm. and Other Departments.* 3 December 2013. www.pbc.gov.cn/en.

People's Bank of China, China Securities Regulatory Commission, China Banking and Insurance Regulatory Commission, Office of the Central Leading Group for Cyberspace Affairs, Ministry of Industry and Information Technology, State Administration for Industry and Commerce, and China Insurance Regulatory Commission (2017a). *The Regulation on the Disposition of Illegal Fundraising (Consultation Draft).* 24 August 2017. www.pbc.gov.cn/en.

People's Bank of China, China Securities Regulatory Commission, China Banking and Insurance Regulatory Commission, Office of the Central Leading Group for Cyberspace Affairs, Ministry of Industry and Information Technology, State Administration for Industry and Commerce, and China Insurance Regulatory Commission (2017b). *Announcement on Preventing Financial Risks from Initial Coin Offerings.* 4 September 2017. www.pbc.gov.cn/en.

Perez, C. (2002). *Technological Revolutions and Financial Capital: The Dynamics of Bubbles and Golden Ages.* Edward Elgar, Cheltenham, UK.

Pierce, H. (2019). *Broken Windows: Remarks before the 51st Annual Institute on Securities Regulation.* 4 November 2019. www.sec.gov/news.

Quine, W. V. O. (1951). Two Dogmas of Empiricism. Reprinted in *From a Logical Point of View*, 2nd Ed. Cambridge, MA: Harvard University Press, pp. 20–46.

Securities and Futures Commission of Hong Kong (2017). *Statement on initial coin offerings.* 5 September 2017. www.sfc.hk.

Securities and Futures Commission of Hong Kong (2018a). *SFC's regulatory action halts ICO to Hong Kong public.* 19 March 2018. www.sfc.hk.

Securities and Futures Commission of Hong Kong (2018b). *Statement on regulatory framework for virtual asset portfolios managers, fund distributors and trading platform operators.* 1 November 2018. www.sfc.hk.

Securities and Futures Commission of Hong Kong (2018c). *SFC's regulatory action halts ICO to Hong Kong public.* 19 March 2018. www.sfc.hk.

Securities and Futures Commission of Hong Kong (2019a). *Proforma Terms and Conditions for Licensed Corporations which Manage Portfolios that Invest in Virtual Assets.* www.sfc.hk.

Securities and Futures Commission of Hong Kong (2019b). *Regulation of virtual asset trading platforms.* 6 November 2019. www.sfc.hk.

Securities Commission Malaysia (2019a). *SC to regulate offering and trading of digital assets.* 14 January 2019. www.sc.com.my.

Securities Commission Malaysia (2019b). *SC Cautions Investors Against Unauthorised Initial Coin Offerings and Digital Asset Exchanges.* 4 July 2019. Media Releases and Announcements. www.sc.com.my.

Suberg, W. (2019b). China: Shenzhen Identifies 39 Crypto Exchanges Defying Trading Ban. *Cointelegraph.* 22 November 2019. www.cointelegraph.com.

Underwood, B.D. (2018). *Virtual Markets Integrity Initiative Report.* Simon Brandler et al. eds. https://virtualmarkets.ag.ny.gov/.

United States Securities and Exchange Commission (2017). *In the matter of Munchee.* 11 December 2017. www.sec.gov.

Winston, C. (2006). *Government failure versus market failure.* Ebook https://www.brookings.edu/.

Yang, K., Akhtar, U., and Dessard, J., (2019). *Asia-Pacific Private Equity Report 2019*, Bain & Company. www.bain.com.

Yoon Y. (2020). *Korea Needs to Allow Financial Companies to Release Cryptocurrency-related Products, a Presidential Commission Says.* BusinessKorea. 6 January 2020. www.businesskorea.co.kr.

Xie, R. (2019). Why china had to ban cryptocurrency but the US did not: comparative analysis of regulations on crypto-markets between the US and China. *Washington University Global Studies Law Review*, 18(2), 457–492.

Xinhua (2020). China Focus: China adopts law on cryptography. *Xinhuanet*. 10 May 2020. www.xinhuanet.com.

Winn, J. (forthcoming). The Impact of Regulation and Governance on Competition and Innovation in Payment Systems. *SWIFT Institute Grant No. 2015–003*.

Zmudzinski, A. (2019). China Passes First-Ever 'Crypto Law' Going Into Effect January 2020. *Cointelegraph*. 26 October 2019. www.cointelegraph.com.

Part III

Disintermediation in Political Economy and Regulation

11

The Political Economy of the Blockchain

Pēteris Zilgalvis

Where would you rather be, floating passively downstream on a platform to destinations unknown, or to be sailing your own boat, painting the landscape of your life?

The following chapter builds on and further develops some of the themes that were presented in my Public Lecture at the Riga Graduate School of Law on 18 December 2018, and then in my panel intervention at the Harvard European Law Association's Spring Conference in March 2019 at Harvard Law School on *Disruption, Innovation and the Future of Europe*. It has also been inspired by observations on the similarities and parallels between the political economy and law of decentralized digital ecosystems and the trading

---

[1] "From humble origins, Venice had risen to true power. Poverty had been its spur, industriousness its secret. Its simple and ancient industries had developed and multiplied; its naval constructions had become extraordinary; its arsenal was unique." Brief History of Venice, Rinaldo Fulin, lineadaqua, June 2019, San Marco, Venezia, Italy, pp. 38–39.

Peteris Zilgalvis: Personal views hereby presented are the authors' only, and should not in any way be construed as to represent an official position of the European Commission.

P. Zilgalvis (✉)
St. Antony's College, University of Oxford, Oxford, UK
e-mail: peteris.zilgalvis@ec.europa.eu

and cultural networks of ports, coastal cities and seafaring peoples such as the Hanseatic League, Venice,[1] Greece and the Mediterranean: open, dynamic, innovative, connected, building various levels of governance, exchanging value and knowledge, finding agreements and creatively settling disputes.

The law and political economy of decentralized technologies could be described more as a philosophical or political concept than as a technical one or as a specified and limited group of existing or future technologies. What characterizes and differentiates them from other technologies is that they are distributed and foster self-determination rather than being centralized, paternalistic or organized in a silo.

This is also a future-proofed definition since the technologies themselves will develop further, progress or be replaced by others, but what should survive and flourish is this concept of individual or citizen-tricity, multi-level governance and democratic experimentation. The general principles of European (EU) Law themselves underline respect for, and the centricity of, the individual. "Because these rules of law, which permit regulation of the economy, directly affect individuals, the procedures must respect the position of the individual. Community law accordingly contains important principles protecting the individual".[2]

The governance tools of regulatory (and technical) sandboxes as instruments of regulatory innovation accompanying the proponents of new ideas align naturally with this technological and philosophical approach as well, though their application can be much broader. I have discussed this more encompassing vision in my article, "The Need for an Innovation Principle in Regulatory Impact Assessment: the Case of Finance and Innovation in Europe",[3] so will not return to it here; other than to note its applicability to the overall innovation and data economy, of which decentralized digital technologies are an important and challenging (from the regulatory and supervisory point of view) subset. It is clear that many European Union economies could benefit from a larger number of innovations and that appropriate application and adaptation of the regulatory framework can enable such innovation while continuing to safeguard vital public interests.

In addition to the political imperative of holistic citizen-centric governance, innovation and creative destruction engendered by decentralized

---

[2]"Cases and materials on EU Law", Stephen Weatherill, Oxford University Press, Oxford, United Kingdom, 2006, p. 58.

[3]"The need for an Innovation Principle in Regulatory Impact Assessment:
 the Case of Finance and Innovation in Europe," *Policy and Internet*, Wiley Periodicals, Malden, USA and Oxford, UK https://doi.org/10.1002/1944-2866.POI374, Volume 6, Issue 4, pages 377–392, December 2014.

digital technologies reflect the renewal of dynamic capitalism, where incumbents are challenged, and adapt or fall into irrelevance, by new competitors proposing new business models or simply incremental improvements to what has been on the market. Joseph Schumpeter has written, "This process of Creative Destruction is the essential fact about capitalism. It is what capitalism consists in and what every capitalist concern has got to live in".[4]

Little is permanent in market economics and this serves a practical purpose in the face of large dominant firms. Are the platform economy and its dominant platforms destined to rule the digital economy on into the foreseeable future or is change afoot?

Platforms are currently dominant in many parts of today's economy and in the Digital Single Market. However, they are facing issues of data privacy, fake news, unfair trading practices and consumer fatigue with some of their products. As Professors Ariel Ezrachi and Maurice E. Stucke have written, "could it be that, after the initial procompetitive promise, these technologies lead to higher prices, poorer quality, fewer options presented to us, and less innovation in things we care about, such as our privacy?".[5]

The rise of decentralized digital technologies: blockchain/distributed ledger technologies, artificial intelligence/collective intelligence, Internet of Things, Big Data, 3D printing and robotics, is a challenge in philosophy and approach to the centralized platform model of the Internet of today. These developments are related to, and also sometimes referred to as: convergence, Web3, protocols not platforms or as being part of the Next Generation Internet.

It is still an open question whether these developments will be good for competition and the consumer, or will simply serve as fodder for absorption by the same Platforms in M&A. As Ezrachi and Stucke wrote, "To cement its leadership, the super-platform may engage in the defensive practices of acquiring or blocking innovation or entry that might potentially undermine its dominance".[6] The moves of several of the biggest platforms to explore applications for payments or for decentralized social media on blockchains can be seen as part of their commitment to new types of innovation or as attempts to squelch future competition from new and dynamic actors in the market who could threaten their dominance of the sector.

---

[4]"Can Capitalism Survive? Creative Destruction and the Future of the Global Economy", originally published as "Capitalism, Socialism and Democracy" by Harper & Row, New York, 1942, pp. 42–43.
[5]"Virtual Competition: The Promise and Perils of the Algorithm-Driven Economy", published by Harvard University Press, Cambridge, Massachusetts, USA, and London, England, 2016, p. vii.
[6]Ibid., p. 175.

Decentralized Decision-Making

Looking at the history of the development of the Internet, it could be deduced that decentralized decision-making was superior for enabling development compared to a centralized process, incorporating entrepreneurial actors with diverse perspectives. Many subcommittees and different actors contributed to building the Internet. The governance was grounded deeply in technical meritocracy and was inspired by the peer review system, and this was later formalized.

A rallying cry of today is "build protocols, not platforms".[7] However, it is interesting to note that while this vision is forward looking; at the same time, it harks back to the spirit and practices of the early Internet and to the innovation ecosystem that it spawned. In his article, "Protocols, Not Platforms: A Technological Approach to Free Speech", subtitled, "Altering the Internet's economic and digital infrastructure to promote free speech", Mike Masnick writes, "To be clear, this is an approach that would bring us *back* to the way the internet used to be. The early internet involved many different protocols—instructions and standards that anyone could then use to build a compatible interface. Email used SMTP (Simple Mail Transfer Protocol). Chat was done over IRC (Internet Relay Chat). Usenet served as a distributed discussion system using NNTP (Network News Transfer Protocol). The World Wide Web itself was its own protocol: HyperText Transfer Protocol, or HTTP".[8]

Further, he observes as I have above, "In the past few decades, however, rather than building new protocols, the internet has grown up around controlled platforms that are privately owned. These can function in ways that appear similar to the earlier protocols, but they are controlled by a single entity".[9]

An analogy that can be found today is in the challenges and opportunities that we see in the development of the next generation of the Internet, the new data economy and the social and economic models that will make the green transition a reality. In addition to new economic opportunities based on disruptive innovation and more competition in the market, the new decentralized digital technologies being developed today can offer even more to science and to society, as I will detail below.

---

[7] "Protocols, Not Platforms: A Technological Approach to Free Speech." By Mike Masnick, Knight First Amendment Institute at Columbia University, published 21 August 2019, https://knightcolumbia.org/content/protocols-not-platforms-a-technological-approach-to-free-speech, accessed on 16/03/2020.

[8] Ibid.

[9] Ibid.

The decentralization element is also important for the development and safety of artificial intelligence and other emerging technologies. "Just for pure computational reasons, making very advanced intelligence is going to involve making communities of intelligent systems because a community can see much more data than an individual system. If it's all a question of seeing a lot of data, then we're going to have to distribute that data across lots of different intelligent systems and have them communicate with one another so that between them, as a community, they can learn from a huge amount of data meaning that in the future, the community aspect of it is going to be essential".[10]

Thinking about industrial policy and new technologies, another, and more European, example is that of Airbus. As Sarah Gordon wrote in the Financial Times, "Airbus' success lies in its political roots".[11] Impressive success was achieved by that bold initiative: within 25 years, Airbus had 50% of the global commercial air market and by 2003, it had become the largest supplier. It can be noted that it was a project that was engineering complex systems demanding low fault tolerance, and in that sense can be seen as instructive for token engineering. There are areas in which Europe can replicate this past success, Fintech and Blockchain, along with other DeepTech, particularly where the decentralized characteristic is present.

Trust

In addition to new economic opportunities based on disruptive innovation and more competition in the market, is there something more that these new decentralized digital technologies offer to society? John Authers wrote, "Trust then died with the credit crisis of 2008 and its aftermath. The sheer injustice of the ensuing government cuts and mass layoffs, which deepened inequality and left many behind while leaving perpetrators unpunished, ensured this".[12] Into this environment of eroding trust came an unexpected innovation.

In 2008, Satoshi Nakamoto (an unknown person or group of people) published the White Paper for "Bitcoin: A Peer-to-Peer Electronic Cash System"[13] It is a fully peer-to-peer system, doing away with any need for

---

[10]Geoffrey Hinton, interviewed by Martin Ford in "Architects of Intelligence", Packt Publishing, Birmingham, UK, 2018, pp. 87–88.
[11]"The European Model", by Sarah Gordon, Special issue: Europe, the Financial Times Weekend Magazine, 24/25 May, 2014, p. 32.
[12]John Authers, "Finance, the media and a breakdown of trust", *Financial Times*, FT Weekend, 6 October/7 October 2018.
[13]https://bitcoin.org/bitcoin.pdf, accessed on 04/03/2020.

a trusted third party, while eliminating the risk of double spending and immutably recording the transaction. The design was that the cryptocurrency Bitcoin functions on a blockchain. The practical application of Bitcoin was limited in scope and, in reality, it is functioning as a crypto-asset primarily for speculation, rather than as a currency.

While its proof of work was a groundbreaking and innovative, distributed approach in 2008, its energy consumption is hard to defend in 2020. The blockchain trilemma of self sufficiency, resource efficiency and no rent extraction provides a framework for reflection. Moving forward, we are able to evaluate a choice of alternative consensus mechanisms to proof of work, such as proof of stake.

The underlying technology has shown itself to be versatile and useful in many domains. Since that time, what could be called "blockchain inspired technologies" have proliferated and overlap with digital ledger technologies, which, for most, they are a subset of, and variants like tangle, hashgraph and others.

The Promise: Make Your Own Revolution and Cut Out the Middleman!

Blockchain is an innovative technology that enables both secure and transparent registers and data sharing. The potential use cases are in societal, economic and governmental contexts and could deliver benefits in terms of transparency, cost savings, efficiency, inclusion and security.

If the technology does not utilize proof of work and mining, which on the other hand Bitcoin does, it can be very energy efficient, especially taking into account reduced downtime for maintenance. It has been succesfully tested, in financial services, supply chain, trade finance, public services, regulatory reporting–RegTech, and more and more examples of deployment are arising daily.

What is rightfully disappearing is the type of irrational expectation that the technology is a magic cure for all problems, which it is clearly not. It has the most potential where a group of actors wish to share data and transfer value but cannot for legal (competition), political or other reasons share a single database while still having a desire to collaborate on specific operations.

The not very well founded assumption that blockchain technology would simply replace intermediaries, middlemen or governments entirely is a casualty of its collision with reality. It clearly has a lot of potential to disintermediate multiple, diverse processes and markets, but such transformation often require changes in legislation which foresees a certain role for an intermediary or in other cases changes in behaviour, business models or assumptions. On top of that, a peer-to-peer market or other collaborative mechanisms must develop to link the different parties.

A blockchain technology can be at the heart of such markets or cooperation but the technology will not ensure them by itself. This realism is reflected in business models of the blockchain companies that have survived the hype cycle and that are developing workable solutions to address private sector and public sector use cases, including for infrastructures. This is seen as well in the program of startup conferences like TechChill,[14] in Riga, Latvia, in February 2020, that are focusing on these solutions and infrastructures, rather than on the "get rich quick" scenario that was evident in much of the cryptocurrency discourse a year or so earlier.

Regulatory Approaches to Decentralized Digital Technologies

Preventing fragmentation, adopting standards, providing legal clarity and promoting public–private cooperation will help blockchain technologies flourish in the European Union and globally. Regulatory approaches should ideally unleash the potential of the private sector and societal actors to develop applications benefitting from peer-to-peer interactions. A set of actions in this direction have been undertaken, starting with the vision and policy.

The European Council (the Heads of State of the EU) recognized this already in October 2017, when they asked the European Commission to present a European approach to blockchain and invited the Commission to put forward initiatives for strengthening the framework conditions that enable the EU to explore new markets and to reaffirm the leading role of its industry.

The European Commission followed soon afterwards with a policy initiative, the *FinTech Action Plan: For a more competitive and innovative European financial sector*,[15] in which the European Commission's follow-up to address

---

[14] Sessions like 'Making Blockchain Work' and 'European Leadership in Blockchain: Innovation, Infrastructure and Regulation' were featured in the second day, 21 February, which had a focus on blockchain: https://techchill.co/agenda2020/, accessed on 17/03/2020.
[15] Brussels, 8.3.2018 COM(2018) 109 final, COMMUNICATION FROM THE COMMISSION TO THE EUROPEAN PARLIAMENT, THE COUNCIL, THE EUROPEAN CENTRAL BANK, THE EUROPEAN ECONOMIC AND SOCIAL COMMITTEE AND THE COMMITTEE OF THE REGIONS.

a wide range of technological, organizational and regulatory issues related to technology-enabled innovation was highlighted, including the use of blockchain in financial services. The Action Plan proposed a *FinTech Lab* where supervisors/regulators could be enlightened about new technologies by solution providers and to ask them hard questions, collaboration on *standards* (technical and regulatory) and *a European Blockchain Initiative.*

In regard to the latter, the Commission announced that that it intended to enable Fintech applications with the EU Blockchain Initiative, envisioning that blockchain and distributed ledger technologies would most likely lead to breakthroughs transforming the way information and assets are exchanged, validated, shared and accessed through digital networks. It was envisioned that blockchain could become a central part of future financial services infrastructure, also connecting RegTech applications to eGovernment platforms.

Intensified cooperation between the financial services players, regulators/supervisors and innovators utilizing approaches like regulatory sandboxes and innovation hubs was seen as beneficial for a rapid uptake and adoption of blockchain technologies in the financial sector. The utility of building an evidence base of where blockchain could produce the most tangible results was also underlined, following the supposition that blockchain/DLT is not a magic solution to all problems but a promising application for a number of broad coordination and collaboration challenges.

The EU Blockchain Initiative was comprised of the EU Blockchain Observatory and Forum, its working groups on legal issues and policy, and on use cases and transition scenarios; the European Blockchain Partnership, the European Blockchain Services Infrastructure, research and innovation funding in the areas of blockchain and DLT, assessment of legal frameworks, an equity investment fund for AI and blockchain, and a global stakeholders organization—the International Association of Trusted Blockchain Applications (INATBA).

Moving from policy to implementation, the European Blockchain Partnership was founded at European Digital Day 2018, when 21 EU Member States and Norway signed the European Blockchain Partnership Declaration,[16] with the aim of creating a European Blockchain Services Infrastructure (EBSI). The EBSI aimed to support the delivery of cross-border digital public services, with the highest levels of security, privacy and sustainability. The Partnership grew to 30 countries, all 28 EU Member States, Norway and Liechtenstein, in 2019, but then stabilized to 29 countries, all 27 EU Member States, Norway

---

[16]https://ec.europa.eu/digital-single-market/en/news/european-countries-join-blockchain-partnership, accessed on 09/03/2020.

and Liechtenstein, with the UK's withdrawal from the EU. The first use cases were confirmed by the European Blockchain Partnership in 2019 for launch in 2020 and were in the areas of regulatory reporting, audit publications and documents, diploma certification and self sovereign identity. It utilized funding from the Connecting Europe Facility (CEF).

The example of the European Blockchain Services Infrastructure (EBSI) shows how the distributed nature of blockchain is particularly suited to the multi-level governance of the EU, with the possibility of introducing nodes at the EU, Member state, regional and municipal levels on a permissioned basis; concurrently, citizens could have a different level of access on a non-permissioned, but identified basis to benefit from public services or for transparency of governmental operations. This decentralization aspect of blockchain offers a further possibility to ensure a citizen-centred and managed data society and economy, based on individual free choice and self-determination.

Moving from policy and implementation to the legal framework that can enable optimal uptake of the technology in the context of a values-based approach, what needs to be done? In terms of law and regulation, the major difference that can be found in addressing blockchain, distributed ledger technologies and other decentralized digital technologies is precisely the decentralized characteristic. Much legislation in the EU has been adopted in the pre-digitalization era or in that of data and platforms controlled and managed by a single entity.

Can, or how can, these frameworks be applied to the new decentralized digital technologies? In order to shape and adapt such new technologies in line with EU law and European values, the aforementioned regulatory sandboxes may be a useful tool. Regulatory sandboxes feature in both the aforementioned FinTech Action Plan and the European Commission's Startups to Scaleups Communication[17] as an approach incorporating regulator/innovator collaboration in testing a new technology or business model that is not foreseen in existing legislation. There are interesting examples of regulatory sandboxes in the Netherlands, in the United Kingdom (the Financial Conduct Authority), Singapore, Taiwan, Lithuania and Denmark, with more under development in the European Union as well as in the rest of the world.

---

[17]COMMUNICATION FROM THE COMMISSION TO THE EUROPEAN PARLIAMENT, THE COUNCIL, THE EUROPEAN ECONOMIC AND SOCIAL COMMITTEE AND THE COMMITTEE OF THE REGIONS Europe's next leaders: the Start-up and Scale-up Initiative. Strasbourg, 22.11.2016 COM(2016) 733 final.

The European Blockchain Partnership can be seen as using this approach itself in the context of creating the European Blockchain Services Infrastructure, where legal frameworks and existing procedures must be applied to a novel technology: blockchain, in the course of creating this cross-border infrastructure and assessing regulatory initiatives that may need to be prepared in order to fully enable an innovation ecosystem utilizing blockchain across all sectors in the EU. This is an approach that is worth exploring also in relation to the "convergence economy": not just blockchain/DLT but also their interaction with the Internet of Things (especially data coming from IoT), 3D printing, robotics, and Artificial Intelligence/machine learning.

Policymakers and legislators then face the question of whether the application of a regulatory sandbox approach is enough or specific legislation needed? There is always rightfully hesitancy to prepare legislation on a technology itself because of the principle of technology neutrality, i.e. we legislate on applications of a technology or to promote positive effects or to prevent impacts but not a regulation "on servers" or "on transistors", etc. However, the FinTech Action Plan launched a tech-review of financial services regulatory frameworks in light of the new digital technologies and a Public consultation was announced by the European Commission from 19 December 2019 to 19 March 2020 on the EU Regulatory Framework for Crypto-Assets.[18]

Is something like a Digital Millenium Act or a "Safe Haven" needed for decentralization? The USA was successful in the Internet race, not only as a first mover with ARPANET, NSFNET, etc., (there was, however, also the Minitel in France) but also by rapidly developing a holistic, proportionate and innovation enabling regulatory framework, exempting the Internet from telecoms and broadcasting requirements. It updated copyright and shielded Internet intermediaries from (copyright) liability.[19] Considering that while the Internet resembled telecoms and broadcasting/publishing in some ways, it was also considered fundamentally different. It created legal certainty for the rise of the Internet and platforms, though in hindsight this approach may also have contained the seeds of some of the problems with fake news, unfair business practices and copyright infringement on the Internet that we see today.

Arguments have been made that blockchain, as a decentralized and disintermediated Internet of value can only thrive if policymakers, regulators and

---

[18] https://ec.europa.eu/info/law/better-regulation/have-your-say/initiatives/12089-Directive-regulation-establishing-a-European-framework-for-markets-in-crypto-assets/public-consultation, accessed on 09/03/2020.

[19] https://www.copyright.gov/legislation/dmca.pdf, accessed on 10/03/2020.

supervisors do not apply requirements to it that were designed for centralized models and intermediaries. The same could be said for decentralized machine learning, artificial intelligence, Internet of Things, 3D printing, robotics, etc. However, this argument is taking a somewhat pessimistic view of the ability of the law to adapt and be flexible as times change, and new technologies replace older ones. It can also be observed that countries that have adopted blockchain/distributed ledger technology-specific legal regimes have been more those looking to attract more blockchain or crypto activity rather than those in which such economic or societal initiatives were already underway, and to which the existing legal framework was being applied to.

It may be moreover possible to deduce what principles were behind the regulation of the centralized models (protection of investors, of consumers, of the natural environment) and to apply them in a proportional manner to the new technology. Unless the law goes into exquisite detail, and thus risks to become obsolete as technology or business models develop, it will always have to be applied as economies progress, "But no matter how technically precise and careful, the law will always be subject to interpretation".[20] Cecelia Watson further noted, "The law is skeletal, a mere naked framework of words, and those words require interpretation for the law to become animate and to act in the world".[21]

Reflecting on a technical and specific legal aspect of blockchain, that of smart contracts, highlights some of the issues at stake, particularly in a cross-border context. It is expected that smart contracts utilized on blockchains can make a new automated and decentralized Internet infrastructure possible, concurrently enabling a decentralized economy based on automated execution and its related business models. A smart contract can be described as a piece of software that is stored and executed by the entire network in a decentralized manner. They make it possible to conduct a transaction online automatically, once the program has established that certain conditions that were set out earlier in the software code have been fulfilled. In the current legal situation, a smart contract may have legal significance, but this is necessarily so.

What are the legal issues that may need to be addressed in order to enable smart contracts while continuing to protect consumers? A question that has been raised is what is actually determinant: the intention with which a smart contract is drawn up or the way in which that intention is coded?

In regard to jurisdiction, it has been asked, if there is a dispute over a smart contract on a blockchain, particularly on a decentralized one, what

---

[20] "Semicolon", by Cecelia Watson, 4th ESTATE, London, UK, 2019, pp. 87–88.
[21] Ibid., p. 88.

is the applicable law and which court is competent? In regard to liability, if something goes wrong in the implementation of the contract, is this the responsibility of the programmer, of the party for whom the programmer worked, of the platform that provided the smart contract functionality?

Cross-border applicability, even in the EU, is an issue, "one specific aspect relating to the validity and enforcement of (smart) contracts is that of cross-border transactions, an element that is very important from a Digital Single Market perspective. Smart contracts are expected to be widely deployed in cross-border transactions, raising the question of whether a smart contract that is recognised in Member State A will also be recognised in Member State B. Our research has revealed that there can be scenarios where this is not necessarily the case, such as where jurisdiction A does not require that that particular contract be in writing but jurisdiction B does require semantic written contracts for that particular kind of contract."[22]

Another area of legal discussion is that of data protection, and the General Data Protection Regulation[23] (GDPR) more specifically, and blockchain. The preparation of this and most privacy regulation took place in a context that was not one of disintermediated and decentralized technologies, but of centralized controllers and storage of data. It would be a pessimistic view of the law that would conclude that it cannot, or won't adapt.

A valuable contribution to this debate is the EU Blockchain Observatory and Forum's Report on Blockchain and the GDPR,[24] which deduces that GDPR compliance is not about the technology, but about how the technology is used. Just as one cannot say that there is a GDPR Internet, or a GDPR-compliant artificial intelligence algorithm, one cannot say that there is a GDPR-compliant blockchain at the technology level. The report concludes that there are only use cases or applications that are GDPR-compliant (or not).

The tensions between GDPR compliance and blockchain revolve mainly around three issues: the identification, and obligations, of data controllers and processors, the anonymization of personal data and the exercise of some data subject rights. To date, these issues have not been conclusively settled by data protection authorities, the European Data Protection Board or in courts, so it is an area where privacy by design and dialogue with the relevant supervisory

---

[22] "Study on Blockchains Legal, governance and interoperability aspects" (SMART 2018/0038), pp. 117–118, https://ec.europa.eu/digital-single-market/en/news/study-blockchains-legal-governance-and-interoperability-aspects-smart-20180038, accessed on 27/03/2020.

[23] Regulation (EU) 2016/679 of the European Parliament and of the Council of 27 April 2016 on the protection of natural persons with regard to the processing of personal data and on the free movement of such data, and repealing Directive 95/46/EC (General Data Protection Regulation).

[24] https://www.eublockchainforum.eu/reports, accessed on 11/03/2020.

authority are an important part of blockchain and other decentralized digital technology design. The upside is that decentralized digital technologies can evolve ever more to become not just privacy compliant but privacy and self-determination enhancing technologies.

An example of such advances and ambitions can be found in the European Commission funded DECODE project: "Technological innovation is the core of DECODE: discover open source and privacy-enhancing tools that have been developed within the project. The decentralized DECODE stack includes a cryptographic virtual machine, a blockchain stack, a modular mobile app to access services privately, a dashboard for data visualization and a passport scanner".[25] The aim is to allow individual citizens to manage their own data, keeping it private, or donating it themselves to address societal challenges.

Another European Commission funded project *My Health, My Data* is in the vital area of sharing healthcare data on demand. It fostered individual citizen empowerment by, "Development of the **dynamic consent** interface, aimed at enabling data subjects to allow, refuse and withdraw access to their data according to different types of potential usage. Build-up of a **blockchain-based software infrastructure** in which individual data exchanges are governed by peer-to-peer relationships between all the stakeholders. Implementation of the **personal data account**, a personal cloud allowing data subjects for direct access to their whole clinical data from any personal device through the blockchain. Use of **smart contracts** to assist data subjects in their right to access, erase, modify delete or even 'be forgotten'.[26]"

An area of legal analysis and debate, which is also relevant is that of tokenization on blockchains. Jamie Burke, CEO and Founder of Outlier Ventures has written, "Cryptographically secure and digitally scarce tokens are the magic sauce, or killer app, of the blockchain movement and represent a new wave of business model innovation. The ability to program both a hard cost and monetary incentive against user behaviors, directly into open source systems, transforms them from purely technical to socio-economic innovations".[27]

There was a big boom of Initial Coin Offerings (ICOs), a new fundraising or utilization tool based on tokenization on a blockchain, peaking in 2017–18 and raising billions of Euro. A division of types of tokens or "coins" could

---

[25] https://decodeproject.eu/, accessed on 26/03/2020.
[26] https://www.myhealthmydata.eu/why-mhmd/, accessed on 27/03/2020.
[27] "Token Ecosystem Creation: A strategic process to architect and engineer viable token economies", https://outlierventures.io/wp-content/uploads/2019/05/Token-Ecosystem-Creation-Outlier-Ventures-PDF.pdf, accessed on 12/03/2020.

be into settlement tokens, currency and other assets; investments tokens, equity or debt; utility tokens, for enabling or consumer use; and donation tokens. Utility tokens are used to enable the use/consumption of services, usually in a decentralized system.

The EU Blockchain Observatory and Forum published a report on Blockchain and the Future of Digital Assets,[28] which provides expert input on this subject. The FinTech Action Plan concluded that an assessment of the suitability of the current EU regulatory framework with regard to Initial Coin Offerings and crypto-assets more generally is necessary. This has been followed up with the aforementioned Public consultation was announced by the European Commission from 19 December 2019 to 19 March 2020 on the EU Regulatory Framework for Crypto-Assets.

Self Determination and Data Management

The issue that platform domination of digital markets raises for consumer choice and competition in the marketplace, but what is the impact of that dominant model on data and citizens' control over it? "Our information, the data, serves as a valuable commodity that translates into targeted advertisements, sales and money. Lots of money. It is therefore no surprise that companies are investing many resources into harvesting and analyzing such data, and many powerful tech firms, as we'll see, view privacy protection technologies as a threat. These trends create new gatekeepers and new forms of market power".[29] The decentralized digital technology promise to reduce the market power of these gatekeepers and make individuals the gatekeepers and holders of market power themselves.

In the digital economy, access to data and control over data is vital. As Ezrachi and Stucke write, "if the critical resource at this point is data – not merely to target advertising, but also to optimize the products and services themselves – the firms with the most data are not merely in the best position to dominate their own sectors – they are also poised to take over adjacent fields".[30] We see in the market, that moves are already foreseen from search or social media and advertising into mobility, payments, currency and the health sector, at scale. At the same time, barriers to entry into the market are

---

[28]https://www.eublockchainforum.eu/reports, accessed on 12/03/2020.

[29]"Virtual Competition: The Promise and Perils of the Algorithm-Driven Economy", by Ariel Ezrachi and Maurice E. Stucke, published by Harvard University Press, Cambridge, Massachusetts, USA, and London, England, 2016, p. 28.

[30]Ibid., p. 31.

very high for startups or SMEs that do not have access to that amount or even far lesser amounts of data. However, Ezrachi and Stucke note, "The real threat to the super-platform generally comes from innovation that disrupts the entire market".[31]

J. Burke has also written, "we believe blockchain technologies, including distributed ledgers & smart contracts, are the mega-trend that allows all other macro-trends to scale securely, converge and combine. They represent the next phase of The Web, Web 3.0 or 'The Trust Web / Internet of Ownership' and will transform how technologies interact with one another and the World around them. Combined they enable a new more decentralised and automated Web infrastructure that brings with it previously impossible economic models. At their core, they represent a fundamental shift from centralized & human-mediated systems to trustless decentralized and autonomous networks".[32]

Decentralized citizen-centred management of data is identified as a potential opportunity in the European Commission's Communication on a European data strategy,[33] which states, "New decentralised digital technologies such as blockchain offer a further possibility for both individuals and companies to manage data flows and usage, based on individual free choice and self-determination. Such technologies will make dynamic data portability in real time possible for individuals and companies, along with various compensation models". The aforementioned European Commission Digital Strategy foresees the adoption of a Blockchain Strategy in the second quarter of 2020.

Elsewhere in the world, Dubai has announced that it is planning to launch "Decentralised Data for Dubai",[34] a program that has announced that it will be setting up an open data "Sandbox" built using a range of decentralized technologies from the Outlier Ventures "Convergence Stack",[35] potentially including blockchain-based companies like Sovrin, Ocean Protocol and Fetch.AI. They have foreseen laying the foundation for Dubai and its citizens to benefit from an open data explosion of innovation, which would be made

---

[31] Ibid., p. 175.
[32] "Blockchain-Enabled Convergence: Understanding the Web 3.0 Economy, by Outlier Ventures Research, https://outlierventures.io/wp-content/uploads/2018/11/Blockchain-Enabled-Convergence-Whitepaper.pdf, accessed on 17/03/2020.
[33] Brussels, 19.2.2020 COM(2020) 66 final COMMUNICATION FROM THE COMMISSION TO THE EUROPEAN PARLIAMENT, THE COUNCIL, THE EUROPEAN ECONOMIC AND SOCIAL COMMITTEE AND THE COMMITTEE OF THE REGIONS, A European strategy for data.
[34] 'Decentralised Data for Dubai Report', published on 19 May 2019. https://www.smartdubai.ae/newsroom/news/decentralised-data-for-dubai-report, accessed on 17/03/2020.
[35] https://outlierventures.io/research/the-convergence-stack/, accessed on 17/03/2020.

accessible to a growing and increasingly diverse range of active participants in the city data market.[36]

Dubai is not alone in moving into formal recognition of this decentralized model, but was daring in making this move early and at the scale of its whole jurisdiction. High potential for this type of approach exists globally, with one example being the citation above from the European data strategy. The scale of EU Member States and of the whole EU, as well as large economies of the world is of course potentially much greater. In the case of Europe, such an approach also recognizes the multi-level governance of the EU in its decentralization and provides great opportunities for private sector, bottom-up innovation, putting the individual citizen and his or her concerns at the centre.

The aim would be to develop a system that puts individuals in control of their data, enabling them to share data securely across suppliers and services in different sectors on an informed basis, with blockchain being an enabling technology for implementation of this policy. It is necessary to underline that this needs to be a technologically neutral and innovatively open approach in that other types of distributed ledger technologies or other new or more appropriate tech would be used if shown to be better. However, the principle of decentralization and individual and community empowerment should not be sacrificed on the alter of speed, which a centralized technology might offer.

Here the tools of smart contracts and tokenization on a blockchain make possible this type of management of data with ease of use and minimal burden for the citizen. This technological approach opens up the possibilities of donation of data with recognition of "good deeds", easy to use subscriptions and receiving compensation in diverse business models.

A goal would be to develop the possibility for dynamic portability of data in real time by individuals and thus make possible many business models serving both individual convenience as well as citizen-directed data sharing to meet societal goals such as the battle against climate change, to provide vital data to address pandemics or to provide relevant data for other medical research or public health goals.

It is clear that such an approach will require much investment in technology, including in the ancillary measures needed in support, but given the needs for evidence-based decision-making and implementation in these areas, it can be justified. In the case of the European Union, some part of this investment will come in relation to implementing the public sector use cases of the European Blockchain Services Infrastructure, coming from

---

[36] Ibid.

the Digital Europe Programme but much more investment will come from the private sector in anticipation of a strong return on investment from the individual-centric business models.

Conclusion

Increased levels of competition between enterprises in the economy to the benefit of consumers would be achieved and SME and startup activity would be encouraged by freeing up access to citizens' data, on their demand, which has been until now concentrated in several recognized and dominant silos. Looking forward to the convergence of artificial intelligence (AI), IoT, big data, 3D printing and blockchain in the next industrial revolution, this policy will foster the provision of many diverse, trustworthy, high quality, standardized, consented to sets of data for the development of machine learning and trustworthy AI models.

A worthy aim is to forge a citizen-centred data economy, a market shaped by forward-looking governments implementing legal frameworks enabling real time, effective portability of data and encouraging and benefitting from widely flourishing innovation bottom-up. The utilization of new decentralized technologies such as Blockchain and Distributed ledger technologies, employing applications such as smart contracts and tokenization can be part of this solution providing real portability of data (social graph portability) at the request of the citizen/consumer in order to receive a better service, or to donate data in order to address a societal challenge. This is a necessity not just for the dynamism of economy but also for individual-based trusted societal initiatives free of manipulation and for the health of our media space and democracy.

Bibliography

Ezrachi, Ariel; Stucke, Maurice E., "Virtual Competition: The Promise and Perils of the Algorithm-Driven Economy", published by Harvard University Press, Cambridge, Massachusetts, USA, and London, England, 2016.

Ford, Martin, "Architects of Intelligence", Packt Publishing, Birmingham, UK, 2018.

Fulin, Rinaldo, "Brief History of Venice", lineadaqua, San Marco, Venezia, Italy, June 2019.

Masnick, Mike, "Protocols, Not Platforms: A Technological Approach to Free Speech." Knight First Amendment Institute at Columbia University, published

21 August 2019, https://knightcolumbia.org/content/protocols-not-platforms-a-technological-approach-to-free-speech, accessed on 16/03/2020.

Schumpeter, Joseph, Can Capitalism Survive? Creative Destruction and the Future of the Global Economy", originally published as "Capitalism, Socialism and Democracy" by Harper & Row, New York, 1942.

Watson, Cecelia, "Semicolon", 4th ESTATE, London, UK, 2019, pp. 87–88.

Weatherill, Stephen, "Cases and materials on EU Law", Oxford University Press, Oxford, United Kingdom, 2006.

Zilgalvis, Pēteris, "The need for an Innovation Principle in Regulatory Impact Assessment: the Case of Finance and Innovation in Europe," *Policy and Internet*, Wiley Periodicals, Malden, USA and Oxford, UK DOI: https://doi.org/10.1002/1944-2866.POI374, Volume 6, Issue 4, December 2014.

# 12

Regulating Blockchain in the EU: Building a Global Competitive Advantage

Eva Kaili

Introduction

In September 2020 the European Commission, the executive body of the EU that proposes regulations to the European Parliament and the Council, introduced the legislative proposal "Markets in Cryptoassets" (MiCA).[1] This was part of a wider strategy, called Fintech Action Plan,[2] introduced few years ago. The aim was to help legacy financial institutions as well as newcomers, mainly Fintechs or financial service providers that use enhancing digital technologies, to operate in the internal market within a regulatory framework that ensures a level-playing field for everybody and enables the use of innovative digital solutions in a responsible way.[3]

The initial critique this text received from the market participants was that it excluded an entire part of the market, called Decentralized Finance (DeFi). As cryptocurrencies (try to) provide a decentralized store of value

---

[1] COM (2020) 593: Regulation on Markets in Crypto-assets (MiCA).
[2] COM (2018) 109/2: Fintech Action Plan: For a more competitive and innovative European Financial Sector.
[3] COM (2020) 591: Communication from the Commission on a Digital Strategy for the EU.

E. Kaili (✉)
European Parliament, Brussels, Belgium
e-mail: eva.kaili@ep.europa.eu

independent from centrally issued fiat currencies, similarly DeFi, tries to decentralize financial services making them independent from centralized financial institutions. The operations of DeFi, ideally, run with smart contracts in decentralized autonomous organizational architectures (DAO) leveraging decentralized applications (dApps). The "Markets in Cryptoassets" regulation, first, omits any mentioning to the technologically interesting case of DeFi altogether, and, second, it "dissuades" the possibility of this innovative business model to operate in the EU by making clear that the providers of blockchain financial services should be *legally established* entities.

In the moment we write this chapter, MiCA regulation is still under revision and negotiation in the European Parliament and the Council, and it is expected to be enacted in the coming one or two years. The initial (informal) response to the DeFi criticism from the side of the EU is that a financial regulation, by necessity manages risks, and it is there to protect investors and consumers. This requires the allocation of liabilities to a specific natural or legal person in case of failure. DeFi, by design, is an entity that lacks these traditional legal characteristics. A less *imaginative* excuse for this omission is that MiCA is about crypto-assets and not about providers of traditional financial services in blockchain.

The notion of "imagination" is rather instrumental here from a regulatory point of view. Regulators facing technological breakthroughs usually have two paths: either to use old rules to new instruments or to create new rules to new instruments. The first needs creativity. The second needs imagination. Could the draftsperson of this regulatory proposal include DeFi in the first regulatory text? Does the inclusion require more creativity or more imagination? Is the decision of the regulators of the Commission to omit DeFi a smart choice, given the techno-social limitations of blockchain technology today? There are no direct answers to these questions. However, it is not the first time we find ourselves in this situation. Traditionally, a regulator who has to intervene in the occasion of a technological innovation has to answer three fundamental questions: (i) how early should I regulate, (ii) how much detail should I include? and (iii) how much narrow or wide in scope should I be?

The answers the regulator will give to these questions determine the growth of the market, the time to reach this growth and the impact of the regulation to other markets. Moreover, there is another critical element: the global dimension of the regulatory regime regarding a technology. In the new global digital economy the concentration of technological capacity to a very small number of blocks, increases the competition between Asia, Europe and America, and makes denser the technological inter-dependences and dependences between the dominant players and the geographic regions they control. Digital products and services are not just elements of international free trade; they are "chips" of power and influence with strong geo-economic implications and they generate narratives such as "digital imperialism" or "techno-nationalism".[4] Thus, the regulatory framework that a jurisdiction generates should be a source of national competitive advantage, as it has (a) to generate robust, innovation-friendly, risk-immune markets, (b) it has to attract human capital to sustain innovation, and (c) it has to attract risky financial capital to fund innovation over time. Market robustness, quality and quantity of human capital and abundant availability of financial resources are considered sine qua non-requirements for global competitiveness in the era of the fourth industrial revolution. No global player can ignore the significance of the regulatory framework in creating competitive advantage.

The Blockchain Resolution of the European Parliament: Context and Content

On 3 October 3 2018, the European Parliament voted, with unprecedented majority and the support of all the European Parties, its "Blockchain Resolution". The author of this chapter was the Rapporteur of this Resolution.[5] This Resolution has its own story, as it is the product of a systematic effort of *political entrepreneurship*. The "demand" for a Resolution on Blockchain in the months of the hype of bitcoin and ICOs should not be taken as given or welcome in a House like the European Parliament.

The political pressure for legal action was fierce but the "reputation" of blockchain as the facilitator of fraud, enabler of illicit payments of drag dealers and terrorists in the dark web, and environmentally irresponsible edifice, created many obstacles for any regulatory treatment of the technology. At the end of the day, *"why to regulate something we want to kill"*? Other jurisdictions (including Korea and China) had banned ICOs and cryptocurrencies altogether and the USA and Canada were very reluctant to create any specific framework. Moreover, technological failures like the Etherium's DAO was in the mouth of suspicious policymakers and regulators who were claiming that blockchain is just a fashionable trend among the members

---

[4] For an interesting account on Techno-nationalism, see at: MIT Technology Review: The techno-nationalism issue, September–October 2020, Vol. 123, No. 5.
[5] EP (2017) 2772: Distributed Ledger Technologies and Blockchain: Building trust with disintermediation.

of (sic) a *semi-legit* community (the crypto-community) and an inefficient "techno-obsession" that *haunts* the imagination of libertarian anarcho-capitalists. Back then (in 2017), only minor jurisdictions like Cyprus, Malta, Gibraltar, Cayman Islands and Singapore where experimenting seriously with blockchain enabling regulations.

If European Union, the most trustworthy regulator in the World, would take steps in giving guidelines for blockchain technology, this would be a bold move from the side of the Union to create legal and, most importantly, *institutional* certainty. It would also give to the EU a considerable first-mover advantage in the new digital economy, as blockchain was already perceived to be, the backbone and the infrastructure of any IoT environment leveraging human-to-machine and machine-to-machine interactions.

The main argument for a Blockchain Resolution was then, that blockchain is not just the enabling technology for cryptocurrencies and crowdfunding tokens. It was the infrastructure for a wide range of applications necessary for Europe to stay competitive in the New Economy. Based on this argument, the Committee of Industry (ITRE) of the European Parliament authorized the drafting of the Resolution: "Distributed Ledger Technologies and Blockchain: Building trust with disintermediation".

This authorization from the side of the European Parliament to draft a resolution on blockchain is of a special significance from a Political Economy perspective. The context around a technology influences a lot the "demand" for a regulatory action. Political entrepreneurship, thus, is of paramount importance to unlock demand for regulation, and the regulator should act as a change-leader when change seems difficult and the appetite of change of risk-averse agents (e.g. of a legacy Institution) is very low.

The Blockchain Resolution of the European Parliament can be seen as a facilitator of demand generation in this techno-regulatory field. The idea of regulation in a technological space can take many different facets; it can be, inter alia, hard regulation, soft regulation, light-touch regulation, smart regulation (Baldwin et al. 2013). As Hacker et al. note, regulation can be used as a *weapon* in the initial "framing struggles" of the supporters and the opponents of the technology to establish regulatory barriers or to curtail the spread of the new technology or it can be used to facilitate the development of the technology. In the second case, the space of regulatory options is really wide and spans from those who support the idea of "discounting" the existing legal norms in order to make space for accelerating the value proposition of a technology, to those who suggest risk-based approaches to regulation and the application of "hard law" (Hacker et al. 2019).

If regulation qualifies as an "embedded technology" per se to facilitate the interactions of the actors in a marketplace (Deakin 2018), in the case of the Blockchain Resolution the priority was wider than that: the aim was to facilitate *the creation of blockchain marketplaces* altogether. This is a detail instrumental to understand, as the requirement here was not just to create a basis of legal certainty but rather a framework of *institutional certainty*.

The Blockchain Resolution, thus, gave the instructions to the European Commission on how to create a framework that could allow the creation of a fertile ground in the internal market for this new technological option to flourish and *make EU the best place in the world to do blockchain*. The most important blocks of the text where the following:

(1) blockchain market places concern many strategic commercial sectors for the EU;
(2) there are many alternative blockchain architectures;
(3) scalability and interoperability of different blockchain architectures is critical;
(4) smart contracts open a wide range of opportunities but also impose significant challenges;
(5) ICOs and cryptocurrencies should be allowed to be used in the internal market and
(6) data privacy is a strategic priority.

The author of this chapter agrees with the view that blockchain is a digital technology of critical strategic importance, because at the same time it touches on three fundamental techno-social aspects: the economic, the societal and the legal (Tasca and Pisseli 2019). The regulator should not fail to take into consideration the opportunities and challenges in all the three aspects and, at the same time, cannot ignore the strong potential of a vibrant blockchain regime in assisting to the transition from a mainly analogue to a mainly digitally enhanced, exponential economy. Blockchain is instrumental in forcing both business and government leaders to imagine:

(i) how the new marketplaces will look like in the coming years;
(ii) what is the appropriate organizational setting in the New Economy; and
(iii) what kind of market structures should we form, in order, not only to survive the economic competition by staying technologically relevant, but also to generate and sustain rates of inclusive growth proportional to the expectations of the society.

What Blockchain Principles the Regulator Should Take into Consideration

The Blockchain Resolution of the European Parliament enjoyed wide support and publicity as it was the first time that a major regulator with global impact and reach made a statement in favour of blockchain, instructing the European Institutions to provide legislation based on specific technology-enabling principles. This text also influenced other major regulators, like the Congress of the United States.

Giving guidelines for regulatory action can be thought of as an *optimization exercise*. Many steps should be taken for a truly enabling regulation. We recommend the following two dimensions to consider:

A. *Define with flexibility the regulated subject*

In mid-2000s, Lawrence Lessig, famous for his dictum that "code is law" (Lessig 2000) introduced his famous "pathetic dot theory", indicating that Internet organizations and service providers (the "pathetic dots") are regulated by four forces: the market, the norms, the architecture and the law. Governments directly affect the legal environment but they use (indirectly) all the four forces to control the behaviour and activities of the internet actors. Lessig also stressed two very important elements: (i) that the architecture of the solution can conflict with the law and (ii) that the higher the level of decentralization, the lower the capacity of the governments to control (Lessig 2006). These two points underscore the regulatory challenge of blockchain as well. In many different blockchain architectures, especially the ones that are based on permission-less blockchains that provide not only disintermediation but also decentralized governance structures with automation properties like the ones we described in the beginning of this chapter (the DeFi case), this "pathetic dot" disappears, as we can see in Fig. 12.1 (De Filippi and Wright 2018).

The left half of Fig. 12.1 shows the Lessig's schema and the forces that regulate the Internet subjects' behaviour. However, in a decentralized environment the entity, natural or legal, that bears the liability in case of misconduct, can be replaced with a network of pseudonymous actors (the right half of Fig. 12.1). Pseudonymity is not compatible with our legal and regulatory tradition. At least not so far. No matter what is the architecture, the design, the process and the characteristics of a product or service, everything and always ends up to a responsible person. The regulation has to be enforced on this person.

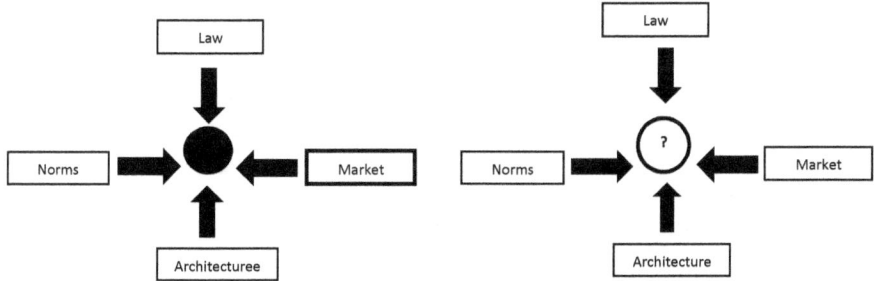

Fig. 12.1 Lessig's four modes of regulation applied to blockchain systems (*Source* De Filippi and Wright [2018])

The DeFi case, reflects exactly this problem. How can we regulate the missing "pathetic dot"? Ruling this problem out does not solve anything in the long-run. In the short-run, indeed, the Regulator has a comparatively easier job. The vast majority of the blockchain applications we experience so far are not *complete*. A *blockchain-complete solution* is one that entails several properties including *distribution, encryption, disintermediation, tokenization* and *decentralization*. This completeness is quite rare and the most use-cases include only the first three or four properties (Furlonger and Uzureau 2019). Decentralization is much more challenging not only for the regulator, but also for the market. Only few technology enthusiasts experiment with purely decentralized governance structures. This rarity is the result of the current limits of the technology. For example, the bitcoin blockchain experiences significant scalability problems. The DAO experiment failed because of the inherent limits of smart contracts to predict everything and the lack of flexibility to make algorithmic changes fast when a problem is spotted. It seems that prediction and scale failures in decentralized architecture designs are solved, at least for the time being, only with painful *forks* (Werbach, K., 2018). However, this is not the way society solves its trust issues and this is something the regulator should not ignore.

In the long-run, though, the problem becomes more pressing. The proliferation of the IoT and the further blending of blockchain with other enhancing digital technologies, like artificial intelligence and hyper-performance computing, will allow new business models to emerge and operate with more clarity. Smart contracts will become smarter; blockchain consensus mechanisms will become more creative and efficient; algorithmic designs will become more resilient to changes and disposable digital identities will penetrate our culture more than today. People will be educated to feel more comfortable in digitally complicated environments and the techno-social environment will be safer and less resistant. In an environment such this, the further shift to *blockchain-complete* solutions will be perceived not as a choice but as a necessary step forward. The actors making this choice, will be mainstream, risk-averse market players, not *just* technology enthusiasts. The regulator should be ready to provide a legal framework that will allow this transition to happen.

Reaching the point where blockchain-completeness will be mainstream, the regulator will be compelled to introduce into the legal and regulatory tradition the concept of *Lex Cryptographia*. Lex Cryptographia are rules administered through self-executing smart contracts and decentralized (autonomous) organizations. To navigate in these territories there will be an increasing need to focus on how to *regulate blockchain technology* and how to shape the creation and deployment of these emerging decentralized organizations in ways that have yet to be explored under current legal theory (Write and De Filippi 2015). This leads us to our second recommendation.

B. *Combine technological neutrality with business model neutrality*

Should we regulate the blockchain technology per se or only its uses and users? In the Blockchain Resolution of the European Parliament, the guideline given to the EU lawmakers reflected the principles of technological neutrality and the associated concept of business model neutrality. Technological neutrality is a long established concept in the European Union regulatory tradition since the early 2000s and re-appears as the guiding principle in technology-related regulations including the Framework Directive for Electronic Communication Networks and Services (2002),[6] and the General Data Protection Regulation (2016).[7] This principle is also reflected in the OECD's recommendations,[8] and the US's "better regulation" initiative.[9]

Technological neutrality is an instrumental concept that can take three different meanings depending on the context. In the first meaning, technological neutrality is equivalent to "standards setting". The regulator tries to limit negative externalities by *setting the targeted result* but leaves the companies free to choose their technology. The second meaning of technological

---

[6]Directive 2002/21/EC of 7 March 2002 on a common regulatory framework for electronic communications networks and services (Framework Directive).
[7]Regulation (EU) 2016/679 of 27 April 2016 on the protection of natural persons with regard to the processing of personal data and on the free movement of such data, and repealing Directive 95/46/EC (General Data Protection Regulation).
[8]OECD (2011), OECD Council recommendation on Principles for Internet Policy Making (December 13).
[9]Obama, B. (2011), Executive Order No. 13563: Improving Regulation and Regulatory Review (January).

neutrality defines the scope of the regulation. In this case, *the regulator defines the principles* without having technological silos in mind. The third meaning of technological neutrality is that the regulator *does not pick technological winners* and uses the concept rather to nudge the market towards a desired direction (Maxwell and Bourreau 2014).

Technological neutrality is an enabling principle, which on the one hand is intended to mitigate risks while at the same time it allows the experimentation and the growth of an innovative solution. Though it can be used as a nudge to influence market and design behaviours and preferences, as per the regulatory concept of *libertarian paternalism* (Thaler and Sunstein 2009) it is much more than that. It aims to pre-determine what risks are acceptable in the society and what not. I that sense it is much more than just a "light touch" regulatory approach. We can define it as rather a "smart regulation" approach, where at any point the regulator can control and safeguard his/her reputation and reliability. We strongly advise in favour of a "smart approach" to regulation rather than a "light approach". It is of paramount importance for the acceleration of the adoption of any new technology, to keep a regime where the scientist and the engineer will tell what the technology can do, but the regulator will keep his authority in determining what the technology cannot do.

But how far technological neutrality can go? First, technological neutrality does not imply that the changes the technology brings are neutral. Blockchain does not produce neutral changes in the market. Market structures are transformed; the scope and the size of the firm is impacted; the governance and decision-making procedures are affected. Second, technological neutrality does not rule out the idiosyncratic technological risks of blockchain. ICOs have technology-specific risks just like the smart contracts. Stressing specific idiosyncratic risks does not imply discrimination subject to the technology.

But this is not the end. Technological neutrality is a necessary condition for enabling technological and market disruption, but it is not an adequate condition. To achieve a genuine result, technological neutrality must be accompanied by business model neutrality. The regulator, as we mentioned before, should not pick technological winners. Sometimes though, he/she discriminates favouring one business model over another. For example, in the first reading of the MiCA regulation, many of the provisions applied to Fintechs, do not apply to legacy financial institutions. Or, as it is specified in the accompanying DLT Pilot Regime Regulation, creating market places for crypto-assets regulated under MIFID2, requires the facilitators of the exchange to be regulated as Multilateral Trading Facilities (MTFs), favouring thus a legacy business model over a new one (e.g. DeFi).[10]

The regulator, consequently, faces a short-term/long-term dilemma. In the short run, pushing an innovative instrument into an old regulatory box, may seem easier, or even politically more desirable. But he cannot cover the skeletons into his closet forever. Competitiveness and growth have inter-temporal consequences on the decisions of a short-termist regulator. By pushing new technological instruments into old boxes the regulator inadvertently (or deliberately) picks winners by favouring legacy business models over the innovative ones creating disproportional costs to the innovative start-ups, neutralizing thus their edge over their legacy competitors. This in the long run affects not only the competitiveness of the economy but also hampers the prospects of a sustainable and organic growth.

Conclusion: Advancing Innovation with Regulatory Sandboxes

Regulating blockchain is a dynamic optimization exercise. The technology is still evolving and its impact onto the real economy is expected to be decisive, although it is not easy to predict in which way and under which conditions. The value of the blockchain comes from its ability to improve or disrupt certain economic functions but also from its convergence with other exponential technologies like machine learning, hyper-performance computing and IoT. We expect that the gradual adoption of blockchain technology over time from different sectors will challenge both market and macroeconomic equilibria. The regulator cannot predict what and how, but he/she can understand the trends in advance by creating an enabling regulatory environment that addresses market and operational risks, idiosyncratic technological risks as well as the risks of no-adoption that may bring disproportionally negative effects in the prospects of a sustainable and organic market growth.

Today, the job of the regulator is relatively easier. Blockchain is here already but not complete. We are closer to the edge of disintermediation than to the one of decentralization, so our regulatory culture seems more compatible to the challenges blockchain brings to us. However, the prospect of having more and more decentralized autonomous organizations in the (near) future, especially with the improvement of DLT design architectures and the merging of blockchain with artificial intelligence, requires us to widen our understanding

---

[10]COM(2020) 594.

of what actually consists a "good regulation". This challenge is not just for Europe but for every jurisdiction in the world. The regulator who will find the solution in the equation between decentralization and regulatory control, will be the one who is going to create for his country a strong regulatory competitive advantage.

However, there are no certainties and prescriptions of how to achieve this end. Markets and scientific discoveries interact in mysterious ways and generate unpredictable dynamics. The unknown-unknowns are many and action in the face of ambiguity (not just risk) requires sometimes an iron feast and sometimes a soft hand. In any case this is a try and error exercise.

We believe that try and error is the most crucial factor to develop internally best practices than to delegate this responsibility to somebody else in hope for "global solutions". Global solutions are uncertain in an environment of ever increasing techno-nationalist trends. Without ruling out cross-border synergies, a vibrant and robust regime of regulatory sandboxes and pilot legal frameworks seems the safest solution in a rapidly changing technological landscape.

A regulator engaged in sandboxes has become strategic partner of the scientist, the startuper and the market participant in accelerating technology transfer from the lab to the market in a most risk-efficient way. Regulatory sandboxes can create a solid but also agile space for innovative creativity, the results of which can be easily trickled down to the low-end of the market in a strongly protected and regulated space. Blockchain is an excellent candidate for such a dynamic framework that will allow both innovators and regulators to build together certainties in an organic way and reduce ambiguity.

* * *

Regulating blockchain is an exciting exercise, first because, in this stage it allows the regulator to build ab initio innovative marketplaces and second, because it makes him build marketplaces having in mind the need for a strong global competitive advantage. This second element is an incentive to be more long-termist and business model neutral. A principles-based approach seems the best recipe as the technology is still evolving and gradually touches more and more industries.

European Union, for the time being is already ahead of the rest in creating an innovation-friendly space, despite the fact that it faces significant market pressures both from the East and the West. In the coming years we expect to see significant changes in the global markets, especially in relation to the decentralization of data that will build new poles of digital power. Blockchain and edge computing is expected to play a significant role in this transformation of the industry and a solid and enabling regulatory regime is the factor that will determine the winners of the future.

Bibliography

Baldwin, R., M. Cave and M. Lodge (2013), *Understanding Regulation: Theory, Strategy and Practice* (Oxford University Press, Oxford).

COM (2018) 109/2: Fintech Action Plan: For a More Competitive and Innovative European Financial Sector.

COM (2020) 591: Communication from the Commission on a Digital Strategy for the EU.

COM (2020) 593: Regulation on Markets in Crypto-assets (MiCA).

COM (2020) 594: Regulation on a Pilot Regime for Market Infrastructures Based on Distributed Ledger Technology.

Deakin, S. (2018), The Evolution of Theory and Method in Law and Finance, at Moloney, N., Ferran, E. and Paynne, J. (2018), *The Oxford Handbook of Financial Regulation* (Oxford University Press, Oxford).

De Filippi, P. and A. Wright (2018), *Blockchain and the Law: The Rule of Code* (Harvard University Press, Cambridge, MA).

EP (2017) 2772: Distributed Ledger Technologies and Blockchain: Building trust with disintermediation.

Furlonger, D. and C. Uzureau (2019), *The Real Business of Blockchain: How Leaders Can Create Value in a New Digital Age* (Harvard Business School Press, Cambridge, MA).

Hacker, P., I. Lianos, G. Dimitropoulos and S. Eich (2019), *Regulating Blockchain: Techno-social and Legal Challenges* (Oxford University Press, Oxford).

Lessig, L (2000), Code Is Law: On Liberty in the Cyberspace, *Harvard Magazine*, January 2020, https://harvardmagazine.com/2000/01/code-is-law-html.

Lessig, L. (2006), *Code: Version 2.0* (Basic Books: New York, NY).

Maxwell, W. and M. Bourreau (2014), Technology Neutrality in Internet, Telecoms and Data Protection Regulation, *Global Media Communications Quarterly* (Autumn, 2014), Hogan Lovells.

Tasca, P. and R. Pisseli (2019), The Blockchain Paradox, at Hacker, P., Lianos, I., Dimitropoulos, G. and Eich, S. (2019), *Regulating Blockchain: Techno-Social and Legal Challenges* (Oxford University Press, Oxford).

Thaler, R. and R. C. Sunstein (2009), *Nudge: Improving Decisions About Health, Wealth and Happiness* (Penguin: New York, NY).

Werbach, K. (2018), *The Blockchain and the New Architecture of Trust* (MIT Press, Cambridge, MA).

Write. A. and P. De Filippi (2015), Decentralized Blockchain Technology and the Rise of Lex Cryptographia (SSRN Paper: March 2015).

Directive 2002/21/EC of 7 March 2002 on a Common Regulatory Framework for Electronic Communications Networks and Services (Framework Directive).

OECD Council Recommendation on Principles for Internet Policy Making (December 13, 2011).

President of the USA, Executive Order No. 13563: Improving Regulation and Regulatory Review (January).

Regulation (EU) 2016/679 of 27 April 2016 on the Protection of Natural Persons with Regard to the Processing of Personal Data and on the Free Movement of Such Data, and Repealing Directive 95/46/EC (General Data Protection Regulation).

13

Advancing Digital Transformation in the Public Sector with Blockchain: A View from the European Union

Emanuele Baldacci and Joao Rodrigues Frade

Introduction

Digital transformation is an essential policy priority for the public sector. The Covid-19 experience set the motion for further acceleration of technological transfer making digitalization a dominant priority for the EU. One of the main findings of the pandemic was that public or private entities with an efficient digital layer were able to absorb better the shocks of the supply chain or the collapse in the demand, compared to entities with purely analogue operational models. The other major finding was that true operational resilience does not come from *digitization* per se (having in place digital capacity), but

---

[1] Weill, P. and S. L. Woerner, What's You Digital Business Model? (Harvard Business Review Press: Cambridge, MA).

Personal views hereby presented are the authors' only, and should not in any way be construed as to represent an official position of the European Commission.

E. Baldacci (✉) · J. R. Frade
European Commission's Directorate-General for Informatics, Brussels, Belgium
e-mail: emanuele.baldacci@ec.europa.eu

J. R. Frade
e-mail: joao.rodrigues-frade@ec.europa.eu

rather from *digitalization* (when digital capacity is coupled with organizational adaptations and procedures that blend digital technologies with human routines).[1]

The European Union public authorities, responding to the major need in creating a European digital capacity in addressing major issues affecting the resilience of the EU economy, adopted a strategy of digital transformation and sustainability. This strategy was reflected in the adoption of a comprehensive Just Transition Mechanism and a set of digital policy initiatives like the Paper of the Digital Future of Europe, the EU Data Strategy and the White Paper on Artificial Intelligence. Blockchain is an integral part of this policy.

The European Institutions responded immediately to the windows of opportunity that blockchain technology opened for better public services. The Directorate-General for Informatics, DG DIGT, of the European Commission is a pioneer in the digitalization of public sector creating a space of innovation and experimentation through a wide range of use cases that, when tested, can be then efficiently trickled down to the public sectors of the Member States. To make blockchain a success story of the EU, this diffusion effort is being carried out in close collaboration with the Directorate-General for Communications Networks, Content and Technology, DG CNECT, and the Member States.

The Blockchain and the Public Sector: Principles and Experience from the European Commission

The hype of bitcoin and the publicity of the Initial Coin Offerings was accompanied by a libertarian political narrative. According to technology enthusiasts, Blockchain has come to replace the existing Institutional setting with a "new one", where an automated decision-making architecture, based on pre-determined rules, will ensure that the agency risks and costs the world experienced in the last global financial meltdown, will not be repeated. In early 2020, we see that the experience accumulated by the blockchain projects around the world of the last four years, lead us to assume that the current technological capabilities of blockchain technology are more modest than the initial expectations of the enthusiasts. It also lead us to assume that disintermediation does not require decentralization, and that the public sector is a very useful field for experimentation for services to the citizens and to public authorities.

Bibliography proposes a wide range of distributed ledger taxonomies and definitions. For simplicity, we can define a complete blockchain solution as the one that includes a set of five digital properties: disintermediation, immutability, encryption, tokenization and decentralization. Though the development of current DLT applications we see in private and public initiatives include many, or even all of these digital properties, the vast majority of successful applications so far rely on the first three.[2] Solutions of this type, can be defined rather as *blockchain inspired* rather than *blockchain complete*. In practical terms, blockchain inspired solutions, also associated with centralized permissioned blockchain architectures, reflect the current limits of the technology and the need to hedge significant scalability risks (like the ones we encountered in the ethereum and bitcoin blockchains) as well as operational risks, including the risks of *forking* and the risk of a *single point of failure*.

Understanding the limits of the technology at a certain point in time is a major challenge for a public sector leader or change agent. This requires leaders in the public sector to spot what a certain architecture can deliver early enough and make bold decisions that reflect the principle "efficiency first" rather than "technology first". In the case of blockchain and the public sector this is sine qua non for two reasons.

First, a public institution that aspires to make a blockchain transformation should be able to select among different governance architectures. Technical experts, in most of the time, propose these governance architectures and the public official should trust his experts. If the proposal comes from a technology enthusiast, an expert who acts on the principle "technology first", the blockchain project could end up with thousands of lines of codes of smart contract, inefficient to deliver and inefficient to scale. For example, in a blockchain solution that aims to verify the educational credentials of a citizen, relying solely on symmetrical smart contract architectures could be, with the current status of the technology, an architectural mistake. An alternative solution, would be to use a standard "digital post" solution, a solution that collects and transmits information between different systems, thereby providing the means for blockchain-based systems to interact with common databases and real-world people.[3] In the degree verification case, if a citizen claims having a graduate degree from a certain university, the access point of the digital post could be used to connect to the database of the university to:

---

[2]Furlonger and Uzureau (2020), The Real Business of Blockchain: How Leaders Can Create Value in a New Digital Age (Harvard Business Review Press, Cambridge, MA).
[3]Primavera de Filippi and Aaron Write (2018), Blockchain and the Law: The Rule of Code (Harvard university press, Cambridge, MA).

- "ask" if the provided metadata is consistent with the metadata of the university, and
- the resulting "yes, it is" or "no, it isn't" would then be recorded in an immutable ledger.

The second reason is that the public sector, when tries to fulfil technological transformation initiatives, takes into its balance sheet every related risk: technological risk, operational risk, financial risk, procurement risk, etc. If a project fails, as it is possible to happen when somebody experiments with a new and still evolving technology, then either new funds should be directed to the project (a situation that is not always convenient from a budgetary point of view), or has to be abandoned (a situation that economically is not desirable if the potential is high).

The European Commission made careful decisions around prudently selected blockchain use-cases taking into account technological, operational, financial and scalability risks with the intention to address the "trust challenge" around the technology and not just to solve a "data synchronicity challenge", as for example in some of the most known cases in the banking sector or in the shipping industry.

When it comes to the public sector, governmental entities are important intermediaries of many transactions happening in our society as the documents they issue or certify are a common way to verify information about people (in the form of identity cards, work permits, driving licences, etc.) and goods (such as their origin, compliance to safety rules, etc.). Official documents and other sensitive information inherit the trust deposited in the governmental authenticities that issue them and therefore become key trust facilitators among the many players transacting in the single market, both within and across borders. In the era of misinformation, it is essential to address the challenge of digital fraud, in particular when digital documents are quite easy to duplicate and to modify. Governments, and society, need technology to verify the authenticity of information it handles. Blockchain is a trustworthy technological option that can increase the transparency of information in the public records, ensure access to the citizens and provide verifiable certified and authenticated data, not only within the national limits, but also cross-border. In that sense, blockchain is a strategic tool for higher quality public services that the citizens can enjoy with limited transaction costs.

Given the importance of the authenticity of information for well-functioning administrative processes, especially when applied across borders, this paper looks at the notarization and reconciliation of information as key functionalities offered by blockchain to public administrations engaged in reducing bureaucracy while increasing efficiency and transparency.

A Short Introduction to Blockchain Technology

"Truly innovative deployments of blockchain require a match between blockchain's specific benefits and use cases that enable realization of these benefits, followed by dedicated hard work to get it right and embed in organizations and industries".[4]

In Europe and elsewhere, blockchain technology is gradually becoming a sound complement to classical trust enabling technologies[5] such as:

- eSignatures, the expression in an electronic format of a person's agreement to the content of a document or set of data;
- eSeals, the electronic equivalent of a stamp that is applied on a document to guarantee its origin and integrity and
- eTimestamps, an electronic stamp issued to prove that a document existed at a point-in-time.

As explained in the picture below, blockchain builds on these technologies to create a highly distributed, tamper-resistant ledger. In short, unlike the above-mentioned classical technologies, blockchain has its information stored across a series of nodes in a network, rather than in a single location. In short, **blockchain does recordkeeping in a verifiable and permanent way** (Fig. 13.1).

A good example of blockchain's disruptive potential is its application for tracking the history and accurate "state" of consumer products in highly fragmented supply chains. It should be noted that there are around 4 trillion consumer products produced and launched onto global markets every year. Each one of these products is composed of several materials, sub-components and ingredients. Each product is subject to many transactions as it becomes sourced, produced, shipped, stored and retailed before being used and eventually disposed of, perhaps remanufactured or recycled. Given the distributed

---

[4]World Economic Forum's White Paper "Blockchain Beyond the Hype—A Practical Framework for Business Leaders".
[5]These definitions are aligned to the eIDAS regulatory framework: https://eur-lex.europa.eu/legal-content/EN/TXT/?uri=uriserv:OJ.L_.2014.257.01.0073.01.ENG.

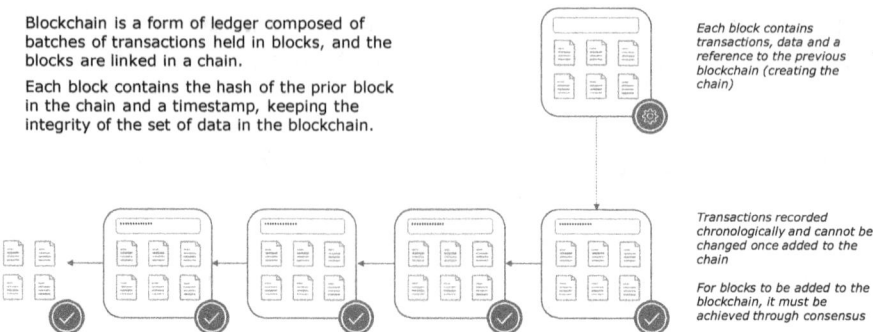

Fig. 13.1 How blockchain ledgers work (*Source* DIGIT, European Commission)

nature of modern supply chains and the many steps that they encapsulate, blockchain technology can be the right answer for keeping trusted records. Trusted recordkeeping and the authenticity of information are of the essence to private sector entities when carrying out their activities and to public sector entities when supervising the events associated to these activities and the lifecycle of consumer products.

Blockchain Applied to the Public Sector

It is important to point out that blockchain is not only interesting to the private sector. Blockchain's unique features are also important for the digital transformation of public administrations. Given the importance of the authenticity of information for well-functioning administrative processes, especially when applied across borders, this chapter explains how blockchain-led disintermediation may be a game changer for the public sector. Blockchain is a very promising technology for partial or full disintermediation of recurrent labour-intensive processes of public administrations. This is particularly important when it comes to:

- **Reconciliation of information;**
- **Notarisation of information.**

The use of blockchain in such processes is likely to advance the digital transformation of the public sector, making it on one hand more efficient (i.e. by saving time and money) and, on the other, more effective (i.e. by increasing trust and transparency). The next sections will look into how blockchain-based reconciliation and notarization of information can be done in practice and the challenges associated to their adoption.

Reconciliation of Information

What Is the Problem to Be Solved?

Reconciliation of information is a quite prevalent activity in a public administration from accounting to human resources processes (internal focus). One good example of such reconciliation processes is the validation of the legal entities[6] with whom a public administration transacts. A legal entity is typically a private company or a natural person that has some sort of contractual relationship with the public administration. These validation processes often involve several standard checks about the legal entity, such as their solvency, and the status of their bank account. A typical validation workflow can be split into two distinct septs:

Step 1. Checks focusing on the entity itself:

- Does the person or company exist?
- Is it a reputable person or company?

Step 2. Checks focusing on the bank account of the entity:

- Does the bank account exist?
- Is it from a reputable bank?

The typical solution to address the reconciliation problem would be to centralize the verification processes in a single central clearing entity. The level of automation and complexity of the clearing entity can be high or low depending on the number of manual checks and the stakeholders involved in providing this information. However, often times, the dependency on a single central entity is not desirable given that it becomes a "single point of failure".

---

[6]Legal Entity File of the European Commission: http://ec.europa.eu/budget/library/contracts_grants/info_contracts/legal_entities/legEnt_privComp_en.pdf.

How to Disintermediate?

Blockchain makes it possible to disintermediate such centralized processes. This can be achieved by using a combination of classical electronic signatures (to verify the origin and integrity of the information) and a blockchain (to ensure traceability and auditability). This means that the reconciliation of information no longer needs to be done centrally by a single entity. Blockchain-based processes can accomplish the same results using a common distributed ledger. Once in place, an increasing number of trusted verifiers can check information in real time without needing to enquire the central entity. At the same time, and as a next step, a number of manual/labour-intensive checks may be suppressed via the use of smart contracts technology. Some of the benefits of such approach are listed hereunder:

- The time cycle to sign contracts is shortened and the overall process accelerated;
- Payment delays, accompanied with their expensive interests are reduced;
- Keeping the register of legal entities in a much more expedient way as re-running the verification process would be done at a fraction of its current cost;
- Virtually costless audit processes as the blockchain maintains information about the transactions associated to the verification process, from its creation to subsequent controls.

What Are the Challenges to Make This a Reality?

As explained by Cathy Barrera[7] in her post "Hidden Costs of Verification", the information about legal entities and bank accounts is not blockchain-native and, in most cases, it cannot be accessed by a smart contract through an application's interface (a.k.a. API). These barriers would need to be overcome for blockchain to fully deliver its potential benefits. Once these barriers are fully suppressed, the use of blockchain would set in motion the disintermediation of centralizing clearing and the associated auditing processes.

---

[7]Hidden Costs of Verification: https://goo.gl/kP5Lsw.

Notarization of Information

What Is the Problem to Be Solved?

Notarization of information is crucial to guarantee the authenticity and integrity of documents, and information in general, when completing administrative processes with a public sector organization such as:

- Requesting proof of registration of birth;
- Submitting a tax declaration;
- Registering a change of address;
- (…)

In some cases, citizens and businesses are still required to provide paper documents that are certified as authentic via a physical authenticity stamp (the so-called apostille). The verification processes of these documents are manual, time-consuming and costly for public administrations providing public services (external focus). When moving to digital processes, the importance of ensuring the authenticity and integrity of documents increases as, in general, a document in digital format is much easier to manipulate and falsify. Hence, in the world of digitized processes, there is a clear need to reduce the cost of verification and auditability of information.

How to Disintermediate?

Blockchain greatly facilitates the auditability of documents by recording their registration time together with key metadata about the document itself and the entity providing it. This not only ensures their authenticity and integrity but also future auditability. All this makes the automation of compliance checks in time-sensitive processes possible. Furthermore, it cuts red tape and guarantees seamless information verification. For public sector administrations to receive effortlessly notarized documents from persons and legal entities, a solution would be to establish a common blockchain-based "registry". This registry would offer notarization services to citizens, businesses and public administrations alike as well as the associated functionality to verify their authenticity/integrity in real time. This would in turn increase the efficiency and transparency of public services at a lower cost.

What Are the Challenges to Make This a Reality?

To make such a solution feasible, data quality is an important element in order to ensure the quality of information. Data quality ensures the accuracy, completeness and consistency of the information that is registered by the person or legal entity.

Another main challenge, not specific to blockchain but common to any online technology, is accurate identity provision and verification. Nonetheless, given its distributed nature, blockchain tries to move towards decentralized Identity/Self-Sovereign Identity (SSI[8]) concepts, involving not one but several identity providers.

The European Blockchain Services Infrastructure (EBSI)

Europe is working on a cutting-edge blockchain infrastructure for public administrations that will offer both notarization and reconciliation capabilities. In simple words, the European Commission and the Member States are currently working together to put blockchain technology at the service of public administrations for the purpose of verification of information, making it trustworthy. The result of this work will be the first EU-wide blockchain infrastructure, driven by the public sector, that respects European values with high level of data security, data protection and privacy. This section will provide detailed information about this EU-wide initiative known as the European Blockchain Services Infrastructure (EBSI).[9]

History

In 2018, the European Commission launched the European Blockchain Partnership (EBP), 26 Member States and Norway, as a preliminary step for the establishment of an EU-wide European Blockchain Services Infrastructure (EBSI). The EBSI will be materialized as a network of distributed nodes across Europe (the blockchain). On 14 February 2019, the European

---

[8] Self-Sovereign Identity is an emerging trend associated with the way identity is managed in the digital world. According it, users should be able to create and control their own identity, without relying on any sort of centralized authority. This may be achieved using Verifiable Claims, meaning that Users can control the pieces of information they want to share with third parties to identify themselves.
[9] https://ec.europa.eu/cefdigital/wiki/display/CEFDIGITAL/EBSI.

Commission published the 2019 Telecommunications Work Programme of the Connecting Europe Facility (CEF)[10] creating the funding conditions for the launch of the EBSI. When fully in operation around 2021, the EBSI will enable the redesign of public services, better security and accountability in line with the approach advocated by current digital policy of the European Union, to which the Member States have committed themselves in the Tallinn Declaration on eGovernment.[11] Furthermore, the EBSI will also contribute and interact with the digital ecosystem of interoperability-enabling technologies that the European Commission is actively promoting through the "Connecting Europe".[12]

Guiding Principles

It is clear that a blockchain focusing on public administrations must be built around strong guiding principles such as:

- **Public Permissioned:** The identity of all participating nodes must be governed;
- **Decentralized:** Each member should run its own node or set of nodes;
- **Scalable:** Support of high-throughput and high number of nodes;
- **Open Specifications:** EU Public License and free from IPR;
- **Sustainable:** Energy-efficient consensus mechanism;
- **Interoperable:** should foster interoperability via alignment with the work of standardization bodies such as ISO, CEN or ETSI.

The table below shows how EBSI compares to other types of blockchain (Table 13.1).

The above means that EBSI Stack Nodes will exist across Europe in the EU Member States. The EBSI stack will provide:

- **Increased resilience** from a network of systems and data that can take over from failed nodes and distributes proofs of actions geographically;
- **Enhanced cyber security** from the enforcement of encryption practices;

---

[10] https://ec.europa.eu/cefdigital/wiki/display/CEFDIGITAL.
[11] All the European Union Member States and EFTA countries signed the 'eGovernement Declaration' in Tallin on 6 October 2017. The text of the Declaration is available at http://ec.europa.eu/newsroom/document.cfm?doc_id=47559.
[12] These include eID, eSignature among others, for more information: https://ec.europa.eu/cefdigital/wiki/display/CEFDIGITAL/Building+Blocks and https://ec.europa.eu/isa2/solutions_enprogram.

Table 13.1 EBSI compared to other types of blockchain—DIGIT, European Commission

	Allow anyone to join the network, to write to the network and to read the transactions from those networks	Whitelisted access is required, all transactions are publicly viewable	Only people with permission can read or write to such systems
Write access	Permissionless	Permissioned	Permissioned
Read access	Public	Public	Private
Topology	Distributed nodes	Distributed nodes	Distributed nodes
Typical consensus model	Proof of Work/Proof of Stake	Proof of Authority	Practical Byzantine Fault Tolerance, Raft
Example	Bitcoin/Ethereum/ECS/Tezos	European Blockchain Services Infrastructure (EBSI)	Hyperledger Fabric/Corda

- **Enhanced performance** for connected systems through the use of local copies of data;
- **Enhanced trust** with the use of blockchain smart contracts and ledgers.

The diagram below shows EBSI's layered architecture, the next section will explain it in more detail (Table 13.2).

Table 13.2 EBSI's layered architecture

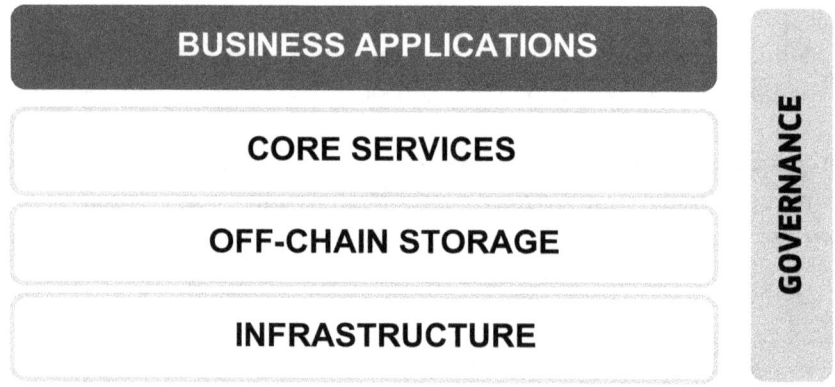

Source DIGIT, European Commission

Architecture

The **infrastructure layer** is EBSI's network of interconnected nodes hosted by the European Commission and the Member States. Each node operates independently of each other and each host organization is responsible for its daily operation. It is worth highlighting that organizations hosting an EBSI node will be subject to the terms and conditions to be reflected in EBSI's governance arrangements.

The **storage layer** is where the data that is not kept on-chain is stored. Similar to the node, the off-chain storage is also under the responsibility of the host organization and will be subject to the terms and conditions defined by EBSI's governance.

The **core services layer** is the interfaces exposed by the EBSI nodes enabling them to support the integration of business applications with EBSI. These interfaces are associated to EBSI's Use Cases. Below are a few examples:

- **Notarization Use Case:** Upon signing information (to ensure its integrity and authorship), public administrations will be able to register it in the EBSI ledger. Technically, this will be done by using the hash of the document in a GDPR compliant way;
- **Diploma Use Case:** Universities will be able to turn diplomas into a set of tamper-evident claims and metadata that cryptographically prove who issued it and who was issued to;
- **European Self-Sovereign Identity Framework (ESSIF) Use Case:** Users of EBSI will be identified through a new type of identifier for "self-sovereign" digital identity known as Decentralized Identifiers (DIDs). Furthermore, the ESSIF being developed alongside, and within, will rely on EBSI's blockchain as its trusted registry.

The vast ecosystem of public and private sector entities will develop EBSI's business applications layer according to the guiding principles shown above.

Next Steps

The EBSI and its services are currently under testing. These tests involve a multiplicity of entities including the European Commission and public administrations of several Member States. Once this phase is concluded, the EBSI will go live. Full operations are expected in 2021.

Bibliography

Regulation (EU) No 910/2014 of the European Parliament and of the Council of 23 July 2014 on electronic identification and trust services for electronic transactions in the internal market and repealing Directive 1999/93/EC. https://eur-lex.europa.eu/legal-content/EN/TXT/?uri=uriserv:OJ.L_.2014.257.01.0073.01.ENG.

Karl Wüst and Arthur Gervais. Do you need a Blockchain? 2017.

European Commission. Legal Entities. https://ec.europa.eu/info/publications/legal-entities_en.

Cathy Barrera. Hidden Costs of Verification. 2018.

Directive 2012/17/EU of the European Parliament and of the Council of 13 June 2012 amending Council Directive 89/666/EEC and Directives 2005/56/EC and 2009/101/EC of the European Parliament and of the Council as regards the interconnection of central, commercial and companies registers Text with EEA relevance. https://eur-lex.europa.eu/legal-content/EN/TXT/?uri=CELEX:32012L0017.

European Commission. https://ec.europa.eu/digital-single-market/en/news/european-countries-join-blockchain-partnership. 2018.

European Commission. https://ec.europa.eu/digital-single-market/en/blockchain-technologies.

European Commission. https://ec.europa.eu/digital-single-market/en/news/european-countries-join-blockchain-partnership. 2018.

Ministerial Declaration on eGovernment—The Tallinn Declaration. https://ec.europa.eu/digital-single-market/en/news/ministerial-declaration-egovernment-tallinn-declaration. 2017.

Regulation (EU) No 1316/2013 of the European Parliament and of the Council of 11 December 2013 establishing the Connecting Europe Facility, amending Regulation (EU) No 913/2010 and repealing Regulations (EC) No 680/2007 and (EC) No 67/2010 Text with EEA relevance. https://eur-lex.europa.eu/legal-content/EN/TXT/?uri=CELEX%3A32013R1316.

Regulation (EU) 2016/679 of the European Parliament and of the Council of 27 April 2016 on the protection of natural persons with regard to the processing of personal data and on the free movement of such data, and repealing Directive 95/46/EC (General Data Protection Regulation). https://eur-lex.europa.eu/legal-content/EN/TXT/?uri=CELEX%3A32016R0679.

Directive (EU) 2016/1148 of the European Parliament and of the Council of 6 July 2016 concerning measures for a high common level of security of network and information systems across the Union. https://eur-lex.europa.eu/legal-content/EN/TXT/?uri=uriserv:OJ.L_.2016.194.01.0001.01.ENG&toc=OJ:L:2016:194:TOC.

World Economic Forum's White paper "Blockchain Beyond the Hype—A Practical Framework for Business Leaders".

European Commission. Blockchain for digital government, an assessment of pioneering implementations in public services: https://joinup.ec.europa.eu/sites/default/files/document/2019-04/JRC115049%20blockchain%20for%20digital%20government.pdf.

14

Disposable Identities? Why Digital Identity Matters to Blockchain Disintermediation and for Society

Loretta Anania, Gaëlle Le Gars, and Rob van Kranenburg

Identity: Greater Than the Sum of Technologies

The most disruptive application in the early bitcoin days was as an alternative form of "liquid currencies". Blockchains became popular for the "digital anonymity" they provided, enabled by a decentralized network. In this model, miners and transactions required an anonymous structure and distributed trust mechanisms based on "mathematical proof". That was then. Ironically, blockchains and digital ledger technologies (DLT) developments now face the far larger and complex matter of identity, where crypto anonymity is not always the rule and may no longer be the attraction. For smart contracts,

---

Personal views hereby presented are the authors' only, and should not in any way be construed as to represent an official position of the European Commission.

L. Anania (✉)
European Commission, DG CNECT, Brussels, Belgium
e-mail: loretta.anania@ec.europa.eu

G. Le Gars
Policy Analyst on Digital and Urban Policy, Brussels, Belgium
e-mail: gaelle.le_gars@mail.be

R. van Kranenburg
Founder of IoT Council, Brussels, Belgium
e-mail: kranenbu@xs4all.nl

© The Author(s), under exclusive license to Springer Nature Switzerland AG 2021
E. Kaili and D. Psarrakis (eds.), *Disintermediation Economics*,
https://doi.org/10.1007/978-3-030-65781-9_14

pseudonymity has advantages (autonomy, privacy, data protection) and legal disadvantages (e.g. as instrument of money laundering).

Blockchains can be used to coordinate actions between different actors, across different locations, under various jurisdictions. Capacity to contract is an issue, since if a party lacks capacity or if a minor is involved it would not be possible to determine whether the capacity to contract exists. Techno-legal limitations of blockchains and DLT applications come in relation to Digital Identities. The necessity to look into disposable digital identities starts with the clear appeal of a fast yet far more decentralized network, and an institutional system able to tackle immediate challenges posed by the Internet of Things (IoT) industry, including, at issue, the locus of liability.

In this chapter, we fit the evolving blockchain/DLT infrastructure in the broader policy context that brings *digital identity*[1] to the fore. As the President of the European Commission Ursula von der Leyen made it clear in her introductory speech to the European Parliament, these technology developments play a part in Europe's "strategic autonomy".

In this chapter, we give the context and explore the meaning of a decentralized alternative to bounded digital identity in light of the strategic goals of the EU and the aspirations of its Treaty-bound citizens. We see a need to develop a coherent legal framework to accompany this novel technology choice of critical importance. We describe some technologies and their implications. We conclude that the future of the EU closely relates to its ability to translate its goals and values laid out in Treaty of the European Union[2] in the digital realm. This can be achieved by embedding the rights of EU citizens, as a digital entitlement: the liberty to act in an internet world.

The Deep Implications of Digital Id

The growing number of online identity solutions is as extensive as the range of purposes. These initiatives are very heterogeneous in nature and origin. Some are well-funded private sector consortia. Public authorities lead some others. Many more are smaller social enterprises constituted "ad hoc" as not-for-profit tech foundations for the social good. A few are gaining great success and support, as we shall see below. Some non-profit co-operatives

---

[1] For the purpose of this chapter's discussion, unless further specified, any reference to "Digital identity" refers to the generic definition of *a computerized record of who a person is, stored in a registry*.

[2] Consolidated version of the Treaty on European Union, TITLE I—COMMON PROVISIONS, Article 3 (ex Article 2 TEU) OJ C 202, 7 June 2016, pp. 17–17.

demonstrate technology solutions with a "social good" purpose that help us understand the open nature as well as the innovation process. Global Good initiatives by the UN and humanitarian NGOs shed some light on the plight of those people who find themselves unable to document their identity. Today, in 2020, choirs of pluralist or corporatist voices debate the implications of identity technologies for the future of society. The sphere of identity and the digital realm intersect, the points of intersection are multiple and—so far—evolving separately, starting from strictly technical systems design to the future of politics online. Engineers set functional requirements of application sectors. Up the value stream banks, philanthropies and large treasury holders see Fintech as a golden nugget that brings home profitable user experiences. The debate now extends to technocratic roadmaps and managerial problem-solving policies, and to market arbitrage.

Meanwhile, recent court cases have to address the implications of surveillance, of privacy infringements, of national sovereignty and of the individual's "right to be forgotten". Big and small court decisions are, at best, patching up small wounds—not a commensurate coordinated cure. The answers to the breadth of societal questions and future implications diverge. Few cases will reach global policy level. The familiar unquestioned narrative is that all digital innovation is for the good. Digital enlightenment and progress is found in many institutional discourses around digital identity, such as in the reports issued by the World Bank, OECD, World Economic Forum or the *IEEE*.

In practice, design and technology choices are established by the specific requirements of those corporate sectors having the most influence. Progress is measured along a timeline set out in global regulatory agreements and the main priority is to select "operational efficiency" as defined by immediate sectors-specific needs and constraints. A good example of this process at play today is that of the global payment system. It relates to new agreements, laws, regulations and standards set around the global application of uniform KYC (Know Your Customer) rules. Much industry activity centers around it; from Fintech to mobile payments and the widespread adoption of digital wallets.

Largely unchanged since from the paper-based era of identification, national authorities remain the core issuers of identity credentials. They hold the only comprehensive record of births and deaths and can verify one's actual existence by time and place. Any public sector identification and authentication system requires legal certainty and enforceability. This is also necessary to process cross-border financial transactions. Individual identity necessarily links to information that is verified by the issuing state authority.

Systems security requires increasingly detailed involvement of diverse public authorities in the technology choices made by operators and the data processing industry. As the newly in force EU second Payment Services Directive (*PSD2*) illustrates, this requires reconciling the goal of stimulating open banking and Fintech with that of protecting personal data privacy regulation. Some analysts predict *PSD2* will also lead to renewed cross-sector partnerships between the already powerful digital and financial players.[3] A growing part of the internet is accessible only to those who can log in as users. This login entry is already evolving into a requirement on users to be verified through a state-id scheme, and their smartphones to be continually tracked thereafter or else repeatedly go through the intrusive verification process.

The US RealID Act of 2005, initiated over security concerns emerging after the 9/11 events, took years to be fully implemented. The *RealID* expands on an already introduced standard, the "new" department of motor vehicles drivers' licence. From October 2021,[4] the *RealID* will be required for US citizens to board inland planes. This is willy-nilly a significant change for US travellers who, until recently, could fly internally without identification. In the USA, as in a few other countries, there are no government-issued compulsory identity cards and a driver's licence often suffices as proof of identity for the few instances when one is required. Standardized identification along the RealID model enables automated ID verification, thus removing the need to employ personnel for that task. For that reason, when tech alternatives are on offer, these may often be another, more intrusive, form of automated verification, such as the requirement to submit to the automated harvesting of one's biometric features.

User Profiling and Digital Privacy

Even small online services with no obvious regulatory need for verified identities have a commercial interest in connecting visitors to a state-verified identity as an alternative to the walled garden logic of inviting login through Google, Apple or Facebook. As one identification systems vendor argues in its sales pitch,[5] *for digital marketers, data is the only currency that really matters, and its value is amplified when that data is tied to a persistent identity graph.*

---

[3]McKinsey. "PSD2: Taking Advantage of Open-Banking Disruption," January 2018. https://www.mckinsey.com/industries/financial-services/our-insights/psd2-taking-advantage-of-open-banking-disruption.

[4]Initially due to be implemented on October 1st 2020, the enforcement of the RealID requirement is delayed by a year following a decision of President Trump made in the context of the Covid-19 crisis. Transportation Security Administration. "REAL ID." Accessed April 16, 2020. https://www.tsa.gov/real-id.

[5]Signal. "What Is Customer Identity?" Accessed February 20, 2020. https://www.signal.co/resources/what-is-customer-identity/.

Common tracking methods allow for some lower level of identification through probabilistic inferences about users. Attaching user profiles to state-issued, ID not only removes some uncertainties but also turns these data profiles into a commodity, generating another value stream by selling metadata to online platforms. Automated real-time micro-bids for digital advertising literally sell individual "impressions" to the highest bidder. An individual's demographic and behavioural data can be instantly connected to their next visit on the site and purpose is to display targeted advertising. Extraordinarily crafty yet intrusive practices lie behind personalized advertising. These are developed for live ad-screens in public spaces; from bus stops to public toilets or waiting rooms. The combined effect further increases the power of money advantage of the largest online advertising platforms over all other stakeholders.

An early Facebook investor turned critic, Roger McNamee, calls the elaborate profiling of all of us by such platforms "voodoo dolls", because, he argues, the ultimate goal is to be tops at monetizing the manipulation of our minds. Gramsci would call it an intended "hegemony", where the information workers form a large social class of "organic intellectuals". As grey-area overlapping markets for our data and profiles grow, the digital business becomes a concern for EU citizens and for EU regulators alike.

Systemic Impacts on Society

Public opinion voices its concern on the intrusiveness of Big Government, Big Brother or the power of State authorities, but also the scale of new data powers related to the practice of covert surveillance. To opponents of big government, data hoarding by private business matters mainly as instrumental alternative to abusive state surveillance of individuals. Public opinion has woken up to the risks for society of this extensive data collection by the largest global corporations. The potential abuse of power to manipulate electoral outcomes is difficult to measure but empirical studies suggest it could be large enough to affect election outcomes.[6] This agenda-setting influencing power over public opinion by the largest platforms is a potential direct threat to sovereignty. It shakes the legitimacy of state authorities, in particular for the diverse nation states that form the EU.

---

[6] "Why Google Poses a Serious Threat to Democracy, and How to End That Threat" Testimony by Robert Epstein, Ph.D. (re@aibrt.org) Senior Research Psychologist, American Institute for Behavioral Research and Technology Before the United States Senate Judiciary Subcommittee on the Constitution Tuesday, June 16, 2019.

To be complete, this picture needs a brief exploration of the alternative model, that of a state-authority-centred model where the state-issued scheme is the reference and a requirement imposed by law on an expanding range of activities in India. The Indian government's citizen ID registration scheme is the largest in the world with 1.2 billion users enrolled. India chose a different path to that of the EU and the USA in the digital identity arena. Their scheme was launched early in 2016. It had a notoriously difficult start (and an evolution from which much can be learned). The legal flaws and early technical failures of India's Aadhaar deployment highlight the risks inherent in translating the centralized approach of paper-based identity to the digital interconnected world. The original design of this ambitious scheme initially failed to properly account for key fundamental rights and principles which then had to be addressed through subsequent supreme court cases and legal adjustments. We conclude that an appropriate legal framework for digital identity cannot be limited to the narrow utilitarian and strictly functional "here and now". To be in the public interest, a government-led initiative has to build on foundational, constitutional principles that resist technology erosion.

Impacts on Individual Lives: From Online to Offline

Until very recently, the needs and rights of the individual holder of a digital ID, as simultaneously user and data subject, were not central to the design and could be entirely absent in the management literature assessing market sector opportunities.[7] The original appeal of blockchain-based identity solutions is precisely that their design intends to account for those rights. Many attempts, regardless of their implementation success or failure, have merit in bringing the entitlement dimension to the fore. At the time, other developments made individual rights a more urgent and more important matter than it had ever been. The implications of digital identity for individuals and for society at large will vastly expand as the distinction between online and offline continues to evaporate across all dimensions of daily life as it does now.

Elizabeth Renieris, a Fellow at the Berkman Klein Center and an academic expert on privacy, recently warned "An identity layer 'for the web' was one

---

[7] See for example: PricewaterhouseCoopers. Digital identity: Changing the way financial institutions connect with consumers [Internet]. PWC India. 2018, Available from: https://www.pwc.in/consulting/financial-services/fintech/fintech-insights/digital-identity-changing-the-way-financial-institutions-connect-with-consumers.html—an overview of the benefits of Digital Identity for the financial sector, where the word "consumers" in the title is the only reference to human individuals behind the Digital Identity.

thing when there was a separation between the online and offline worlds. Now, as we bring everything online through connected devices, smart cities, augmented humans, and (yes) blockchain too, the digital is 'eating the real world' to put it in software terms. If we bake identity into all things connected, we bake it into everything. We create a world where the default practice will be to identify in all contexts and all settings. In other words, adding identity to the web isn't just adding it to the web anymore".[8]

Among the variety of ID schemes currently emerging, the common characteristic is a near total lack of agency for the individual as data-subject past the choice she/he made of joining ("onboarding") the particular scheme. This situation may be "as-expected" when the Digital ID is experienced as the merely "digitalized" version of a familiar public-authority-issued ID, as in the case of government-led schemes. The user ID solutions provided by digital platforms (Facebook, Amazon, Google, Microsoft, etc.) is used to access many other sites. It seemed benign as an easy alternative to collecting multiple passwords. The implicit and ever growing power imbalance between the Digital ID provider and the data-subject takes on a completely different significance when participation in a given Digital ID scheme becomes a prerequisite to a growing range of basic but essential actions of daily life from paying for purchases, making a call, accessing public transports, travelling on motorways, parking or entering the door of one's own house.

The disruptive impact to one's life is clearly experienced when loosing temporary access to an ordinary taken-for-granted entitlement. This risk dwarfs in comparison to the potential harm to individuals that would come from being locked-out of multiple vital services at once. It is already an envisioned possibility with the current versions of digitalized personalization of access to essential services (water/energy) and daily use devices (car, phone, accommodation). Stories of such individual cases of bad experiences are already appearing, ranging from digital keys locking people out of vehicles,[9] to biometric systems refusing access to homes[10] to the much more dramatic cases of losses and deaths caused or attributed to Aadhaar.[11]

---

[8]Renieris EM. An Identity Layer for the Web Would Identify Us Everywhere [Internet]. CoinDesk. 2019 [cited 2020 Jan 12]. Available from: https://www.coindesk.com/an-identity-layer-for-the-web-would-identify-us-everywhere.

[9]"5 Symptoms of Engine Immobilizer Problems." CarTreatments.Com (blog), March 13, 2019. https://cartreatments.com/car-immobilizer-systems-function-and-bad-symptoms/.

[10]Independent.i.e. "This Man Was Locked out of Home When His Smart Doorbell Thought He Was Batman," September 18, 2018. https://www.independent.ie/world-news/and-finally/this-man-was-locked-out-of-home-when-his-smart-doorbell-thought-he-was-batman-37329890.html.

[11]Ratcliffe, Rebecca. "How a Glitch in India's Biometric Welfare System Can Be Lethal." *The Guardian*, October 16, 2019, sec. Technology. https://www.theguardian.com/technology/2019/oct/16/glitch-india-biometric-welfare-system-starvation.

So far, most causes are attributed to multiple failures or teething malfunctions of the system itself. The wider appeal of the digitalization of identity, even in those sectors where adoption of the scheme is not a regulatory requirement, is usually found in the monetization of personal data and, increasingly, in the monetization of access. Without adequate legal framing, this conditional access could rapidly evolve in the multiplication of digital tollbooths. Crossing a bridge or turning on the water tap may be an instance, conditioned on one's real-time ability to pay or, more perniciously from the user's standpoint, to one's consumer score established from big data shared across services and digital identity platforms.[12] Hegemony of a profit-driven scheme could easily lead to loss of rights previously so obvious that no one thought of enshrining them in law. This ill beginning is already manifest in those cases that made it necessary to campaign for the "right of repair". In such circumstances, as the Indian government itself learnt,[13] it is imperative that the public authority be empowered to deter and stamp out abuses through an immediate intervention. An unchecked generalization of abusive practices would inevitably be deleterious to society as a whole, eroding the legitimacy of the public authority, now exposed as powerless. Yet this is precisely the risk governments would take unless a proactive effort to ensure the protection of rights of ID holders in the design, operations and applications of Digital ID schemes they authorize is part of it.

To strengthen citizen's rights, legal framing is a critical mechanism that cannot be substituted by insisting on expedient government-led mechanisms, crisis or no crisis. The case of the Chinese social score shows,[14] that the drive to achieve "effective" behavioural control on the population can impact the rights of individuals, arguably more comprehensively and rapidly, with even less opportunities for collective or individual recourse.

---

[12] An early version of this "backroom" surveillance scoring already exists between the largest retailers in the US as was revealed through a petition by a consumer watchdog org. To the FTC and letter to the NY Attorney General in 2019 "As the enclosed petition explains, at least 11 tech companies—none of them known to Americans, much less household names—are applying secret algorithms to tens of thousands of pieces of private information about each American to create a variety of scores that enable corporations to overcharge, mistreat or even refuse to do business with those with poor scores" representconsumers.org. "Secret Surveillance Scoring: Request for Investigation and Enforcement Action," September 11, 2019. https://www.representconsumers.org/surveillance-scoring/.

[13] Georgetown Journal of International Affairs. "It's Now Aadhaar with Caveats," February 15, 2019. https://www.georgetownjournalofinternationalaffairs.org/online-edition/2019/2/15/its-now-aadhaar-with-caveats.

[14] See Engelmann, Severin, Mo Chen, Felix Fischer, Ching-yu Kao, and Jens Grosskalgs. "Clear Sanctions, Vague Rewards: How China's Social Credit System Currently Defines 'Good' and 'Bad' Behavior." In Proceedings of the Conference on Fairness, Accountability, and Transparency, 69–78. FAT* '19. Atlanta, GA, USA: Association for Computing Machinery, 2019. https://doi.org/10.1145/3287560.3287585.

Geopolitical Impacts

Digital ID implementation can have a profound impact on geopolitics. The sovereign prerogatives of States to define citizenship and protect their security relies on their ability to address legitimate expectations of citizens and to continue to deliver entitlements, including some regarding privacy and security from cyber threats. In what the Indian think-tank *ORF* argues is "governance by technical standards",[15] States are already relinquishing some of the sovereign prerogatives attached to the definition of citizenship and territory for the purpose of efficiently implementing Digital ID along technical lines as endorsed by the World Bank and the *ITU* and emanating from industry-led standards of the *ISO*. The ORF also envisions the risk that the generalization of e-residency schemes such as the one offered by Estonia could lead to a novel trend: State-affiliation shopping by individuals seeking virtual residency in those States offering more favourable legal and tax regimes. Virtual offshoring by digital identity would entice a much larger population set and divert national tax revenue streams from State to State.

Another key consideration for raising the geopolitical standing of States is the national security implications of the deployment of national digital ID schemes. Doing it wrong potentially creates new risks for critical infrastructures and greatly complicates the protection of "Politically Exposed Persons". Doing it right brings attention. An example of this happening is seen at the UN. Estonia, acting in the UN Security Council in January 2020, sought and was elected (for the first time) to one of the temporary seats on the strength of their ambitious digital ID policy and proactive cybersecurity agenda.

Identity is a sum of all our social relationships. For individual and collective empowerment, it will be necessary to safeguard or secure identity, interoperability, transparency and controllability, data portability, ethics and equity. To the extent that we embrace the growing overlap between the digital and the non-digital parts of daily life, we will need a careful reconsideration of legal framing and safeguards that protect each of us as individuals from a number of new risks. These include falling hostage to predatory practices of business operators, having one's choices unfairly restricted by arbitrary or malfunctioning application of automated decision-making systems, being exposed to criminal abuse of personal data through poor security. Legal

---

[15] Sukumar, Arun Mohan. "Governance by Technical Standards: Do Digital Id Platforms Re- Order or Reinforce International Relations?" ORF, November 6, 2019. https://www.orfonline.org/expert-speak/governance-by-technical-standards-do-digital-id-platforms-re-order-or-reinforce-international-relations-57367/.

remedies can address the societal costs of mass surveillance—or the similarly damaging general assumption that it goes on—as well as other harms to individuals from abusive "scoring" practices by parties invisible to them. But dealing with remedies and each new case individually would put an enormous burden on public regulators, legislators and the justice systems. It can also be damaging to inter-personal and institutional trust at system level. These dystopic outcomes are possible thanks only to the continuous stream of personal data trailing our online identity. The effects of digital identity cannot be limited to a technological or economic choice made on basis of technical performance for expediency and efficiency.

State of Play

In the last decade, individual data privacy has become a subject matter of civil liberties. A legitimate expectation of this liberty has gained visibility through substantial reporting in the global media. Much has been reported in the form of lament over the precariat of these "rights" in the dark digital enterprise age of biased AI decision-making intelligence, or powerless outrage over revelations of yet another large-scale breach. Matters of civil liberties and expectations of privacy protection for individuals as "data-subjects" have substantially gained with the GDPR. Before it reports took the form of lament over the precariousness of these "rights", as in Big Brother haunts the digital age. Powerless outrage over revelations of yet another large-scale breach called out to "take back control". On occasion, a few determined individuals managed to obtain institutional recognition of the specific harms to each and all individuals of specific abuse over personal data as was the case for the now-famous Max Schrems, and his successful legal campaigns have ripple effects in the courts, policy and the media (a battle still ongoing).

In December 2019, in the USA, a public opinion poll of registered voters found that 79% said Congress should make crafting a bill to better protect consumers' online data a priority and 65% said data privacy is one of the biggest issues our society faces and legislation is needed to stop data breaches. This matches other survey findings globally, showing increasing support for public regulation of private data collection businesses. The digital ID schemes deployed primarily reflect the respective immediate priorities of three core stakeholders: governments, the financial sector and the digital tech sector. The three link, especially the largest corporations and the most powerful governments eager to set the global agenda through soft-law and informal forms of concertation rather than multilateral binding legislation implementation.

This top-down first-in approach can change. The EU *GDPR*, in force since May 2018, is the first comprehensive regulatory instrument primarily aimed at protecting individual digital privacy rights. Much maligned at first, The EU regulation was imitated across other jurisdictions, including California, Canada, Japan, etc. There is a signal of broader multi-stakeholder support for proactive regulatory protection of digital rights. Whether this is a bold enough first step in rebalancing powers remains to be seen. For the EU, the content of the legislative proposals announced by the Commission Presidency on data protection and data flows (a digital single market for data) will constitute a first indication of how far and with what effect.

UN, World Bank and the Sustainable Development Goals

The World Bank, together with the UN promotes the adoption of Digital ID for development as a way to address the needs of 1.1 billion people it found currently lacking any form of verified identity. They assess it will take $12 billion to achieve identification for all. Key players from both financial and digital sectors are represented in a UN multi-stakeholder coalition[16] launched in 2018 at the Davos WEF meeting.

The World Bank promoted a global digitalization of identity since 2010 under the banner of *Financial Inclusion*. This program aimed at including a billion unbanked into the global financial system by 2020. Sponsoring universal digitalization of ID initially was presented as a means to reach the one billion unbanked mainly living in poorer parts of the world. As means to reach the goal of "Universal Financial Access by 2020" (UFA2020 program), the World Bank then intended to support *a platform approach including three basic functionalities : a biometric identity database, virtual payment addressing a digital payment interoperability as well as national policies that provide scale through combinations of digital ID, digitized G2P payments.*[17] The *G20* partnered with the World Bank in 2016 to take up financial Inclusion as a goal and to promote similar measures across all countries. A group of private partners supported this goal: financial institutions, telecom associations, many organizations and foundations with links to the payment system operators

---

[16]Including The UNHCR, World Bank, World Food Programme, Consumers International, Omidyar Network, the Linux Foundation, FIDO Alliance, GSMA, Hyperledger, ID2020, Open Identity Exchange, Sovrin Foundation, World Identity Network, Accenture, Barclays, Deutsche Bank, Mastercard, Microsoft, Sedicii and Visa.

[17]World Bank. "UFA2020 Overview: Universal Financial Access by 2020," October 1, 2018. https://www.worldbank.org/en/topic/financialinclusion/brief/achieving-universal-financial-access-by-2020.

(Visa, Mastercard) and to the Digital sector (Bill & Melinda Gates foundation). All joined in as partners in these initiatives for *Financial Inclusion*[18] as they would later do under the *UN SDGs* under the objective of "an identity for all".[19]

Some challenge the merit of promoting financial inclusion as a benefit to the "unbanked" as a priority when those communities and individuals often also experience other, more critical forms of deprivations. The programs were criticized also for implementing what amounts to digital financialization, with results that end to the detriment rather than the benefit of target populations.[20] The World Bank has since reframed its agenda in favour of the global adoption of digital ID within the broad societal and political agenda of the *UN SDGs*.[21] That initiative aims to coordinate public and private sectors initiatives around the *UN SDG* target 16.9: *giving everyone over 5 an ID by 2030*. This was again criticized for neglecting the privacy and civil liberties issues. High-level coordination between private sector and public authorities conducted under the aegis of the UN and the World Bank, has generated concrete plans for national ID schemes, notably in Africa, some already at deployment phase, and not always running entirely smoothly.[22]

High-level coordination between funding bodies, business stakeholders and public authorities resulted in schemes prioritizing technical feasibility and cost efficiency for their issuing authorities. Some of these projects were challenged in court for failing to deliver on the basic promise of inclusion made to the population concerned.[23] As with the *SDGs* overall, the UN and the World Bank rely on a public–private partnership strategy from conception to implementation as well as big projects co-funding. As a result, rather than enabling a broad consensus, the outcome of the World Bank's efforts may potentially have the opposite effect of reinforcing imbalance in favour of specific private sector stakeholders.

---

[18] https://www.worldbank.org/en/topic/financialinclusion/brief/achieving-universal-financial-access-by-2020.

[19] https://blogs.worldbank.org/digital-development/joining-forces-make-ids-accessible-all.

[20] See for example Soederberg, Susanne. "Universalising Financial Inclusion and the Securitisation of Development." *Third World Quarterly* 34, no. 4 (May 1, 2013): 593–612. https://doi.org/10.1080/01436597.2013.786285.

[21] Under SDG 16 The World Bank leads and coordinates activities aimed at Target 16.9—by 2030 provide legal identity for all.

[22] World Wide Web Foundation. "Digital ID Tech Must Be Transparent If It Is to Work for Citizens," August 28, 2019. https://webfoundation.org/2019/08/digital-id-tech-must-be-transparent-if-it-is-to-work-for-citizens/.

[23] "Digital IDs Make Systemic Bias Worse." Wired, February 5, 2020. https://www.wired.com/story/opinion-digital-ids-make-systemic-bias-worse/.

5G, Open Banking and Global Corporate Strategies

To address what is widely acknowledged as an unsatisfactory status-quo,[24] major stakeholders along with proxy philanthropies and sector associations coalesce to enable the emergence of global identity standards.[25] The key to broad acceptability within the business sector is to find a solution satisfying global standards of trust, security and interoperability at financially sustainable costs. This is all the more critical that both the deployment of 5G and the merging of financial and digital services under open banking regimes are predicted to fundamentally reshape the distribution of power between the corporate sectors 2 and 3 to billion digital native will enter the financial services space between the years 2010 and 2030 and 95% of those will bank online only and mostly through mobile phone. Financial authorities foresee *bigtech* as the most likely winner in this new global regime leading to further accumulation of their already exorbitant power. In June 2019, the Dutch Central Bank issued a briefing note assessing that *the combination of payment data with large volumes of personal data could lead to privacy concerns on the part of the general public. Given the international nature of these developments, central banks and supervisory authorities are discussing at the international level whether the current supervisory frameworks are adequate to address them.*[26]

This current moment of uncertainty is when political signals by powerful sovereign states race to have influence, as the hot debate around Huawei exemplifies. Once substantial investments have been made by powerful public and private players, path dependency sets in and the changing course becomes near impossible, barring a societal breakdown of global magnitude.

The EU Legislation Shaping Digital ID

Depicted in Fig. 14.1 is the "Governance Stack", a set of EU legislation in force by early 2020, which, added together, shape the models of digital identity for broader use. As it stands, this governance stack is made of multiple legislations produced for various purposes and aimed at various sectors. It

---

[24] Burt, Chris. "Digital Identity Gets Mediocre Marks in Annual Progress Report." Biometric Update, February 8, 2019. https://www.biometricupdate.com/201902/digital-identity-gets-mediocre-marks-in-annual-progress-report.

[25] Such as the https://fidoalliance.org/ which Apple joined in 2020 or ID2020 which includes Microsoft, Open Identity Exchange, or Kantara.

[26] De Nederlandsche Bank. "DNBulletin: BigTech Companies Increasingly Active in European Payment Markets," June 4, 2019. https://www.dnb.nl/en/news/news-and-archive/DNBulletin2019/dnb384278.jsp.

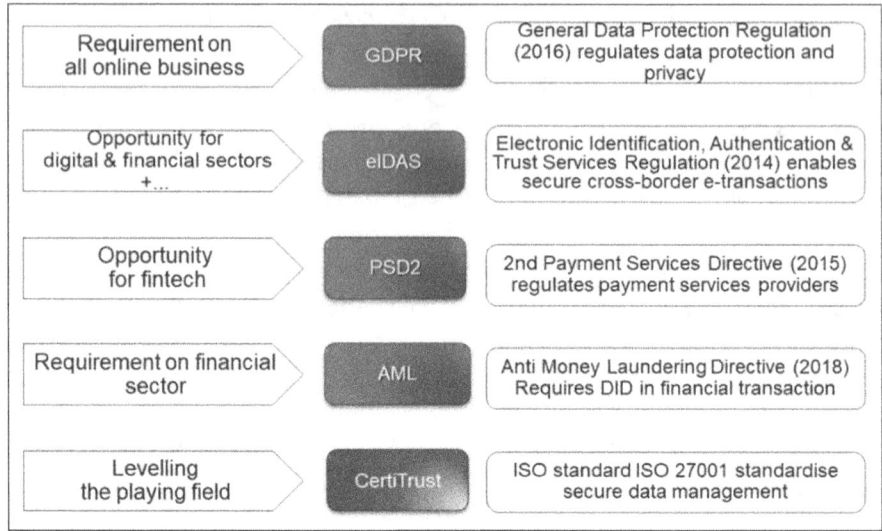

Fig. 14.1 The EU legislation shaping the Digital ID "governance stack" (*Source* Authors)

evolves, so far, without a coherent single digital identity model or policy driving them.

The *GDPR*[27] is a landmark regulation by which the European Parliament, the Council of the EU and the European Commission intend to strengthen and unify data protection for all individuals within the European Union. Adopted on 27 April 2016 it came into force 25 May 2018, after a two-year transition period. In addition to legitimizing stronger consumer protection and data privacy principles (noticed worldwide) it facilitated support for privacy-enhancing technologies and for promoting change in shaping data processing innovations (e.g. Cloud). Sustained influence of the *GDPR* greatly depends on the extent to which it is enforced.

The *eIDAS*[28] regulation was first adopted by *piggy-backing* on previous efforts of the European Commission to have digital signatures recognized cross-border. Today's core legislation on identity credentials remains the *eIDAS regulation and its implementing rules*. Originally, *eID* was promoted

---

[27] Regulation (EU) 2016/679 of the European Parliament and of the Council of 27 April 2016 on the protection of natural persons with regard to the processing of personal data and on the free movement of such data, and repealing Directive 95/46/EC (General Data Protection Regulation) (Text with EEA relevance).

[28] Regulation (EU) No 910/2014 of the European Parliament and of the Council of 23 July 2014 on electronic identification and trust services for electronic transactions in the internal market and repealing Directive 1999/93/EC, Pub. L. No. 32014R0910, 257 OJ L (2014). http://data.europa.eu/eli/reg/2014/910/oj/eng.

top-down as a way to simplify the citizen's relationship to the public administration (e.g. welfare receipts, taxation). *eIDAS* standardization took many years to be agreed. Alongside that EU-centric effort, global negotiations addressed the matter of mutual acceptance for e-signatures and digital authentication, relying on a common set of reputable validation mechanisms. It worked and served its purpose even in the transatlantic context.

For EU Member States, *eIDAS* now requires at least one working central node plus a bridge to facilitate the exchange of records to all other nodes, thus functioning in an interoperable manner. There is now a recognized need to address some complications, both in terms of cross-border data flows and in terms of certified intergovernmental solutions. Blockchains and non-blockchain solutions are allowed in *eIDAS*. For identity, self-sovereign identity (SSI) is one of the options under consideration. SSI was spearheaded by Estonia, chosen by Finland, Austria, and may soon be selected for other Member States. For over a year there are SSI infrastructure implementation projects in Canada and in the USA with the backing of the Department of Homeland Security.

The current college of EU Commissioners has the transition to digital as a priority and needs to ensure that all Member States move faster or in a more coordinated manner. The covid19 crisis is a first test case on applications in eHealth, especially in cross-border settings. The Digital Services Act is a new framework proposed by the Commission in 2020, to update its decades-old eCommerce directive. Possibly, these legislative efforts can go further, establishing new rules governing the internet.

PSD2[29] is the EU's revised Payment Services Directive. It is fully in force across the EU from the 1st of January 2020. Its goal is to create a single integrated market for payment services by standardizing the regulations for the banks and for new payment services. It enables the provision of third-party service around user data by requiring that banks share their customer data for purposes agreed upon by the customer. It also reinforces a legal requirement for strong customer identification across the digital payment chain on the basis of standards approved by the European Banking Authority. This directive supports the development of Fintech innovations, by offering services built on continuous access to consumer data, completing the dematerialization step of the customer's relation to the bank.

The relationship between *PSD2* and *eIDAS* seems that of a happily married couple. Harmonious complementarity, further facilitated by the

---

[29] Directive (EU) 2015/2366 of the European Parliament and of the Council of 25 November 2015 on payment services in the internal market, amending Directives 2002/65/EC, 2009/110/EC and 2013/36/EU and Regulation (EU) No 1093/2010, and repealing Directive 2007/64/EC.

adoption of a first-born *ETSI* standard provided the technical bridge between the two.[30] The respective requirements of *GDPR* and *PSD2* generated a great deal of confusion, especially for the banking sector, possibly because reconciling interests of both sets requires "a granular understanding" of personal data attached to the identities of customers. The resulting environment of those two legislations combined could give the upper hand to the digital sector in the global convergence of the digital and financial that the era of "open banking" would produce. The financial stability board recently noted this advantage to the digital sector as an issue worthy of scrutiny.[31]

AML[32] is the fifth box depicted in Fig. 14.1. The current AML is the 5th version of the EU Anti Money Laundering Directive. It was introduced in 2016, amending the Fourth *AML* of 2015. The rush to amend the fourth version was driven by the political urgency to set limitations on the anonymity related to virtual currencies, digital wallet providers and pre-paid cards. The new AML sets up central bank account registries in all Member States. It also deepens the cooperation between anti-money laundering supervisors and the European Central Bank. AML builds on the recommendations of the Financial Action Task Force (FATF) and was introduced with a bang, presented as response to terrorist events of 2015 and 2016 and to the Panama Papers revelations of that same year.

The EU EID Landscape

In the EU, the current state of play is an heterogeneous landscape of Identity schemes.

The state of play in 2020 is a protean and unstable one. The mapping, in Fig. 14.2, represents a small snapshot of the EU landscape as it stood in early 2018, that is immediately prior to the coming into effect of critical parts of both the GDPR and PSD2. The patchwork of relatively small schemes run through a variety of public- and private-led governance mechanisms, may have misled many into thinking of digital ID as a narrow matter

---

[30] "ETSI TS 119 495 V1.4.1 (2019-11) Electronic Signatures and Infrastructures (ESI); Sector Specific Requirements; Qualified Certificate Profiles and TSP Policy Requirements under the Payment Services Directive (EU) 2015/2366." Accessed March 8, 2020. https://www.etsi.org/deliver/etsi_ts/119400_119499/119495/01.04.01_60/ts_119495v010401p.pdf.

[31] "FSB Reports Consider Financial Stability Implications of BigTech in Finance and Third Party Dependencies in Cloud Services," December 9, 2019. https://www.fsb.org/2019/12/fsb-reports-consider-financial-stability-implications-of-bigtech-in-finance-and-third-party-dependencies-in-cloud-services-2/.

[32] Directive of the European Parliament and of The Council amending Directive (EU)2015/849 on the prevention of the use of the financial system for the purposes of money laundering or terrorist financing, and amending Directives 2009/138/EC and 2013/36/EU.

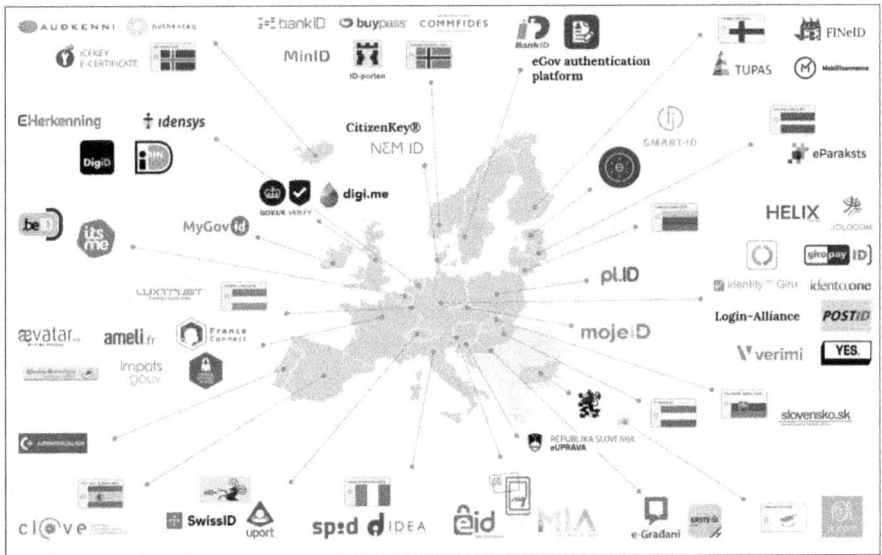

Fig. 14.2 The Europe's heterogeneous ID landscape (*Source* Asquared, 2018)

of agreements on standards. Although the full impact of the governance stack described above is not yet visible to most people, the combined effect of these legislations amounts to a major push for a broad adoption of Digital ID. It is easy to predict that in the coming months and years, the EU landscape of eID will look very different to the uneven set of smaller schemes which existed in 2018. But this will be the result of legislative changes rather than technological determinism. The review of the eIDAS regulation, due to start in 2020, is the first opportunity for legislators to consider introducing a comprehensive approach to eID policy framing that trend and driving it towards a desirable outcome. Meanwhile, the race is on between a small number of private-sector-led schemes which are onboarding users/holders at a very high rate of growth. The prize is the most attractive segment of digital identification: the secure mobile ID for banking and payment.

The Case of ITSME

The case of the Belgian born *itsme*[33] solution is illustrative of one possible outcome of the many forces at play. At the user's end, it comes as a mobile application that "*allows you to safely, easily and reliably confirm your identity and approve transactions*". It claims full compliance with EU regulation and

---

[33] www.itsme.be.

ISO standards including *GDPR* and *eIDAS* Level of Assurance "High" for operations in Belgium, Qualified Electronic Signature, alignment to *PSD2* Strong Customer Authentication in payments, *AML5*, *ISO 27001*. All these accreditations took the company more than two years of effort to acquire. Accreditation from *eIDAS*, was requested by the Belgian federal authority for the national eID card scheme and the mobile *itsme* scheme jointly, That makes both schemes valid to be used by Belgian users enrolled to access eGovernment services and (potentially) *PSD2* regulated financial services across EU Member States. *Itsme* expects to grow well beyond the borders of Belgium and become the preferred "once-only" mobile ID operator across other EU Member States and some overseas neighbours. Their claimed competitive advantage is to offer a uniform customer experience and faster access to market for scheme participants, in particular retail banks. The scheme's adoption rate in Belgium greatly benefited from trust and support of the federal authorities. Behind *itsme* is an entirely private-sector-based operation created by four major banks (KBC, BNPP Fortis, Belfius and ING) and a leading telecom operator (Proximus). Thus *itsme* has strong financial backing, and a large user base of customers.

By the end of 2019, after less than two years of operation, *itsme* claimed no less than 20% of the Belgian population as users (see Fig. 14.3). This represents a significantly faster onboarding than experienced by other private-sector-led schemes apart from those run by the major digital operators.

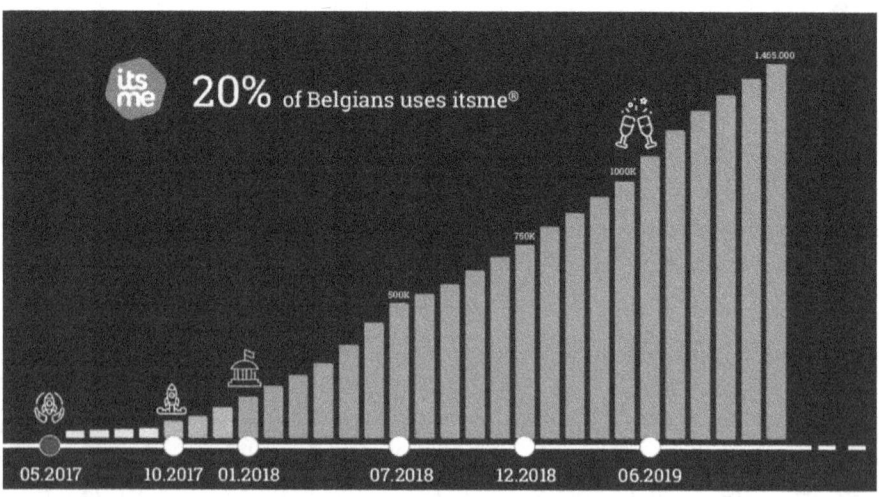

Fig. 14.3 Belgian user's of ITSME since 2017 (*Source* ITSME presentation, Rotterdam December 2019)

If EU expansion beyond Belgium succeeds, *itsme* has the potential to become a big player, able to muster a privileged position with institutional state actors. At this point it would control a significant portion of our data. When such systems emerge to broaden usability to new applications, they inevitably expand the range of data collected per individual and in a cross border and cross-sector context. A structural separations policy and problems of centralization/control of user data issue will become more problematic for regulators.

Some fear that *Itsme*'s structure renders control over our previously national identity data an inevitability and predict that as a model it can be challenged in the future to respond to the pressure from citizens expecting to retain true control over their data. By positioning itself in the facilitator middle of a hugely scalable large amount of transactions between different organizations, it brings a new replica of first-player advantage, the similar problematic unbalance of power as presented previously by the platform model.

In the Netherlands, we see another example, an alternative scheme called *IRMA*, as a contrasting example. If *itsme* is a prima donna, *IRMA* is a Dutch professor's modest proposal, with early funding from an EU NGI project. The *IRMA* Digital ID platform grew organically in an open source non-profit 2008 academic prototyping research environment. The acronym *IRMA* stands for *"I Reveal My Attributes"*, a privacy-friendly way of logging in with, for example, your health insurers and your local authorities. The user reveals only as much personal information ("attributes") as strictly necessary, by controlling the process with the *IRMA* phone app. In 2019 *SIDN* the internet domain name manager for the Netherlands and *IRMA* joined forces, so *SIDN* provides *IRMA*'s infrastructural backbone. *IRMA* has an active user base estimated at around 10,000 people. By comparison *itsme* has reached 38.5 million transactions. The ISA2 EU framework for public service interoperability for the Netherlands is based on the bank and tax digital ecosystem. This would reinforce the *itsme* approach.

As common sense might suggest, having a homegrown potential digital identity champion may attenuate the risk of a complete take over by cash rich extra-EU platforms. We argued that in digital id field, due to the data problem, this could still replicate the major imbalance of power observed in other parts of the digital environment. That imbalance of power would eventually also come at the expense of the state's own traditional power. When it comes to something as critical and core as our identity system, it seems too important not to consider what the alternative choices are, before we collectively reach a threshold, the tipping point of no return.

Making the case for the emergence of technological solutions based on disposable identities stems from our understanding that the future of digital ID is not a matter of technological determinism but a policy choice with ethical and equity implications. The notion of "digital inclusion" is a desirable design principle for ID policy provided the myth of universality is not limited to merely extending a surveillance-driven network to other new population groups. A human-centric digital society is one in which individual agency and collective rights come in combination with responsibilities to enhance self and society combined. Our ideal rests on a system where transparency is sought first from the powerful "haves". Disposable identities must maintain a mean of accountability, but a vital amount of anonymity must be ensured for everyone because it serves creativity and preserves opportunities for cooperation and an entry ticket to the free-entry space of permission-less innovation.

The Once-Only-Principle at EU Scale

The *once-only-principle*, most eloquently defended by the Estonian government,[34] is defined in the eGovernment Action plan[35] as the principle by which public administrations should ensure that citizens and businesses supply the same information only-once to a public administration. The meaning and means through which this principle applies to verified identity is still evolving matter and there is much at stake.

Several key EU legislations are due for review in the coming years. An EU official we interviewed explained how important it is for legislators to clearly lay out in future texts the definitional differences and relationships at play, in distinguishing between (1) "identity", (2) "digital identity" and (3) "digital entitlements/credentials". This approach requires legislation to differentiate the need for identification—substantiated by an identity—and the need for authentication—substantiated by entitlements and/or credentials.

Ultimately, what is at stake for the EU goes beyond merely oiling the digital machinery that is an engine driving across the single market for economic operators. The goal of a digital ID infrastructure is to produce, through the successful implementation of the *once-only-principle*, the actual experience of a single space within which European citizens can enjoy their

---

[34] https://ec.europa.eu/info/sites/info/files/economy-finance/digital_identity_once-only-principle_and_reducing_administrative_burden.pdf.

[35] Communication from the Commission to the European Parliament, The Council, The European Economic and Social Committee and the Committee of the Regions EU eGovernment Action Plan 2016–2020 Accelerating the digital transformation of government.COM/2016/0179 final.

rights guaranteed in the treaties. For one the guarantee that a passport or digital signature has EU added value, a mutual "once-only" verifiable recognition. So far the citizen's experience of the digital transition so far typically translated in the obligation to identify oneself when seeking government services. We saw translation of this into a technical problem, with many vendors competing to offer their single best solution based on requirements of governments—theoretically—putting the digital citizen in the driving seat. Putting the technology first, we argue, is the wrong approach. Separate and discard online identities to empower the holders of digital identification. Entitlements are designed as technological means of availing oneself of pre-existing political entitlement and preserving one's rights.

The Potential for an EU Solution to Emerge

The EU, it turns out, may be better placed than institutions such as the World Bank or even the UN, to deliver a solution that prioritizes expectations of privacy and civil liberties for EU citizens and potentially beyond. Here is why:

- Its legislative and enforcement powers over the single market translate into direct and indirect leverage over the most powerful players from those two sectors cited above.
- It is empowered to act on behalf of its member states *and* on behalf of EU citizens and residents.
- Its *Charter of Fundamental Rights of the European Union*, binding on member states since December 2009, enshrines into primary EU law, rights enjoyed by EU citizens and residents including personal, civic, political, economic and social rights plus specifically and directly relevant rights of data protection and privacy.

It is also relevant that, in a significant departure from prior eras, the current Commission has officially[36] included among its political priorities, its intent to intervene to protect both the rights of EU citizens to digital privacy and EU's technological sovereignty. To address the coming challenges, it can make use of the promising results and findings of EU funded developments, including those produced by the ecosystem of projects funded under the Next

---

[36]As stated by President von der Leyen in her speech to the European Parliament presenting the political priorities of her Commission.

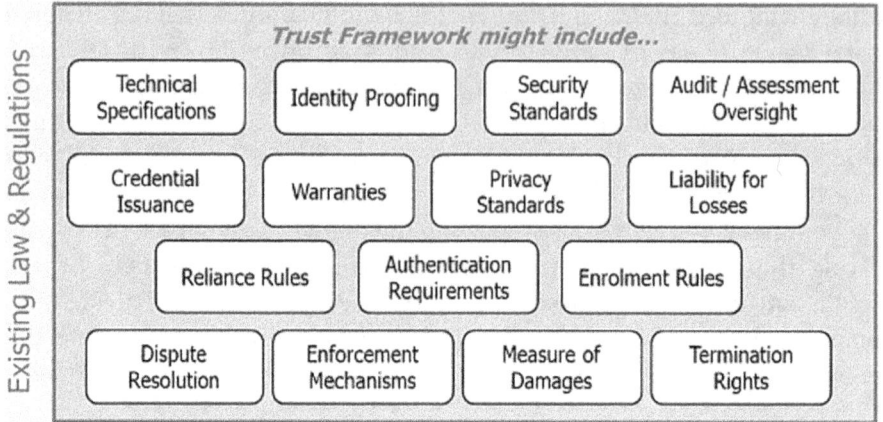

Fig. 14.4 Components of a Trust Framework (*Source* Makaay, E, T Smedinghoff, and D Thibeau. "OpenID Exchange: Trust Frameworks for Identity Systems," 2017)

Generation Internet (NGI)[37] which demonstrate the concrete feasibility of an alternative path to digital identity.

Findings from EU NGI Projects

Trust Frameworks

One fruitful experience emanating from the NGI ecosystem is the application of the Trust-Framework[38] to the governance of personal information at city level which is currently tested in Amsterdam. Trust frameworks are established mechanisms for the digitalization of a combination of agreements and rules between heterogeneous parties relying on a common system for which trust frameworks serve to combine interdependent bilateral agreements and common requirements into a single set of operating rules. Their theoretical applicability to the identity ecosystem is explored in a 2017 white paper[39] published on the Open Identity Exchange in which the authors provide the following graphic representation (Fig. 14.4).

---

[37] https://www.ngi.eu/.

[38] The program to realize this infrastructure has just started its design phase in January 2020. Feedback from, among others, the recent (December 2019) NGI FORWARD Thingscon workshop will be included. It will be a continuous learning cycle.

[39] Makaay, E., T. Smedinghoff, and D. Thibeau. "OpenID Exchange: Trust Frameworks for Identity Systems," 2017. https://www.openidentityexchange.org/wp-content/uploads/2017/06/OIX-White-Paper_Trust-Frameworks-for-Identity-Systems_Final.pdf.

The NGI Amsterdam pilot focuses on the application of that approach to a range of welfare services provided by third party on behalf of the city to vulnerable population groups. These range from urgent health and safety assistance to the elderly to ad hoc financial support to overindebted residents. It enables mobile transmission to the relevant third-party services of needed information regarding individual residents at crucial moments for the person concerned, but framed by law and by rules agreed with that particular person in advance. The trust framework protects what is often very intimate individual information from unwanted and unnecessary sharing with third parties while ensuring that the part of it serving the emergency purpose is made instantly available to the party intervening to assist the resident. Manon den Dunnen, working at the Dutch Police as a strategic specialist on digital transformation, an expert in the NGI FORWARD ecosystem, presented the promising results at a *Thingscon* event in December 2019. She noted that the trust framework approach, at a fundamental level was also the means of safeguarding constitutional values, the notion of an inclusive society and a focus back on real people and their needs, wants and dreams.

This experience is still ongoing and the concrete challenges addressed include:

- Ensuring individual understanding and decision-making over one's own data, its content, collection and use
- Availability of individual data for agreed-upon social purposes by designated parties
- Manageable cost and efficiency of data exchange process for all involved.

Beyond trust frameworks, projects belonging to the NGI ecosystem are also operating a common trust infrastructure. It consists of data collaboratives that ensure responsibly functioning data markets between participants. Participating organizations develop data sharing agreements, draft related consent agreements and manage the granted permissions. For the verification of identities and data sharing permissions, these organizations use the generic provisions of the DVI. The incentive to do so is that it allows them to access data in a *GDPR*-compliant, low cost and easily accessible way. In return, they must meet the requirements in terms of transparency and privacy & security by design.

"Disposable Identities".[40]

Disposable identities are temporary attribute-based identities integrated in any smart contract between a receiver and a supplier. A digital context-based sharing of data that is generalizable: to apply a digital id internet layer to any existing communication service.[41]

The complete ecosystem in which Disposable Identities would operate, requires a similar trust infrastructure where the combination of seamless connectivity and personalized support is not build on continuous and real-time tracking and tracing of identified users. Instead it operates with attribute-based relational identities, generated for each single interaction between user and service (or object and service) and disposed of, immediately afterwards.

With disposable identities, new applications can be added to this ecosystem using a strict attribute-based solution, needs no full disclosure (of identity) just beyond age, ability to pay for the service, legal compliance in terms of insurance and accountability. Digital services can be delivered to authenticated users without requiring the need for a single full set of identifying data to be shared.

The diagram above is a schematic representation of the model of disposal identity developed by the DECODE project which relies on the Zenroom Virtual Machine.

This schema minimizes risks of data leaks and unauthorized reuse of personal data by third-party service providers. The proposed technical framework of provable computing developed by zenroom.org, runs on *Virtual Machines*[42] embedded in the chip used with any personal communication device and any connected object. These chips representing the key material component of the approach, they could be regarded as the digital era equivalent of the secure ID of Passport and require comparable level of confidence in the fabrication process. This argues in favour of relying on chips manufactured under EU jurisdiction. While this represents a major change from the current supply chain for commercial chips which are almost entirely sourced

---

[40] disposable.id is registered on blockstack based on a subdomain id it is possible to generate disposable identities and credentials with the Zenroom tool that can be conversed in W3C compliant digital Ids and verifiable credentials.

[41] https://atos.net/en/blog/the-next-identity-management-evolution-self-sovereign-identity.

[42] In computing, a virtual machine (VM) is an emulation of a computer system. Virtual machines are based on computer architectures and provide functionality of a physical computer. Their implementations may involve specialized hardware, software, or a combination. "Virtual Machine." In Wikipedia, March 29, 2020. https://en.wikipedia.org/w/index.php?title=Virtual_machine&oldid=947995885.

from China for the EU market, it is also a move that may serve other geopolitical and environmental Commission priorities. Zenroom, which can also run on existing integrated chips,[43] was developed as European alternative for achieving a level of accessibility, provability and certification of computing.

The NGI ecosystem is driven by stakeholders that organize themselves along the multi-stakeholder non-profit model already used for consensus building structures in the digital sector (e.g.: ICANN). Among ongoing developments, NGI participants also work on digital signatures for services such as banking, payment, energy, education, care, mobility, connectivity as well as digital signatures for architectures (virtual and analogue enablers of connectivity). With these tools, participants intend to complement innovative procurements actions and extend opportunities for their stakeholders to access original data sets and analytical platforms even when they are formally controlled by another part of the ecosystem.

These means of cooperation have led to a significant breakthrough: the definition of core characteristics for the disposable identities concept. It relies on the application of a trust-framework certifying conditions for the disposability as well as verifying and attesting to the disposing of the disposable identity. Disposable identities are temporary attribute-based identities integrated in a smart contract between a receiver and a supplier of a service, implementing the following:

[actor]\may [action] with [actee = disposable identity] under [condition] so that [purpose], and can apply to any service that demands for context-based sharing of data such as leasing a car, sharing energy between homes or paying taxes.

In practice, disposable identities require a provable computing environment. That environment is not an option available on the EU single market at present. The next step is a possible *ETSI* standard for disposable identities which is currently under discussion at *ETSI*. Disposable identities could also be a foundation for an *eID* NGI framework.

Disposable Identities are framed within existing legislation by reference to Article 2 of the Treaty on the European Union and Article 5 of the *GDPR* setting seven key principles as a first step to a digital governance regime: *"lawfulness, fairness and transparency"; "purpose limitation"; "data minimization"; "accuracy"; "storage limitation"; "integrity and confidentiality"; "accountability".*

---

[43] Including the Portenta H7 by Arduino.

Security in our governance context is cybersecurity in the broadest sense of the term. Cybersecurity is a fast evolving field and keeping up with global technology developments is a real challenge.

Regarding governance, one case to draw from is the Dutch New Trust Foundation framework: a scheme kick-started in January 2020 by a small number of creative public institutional actors. One of the ideas at the heart of the Dutch approach is a translation of the ROLO concept (Register of Legal Organisations) and the adoption of Distributed Dynamic Authentication Attributes. As stated by one of the architects[44], it relies on the combined implementation of Trust Anchors,[45] Zero Trust Architectures,[46] Verifiable Claims[47] and alignment to the standard *ISO* 29115, a framework for managing entity authentication assurance in a given context. The levels of identity proofing and requirements to achieve these levels, are specified as set by ISO 2900. TC307 standardization for blockchain technologies and distributed ledger technologies. At the heart of it is the realization that physical objects that are more and more 3D printed in our current world—literally are solidified bits of data that are hackable on a material level. Another example of governance tech is SRAM PUF solutions (e.g. Intrinsic ID), as are currently running in the Estonian framework.

As every individual chip manufactured has its own unique pattern of impurity, each one is uniquely traceable. A solution developed by the US agency DARPA and Draper labs, the Dover's CoreGuard,[48] integrates with processor architectures to monitor every instruction executed to ensure that it complies with a defined set of security, safety and privacy rules. It is possible to conceive that a similar model and hardware and software solutions could be developed and applied to support features designed along the goals of the *GDPR*

---

[44]Vincent Hoek, Rijksoverheid.nl.

[45]A trust anchor is an authoritative entity represented by a public key and associated data. The public key is used to verify digital signatures, and the associated data is used to constrain the types of information or actions for which the trust anchor is authoritative. Housley, Russ, Sam Ashmore, and Carl Wallace. "Trust Anchor Format." Internet Engineering Task Force, 2010. https://tools.ietf.org/html/rfc5914.

[46]*Zero Trust*, *Zero Trust Network*, or *Zero Trust Architecture* refer to security concepts and threat model that no longer assumes that actors, systems or services operating from within the security perimeter should be automatically trusted, and instead must verify anything and everything trying to connect to its systems before granting access. The term was coined by a security analyst at Forrester Research. *Secret Double Octopus*. "What Is Zero Trust? | Security Wiki." Accessed April 12, 2020. https://doubleoctopus.com/security-wiki/network-architecture/zero-trust/.

[47]A verifiable claim is a piece of information that is cryptographically trustworthy. Sovrin. "What Is a Verifiable Claim?" Accessed April 24, 2020. https://sovrin.org/faq/what-is-a-verifiable-claim/.

[48]Dover Microsystems. "Learn More About CoreGuard®." Accessed March 13, 2020. https://www.dovermicrosystems.com/solutions/coreguard/.

and other instruments mentioned in our governance stack. This approach amounts to hardcoding the set of chosen governance standards.

The same system can generate "event identities" as resources for Big Data, AI analytics, quantum computing and without exposing unnecessary parts of personal data. That digital identity space is able and certified for creating Digital Signatures. However, if the router—application—device "takes three to tango" trust relationship triangle is not apparent, then nothing happens. In other words, there is no need to identify natural persons or for these persons to expose themselves as natural persons. The event identity remains accessible and searchable for future big data analytics.

The provable computing framework we envisage for Europe as a 460 million zone of people (and 55 billion *IoT* devices by 2025 worldwide) rests on the assumption that data frameworks and identity management cannot be separated. It would take a deliberate policy to achieve this at the EU and Europe-wide scale including the will and means to retain and sustain the results of EU-funded developments from the chips to the applications. Case in point, Zenroom which provides the cryptography and the sensitive data manipulation for the DECODE project, relies to do so on implementing the *Coconut* credential scheme developed by a UCL team in 2018 in the context of an EU project.

The Zenroom part of the approach has now reached the stage of validation for commercial use. However, in 2019, Facebook managed to "*aqui-hire*" the key cryptologists from the UCL team who moved to the USA and now work on building Facebook's LIBRA currency and its related identity system. In addition, more recently, Microsoft announced their variation on a Coconut credential scheme.[49] Without a policy to frame and support current developments, these moves by extra-EU corporate players will likely keep on happening. On the other hand, security considerations may also lead to a different approach to market regulations applying to the router the chip market and requirements for embedded computing. From a technical standpoint, opting for VM on chip implies a different approach to security requirements.

In 2020 three key components of the EU legislative framework will be reviewed: the GDPR, ePrivacy and eIDAS. This represents an opportunity to adopt a more comprehensive approach to identity that considers what is technically feasible and politically desirable at this stage. At the core of

---

[49] Simons, Alex. "Toward Scalable Decentralized Identifier Systems." TECHCOMMUNITY.MICROSOFT.COM, May 13, 2019. https://techcommunity.microsoft.com/t5/azure-active-directory-identity/toward-scalable-decentralized-identifier-systems/ba-p/560168.

this comprehensive approach, it is possible to envision a European identity-scheme fit for a sovereign area encompassing a population of nearly 500 millions, designed on a principle of multi-stakeholder governance. Beyond the EU, such a model could also be attractive to Africa where the same issue of reliance on imported technology also raises sovereignty issues.

Figure 14.7 depicts an alternative to the Governance Stack which could deliver a European Trust Framework (ETF) stack. Such ETF could play a role in advancing Digital ID developments and the policy move to safeguard the "disposability" of digital identities. Fully commercial providers will need to facilitate the interoperability and business value (compliance with the middle part of the stack) from GDPR to ISOA27001 standards.

Three layers form a comprehensive regulatory framework: embedded security and interoperability on chip (a European Operating System on a Virtual Machine), hardcoding the EU Green Deal based on that technical infrastructure from the chip up supported by an approach to procurement favouring decarbonized and renewable manufacturing solutions delivering the components for that layer and that system. Reputation systems and trusted ID Technologies need to be harmonized. The ID layer brings new understanding and insight into the digital behaviour of people and machines at the edges (at the level of wearables, in the smart home appliances such as cameras and voice-activated assistants, as well as things and artefacts such as in the surveillance infrastructure of smart cities). Substantially more intrusive proposals, preparing to exploit vast array of personal data produced from IoT in the future, such as that emanating from coelition.org and its coel standard aiming to label and recognize data from the most intimate moments of life,[50] might need to be regulated into joining a level playing field.

Figures 14.5 and 14.6, together represent the proposal for a digital approach to identity. This approach involves a comprehensive review of the current identity regulatory stack and the implementation of a technological solution enabling the system-wide use of disposable identities. Beyond the legal and technological dimensions, this is also a political matter. Embedded within and determined by the future digital identity model is the continued preservation individual rights of EU citizens and the assertion of EU sovereignty which can be summarized in one picture (Fig. 14.7).

In sum, EU sovereignty will be maintained and sustained starting with Identity and re-asserting it through this entire stack. To be coherent with that objective, an EU Digital Strategy should cover the full range of connectivity and identity dimensions including people, objects and events and,

---

[50] https://coelition.org/business/resources/visualising-life/.

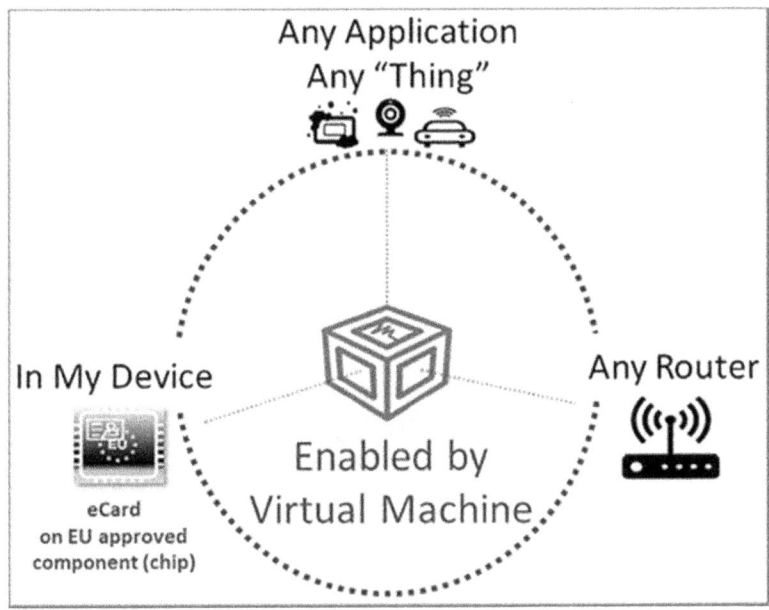

Fig. 14.5 A diagram of disposable identity enabled by the Zenroom VM developed by DECODE (*Source* Authors/decode)

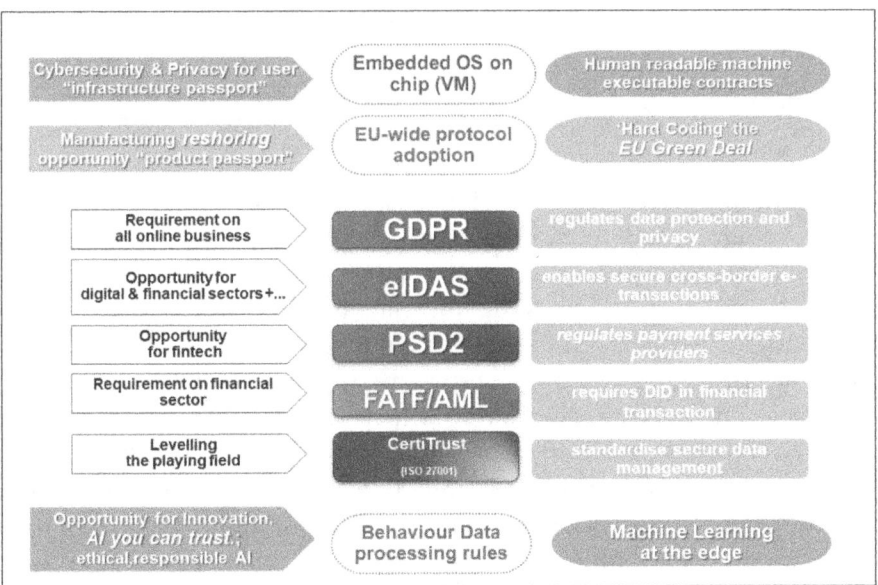

Fig. 14.6 The European Trust Framework: An alternative to the governance stack (*Source* Authors)

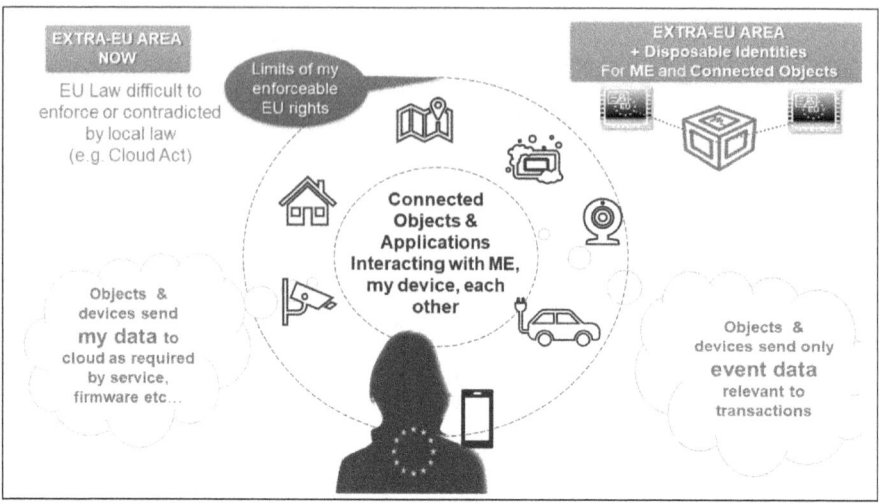

Fig. 14.7 EU citizen rights and EU sovereignty (*Source* Authors)

even, formats of behaviour created by AI. The hardware dimension of such an approach also involves considering embedded security on the chip. The coming review of eIDAS offers an opportunity to extend the achieved cross-border mutual acceptance on digital signatures extended to legal and natural persons to digital signatures for services and infrastructures. The complex matter of privacy might find a more comprehensive solution and more trust if a clear consensus can emerge around fundamental principles, such as individual behavioural autonomy and collective human dignity.

The coming review of the GDPR is an opportunity to explore the value possibilities and to move forward, because minimal data disclosure is difficult in the current system. A paradigm shift is needed: centralizing public infrastructure (and boosting investments), decentralizing services (and data/identity in a mixed SSI framework) under an appropriate form of multi-stakeholder governance (citizens, corporates, governmental coordination).

We envision Europe to be able to achieve a 500 million residents' zone of strong, bottom-up, distributed connectivity, based on attribute-based onboarding of people and objects into this ecosystem. This can be hard-coded on each "sovereign eurochip" (in router, in application, in 5G base stations, in the chips for phones or cards (e.g. the Estonian e-card +). Citizens seeking relief and protection from full tracking and tracing would welcome an opportunity to adopt the solutions produced through this novel value-driven EU-wide ecosystem.

Conclusions

The tech giants and the banking sector are already in competition to become the frontline providers of digital identity. Leaving the eID domain to market forces risk a repeat of the concentration of power outcome already decried in other parts of the digital market. But if there ever was a matter too great to be left to market forces in our collective digitalized existence, eID is it.

Soon the EU will need to act in response to Member States under pressure to defend their sovereignty in the expanding digital sphere. Citizens will rightly demand that their freedom of expression and autonomy is ensured in the digital realm. The EU, itself, will need to ensure that its own laws remain enforceable, as it allows an ever greater share of every life to undergo digital transition. Online reputation systems and ID technologies will require broader accountability and diligent regulators. Equity and inclusion sustain our democratic system and that is also true online. This requires a deliberate approach and will not happen without the deployment of appropriate legal and technological approaches.

In this chapter, we described the context and evolution of digital identification technologies and proposed a novel approach, a possible solution that would simultaneously defend individual autonomy and EU sovereignty. Any eID approach that would cover the entire EU must be inclusive by design. A Disposable Identity approach would deliver in the digital realm, the level of privacy and security that are entitlements of EU citizens. The "provable computing on a chip" would ensure the level of security required for law enforcement purposes. Finally, issuance decisions would be kept under the control of legitimate and accountable state authorities.

Technologies of freedom require safeguards aligned to Article 2 of the Treaty on the European Union. Our treaty explicitly safeguards a "gathering of individuals" as opposed to institutions. At a fundamental level, the human right to retain agency in a digital world is as important for the EU to safeguard today as the four freedoms introduced in the Treaty of Rome (1957) or the rights brought about by the introduction of EU Citizenship in the Maastricht treaty (1992). The EU evolved from coal and steel and the common market to a union of citizens. Beyond the Single Market, this union is what is at stakes here.

We conclude with this inspiring quote from the Swedish MEP, David Lega:

> Because it is about **identities** isn't it? My disability is, and will always be one of my identities. But it will never be all of my identity. I was an athlete, I was an entrepreneur, I was a speaker. I'm a boyfriend, I'm a brother, I'm a friend, and I'm in a wheelchair.

Conclusion

Eva Kaili and Dimitrios Psarrakis

This volume was a systematic effort to explore the impact of blockchain technology in markets, corporate strategies, firm structures, data management, smart identities, smart contracts, monetary economics, stablecoins, finance, ecosystem development, the private sector and regulation. We adopted a global view as the contributors of this volume represent different perspectives, different roles and different geographic origins.

Starting from the blockchain technology as it stands right now and considering the adoption dynamics we see in the markets so far, we observe a certain preference to specific types of engineering of DLT solutions that use combinations of properties such as immutability, encryption, distribution and tokenization in arrangements that are more compatible to hierarchical and centralized governance designs than more "democratic", equitable and flat. Despite the fact that many innovative organizations emerge and advance decentralized autonomous designs, e.g. DeFis, the vast majority of the blockchain projects are centralized in nature and focus, mainly, on creating economies of scale aiming to the reduction of verification and transaction costs.

Governments and trans-governmental organizations, like the EU and the UN, seem eager to adopt a similar path in improving their services to the citizens and expand financial inclusion, transparency, accountability and access. Property rights get into a new orbit and innovative applications like distributed data, disposable identities and smart contracts promise a new era of marketplaces that the interaction of humans with humans, humans with machines or even machines with machines will be the new standard. Blockchain is possibly the infrastructure that will enable a robust IoT economy to emerge and flourish.

Money and Finance also get into a new era. Central banks and major corporations realize that programmable money is the next step in removing fragmentations in the payments systems and compete for solutions that can create new sources of value, as well new sources of control. Similarly, the financial sector experiences the challenge of tokenization in various ways. Blockchain disrupts traditional value chains (e.g. the trading, clearing and settlement systems) and introduces new types of securities and tools for crowdfunding.

Regulators are challenged by the new technological options that blockchain brings and are forced to move away from old-type mindsets to address new sources of liability as well as more flexible designs of market structures. The battle for standards becomes a new source of competition for major technology providers. Regulators are invited to strike a balance that will allow the forces of innovation to play their role in a legally certain environment that enables experimentation without compromising quality standards and investor/consumer protection principles.

It is our prediction that this disintermediation-oriented blockchain paradigm is not the last stage of blockchain evolution. A new stage, more decentralization-oriented, will emerge as blockchain technology matures, as people become more comfortable with flat organizational systems and as the evolution of other exponential technological settings like the IoT, machine learning, hyper-performance computing, edge/fog/mist computing and cybersecurity systems will become more widespread. The transformation of the society will play also a significant role as gradually the majority of the population, as well as the majority of the regulators and government officials, will be composed by digital natives.

From an academic point of view, this volume introduced concepts and made some initial recommendations for further exploration. It was by no means our intention to give conclusions and definite answers but rather to start a debate about Blockchain Economics taking into account the technological and social limitations of our time. We believe, that in the current environment the economic value of blockchain is built around the concept of disintermediation. This concept generates a specific type of economic impact. This is what we call "Disintermediation Economics". From an evolutionary point of view, we expect that the next stage of Blockchain Economics will need a new theoretical framework, the "Disintermediation Economics". In this case, new challenges and new economic impacts will affect the disciplines of Microeconomics, Macroeconomics, Finance and Political Economy.

Index

A
Anti-money laundering (AML) 189, 195, 214, 226, 312
Authentication xii, 12, 149, 190, 299, 311, 314, 316, 322

B
Bitcoin 3, 4, 6, 20, 48, 56, 61, 93, 99, 112–120, 125, 145, 147, 149, 155, 160, 167, 173, 175, 182, 187, 189, 203, 216–218, 220, 221, 223, 224, 253, 254, 269, 273, 282, 283, 297
Blockchain 2–12, 17–29, 33–38, 40–44, 48–55, 57–65, 69, 70, 76, 83, 86, 88, 93–104, 108, 112–116, 118, 119, 123, 124, 129, 146, 147, 149–154, 156–163, 165, 174–176, 179, 180, 182, 183, 185, 186, 189, 190, 194, 201, 204, 213, 214, 217, 218, 221, 227, 228, 230, 233, 251, 253–265, 268–277, 282–293, 297, 298, 302, 303, 311, 322, 329, 330
Blockchain-based solutions 12, 22, 57, 58
Blockchain ecosystems 24, 62, 63, 113
Blockchain narrative 2, 19, 20, 24
Business model neutrality 12, 240, 274, 275

C
Central bank digital currencies (CBDC) 9, 10, 56, 76, 88, 113, 121–125, 127–138, 142, 145–154, 156, 157, 161, 164, 167, 168, 173, 175, 178, 183–186, 214, 227
Central banks 6, 55, 56, 93, 121–125, 127, 128, 132–136, 139, 142, 143, 146, 148–152, 154, 157, 159–161, 167, 168, 183–188, 214, 227, 309, 312, 330

Central securities depositories (CSDs) 26, 198
Consensus 2, 7, 20, 21, 27–29, 35, 41, 43, 59, 61, 102, 113, 115–117, 119, 121, 182, 234, 254, 273, 291, 308, 321, 326
Coordination costs 7, 19, 24
Corporate transformation 62
Crypto-asset-backed-securities (DABS) 230
Crypto-assets 9, 10, 25, 42, 275
Cryptoassets 120, 193–195, 197–200, 203, 204, 206–213, 215–219, 221–224, 226–229, 231–234, 236, 238, 254, 258, 262, 268
Cryptoassets taxonomy 199, 233
Cryptocurrencies 9, 10, 57, 93, 101, 112–122, 124, 125, 131, 145–147, 155, 158, 160, 169, 173, 174, 180, 182, 184, 186, 216, 219, 222, 223, 228, 238, 254, 255, 267, 269–271
Cryptoexchanges 217–222, 224, 226, 227, 229, 231, 232, 234
Cryptographic consensus technology (CCTech) 215, 217, 222, 230–241

Dark internet 269
Data economics 8, 69, 73, 74, 87
Decentralization 3, 5, 11, 27, 29, 40, 42, 64, 65, 176, 272, 273, 276, 277, 282, 283, 330
Decentralized applications (dApps) 42, 119, 146, 268
Decentralized architectures 64, 273
Decentralized decision-making 252
Decentralized Finance (DeFi) 6, 42, 119, 120, 267, 268, 272, 273, 276, 329

Determined-by-architecture (DBA) 234, 235, 240
Digital identities 13, 39, 95–97, 99, 184, 273, 293, 298, 299, 302, 304–306, 309, 310, 315, 316, 318, 323, 324, 327
Digital numismatics 176, 179
Digital signature 3, 4, 125, 310, 317, 321–323, 326
Digital transformation 8, 10, 12, 21, 22, 47–50, 53, 54, 64, 105, 164, 173, 177, 180, 184, 188, 205, 281, 282, 286, 316, 319
Digital wallet 13, 179, 184, 185, 187, 299, 312
Disintermediation 3, 5, 6, 11, 40, 48, 49, 51, 64, 197, 269, 270, 272, 276, 282, 283, 286, 288, 330
Disintermediation economics 11, 330, 331
Distributed data 7, 8, 69, 70, 80, 82, 84–89, 329
Distributed ledger technologies (DLT) 2, 11, 25, 33, 48, 86, 123, 173, 190, 193, 204, 217, 251, 256, 257, 259, 264, 265, 269, 270, 322
DLT MTFs 26
DLT Pilot Regime 10, 25, 26, 275
DLT securities settlement system (DLT SSS) 26, 206

Encryption 3, 5, 23, 40, 64, 86, 186, 202, 283, 291, 329
Etherium 269
European Blockchain Service Infrastructure (EBSI) 12, 256–258, 264, 290–293
Exponential technology 180, 276

F

Financial inclusion 94, 95, 97, 112, 125, 129, 183, 184, 186, 307, 308, 329

Financial services 10, 25, 26, 51, 60, 61, 73, 89, 95, 97, 112, 146, 147, 169, 173, 175, 176, 180, 181, 183, 184, 190, 191, 194, 196–199, 205, 207–209, 216–218, 233, 254, 256, 258, 267, 268, 309, 314

Fintech 45, 52, 101, 119, 123, 159, 162, 166, 167, 175–177, 179–183, 188, 191, 196, 216–218, 234, 253, 256–258, 262, 267, 275, 299, 300, 311

Fintechnocrats 180–182

Fraud 44, 51, 53, 54, 71, 112, 120, 128, 180, 187, 191, 217, 269, 284

G

Geopolitics 117, 190, 305, 321

Growth 6, 9, 22, 49, 54, 72, 79, 88, 94, 95, 98, 105, 106, 112, 129, 167, 177, 217, 218, 220, 230, 236, 239, 268, 271, 275, 276, 313

I

Immutability 3, 37, 38, 113, 119, 130, 217, 283, 329

Initial coin offerings (ICO) 10, 55, 93, 120, 173, 195, 198, 204, 216, 261, 262, 282

Innovation 3, 6–8, 10, 11, 13, 25, 48, 54, 58, 62, 70, 83, 88, 89, 94, 99, 103, 105, 107, 123, 124, 127, 131, 138, 142, 145, 146, 148, 150–152, 167, 174–176, 179–184, 186, 188, 191, 196, 197, 204–206, 209, 213, 234, 236, 239, 241, 250–253, 256, 258, 261, 263–265, 268, 269, 277, 282, 299, 310, 311, 316, 330

L

Lex cryptographia 41, 274

Libra 10, 48, 52, 56, 76, 121, 127, 144, 152, 154, 156, 169, 323

M

Markets in Cryptoassets (MiCA) 10, 205, 208–214, 267, 268, 275

Market structure 6, 7, 9, 12, 25, 26, 64, 65, 271, 275, 330

Multilateral trading facility (MTF) 26, 206, 276

O

Oracles 8, 42–44, 53, 154

Organizational design 19

P

Payment system 111, 118, 123, 124, 126, 128, 139, 141, 142, 145, 148–152, 155, 156, 167, 178, 186, 188, 216, 299, 307

Permissioned blockchains 20, 28, 61, 119, 121, 283

Permissionless blockchains 3, 61

Privacy 52, 53, 61, 71, 76–81, 85, 87–89, 114, 119, 128, 130, 131, 151, 154, 182, 184–186, 189, 190, 251, 256, 260–262, 271, 290, 298–300, 302, 305–308, 310, 315, 317, 319, 322, 326, 327

Programmable money 10, 154, 177, 189, 330

Public sector blockchain 6, 12, 283

R

Randomness 2–6, 23, 27
Regulation 10, 11, 25, 26, 75,
    79–82, 87–89, 100, 104, 115,
    123, 130, 131, 136, 142,
    145, 146, 151, 155, 156, 158,
    167, 168, 180–182, 191, 194,
    198–202, 204, 205, 207, 208,
    210–212, 216, 223–225, 228,
    229, 231–234, 236–240, 250,
    257–260, 267, 268, 270–275,
    277, 299, 300, 306, 307, 310,
    311, 313, 323, 329
Regulatory incrementalism 11, 236,
    237
Ricardian contracts 8, 44
Rule of code 283

S

Sandboxes 11, 25, 26, 182, 196,
    197, 226, 250, 256–258, 263,
    277
Security token offering (STO) 120,
    220, 221, 225, 230, 237, 238
Self-sovereign identity (SSI) 290,
    311, 326
Smart contracts 5, 7, 8, 11, 12, 20,
    24, 28, 33–45, 51, 53, 57, 59,
    61, 62, 65, 94, 95, 101, 102,
    112, 114, 118–120, 128–130,
    152, 154, 259, 260, 263–265,
    268, 271, 273–275, 283, 288,
    292, 297, 320, 321, 329
Stablecoins 9, 10, 119, 120, 168,
    169, 175–177, 182, 184, 187,
    209, 210, 213

Sustainable Development Goals
    (SDGs) 9, 93–95, 98–103,
    105, 108, 307, 308

T

Tamperproof 5, 114
Technological neutrality 12, 194,
    274, 275
Techno-social factors 7, 19, 24
Timestamping 20, 23
Tokenization 3, 23, 40, 49, 62, 64,
    124, 217, 230, 283, 329, 330
Tokens 20, 42, 48, 55–57, 61, 69,
    101, 102, 113–115, 120, 121,
    123–127, 130, 143–149, 175,
    177, 179, 186, 203, 204,
    209–212, 215, 219, 221, 224,
    225, 228, 232, 236, 237, 253,
    261, 262, 270
Transaction costs 23, 24, 27, 44, 51,
    56, 94, 98, 141, 284, 329
Trust 1, 2, 4, 6, 12, 13, 20, 27,
    48, 49, 54, 58, 65, 102, 112,
    118, 123, 127, 129, 130, 138,
    142, 143, 146, 155, 156, 175,
    181, 184, 185, 187, 189, 190,
    202, 237, 253, 269, 270, 273,
    283–285, 287, 297, 306, 309,
    310, 314, 318–323, 325, 326

V

Variegated capitalisms 7, 19
Verification costs 3, 26
Virtual assets service providers
    (VASPs) 176, 226

GPSR Compliance

The European Union's (EU) General Product Safety Regulation (GPSR) is a set of rules that requires consumer products to be safe and our obligations to ensure this.

If you have any concerns about our products, you can contact us on

ProductSafety@springernature.com

In case Publisher is established outside the EU, the EU authorized representative is:

Springer Nature Customer Service Center GmbH
Europaplatz 3
69115 Heidelberg, Germany

www.ingramcontent.com/pod-product-compliance
Lightning Source LLC
LaVergne TN
LVHW010335260326
834688LV00036B/722